STARDUST MELODY

STARDUST MELODY

The Life and Music
of Hoagy Carmichael

RICHARD M. SUDHALTER

OXFORD
UNIVERSITY PRESS

OXFORD

UNIVERSITY PRESS

Oxford   New York

Auckland Bangkok Buenos Aires Cape Town Chennai
Dar es Salaam Delhi Hong Kong Istanbul Karachi Kolkata
Kuala Lumpur Madrid Melbourne Mexico City Mumbai Nairobi
São Paulo Shanghai Taipei Tokyo Toronto

Copyright © 2002 by Richard M. Sudhalter

First published by Oxford University Press, Inc., 2002
First issued as an Oxford University Press paperback, 2003
198 Madison Avenue, New York, New York 10016

www.oup.com

Oxford is a registered trademark of Oxford University Press

Library of Congress Cataloging-in-Publication Data

Sudhalter, Richard M.
Stardust melody : the life and music of Hoagy Carmichael
by Richard M. Sudhalter.
p.   cm.
Includes bibliographical references and index.
ISBN 0-19-513120-7 (cloth)
ISBN 0-19-516898-4 (pbk)
1. Carmichael, Hoagy, 1899–1981   2. Composers—United States—
Biography.   I. Title.

ML410.C327 S83   2002
782.42164'092—dc21   [B]   2001034612

Book design by Adam B. Bohannon

1   3   5   7   9   8   6   4   2

Printed in the United States of America
on acid-free paper

For TSP, Bunzer, and their friends

CONTENTS

INTRODUCTION

Our United Airlines 767 had barely lifted off the runway at Santiago when I found myself in conversation with my two immediate neighbors in row fourteen. Young, female, and blonde, they radiated a particularly American, particularly effortless, brand of assured good health.

They were college juniors, they said, and had just backpacked their way across the Andes, actually scaling some of the glaciers viewed distantly from the cruise ship I'd just left at Valparaiso. For the next hour they held me in thrall with tales of towering ridges and tenebrous valleys, mystical dawns and dazzling sunsets—all with a verve and immediacy hard to resist.

Finally, with things starting to flag a bit, came a few questions. What was *I* doing down here? What did *I* do in life besides ride in airplanes? Well, I explained, I played the trumpet, specialized in jazz, and had just finished entertaining passengers on an ecocruise with the music of Hoagy Carmichael—

Their blank stares halted me in mid-sentence. "Hoagy ... Carmichael ... ?" I repeated, enunciating each syllable slowly and clearly. "You know—'Star Dust?' " Not a blink of recognition. " 'Georgia on My Mind?' 'Rockin' Chair?' " I reeled off the familiar titles. " 'Ole Buttermilk Sky?' " Still no sign. Nothing. Oh come on, kids, I thought—and started humming the opening bars: "Sometimes I wonder why I spend the lonely night ..."

"Oh, right," one of my companions declared, furrowing a radiant blonde brow. Haltingly, as if summoning the Pythagorean Theorem from the darkest recesses of memory, she ventured, "I'm sure I heard my mom singing that once ..."

Perhaps that's just the natural way of things: America is world-famous, after all, for celebrating the new, living in the moment. How quick we are to discard, to expunge what's not immediately relevant to us. Surely it wasn't all that long ago that Hoagy Carmichael—wise, thoughtful, casual in a grown-up, seen-it-all way—was a familiar, even reassuring, presence in our midst. But a lot of mileage now separates his times and ours: change remains the constant, and we dare not forget that those sorts of seismic shifts have always gone on, were even going on in Hoagy's own lifetime.

He spent his first songwriting years in Indiana and New York, immersed in the almost gnostic subculture of hot jazz, a music that burst into 1920s America in its own kind of youth rebellion. By his mid-thirties he was in California, rebel no more, blending into the movie establishment, and he spent the rest of his career writing songs for, and acting in, films.

But then as now, Hollywood trafficked in ephemerality, and too many of the movies that brought Hoagy Carmichael—his face, his image, his songs—to a mass public now repose quietly on video store "classics" shelves, ignored by anyone not expressly seeking them out.

Various of the tunes escaped their films to join the roster of much-loved popular standards, alongside "Georgia on My Mind," "Skylark," and of course the incomparable "Star Dust." But all that exists on the far side of an immense generational divide. From time to time a k. d. lang will recycle "Skylark," or ex-Beatle George Harrison will have a go at "Hong Kong Blues." But for the most part there's no reason why today's kids would have the slightest idea about—or interest in—an old song celebrating the purple dusk of twilight time.

Broadway composers seem to have made out better. Perhaps it's because George Gershwin celebrated life and romance in fast-moving, superhip New York, Cole Porter's reach extended to high-society Paris and Venice, and the melodies of Richard Rodgers melded smartly with the acidulously world-weary lyrics of Larry Hart. Those songs never need reviving because they always seem to be around, and surely more youngsters today know them than know those of Hoagland Carmichael.

But anyone with enough curiosity to stop, look, and listen is bound to find that Hoagy and his songs are still very much alive and—here's the key word—relevant, occupying territory recognizably theirs alone. His melodies and (more often than is popularly realized) lyrics have little in common with the Ruritanian conceits of Jerome Kern, the arch topicality of Porter, or the cutting-edge smarts of the Gershwins. But they have unrivaled strengths of their own.

Hoagy Carmichael's songs can evoke place and time as vividly as the work of Edward Hopper or Sinclair Lewis, the essays of H. L. Mencken, or the humor of Will Rogers. But they're not period pieces. They deal with eternal things: youth and age, life and death, a longing for home. Relatively few of the best known Carmichael songs, in fact, are about love—at least in any explicit, boy-girl, moon-June sense. Hoagy's love songs have their own spin: "I Get Along Without You Very Well," for all its bereavement, remains stoic, never approaching standard-issue "Body and Soul" self-pity. "Skylark" and "Baltimore Oriole" apostrophize birds in the service of amour; "Two Sleepy People" looks back on young romance with wry affection.

Finally, and above all, there's "Star Dust." Rangy, arpeggiated, structurally unconventional in its ABAC format, it stands alone; outfitted with its Mitchell Parish lyric, it's a song about a song about love. No other song even begins to challenge its unique primacy as a kind of informal American national anthem. Even the resolutely yuppified National Public Radio, selecting its "100 most important American musical works of the twentieth century," found time for a lengthy, affectionate Susan Stamberg ode to "Star Dust."

Numerically speaking, Hoagy didn't write many songs—perhaps 650 at a conservative estimate, a mere handful compared to, say, the prolific Irving Berlin. But quantity is at best an unreliable unit of measure: Carmichael's songs are personal statements, most often nourished and reinforced by his own performances. Beyond argument, he's the key precursor of that phenomenon of our own times, the singer-songwriter. Whether Billy Joel or Elton John, Dave Frishberg or Bob Dorough, or the countless others who have made an industry of devising and performing their own material, all share a common ancestor in the wiry little guy at the piano, hat back on his head, often bathed in cigarette smoke as he chides "Lazybones" or "Small Fry," exhorts an "Ole Buttermilk Sky" to be mellow and bright, or extols the fragrant memory of "Memphis in June."

It's possible to talk of songs as having a "Carmichael flavor." Not that they all sound alike or conform to any one model: far from it. Overall, in fact, they're a pretty diverse lot. Yet they remain unmistakably his, and, in all but a very few cases, it's hard to imagine them having been written by anyone else. If such perennials as "Georgia on My Mind," "New Orleans," and "Moon Country" evoke the Southland, it's worth noting that Indiana, set on a firm east-west axis alongside Ohio and Illinois, can also be seen latitudinally, contiguous geographically and socially with Kentucky, Tennessee, and the Carolinas.

Except for Duke Ellington, whose primary activity was not songwriting, Carmichael is arguably the only major tunesmith whose musical roots are discernibly in jazz. Though his later career grew in another direction, he never lost his early affinity for, and love of, the dynamic music of his youth. No coincidence, that some of Louis Armstrong's most majestic recorded moments are in performances of "Star Dust," "Rockin' Chair," and other Carmichael songs.

I discovered Hoagy Carmichael early in life, through the crystalline miracle of Bix Beiderbecke's cornet. Seeking out Bix inevitably meant running across Hoagy's "Riverboat Shuffle," "Washboard Blues," and the original, medium-tempo incarnation of "Star Dust." To a kid growing up in the Boston suburbs of half a century ago, the pair of them seemed American exotics, equal parts roaring-twenties college hepcats and *Saturday Evening Post* Norman Rockwell archetypes.

Imagine all that farmland. Those golden wheatfields and deep blue big-sky summer horizons. Lakefront ballrooms, with no ocean within thousands of miles; nocturnal expeditions into Chicago to find hot jazz in basement cabarets and South Side dance halls. What a wondrous world of discovery and exuberantly, timelessly youthful music!

How easy, too, and how welcome, to bask in the magenta glow of Carmichael's two published memoirs, *The Stardust Road* and the more matter-of-fact *Sometimes I Wonder*. But what about a biography? Books on Gershwin, Porter, Youmans, Kern, and the rest were easy enough to find, as were studies of Armstrong, Ellington, Benny Goodman, and other jazz notables. But no Hoagy. Had his own two books said everything that needed to be said?

Even shorn of its subject's embellishments and elisions, the story asked to be told, and the music badly needed addressing. Alec Wilder's brief Carmichael section in *American Popular Song* had made a start; various estimable writers, from William Zinsser to John Edward Hasse, had added much of value. But a full biography, of both the music and the man, was still yet to come.

I'd like to think that future generations, backpackers and music scholars alike, will read here about Hoagland Carmichael and respond to the American vision so lovingly preserved in his music, a vision now receding much too quickly from view. It's an idealization, of the people we'd like to think we once were and those we want to believe we still can be: open and decent, worldly but appreciative of simple pleasures; pragmatic yet principled, secular yet deeply moral. In our quest to find what's best in ourselves we need all the help we can get, and there's nothing like a *Vorbild* or two to speed things along. Above all, great songs are indestructible artifacts, impervious to time and changing fashion.

With all that in mind, then, I invite you (and my quondam traveling companions, wherever they are) to enter Hoagy Carmichael's world—a world sprinkled, in the most truly magical sense, with stardust.

SOUTHOLD, NEW YORK   R. M. S.

JUNE 1, 2001

"Play me a Hoagy Carmichael song and I hear the banging of a screen door and the whine of an outboard motor on a lake—sounds of summer in a small-town America that is long gone but still longed for."

—William Zinsser
The American Scholar, 1994

STARDUST MELODY

✻ *I* ✻

Daybreak

Sonny—ain't but one thing to remember when you gets to be a man:
You saves your money, and does the best you can.
—HOAGY CARMICHAEL (*Undated, unused lyric*)

Anyone wanting to drive from Indianapolis to Richmond, Indiana, these days simply picks up Interstate 70, which bisects the city, heads east, and steps on the gas. Provided the traffic is relatively light, the weather reasonable, and the police not too attentive, a driver can cover the seventy-three miles in little more than an hour.

That's the way most people in this adrenalized age do it. Driving an interstate in central Indiana, after all, is much like driving one anywhere: self-contained, insular, passing by but never through; experiencing but never partaking. Penetrating, even—but never touching.

At certain points along I-70 it's possible to look south and see, off in the middle distance, another road, running parallel. The map identifies it as Route 40, though most folks in this part of Indiana still call it the "National."

Built in 1827 as a stagecoach route, it cuts right across the middle of the state, from Terre Haute, over by the Illinois line, through Indianapolis, then wanders east toward Ohio; the names of Dunreith, Straughn, Dublin, and East Germantown trace settlement patterns, waves of immigrants moving west, naming new places for those they'd left in search of lives better than what they'd journeyed all those miles, crossed oceans, to escape.

Indiana achieved statehood in 1816, but even before that it was a cross-roads place. Anyone wanting to get from New York, Philadelphia, or Boston to Chicago or Kansas City, St. Louis or Omaha, Des Moines, Minneapolis, or points further west, had to go right through Indiana Territory, on either the train or the National Road. As nineteenth-century America grew, that came to mean meat and grain heading one way, people and supplies moving the other, a burgeoning economy flooding across the heartland.

Few were surprised when the 1890 census placed the statistical center of the U.S. population on Lewis Wells's farm outside Greensburg, some fifty miles southeast of Indianapolis. By 1900 it had marched thirty miles west to another farm, that of Henry Marr, near Columbus, Indiana. B. M. Hutchins, whose firm cut gravestones for just about every family thereabouts, carved a monument for the spot, and the *Indianapolis News* remarked on December 16, 1902, that "farmers for miles around watched the work with interest. Quite a number of Columbus people drove to Marr's farm during the day."[1]

The land was arable, and between 1860 and 1900 the number of Indiana farms increased from 132,000 to 222,000. Newcomers from Germany, from Ireland and Scotland, Scandinavia and Holland, brought a love of the soil and knowledge of what riches it could yield. Indiana forests provided timber. Men quarried limestone from the vast shelf on which much of the state rested.

If modern-day Indianapolis resembles most other medium-sized American conurbations in its ever more cluttered skyline, traffic jams, and labyrinthine one-way systems, its restaurants, motels, and shopping malls, the similarity ends abruptly at the city limits. The National Road may parallel the interstate, but the difference between them—in appearance, tempo, meaning—betokens a gulf of time and culture.

Driving the National eastward, the visitor traverses a gently rolling landscape dotted by old wood-frame houses, stately brick school buildings, churches and Moose lodges, Shell stations and savings banks. Discreet signs extol the Riley Family Restaurant or Suzy's Cafe (no fancy French accent *aigu* here, please), where the Sunday fried chicken dinners are still the best around. Barbershops and "beauty parlors," Jim's Hardware and John Deere dealerships, line the main streets.

As William Least Heat-Moon (in *Blue Highways*, 1982) and other peripatetics have discovered, these towns still speckle the U.S. landscape, their people living out daily lives not so much in spite of as simply alongside and apart from the hurry-up cities. "You enjoy your beepers and cell phones and too-busy-to-bother existence," they seem to say, "and we'll just carry on here, at our own pace, the way we always have."

✻ ✻ ✻

Abraham Lincoln, born in neighboring Kentucky, spent his boyhood in southern Indiana's Spencer County; when he ran for president in 1860, Hoosiers (the origin of the term is unclear) helped vote him in, remaining loyal to the Union throughout the Civil War. Apart from a raid in 1863 by Confederate General John Hunt Morgan, Indiana kept out of the war—making it a prime, 36,000-square-mile postbellum destination for waves of southern blacks moving north to the promise of better lives.

They and other groups at society's margins left their cultural mark—not least on an audience eager for entertainment. In the words of historian Duncan Schiedt, turn-of-the-century Indiana

> was a favored place for touring musical shows of all kinds. The circus, the opera, musical comedy, burlesque, and even the lowly medicine show ... all regarded the Hoosier state as fertile ground. A major circus, the Hagenbeck Wallace organization, was but one of several which wintered at the town of Peru. In Indianapolis, black stage producers got an early start as they sent companies on the road.[2]

Among the visitors were musicians, many of them members of town and traveling tent show bands, representing myriad backgrounds and traditions. As Schiedt puts it, the Germans brought their choral legacy, the Anglo-Saxons their folk melodies, the blacks their rhythmic vitality—and the unique, compelling accents of the blues.

By the late nineteenth century, Indiana folk were living a rich, varied, ever-expanding musical life. It erupted into the national consciousness on the very eve of the twentieth century, when Paul Dresser, brother of novelist Theodore Dreiser, published "On the Banks of the Wabash," his sentimental ode to his home state. Not long after came James Hanley and Ballard MacDonald's "(Back Home Again in) Indiana," reverentially borrowing several key phrases from Dresser's tune.

It didn't take long for songs celebrating Indiana to become staples of the popular repertoire—even if they did run a distant second to Tin Pan

Alley's eternal fascination with a romanticized (and largely fictitious) antebellum South. The first decades of the twentieth century brought nationwide popularity to "Indiana Moon," "You're My Little Indiana Rose," "Wabash Moon," "Dreaming of My Indiana Sweetheart," the punningly titled "Hoosier Sweetheart," and even Dresser's own "Way Down in Old Indiana." Songwriter Harry Von Tilzer, who as Harold Gumm had lived several boyhood years in Indianapolis, expressed fond longing for home in his 1920 "A-B-C-D Blues."[3]

It's perhaps no coincidence, moreover, that Richmond, the last major town on the National Road before it crosses into Ohio, should have been the site of a small pioneer company whose phonograph records chronicled, and in turn helped shape, the history of American twentieth-century music, in particular the unique hybrid form ultimately to be known as jazz.

✻   ✻   ✻

A visitor driving along the National Road today still glimpses bits of earlier Indiana life. A ten-mile stretch between the towns of Cleveland and Charlottesville, say, remains much as it must have been: solid old Victorian houses, set well back on open farmland, frowning at the passage of years like slightly disapproving village elders. Stop along here for a moment, and it's easy to imagine the chill predawn hours of Monday, January 26, 1925, and an open Ford bumping eastward along the two-lane road, two young men scattering the darkness with their laughter.

> We were halfway to Richmond . . . when we stopped and for some reason Bix took out his horn. He cut loose with a blast to warn the farmers and start the dogs howling . . . Clean wonderful banners of melody filled the air, carved the countryside. Split the still night. The trees and the ground and the sky made the tones so right.[4]

That's Hoagy Carmichael talking. When we find him, out there on the National, he's twenty-five, long-faced and solemn; stands a skinny five-eight; plays piano and a little cornet, and is allegedly studying law at Indiana University in his hometown of Bloomington, about fifty miles southwest of here. He's never going to be a lawyer: that much he knows in his heart, though at this point he's nowhere near ready to admit it to himself or anyone else.

Hoagland Howard Carmichael, born in Bloomington on an overcast Wednesday, November 22, 1899, has music on his mind—music, in fact, as embodied in his companion of this night, a quiet, huskily good-looking guy from Iowa, three years his junior, named Leon Beiderbecke. No one ever calls him Leon, of course, except the occasional schoolmarm or maiden aunt. To the rest—parents, friends, an ever-widening circle of admirers— he's "Bix."

His instrument of choice is the cornet, though he's also quite good at the piano. He's already emerged as a minor celebrity in the underground fraternity dedicated to playing "hot music." Enjoying themselves together on this coldly moonlit night, the two friends are bound for quite different destinies: Beiderbecke, impelled by dark inner forces, will burn briefly and brightly, and barely survive the decade. His friend Hoagland, the sometime law student, will walk another path; throughout a long and productive life, he'll bear the imprint of these nights, of the trees and the ground and the sky that "made the tones so right." His friendship with this star-crossed young man, and the music that cascaded so effortlessly out of his horn, will go on shaping the aspiring lawyer's life, ringing bright and forever in the stillness of memory.

✣   ✣   ✣

A first child, Hoagland Carmichael was born at home, in a four-room cottage on Bloomington's Grant Street, only boy in what ultimately became a family of girls. Sometime during his mother's pregnancy, said boyhood friend Harry Orchard, "there was a traveling troupe of circus people stranded in Bloomington and the Carmichaels took in the Hoaglands." The guests went their way, and the name remained.[5]

Howard Clyde Carmichael made a steady if uncertain living running horse-drawn taxis. "He had courted my mother, Lida, while banging a whip into the rump of a fast-pacing horse," the son later recalled, and she "promised to marry him if he'd only slow up."[6]

One of seven children born on Michael Taylor Carmichael's livestock farm near Harrodsburg, twelve miles south of Bloomington, Howard had been a high-spirited boy, especially good with horses. In the U.S. Army during the Spanish-American War, he'd won the nickname "Cyclone" for his uninhibited style in regimental middleweight boxing championships.

A newspaper announcement of his marriage to Mary Lida Robison on

May 24, 1899, describes him neutrally as "a young man of character and promise." His sister Florence remembered him as "the family comedian," entertaining social gatherings with "mimicry and soft-shoe dances . . . a jolly friend of everyone."

Howard Carmichael's photographs show a stocky, stiff, rather solemn man, clearly uncomfortable in front of the camera. A bit rough-and-ready, even intimidating (said his son), but overall "a great guy, an easy mark, a soft touch . . . who was always being bamboozled into something yet not getting riled up about it." Not that he didn't get "riled" once in a while: sudden outbursts of temper could reveal "a primitive instinct that made him a fighter when he was enraged."[7]

Howard's wife, by contrast, was "a shy, poetic young girl" barely five feet tall. Her hairdo and manner of dress emulated those of the "Gibson Girl" ideal created by turn-of-the-century magazine illustrator Charles Dana Gibson, those "classical-faced beauties, smart under their piled-up hair, with studied, superior smiles ready to trap a male."[8]

How close Lida (pronounced "Lye-dah") Robison Carmichael actually came to such perfection is hard to tell. But she possessed at least one striking attribute, owing nothing to Gibson's idealized sophisticates: she was an adept and dynamic pianist. When silent movies came to Bloomington early in the new century, theatre owners hired Lida to improvise piano accompaniments; among her regular places of employment were the Vaudette Nickelodeon, on South College, and the Wonderland Air Dome, on East Sixth Street. When fraternity and sorority houses at Indiana University held weekend dances, Lida was usually at the keyboard, often accompanied on the traps by a man remembered only as Mr. Woodward, who worked days as a clerk in Whitaker's Grocery Store.

She could give a respectable account of "classical" favorites, cobble together impromptu Gilbert and Sullivan medleys, draw on familiar themes from opera and operetta—and toss off such favorites of the day as "The Stars and Stripes Forever" or Scott Joplin's "Maple Leaf Rag," written in the year of young Hoagland's birth. Reportedly she also wrote verse and short stories, though no examples have survived.

Lida lost her heart to "Cyclone" Carmichael from the start. Quick comparison of the dates of their May wedding and the boy's birth six months later indicates that romance bloomed early and ardently. But Cyclone's jobs somehow never seemed to last very long, and when "horseless carriages" began to replace the horse-drawn rigs of his taxi service, he tried

8

his hand awhile as an electrician. Admitting to friends that he was "no Tom Edison," he soon started looking for better-paying work to support his new family.

That meant moving around, going where the jobs were. Sometimes he'd be gone weeks at a time, leaving Lida, her mother, and various aunts to run the home and care for the boy. Feast or famine, with the emphasis too often on the latter. "We were poor white trash," Hoagy Carmichael declared during a 1972 interview, in a surprisingly harsh assessment of the family's economic and social circumstances—and contrasting sharply with the more affectionate tone he usually adopted. But that careless utterance was far from the only hint that life for the Carmichaels had a hardscrabble side, and young Hoagland soon learned to be canny with what little money he had.

Boyhood friend Harry Orchard, later a respected Bloomington banker, recalled Hoagland watching carefully from the sidelines as he and some high school fraternity boys shot craps. "I was up and down and up and down and finally lost every cent I had," Orchard said in a 1983 letter. "I approached [Hoagy] when I had lost all my money and asked for a loan. He wanted to know what I would give him for security and I pulled out my prize Christmas billfold and told him I would give him that as security for a $5 loan. The billfold had cost my mother $10. Hoagy said it wasn't worth $10 but he would lend me $2 if I put it up for security. I gave the billfold to him and he gave me $2, which I later paid back and got the billfold back."[9]

In 1904, his cab business a failure and work as an electrician not forthcoming, Cyclone packed up his little family—including his now-pregnant wife—and headed up Route 22 for Indianapolis. They found an apartment at the corner of East and Lockerbie streets, where, on the second day of November, Lida gave birth to a second child, a daughter they called Georgia.

Three houses down Lockerbie Street lived the rotund, beloved "Hoosier poet" James Whitcomb Riley. By then in his mid-fifties, he'd written such sentimental children's classics as "Little Orphant [sic] Annie" and "The Runaway Boy." Hoagland, no runaway, remembered the poet as "a fine, fat figure of a man," often wobbling around the neighborhood on a bicycle.

He used to carry me on his shoulders to the grocery store, and when the fire engines passed, he counted them for me. There were always fifty. I don't care how many fire engines there are in Indianapolis today, there were always fifty then.[10]

The Indianapolis sojourn didn't last long. By January 29, 1906, Cyclone, his wife, and their two children were back in Bloomington, living at 214 South Dunn Street, a short walk from both the Indiana University campus and its football practice field.[11]

For the lad who later wrote that "change always upset me," it was a time of happiness and—most important to him—stability: "Bloomington offered everything," he wrote. "Creeks, ponds, rabbits, circuses and wide open spaces. I could cross a dusty street here in my bare feet without the aid of a traffic cop."[12]

There were baseball games in summer, and football in autumn, on Dunn's Meadow, a onetime community pasture; winter ice skating on the Jordan River, a local creek named for a past president of the university. Young Hoagland joined in eagerly, showing up regularly at the football field to "become a nuisance generally to the Indiana varsity players."[13]

Gradually he gained a circle of friends, among them cousins Hugh "Percy" Campbell and Sammy Dodds, as well as "Pee Wee" Johnson and "Klondike" Tucker, both from Bucktown, Bloomington's black neigborhood. It established an ease of association across lines of color and class that remained with Carmichael the rest of his life.

Spring brought the Gentry Brothers Dog-and-Pony Show out of its Bloomington off-season quarters, to set up and rehearse on Dunn's Meadow. Then, in high summer, came the big one, the Hagenbeck and Wallace Circus, which wintered in Peru, Indiana—where it had captured the imagination of a well-to-do local boy named Cole Albert Porter.

The days leading up to such big events saw young Carmichael and his pals collecting empty flour sacks from local boardinghouses, then selling them back to Whitaker's grocery for a penny each—just enough to cover the cost of setting up a soda pop stand on the meadow perimeter.

The day before the circus, all hands got together to build a sleeping-out camp with straw beds, tent, and everything. A grape arbor usually provided the best site. Into this we crawled with the flies and mosquitoes. An alarm clock was set for 4 A.M., and we tried our best to go to sleep in the unmercifully hot place at 5 o'clock in the afternoon so we would be wide-eyed and alert to watch the circus unload at an early hour in the morning.[14]

Entry into the first grade at Central Elementary School in early 1906 did little to ruffle the lad's sense of being just where he belonged. Even Cyclone's prolonged absences had a bright side: evenings, when Lida left the house to play the piano at a sorority dance or local movie, the slight figure of her son was more often than not at her side. He recalled doing little dances for the customers—and later putting two folding chairs together and stretching out blissfully beside the piano, letting the music float him far away.

Cyclone Carmichael, meanwhile, "tested my mother's love by his desire for moving and wandering, tearing up roots to try new places, new ideas, new plans . . . He was born too late: he belonged with the wagon trains in the gold rush days." In 1910, like the covered wagons, he headed for the far West, bringing his son's Bloomington idyll to an abrupt end and pitching the boy into despair.[15]

European merchants had settled far western Montana's Bitterroot valley in 1860, and a small town gradually sprang up around the trading post run by C. P. Higgins and Francis Worden. Known at first as "Hellgate Village," it soon had both a sawmill and a flour milling operation—leading newcomers to style it "Missoula Mills" (later shortened to just Missoula), from a Salish Indian word meaning "near cold, chilling waters."

Set in an old glacial lake bed near the three-way juncture of the Clark Fork, Blackfoot, and Bitterroot rivers, it was a place of towering mountain vistas and big skies—and, as Cyclone Carmichael had heard it, limitless opportunity for any man willing to put in a hard day's work. With electricity and telephones just coming in, there were immediate jobs stringing wires south along the Bitterroot to Hamilton.

He went. It's impossible now to know what thoughts went through Lida Carmichael's mind in those weeks, packing up her household, storing her treasured Armstrong golden oak upright piano in her parents' parlor, and, finally, boarding the Monon Line train with her two children, bound for heaven knew where.

Dunn's Meadow, the Jordan, the circus, the magic nights in darkened theatres listening to "Maple Leaf Rag"—all that had meant security for the boy, something to grasp, hold, make his own. Now, in their place, was this raw, inhospitable outpost, where the scale was too vast, the mountains too distant, the wind constant, cold, and hostile. "I was so homesick," he wrote, "I could gaze over Elephant Mountain and imagine I could see the smoke from the tall stack of the Bloomington gas plant curling over it."[16]

Around the same time, and for many of the same reasons, the family of future songwriter Harry Owens left Holt County, Nebraska, and trekked west, first to Hamilton, then up the valley to Missoula. In later years, living comfortably in Hawaii, Owens recalled the selfsame bleak existence.

> As I look back upon that early beginning, memory spells hardship. All summer we would stack the winter fuel supply in the woodshed but the winters were incredibly cold and our wood supply would never quite survive the winter's demands . . . though the word "depression" had yet to come into usage, "bad times" was an expression we learned to know by heart.[17]

"Dad went back there for location work on the movie *Timber Jack*," his elder son, Hoagy Bix Carmichael, told the author in 1998. "I was just fourteen, and came along with him. We drove out to where the family had lived all those years ago—and amazingly enough the little clapboard house they'd rented that winter was still there. Imagine—this teensy piece of land, maybe the size of a garage, in front. That was the 'lawn,' his playground, where he played the little games he writes about in his 1965 memoir, *Sometimes I Wonder*—created a whole imaginary farm, in miniature. He even fenced in the 'lawn' and flooded it with water, just so he could ice-skate, the way they'd done in distant Bloomington.

"The house—it was so small—was right at the brow of a hill. You'd look out and down, and there were the railroad tracks, and beyond them this line of brick row-houses, the brothels, where the lumbermen and other workers took their pleasure. In a funny way that was a good thing: it wasn't long before he discovered that lots of those houses had piano players, black ones, and they played hot ragtime, sort of the way his mother did. He'd had his black pals in Bloomington, and it seemed the most natural thing in the world for him to steal down there and listen to 'em. I don't think his mom ever found out."

Even with such diversions, it was a forbidding place for a ten-year-old. A place of exile. "He felt alone, abandoned in a foreign land . . . In talking to me about it in '54 he was still able, after all those years, to feel those feelings; and his mother, however strong she was—and for all her small size she was as strong as steel—must have shared it. A feeling of utter misery, of being at the very bottom of the barrel, marooned out there at the edge of nowhere. I think it strengthened a resolve in him. No matter what it took, he wasn't going to live this way ever again."[18]

As usual, the big opportunities Howard Carmichael had anticipated—and the good money—never materialized, and by spring 1911 the family had returned to Bloomington, first at the Dunn Street house, then at 325 South Fess Avenue, just two blocks away. Lida, "this little 80 pounds of wire and sweetness," sat down to a dish of her mother's apple pie, recovered her beloved golden oak upright, and got right back to the business of making "a nickel go more places than it does in a dice game," shoring up the family's meager finances with her music.[19]

But something had changed. No one knew why, but suddenly young Hoagland began to show signs of something like musical aptitude. It came oddly wrapped, in an almost obsessive interest in the 1891 sentimental ballad "Little Boy Blue." With the kind of single-mindedness only an eleven-year-old knows, he implored his mother to teach him the words, penned by nineteenth-century American poet Eugene Field (music by Ethelbert Nevin, best known as the composer of "Mighty Lak a Rose").

After what he remembered as "weeks of practice" he was able to sing melody and words. "The story of the angels taking Little Boy Blue away, and how his 'tin soldiers and toy dog stood staunch and sturdy in their rust' to await his return, had made a firm impression on my memory long before."[20]

He quickly graduated from singing his new *tour de force* just for the family to doing it in public. "The entire grade school turned out en masse in the great halls of the school building to hear the young maestro as he stood beside a grand piano and 'chilled' them to the accompaniment of the best-looking red-headed teacher in town," he wrote.[21]

Even allowing for some embroidery in the telling, it seems inevitable that such musical prowess would have led various Carmichaels and Robisons to recommend lessons on the violin or piano. Lida's answer was characteristically forthright: "We don't see any point in forcing something on the child that he doesn't have a hankering for. We'll know soon enough if he has any talent."[22]

Carmichael himself later agreed. "Kid days are short enough," he said, without the regimen of time-consuming practice required by serious instrumental study. What neither Lida nor Howard, and certainly not their son, could have known was how soon that "hankering" would show itself and what an extraordinary form it would take.

✳ *II* ✳

Discovery

John Porter Foley had every reason to be happy. Since 1896, his first year as a student at Indiana University, he'd held the post of campus electrician and "mechanician." Any problem with an electric or mechanical device and—well, just find Mr. Foley. He'd know what to do.

So it was that when, on Saturday, January 20, 1906, the bells for the university's brand-new clock tower finally arrived, John Porter Foley oversaw their installation. They'd been expected in mid-December, in plenty of time to be mounted, adjusted, and rung out on New Year's Eve. The McShane Bell Company of Baltimore had shipped them on time, but something had gone wrong in transit, and they'd arrived a month late, much to the chagrin of school administrators.

The $120,000 Student Building, housing a six-hundred-seat auditorium, a cafeteria, barbershop, film theatre, billiard room, swimming pool, and men's and women's gymnasium facilities, was due to open in June; it would take weeks to lift the eleven massive bells to the top of its hundred-foot clock tower, mount them, attach them to their keyboard mechanism, and get them working. A month's delay, even at the start, could affect the dedication ceremony, scheduled for commencement week.

Nor were alumni of the classes 1899 through 1902 overjoyed. They'd beat bushes and twisted arms to raise the $3,650 (valued at nearly $66,000 by today's standards) it cost to purchase and ship the bells. The idea that they might not ring out for the first time until summer recess, with nobody but local merchants and townsfolk to hear them, was almost too much to bear.

Only John Porter Foley seemed unruffled. The job would be done, he assured them, properly and on time.

And so it came to pass. On Tuesday, June 19, 1906, students and teachers stood by proudly as university president William Lowe Bryan dedicated the new building, hewn of the Indiana limestone so plentiful in Monroe County. With Mr. Foley working the big broom-handle keys, the clock-tower bells struck the hour, then pealed out the school's newly adopted alma mater, "Hail to Old I.U."

They resounded from one end of campus to the other. There seemed no place in Bloomington where they could *not* be heard loudly, proudly—and, above all, clearly. Every weekday afternoon at six, for years thereafter, all Bloomington turned an ear to Mr. Foley (or, for a while, his deputy Archie Warner), tolling out "Hail to Old I.U."[1]

Mr. Foley's rendering of the melody was clearly audible one rainy six o'clock at 325 South Fess Avenue, to the young ears of Hoagland Howard Carmichael. As he later told it, a regular Saturday afternoon baseball game at Dunn's Meadow had been rained out. He'd been standing there in the family's parlor, he said, looking out at the rain and banging his fists in frustration on the keyboard of his mother's upright piano—and, as if in reply, the strains of "Hail to Old I.U." came floating back to him. A simple melody, spanning less than an octave, it moves scalewise from the tonic—in this case in the key of A-major. Imagination needs no prompting to picture the boy reaching over and picking out the theme with one finger on the piano keyboard.[2]

"I had been exposed to the piano all my life, but no one ever told me to try it, to touch its keys," he recalled later. "Yes, I had discovered a whole new world, and found a new true love." Sometime after this epiphany his mother came home, and "put her arms around me from behind, and held me ever so tightly and I felt her tears falling on my shaggy neck. I didn't turn around. I went on playing. I knew then that my mother had realized a secret goal and that neither of us would be lonely again, as long as we kept that piano."[3]

(In his various memoirs, Carmichael places these events on a Saturday afternoon. But the chimes sounded "Hail to Old I.U." at six P.M. only on weekdays, never weekends. Young Carmichael may indeed have been frustrated because the rain thwarted his after-school plans—but where were his mother and sisters at what was, after all, nearly the family dinner hour? In all probability the story, even if basically true, contains a liberal amount of embroidery.)[4]

Lida Carmichael soon began to acquaint her son with some keyboard rudiments. "Mother showed me the simple construction of the bass and occasionally the fifth," he wrote. "That seemed an impossibility to find in a tough key like three flats, but she always left me with something difficult to solve. This was good psychology and was most helpful to one who was picking it out by 'ear.' "[5]

Exact information is scarce. But it's obvious that young Carmichael's interest in music, and skill at the piano, grew apace. The very fact of sharing a musical life with his mother, he has written, allowed him to "let myself go a little more. I wasn't even too annoyed at my father's loud ways, his hunt for a crazy rainbow at the end of some uprooting journey. I was learning to observe, to file away my emotions, the way a big-eyed, silent kid will."[6]

✻   ✻   ✻

There is a miniaturized, and idealized, flavor to all this, making it all too easy to imagine the actors in Bloomington's small drama living their lives oblivious to a world dominated by real, even apocalyptic, events.

But that world was out there, waiting. On Sunday, September 6, 1914, one ocean and thousands of land miles from Indiana, a war unlike any other in history was sputtering into action. French troops, under the imposing figure of sixty-two-year-old General Joseph Jacques-Césaire "Papa" Joffre, fell upon General Alexander Von Kluck's exhausted German forces near the river Marne, outside Paris. When the battle smoke lifted at week's end, hundreds of thousands of men lay dead, and what quickly came to be called "the Great War" had engulfed Europe. The United States, at least for the moment, stayed out; but that would not last long.

If these five days that shook the world attracted any notice at all in communities such as Bloomington, Indiana, it was distant, abstract. The life of small-town America went its sealed, still relatively pastoral, way. And on an Indiana Wednesday in the week of the Marne, Hoagland Carmichael entered Bloomington High School.

He speaks affectionately of his first "long-pants suit that took $19.50 of Dad's hard-earned cash"; recounts his "crushes" among the girls, and his efforts to win dates with his favorites. When, that March, classmate Ruth Orchard hands him her "character book" to sign, he inscribes his answers to its many questions with a blend of whimsy and high seriousness. "Give a description of yourself," it demands. Answer: "Red eyes, pink hair, pointed nose." What is the signer's highest ambition? "To be something." What is his mother's maiden name? "Ko Chug Ling Chi." Favorite pastime: "Playing the piano." His ideal of a man: "True, honest, brave, strong, good disposition." Kind of life he prefers: "Happy, fast, go-lucky."[7]

The overwhelming impression is of a youngster born into slender means, immersing himself ardently in music, a diversion that will shortly expand into a world for him. More and more, his every waking moment reflects fascination with his mother's keyboard skills. Two-steps, he recalls later, "were the rage, and mother could play them in swell style. Her tiny right hand that stretched to reach the octaves had the power of a man's, and her left never missed a beat of the difficult rhythm."[8]

In 1912, shortly after the birth of a second daughter, Martha Claire, Cyclone Carmichael found work in Bedford, some twenty miles south of Bloomington. His son speaks of it as if the family, uprooted again, had moved there and suffered for a year before returning to Bloomington, but that's unlikely: Bedford is not far enough away to warrant such a convulsion, and no break appears in the boy's public school records. Hoagland often baby-sat evenings for his sisters—another indication that Lida's piano-playing jobs went on as usual. Another lonely patch, yes, but this time the piano "had me body and soul," and "the days without companionship gave me hours of much needed practice."[9]

The cottage on South Fess Avenue lay directly behind Beta Theta Pi, one of the more imposing and well-to-do houses on Third Street, in those days Indiana University's fraternity row. It stood on a natural promontory some fifteen feet above the Carmichaels' low-lying backstreet dwelling, enhancing its sense of exaltation in the boy's mind. "I had my own tiny bedroom with a slanting ceiling and I would lie on my bed nights, listening to the college boys carry on," Carmichael writes. Among them was Wendell Willkie ('13), a future Republican presidential candidate, and Paul V. McNutt ('13), one day to become governor of Indiana.

But above all there was Hubert Herschel Hanna, whose father taught mathematics at the university. His field, officially, was economics, but most fellow-students knew "Hube" as a ragtime pianist. "Not only was his left hand a whiz-bang, but his right was the miracle of the times as it ran octaves at lightning speed," Carmichael writes. "Unconsciously, his bass made the firmer impression on me as I lay night after night near my window to take in his chords amid the whoops and howls of the dear old Beta Theta Pi boys."[10]

Hanna also led the university's only dance band, a quintet that included Francis "Hank" Wells on "hot" fiddle and "Red" Carmichael, no relation, on C-melody saxophone; they were good enough to play weekends at the Crescent movie house, where young Hoagland became a regular attendee. Soon various of Hube Hanna's fancy bass figures began showing up in the boy's own "treatments" of popular tunes of the day. "It wasn't long until I noticed students hesitate occasionally as they passed our house to get an earful of the 'Maori' I was copying from Hube . . . This excited me to a louder bombardment of the keys with the piano lid wide open and my left heel pounding the floor."[11]

(Composed in 1914 and identified on its published sheet music as a "Samoan Dance," *The Maori* gained wide popularity, along with the slightly earlier *The Trocha*, at the height of the first tango craze, as one of the first tangos written by a home-grown American musician. Its composer, William H. Tyers, was assistant conductor of the famed James Reese Europe Clef Club Orchestra, whose performances were at that time the talk of New York. Tyers, a pianist and arranger, also composed such straightforward ragtime pieces as the "Barn Yard Shuffle" and, notably, "Panama," which went on to become a staple of the early jazz band repertoire. He died in 1924.)

According to one account, only a thin wall separated the Carmichael home from the house next door, and the young man's left heel stomping out *The Maori*'s tango rhythms was only too audible to the neighbors. "Every minute I could I banged away, hunting chords on the old upright," Carmichael recalled; "there are no sounds more irritating than unfound music." One neighbor, a man who worked nights, seemed to agree, confessing later that the boy's before-school pounding had indeed kept him awake. "He has some talent for composing and it's important to encourage him" was Lida's no-nonsense reply.[12]

Hoagland "continued to pound out notes on the piano like a madman, trying to impress the peg[ged trouser]-legged college boys in tailored clothes as they walked past our window. *I wanted them to see how refined I was* [emphasis added]. I was amazed that they never seemed to pay any attention to me. I thought I was good; at least I played loudly, and in stylish ragtime."[13]

Mark well that statement: "I wanted them to see how refined I was." A small, wiry kid, growing up on the wrong side of Bloomington's town-gown divide, living for the first time in a house with indoor plumbing, perceives another world over his backyard fence, a world of comfort and substance, in which people can afford to hire a black cook to prepare their meals, to dress in tailored clothes, and in general lead lives that are "happy, fast, go-lucky."

He makes little of this in his memoirs, even less in the many polished interviews he gave over the years. But it doesn't take much reading between the lines to feel the longing of his emotionally locked-up imagination to transcend the small world of itinerant labor, nickel-and-dime saving, and making-do. And it is the music, clearly, that will make his escape possible.

In early twentieth-century America, the role of professional music differed widely in the aspirations of people of different classes. In the imaginations of such bourgeois families as the Beiderbeckes of Davenport, Iowa, or even the rather less affluent Dreisers of Terre Haute, Indiana, a life in popular music was a step down, usually into a *demi-monde* inhabited by gamblers, thieves, pimps, whores, and petty crooks. "Music," as historian Neil Leonard puts it, "was considered an enjoyable avocation, but a musical career was thought to be unfit for a gentleman." Conductor-educator Walter Damrosch amplified the point: "A strong feeling existed," he wrote in his 1923 autobiography, "that music was essentially an effeminate art, and that its cultivation by a man took that much away from his manliness." The 1910 census found 84,000 American women working as musicians and music teachers, compared to only 54,000 men. Little wonder that Paul Dreiser, whose younger brother Theodore aspired to a literary life, changed his name to Dresser long before his song "On the Banks of the Wabash" became a national rage.[14]

Prospects for poor blacks were quite different. The Civil War and Reconstruction still burned painfully in memory; slavery was no longer the law of the land, but free black men and women still confronted "Jim Crow" racism in a segregated society. With most "respectable" professions closed to all but a relative few, there was little choice but to take opportunities where they occurred: the life of a professional entertainer or band musician offered travel, earning potential, even possible fame and (especially as in the case of such figures as James Reese Europe or the venerated conductor, composer, and Oberlin Conservatory alumnus Will Marion Cook) dignity. Such allure drew to ragtime, and later to jazz, a disproportionate number of young men who might otherwise have distinguished themselves as concert artists, composers, painters, authors—and even, by extension, physicians, scientists, and academics.[15]

The Carmichaels worked hard at maintaining a modest version of the gentility they perceived in those more privileged than they. Even a morning's walk up Main Street was a lesson in comparative sociology. Booth Tarkington, writing about turn-of-the-century Indianapolis in *The Magnificent Ambersons*, describes houses that

> lacked style, but also lacked pretentiousness, and whatever does not pretend at all has style enough. They stood in commodious yards, well shaded by left-over forest trees, elm and walnut and beech, with here and there a line of tall sycamores where the land had been made by filling bayous from the creek.[16]

A burgeoning, industrialized twentieth-century economy was beginning to open a new sense of social mobility among members of all classes. It mattered ever less what you did or what you came from, as long as you somehow got where you wanted to go. Music would be young Carmichael's means of ascent, up and away toward a wider, more promising life.

He felt at ease among black families, and from all indications they felt no less so with him. In a 1982 reminiscence, Bloomington resident Mary Cardell Johnson recalled the young man always receiving a warm welcome at the Tenth Street home of Collet and Vertis Johnson. "We liked to see him because we liked to dance and he played the piano for us," she said. "He was a swell guy."[17]

For Hoagland—or "Hogie," as he was beginning to be called—the piano meant both his mother's ragtime specialties and the flashy keyboard feats of Hube Hanna. Saturday nights usually found him in the darkness of the Crescent Theatre, listening to Hanna and Hank Wells beating out such lively tunes as "Mammy Jinny's Jubilee," a 1913 hit by L. Wolfe Gilbert, composer of "Waiting for the Robert E. Lee," "Down Yonder," and the later "Jeannine, I Dream of Lilac Time."[18]

Hank Wells is a pivotal figure in Carmichael's young life. Arriving at the university in 1914, he created an almost immediate stir with what a later newspaper account called "original ideas about dance music. Wells had such an unusual technique, back in those days of the more graceful steps, that his efforts were wasted on the campus socialites."[19]

"Hank Wells," said Indiana bandleader Charlie Davis, "could inspire anyone. He played a lot of jazz fiddle, could romp all over a piano, and write a sensitive lyric with the best of 'em." At the piano, Carmichael added, Wells "knew what he was doing when he brought his left thumb down on the seventh of a chord that his right hand already had struck. This was to emphasize the dominating [*sic*] harmony."[20]

Home recordings of Wells playing and singing his own songs, made years later, reveal a sure touch at the piano and a gently reflective way with melody and lyric. The sensibility occasionally resembles that of Willard Robison (1894–1968), a Missouri-born singer-pianist who wrote such evocative and homespun songs as "Old Folks," "Guess I'll Go Back Home This Summer," and the poignant "Deep Summer Music." Indiana historian Duncan Schiedt has referred to Wells as "a sentimental songsmith, whose influence on Carmichael can be detected in songs like Hoagy's *Little Old Lady* and *The Nearness of You*." Among Wells's outstanding creations is "Falling Star," a sixteen-bar waltz with a dreamy, nostalgic flavor.[21]

Another local figure who plays a role in the boy's early development is the pianist, singer, and occasional banjoist Edwin East, known variously as "Big Ed" or the slightly less flattering "Heavy." Proprietor of a Bloomington music store, he worked frequently around town, amusing audiences with original comedy songs bearing such titles as "Louise, Louise, Come out of the Trees," and "Hello, Hoosier Town." For a while he worked with Charlie Davis's Indianapolis band, playing banjo and doubling at the keyboard during change-of-instrument novelty numbers.[22]

A world was beginning to open up for the boy: silent-film thrillers at the Princess Theatre; a weekend job as ticket taker at the Harris Grand Opera House, despite its high-flown name a cinema with a largely black clientele; and, too, there were the high school fraternities, Beta Phi Sigma and Kappa Alpha Phi, and the Greek Candy Kitchen, frequented by high schoolers, run by the Poolitsans, the family that owned the more popular Book Nook, a collegiate hangout on Indiana Avenue.

Neighbor Bill Kenney remembered the times young Carmichael "came over to our house and my mother used to let him bang away on our piano in our parlor. He had a one-finger base [*sic*] then and played a tune called 'The Little Red House on the Hill.' Years later, when Hoagy became famous, my mother was very proud of that piano, as she used to tell people the above incident."[23]

✻　　　　✻　　　　✻

This hometown idyll came to an abrupt end in early 1916, when Howard Carmichael's errant fortunes took him back to Indianapolis. This time the family came to rest at 27 North Warman Street, remembered by Hoagland as "the thin dark side of a double-fronted place" on the capital's west side. Directly across the street, the Central Indiana Hospital for the Insane cast a hulking, gloomy shadow across the neighborhod.

In mid-February the boy enrolled at Manual Training High School on South Meridian, a two-and-a-half-mile walk from Warman Street. He remembered the school as a bleak, lonely place ("I never had a friend or knew a girl or a boy as a human being"), and this time in his young life as even bleaker. "I was a mixed-up kid, living at school like a monk with a vow not to talk or enjoy anything if he could help it" is a typical reminiscence.[24]

He was there a little more than one miserable year. Lacking friends or diversions, he tried vainly to apply himself to his studies. Finally, "when the teacher tried to show me how to shingle a roof"—something he'd already learned better from his Grandpa Robison—"I knew my school days were numbered." Declaring Manual Training High School "no go with me," Hoagland Carmichael, age sixteen, left on April 25, 1917, and went out looking for a job.

Short for his age, pale of complexion and slight of figure, he was nonetheless strong enough to work, sometimes alongside his peripatetic cousin Sammy Dodds, on a construction gang putting up the city's brand-new Union Station. He dug ditches; pulled twelve-hour night shifts running a cement mixer; stood on an assembly line making bicycle chains; spent a few bootless weeks as a grocery store delivery boy. But his fortunes and morale hit bottom with a three-week ordeal at the Kingan meat-packing plant, extracting and cleaning the bloody entrails of freshly slaughtered pigs in "a forgotten dungeon, a hell-hole full of death."

This was no less desperate a time for his parents. Arrival of a third daughter, Joanne, in mid-1915 swelled the family to six, taxing even Lida Carmichael's ability to stretch a dollar. At one point a charity worker, well meaning, came calling with an offer of food and clothes—only to collide headlong with Lida's fierce pride: "Young woman, what are you *talking* about?" she demanded, showing her visitor the door.

"My father tried to make us a home," Hoagland recalled. "He went to a cheap furniture store and bought, on time, some of the worst furniture one could possibly imagine . . . the cheapest sticks of wood, highly varnished with a junky finish." Beyond the loneliness, the sense of desolation, and—yes—an element of self-pity, something else is at work here, a sense that even this difficult time has a role to play.

"It's easy to paint too dark a picture of one's unsettled youth," Carmichael writes, "and I don't want to grime up my own early life as nothing but a struggle, all dark edges and hard times, with me fighting onward and upward against odds . . . Mother had seen to it that her piano was there and that was all that mattered to us. We rattled away at four-handed noise."[25]

And, too, there was Joanne: golden-haired, affectionate, the little girl seemed a reason for endless rejoicing. Even when she misbehaved, she won every heart. Hoagland's memory of one tantrum in particular seems to glow on the page:

> Almost two hours of struggle and howling took place and then all of a sudden there was quiet. I kissed her on the cheek and said, "I love you," and she kissed me back and said in a small voice, "I wove you." That was the end of the tantrums and, after that, no sweeter, [more] obedient child ever existed.[26]

So sometimes, after all, "the sun shone, life felt good, I smiled and laughed, we enjoyed our food and took our little pleasures." And, as he writes elsewhere of himself and cousin Sammy, "if there was anything to get our noses into, we found it." Did he and cousin Sammy, by all accounts a precocious young man of the world, actually spend so many evenings exploring the fleshpots of greater Indianapolis, especially those with black ragtime piano players, as Hoagland later suggested? It makes a fine story—but it's hard to imagine his conscientious mother voicing no objection at the idea of her young son out carousing after work, often in parts of town that were at least questionable. Whatever their frequency and nature, the boys' nocturnal adventures seem to have included anywhere that had a piano, be it the Columbia Burlesque House (with ragtime whiz Harry Bason at the keyboard), some nameless backstreet Greek restaurant, or even a co-worker's shabby parlor.[27]

There may also have been a few expeditions to Indiana Avenue, center of the city's black nightlife—and, perhaps on one of these forays, a chance meeting with the pianist Reginald Alfred DuValle, whom bandleader Charlie Davis and others have called "the elder statesman of Indiana Jazz." Born in Indianapolis in 1893, DuValle first surfaced around 1912, playing second (ensemble) piano with the popular Indianapolis dance orchestra of pianist Russell Smith (no relation to New York trumpeter Russell "Pop" Smith) at the Severin Hotel. Kentucky born, Smith gained some early renown as composer of such pre–World War I novelties as the "Princess Rag."[28]

But ragtime, like the hot jazz that would soon grow out of it, was still largely a regional phenomenon. Itinerant dance band musicians, on the road, generally knew who the good players were in far-removed places. But such communities as Denver and San Antonio, Indianapolis and Louisville, though musically active, were too far from New York or even Chicago to make much impact on popular consciousness. Nevertheless, recordings by "territory" bands of both races reveal the vigorous, often creative, musical life of such locales.

Throughout the century's second decade, Russell Smith led Indiana-based groups of consistently high quality, played Florida society affairs for James Reese Europe, and later settled in New York City, where he worked for W. C. Handy, knew and was respected by fellow-pianists James P. Johnson and Perry Bradford, and toured with the hit musical *Shuffle Along*.

Reg DuValle, meanwhile, remained in Indianapolis, leading his own band, with himself at the piano, providing society dance music for the ballrooms and "dancing academies" (Brenecke's, on downtown Meridian Street, was one) proliferating in the capital, playing dances at local facilities and at area schools, including Purdue and Indiana universities. When the Walker Theatre, financed by and named for cosmetics magnate Mme. C. J. Walker, opened on Indiana Avenue in 1927, DuValle's "Blackbirds" were the resident band.[29]

Did the adolescent Hoagland Carmichael really first cross paths with this respected musician "in a crumbum dive," as he later asserted? Did DuValle actually tell him that "a brown man plays where he can?" It's possible, though it fits uneasily the image of the handsome, dignified pianist of Brenecke's, the Severin, or the no less toney Lincoln Hotel. What's beyond dispute is the effect that hearing DuValle had on the young man. "Reggie had the new black music tricks and he made ragtime sound old hat. With his head hanging to one side, as if overcome with ecstasy, he'd play and play—and grin. 'You listening, boy?' I would sit, absorbed, watching the movements of his crazy hands."[30]

What was it DuValle was actually *doing*, Carmichael wanted to know.

"You bring your thumb down on the chord right after you've hit it with your right hand."

"Yeah," he grinned. "I want that harmony to *holler*."

"To laugh?"

"Look, Mr. Carmichael," Reggie said . . . "Never play anything that ain't *right*. You may not make any money, but you'll never get mad at yourself."[31]

"He showed me the art of improvising" is Carmichael's evaluation, "using the third and the sixth of the chord as a basis for arpegii [*sic*]. In this manner, Reg departed from the stilted rag-time I had known." Another musician shortly to impress young Carmichael, saxophonist Bradford "Batty" De-Marcus, referred to DuValle's "fine solid tenths and rolling bass."[32]

DuValle's son Reg, a skilled trombonist born in 1927, remembered hearing his father play "a style with the left hand working in a sort of stride manner. He had such big hands, he had a big stretch, and could voice chords interestingly. He was way ahead of his time, especially with his chords—though his 'feel' was still ragtime. Not that his harmonies were what you'd call 'way out'—he stuck largely to the melody, and embellished that. One thing nobody knows is that he wrote the melody for at least part of what became 'Copenhagen.' Sold it to [white bandleader] Charlie Davis for five dollars."[33]

Young Carmichael became a frequent guest in the DuValle home, at 1202 Harlan Street on the largely black south side of Indianapolis. "In our neighborhood we seldom had any white people," the younger DuValle said. "So he kind of stood out, if you know what I mean."[34]

Billed as "the Rhythm King," Reg DuValle also broadcast regularly on Indianapolis radio station WFBM (later known as WKBF). A printed program from a February 25, 1927, concert sponsored by the "Colored Men's Branch Y.M.C.A." lists his eleven-piece orchestra, fronted by violinist Theo Cable, playing such favorites of the day as "Moonlight on the

Ganges," "On the Road to Mandalay," "Indian Love Call," a Hawaiian medley, and a selection of hits from Rudolf Friml's 1925 operetta *The Vagabond King*—as well as Fred Rose's much-recorded 1926 stomp "Deep Henderson."[35]

Though business fell off with the Depression, DuValle continued to lead bands during the 1930s, while holding down a day job with the Linco Gas Company. Later, using his second instrument, the accordion, he toured widely on the Ohio Gas Company's promotional "Lincoln Safety Train," remaining widely known, and beloved, among veteran musicians; members of major bands, including those of Cab Calloway, Eubie Blake, and Noble Sissle (who had gotten his start in Indianapolis singing with Russell Smith), frequently stayed overnight at the DuValle home—a pleasant and gracious antidote to the segregation still in force in area hotels. Reginald DuValle died in 1953.

✤   ✤   ✤

It's not clear just when the Carmichael family's Indianapolis exile ended. Harry Orchard's diaries have "Hogie" back in Bloomington in early autumn of 1917, determined to reenter high school there. *Jazzbanders*, his unpublished first memoir, speaks of a return to the college town in early 1919, with ten dollars in his pocket, and Bloomington High School records show him rejoining the student body for the spring term of that year.

With his family still living in Indianapolis, it's likely that the young man took several trips home, renewing old friendships and hatching plans to return, even if on his own. Others, including neighbor Bill Kenney, refer to him staying with his grandmother and grandfather Robison at 907 Atwater Street, in the same West Bloomington neighborhood as the Dunn Street and South Fess Avenue houses.[36]

And, as if all the hardship and aimlessness hadn't been catalyst enough, there came a day dark beyond words—an event that hardened his resolve to escape the family's shabby, hand-to-mouth life of matchstick furniture and social-worker solicitude, the constant upheaval, the nightmarish jobs in the slime and gore of bloody animal entrails.

That was the day in 1918 when three-year-old Joanne, of the golden curls and cherub's laughter, died, victim of remorseless illness. A passage in *Jazzbanders* powerfully describes the effect on his father—and, by implication, on himself:

He walked into the house after a twenty-four hour ride in a cold day-coach with the hope that diphtheria was not very serious. He found his child in her little white dress. Only a week before he had given her the most prolonged farewell any girl ever got as he struck out for a "boom" town in Alabama to make enough money so we all could eat. Because it was a diphtheria case, there were no services, but Mother had the courage to play a hymn on the old upright piano we had carted all over the country and which I had banged out of tune long before.[37]

Among Hoagy Carmichael's private papers is a small photograph of Jo-anne, sunlit, winsome, happy in that very same white dress. On the back, scrawled in her brother's unmistakable hand, is the briefest of inscriptions:

My sister Joanne—the victim of poverty. We couldn't afford a good doctor or good attention, and that's when I vowed I would never be broke again in my lifetime. She died from dyptheria [*sic*] and it broke my heart that I didn't have the knowledge or where withall [*sic*] to help her. It broke my dad's heart, too.[38]

And, on a separate scrap of paper: "It's strange, but even to this day [1957] I get wet eyes when I think of her. I think Dad . . . would rather have seen me go."[39]

Was it truly diphtheria? At first unnoticed, almost undocumented, a deadly influenza epidemic had spread across the nation, carrying off thousands, especially children and young people in the prime of life. A mysterious killer, it struck without warning; young and old suddenly "took sick" and, after a few days of bleeding, failing respiration, and raging fever, died in agony, leaving families shocked, disoriented, demoralized. It had first appeared that spring, with an outbreak at Fort Riley, Kansas, spreading to Michigan, Georgia, and other military bases all over the country. In early summer it disappeared awhile, only to resurface in civilian Philadelphia and other eastern cities.[40]

By Carmichael's own account, the family could not afford adequate medical care; diphtheria and influenza shared enough symptoms in common to make misdiagnosis—especially by a less than perceptive physician—a real possibility. Without firm documentation, and in view of recent discoveries about the 1918 influenza virus, it is plausible to surmise that Joanne

Carmichael's death was the result not of diphtheria but of "Spanish flu," which by early autumn had assumed epidemic proportions nationwide.

By this time America was in the Great War, with young men of Hoagland's age signing up by the thousands. The thought of going to war must have seemed appealing: order, purpose, a clean uniform—a chance to fight for Uncle Sam against the demonized "Hun." And, perhaps most of all, a way out of bereavement and penury at home, driven by a pervasive fear that he "didn't have anything to give. I was not attractive in a collar-ad way. I had an inferiority complex as long as a tape worm. I felt unattractive, unpopular, untalented."[41]

Eighteen years old, ignorant of the carnage of the Marne and the Somme, "Hogie" saw this as "the last of the great romantic wars . . . I wanted to get into it and away from my miserable jobs." Wartime food shortages and generally straitened circumstances, moreover, were making it ever harder for Lida to feed her family. With Joanne gone and Hoagland in uniform, things would surely be easier, if not happier.

Word had spread that the first American to fire a shot in that war was a South Bend boy named Alexander Arch, who discharged an artillery piece on October 22, 1917. The shell casing was later sent to President Woodrow Wilson. The first American casualty was reportedly also a Hoosier. Men from Evansville and Madison, members of the famed "Rainbow Division," were among the conflict's first recognized American heroes. Even much-admired Hube Hanna was stationed in a field artillery unit at Camp Taylor, near Louisville.[42]

In all, about 118,000 Indiana men signed up for duty. "The farm boys and clerks put on the itchy, high-collared, pinch-hipped uniforms, and I decided I soon would, too," Carmichael writes. But would the U.S. Army take a long-faced, solemn, skinny kid who stood not much over five feet and weighed a scant 110 pounds? After weeks of consuming gallons of water and stuffing himself with bananas and milk (widely thought, in those days, to put quick and temporary weight on any frame), he reported to a recruiting office in downtown Indianapolis. He passed—and walked out reborn as Private Hoagland Howard Carmichael, U.S. Army.[43]

The date, as he gives it, was November 10, 1918, a Sunday. The following day, November 11, Allied and Imperial German forces signed an armistice in a railway car on a siding in the French forest of Compiègne. The "Great War" was over—and with it, says Carmichael, his career in uniform.[44]

The historical record does not support his account. Army recruitment centers had never been open on Sundays; on August 8, 1918, the U.S. Army had ordered its recruiting service to discontinue all voluntary enlistment of men under age forty-six. Under the new Selective Service Act, able-bodied men eighteen to forty-five would be drafted, filling the nation's mobilization needs. September 3 brought a second order, shutting all Army recruiting stations until further notice, and on October 7, with influenza sweeping through military camps from coast to coast, General Enoch Crowder, provost marshal general of the Army, canceled the October draft altogether.[45]

There is no reason to think Carmichael fabricated the entire story. But given this information it's reasonable to conclude either that his brief Army hitch was the result of being drafted earlier or that whatever attempt he made at enlistment occurred at a different time.

He has written of being in Indianapolis for that year's Indiana–Notre Dame football game, but university records show no such game in 1918. Better to heed the meticulously kept diary of Harry Orchard, which has him in Bloomington, hanging out with some high school friends at the Kappa Alpha Phi fraternity hall, the day after Christmas, December 26, 1918:

"It was around 3 o'clock in the afternoon and coming up the hall we heard a noise of something being dragged along, and in a minute or two here came Mr. Steinmetz and his son Hilas, a member of Kappa Alpha Phi, carrying a set of drums . . . They went into the dance hall and set them up. Mr. Steinmetz came into the room where we were sitting and said, 'Hoagie, play some on the piano so Hilas can accompany you on his new drums he got for Christmas.' Hoagie said, 'Play piano! Play piano! Play piano! That's all I hear: Play piano! Play piano! Play piano!' And he just sat there on his chair.

"Finally he got up, gave a deep breath and went into the dance floor and started playing, Hilas trying to improvise on his new drums. We were behind many months with our rent to Mr. Sudbury, the owner of the building, and had just about decided we were going to have to move out. Bob Strong sat there listening to Hoagie on the piano and Hilas on the drums and got the idea for Saturday night dances. He was president of the fraternity, and pushed it through at the next meeting. The charge was to be $1.00 per couple, and from then on every Saturday night until Indiana University let out we had dances. Paid our back rent and had money in the bank."[46]

Carmichael, too, remembered those events: "Hilas had grown up since the days I knew him as Mr. Steinmetz's little boy, and it had never occurred to me that he was interested in music. But Hilas was smart enough to know where the dollars came from and was eager to get hold of a few so he could carry on with the girls in the Greek Candy Kitchen without having his style cramped."

One of the first numbers they tried together was "Pretty Little Baby," a song by Phil Baker, whose song-and-dance act with future bandleader Ben Bernie was one of the hottest tickets in vaudeville at the time. After a few tentative bars, the two young musicians settled down. For Hoagland Carmichael the moment was an epiphany. "I had never played with drums before and had no conception of the surging emotion that I felt in my head. It was like a machine, a perfect machine that automatically placed my fingers on keys that I never had played before."[47]

It was "the second big thrill of my life . . . The years spent in Indianapolis hadn't been for naught." He wound up after the first Kappa Alpha Phi dance with five dollars in his pocket, and a brand-new musical career under way at last.

✳ *III* ✳

Initiation

Young Carmichael's first dance engagement at Kappa Alpha Phi was more than just a musical turning point; perhaps more important to him at the time, it was his ticket of admission to the sacred precincts of the Book Nook.

First opened in 1908, the place actually had been a book (or, some said, news) shop, run in a one-story frame house by Charles W. Jewett and his partner, a man remembered only as Fetzger. An architect named John Nichols had helped them convert the building into a white-brick, gabled storefront at 114 Indiana Avenue, directly across from what is now the Law School. Jewett took office as mayor of Indianapolis in 1917, and two years later he and Fetzger sold the property to an enterprising Greek immigrant named Georgios (or George) Poolitsan and his wife Angelika, who ran it as a sandwich and soda shop, catering at first to town kids. Their Greek Candy Kitchen, on Bloomington's Main Square, already was a popular haunt for high schoolers.[1]

"The students hadn't yet acquired the art of loafing that the town boys had," Carmichael writes, "but it wasn't long until the Poolitsans remodelled in order to make room for them. It was an ideal spot. There were side booths for the girls who were bold enough to frequent the place, and there were chairs and tables unconventionally arranged in the centre."[2]

Soon enough, it became a key hangout and social center for Indiana collegians. Anyone who could meld with the Book Nook crowd could boast of having penetrated an inner circle. The centerpiece, the Nook's reason for existing, some said, was its piano. A battered upright of uncertain pedigree, top and bottom front panels long since stripped away, it occupied a place of honor near the front door. Not just anyone could sit down and play it: that, too, required approval by the Nook's elite.

Such campus musical celebrities as Hube Hanna and Hank Wells were Nook "regulars." "Hoagie" (the spelling still varied) had attended a few times but had remained an outsider, a "townie," a high schooler among the university men. After the Kappa Alpha Phi dance, "I, too, hung out in the Book Nook for Cokes and coffee, and the tense, high-pitched enjoyment of just living. It was a step up for me. My high school bunch patronized the Candy Kitchen, but the Book Nook was a real honest-to-God college hangout for cave-type footballers, hair-oiled Don Juans—already in the [cartoonist] John Held, Jr., styles."[3]

Another Book Nook habitué was a redheaded beanpole named Bradford Bratcher "Batty" DeMarcus. Born in 1901, he'd learned alto saxophone as a boy growing up mostly in Danville, west of Indianapolis; by early 1918, when he enrolled at the university, he'd mastered the horn. His elder brother Bruce, adept on C-melody saxophone, was already at the school and picking up decent money playing dance jobs.

Batty's path soon crossed that of fellow-student Malcolm C. "Johnny" Johnson, who played good, sure piano, and they formed a band, also including the versatile cornet-banjo doubler Dwight van Osdol. The new group was soon playing for campus dances and expanding its reach throughout Indiana and neighboring states, sometimes as a trio, occasionally with up to eight pieces. By the time Hoagland Carmichael started spending his leisure hours at the Book Nook, Johnson and the DeMarcus brothers were among the biggest of the Big Men on Campus.[4]

Inevitably, there came a night when someone urged the hopped-up high school pianist to the Book Nook upright, to play along with Batty's alto. For a kid whose chief prior experience performing for a seated audience had been as a monkey in a high school pageant, this was a heady moment. "Never had I dreamed of notes such as came out of his horn—fast arpeggii and every one of them tongued . . .

"Bruce told me Batty learned the instrument in three weeks—a natural! Batty played an entire chorus, taking but one breath. His face grew red and he gasped for air as he hit the last high note of a long phrase as we came to an end."[5]

DeMarcus played in the manner of Rudy Wiedoeft, whose prowess on C-melody (and occasionally alto) sax was the toast of the pre-1920 popular music world. Born in Detroit in 1893, Wiedoeft had come up in vaudeville, almost single-handedly popularizing the saxophone as a solo instrument. Like Fritz Kreisler and others on whose composing styles much early popular saxophone literature was based, he played in two distinct manners: one, elegaic, suited the countless salon pieces then in vogue; the other was a "novelty" style—vigorous, technically intricate, full of lightning runs, fast tonguing, and other acrobatics. Wiedoeft's influence on all saxophonists of the 1920s, white and black, "legit" or "hot," was profound and lasting.

"When we finished," Carmichael wrote with a mixture of triumph and relief, "Batty was calling me dirty names and running his big freckled hands through my uncut hair." Only then, he remarks, did it dawn on him that he'd just passed an audition.

Within only a few years Batty DeMarcus would be the talk of New York, widely in demand as a recording and broadcasting musician, giving even the great Wiedoeft a run for his money. But now, in this student hangout in Bloomington, Indiana, he'd just put his *imprimatur*, his seal of approval, on Hoagland Howard Carmichael. As if by magic, job offers began finding the young pianist; for some of them he even borrowed Dwight van Osdol to play cornet.

From most independent testimony, "Hoagie" at this point displayed more enthusiasm than polish at the keyboard. "He played in bastard keys," DeMarcus told interviewer George W. Kay, "which was fun for me but confusing to the other fellows." Johnny Johnson, too, recalled the kid he called "Carmichelle," who "spent the entire year of 1917 learning to play *After You've Gone*. I remember how many times I had to leave my English 20 studies at the Phi Gam[ma Delta] House and rush over to the Kappa Sig[ma] House to correct a sour note he was playing."

Johnson's dates are off: "After You've Gone" became popular in 1918, and Carmichael didn't pledge to the university's chapter of the Kappa Sigma fraternity until 1920. Still, both recollections seem accurate depictions of an emergent talent, a newly hatched chick struggling free of its shell.[6]

DeMarcus also remembers Reg DuValle's band playing dances at IU, and speaks admiringly of saxophonist Bert Evans, who later moved to New York and won respect as a Harlem-based music teacher. Now and then the

DeMarcus brothers played at the august Severin Hotel in Indianapolis, frequent home base for DuValle and his men.

In late 1919 Batty headed east, soon joining up with Johnson and fellow-Hoosiers Gene (saxophone) and Dudley (mellophone) Fosdick. An early 1920s photo of a saxophone sextet sponsored by Paul Whiteman includes DeMarcus, Gene Fosdick, and the brilliant but now largely forgotten Loring McMurray, who made several outstanding records at the time but died young, before mid-decade. Between 1920 and 1923 DeMarcus enjoyed a successful New York career, working with major bands and recording widely. In 1923 he accepted an invitation to join the house band at London's Savoy Hotel, the Savoy Orpheans, alongside fellow-Americans Al and Ray Starita and pianist-songwriter Carroll Gibbons. There, too, he recorded widely.[7]

✻   ✻   ✻

College campuses had by far the strongest and most consistent following for "hot music" throughout most of the '20s. Every school seemed to have at least one student band, and records by groups at Princeton, Yale, Harvard, Williams, and elsewhere demonstrate their often near-professional skill. "These young men," says Indiana historian-chronicler Duncan Schiedt,

> were rapidly moving through the period of transition to jazz. They were, like Carmichael, taking their inspiration from the black musician, and working out the style in endless hours of jamming around out-of-tune fraternity house pianos, in movie theatre pits, and hanging around the bandstand when visitng orchestras played.[8]

Carmichael, by his own testimony (and that of others), was running just a few laps behind such pace-setters as Johnson and the DeMarcus brothers. It was still too early, in 1919 and 1920, for him to have been exposed to the first wave of key musicians about to make "hot" music history in Chicago. But his passion for music was irresistible: he drew few distinctions between black and white, northern and southern, the Victor records of the Original Dixieland Jazz Band and those of "novelty" clarinetist Wilbur Sweatman. If it was exciting and had a beat, he wanted to hear it. "I was as interested in hearing good music as making it, and soon I was a kind of booker as well as a band leader, beating MCA into the racket."[9]

"Carmichelle" used his new prominence at Kappa Alpha Phi to hire a black band from Louisville, led by saxophonist Howard Jordan, to play the fraternity's 1919 annual ball. Remembered as two saxophones, trombone, piano, and drums, the Jordan quintet came with some reputation as a "hot" combination. As they took their places and tuned up, Carmichael—as had happened with Batty DeMarcus—fell into his own private kind of trance. "I heard the little piano player with the big white teeth play an introductory crescendo to try out the piano and also a few chords of 'Fate,' that masterpiece in minors which was coming into popularity. My knees nearly gave way, and Kate [Cameron, his date] and I laughed hysterically. Something was going to happen that night, sure as hell! It did."[10]

In both *Sometimes I Wonder* and *The Stardust Road*, a slightly older, more seasoned Carmichael tempers such youthful zeal with more restrained language. But *Jazzbanders*, written in the early 1930s, preserves the fevered ardor of the moment:

> The band started in with a bang, playing "Russian Rag" as a grand march. Immediately, a piercing yell broke loose from the crowd! No one marched; everyone broke into a wild swing, and Jordan's changed the rhythm to a one-step. This was too much! When those "dinges" whipped that tune into a wild, almost blood-curdling shriek of weird harmony as they came into the last chorus, I got the spirit of jazz like a Congo medicine man. I wilted to the floor! I was half insane! Kate only stood there, hysterical . . . At first, Jordan's men acted like scared monkeys behind a cage; they had never seen anything like it, but they soon got the spirit themselves and were off again in a frenzy. We recovered, but never fully. I couldn't recover from that. The dance was over in a few minutes, it seemed.[11]

Afterwards, band and followers adjourned to another local hangout, Beard's Blue Lantern restaurant. A few peremptory phone calls routed the DeMarcuses and other sympathizers out of bed, and a combination party and impromptu jam session got under way.

> "What was different about it?" we asked ourselves. Nothing, particularly, except that the two saxophone players played their screaming arpeggii in a unison of harmony and their notes were "blue." That

was it! Their notes were bluer than ours. Also, the muted trombone added a tinny effect that was piercing. It added background when it was played without a mute. The big black boy hit the notes on the head and made them pop at you; they went clear through and excited our insides.[12]

Jordan's Louisville band soon became a favorite at Indiana University dances, with Carmichael and fellow-acolytes invariably in attendance. They even did Sunday afternoon appearances at the *sanctum* itself, the Book Nook. "Carmichelle" and his pals meanwhile incorporated things they'd heard into their own efforts and took to pestering Big Ed East and other local music dealers for any record containing even a few bars of "hot" music. Every new tune "was a big event," he recalled.[13]

They played informal dances in the gym at the Student Building, whose clock-tower chimes had started the young man on his musical way just a few short years before. They imitated records, and the "drummer played four beats to the measure on his bass drum," rather than the first-and third-beat accentuation common in ragtime and popular dance music of the time.

Johnson, van Osdol, and the DeMarcus brothers, good readers all, were meanwhile ranging far afield, picking up more varied kinds of musical work. But Carmichael remained strictly "one of 'them ear players,' as the Brown County Folk called us. Learning to read was a mechanical accomplishment that held no appeal for me, but it was one of the biggest mistakes of my life that I didn't buckle down and do it."[14]

"Hogey's fame as a musician is known far and wide," the editors of the *Gothic*, Bloomington High School's student yearbook, remarked in its Class of 1920 edition, and schoolmates eagerly seconded the testimony. "He'd come to our house once or twice a week, sit in the living room, talk to my family, and play the piano," said neighbor Leland "Tinker" Bell. "It seemed he wasn't happy unless he was sitting near a piano."[15]

The Carmichael family was still in Indianapolis, in a slightly larger house at 130 Neal Avenue, less than a mile from the Warman Street place; the boy, meanwhile, had moved in with his grandparents on Atwater Street in Bloomington and was often too broke, said Kathryn Moore, a "crush" of those years, to scrape together even a dollar to treat a girl to a movie, a hamburger, and a Coke. Nevertheless, she resolved at some early point that this strangely zealous young man was just right for her and that they would someday get married. "Kathryn," her mother remonstrated sternly, "he's just not the kind of boy you should go with." Another parent, echoing the sentiment, declared that "that man will never amount to a cent."[16]

For all that, the *Gothic* added, "Hogey" was "a great favorite with the girls," even if, in the reminiscence of another Bloomington contemporary, sometime drummer Dale Ferguson, "a lot of people didn't want him over because he'd tear up their pianos."[17]

❖   ❖   ❖

Images of this life take on an insular, almost idyllic quality when set within the larger picture of what was going on in America, and even the rest of Indiana, in 1919. From Carmichael's descriptions of his sessions with Reg DuValle, his zeal for Jordan's Louisville Quintet, and other features of this coming-of-age time, it would be impossible to know that racial strife had swept America on a near-unprecedented scale during the summer. Race riots erupted in Nebraska, Arkansas, Texas—and, beginning July 27, on Chicago's mostly black South Side. The Civil War had ended more than half a century before, but altogether seventy lynchings were reported nationwide in 1919; there is no telling how many went unreported. The Ku Klux Klan, which had flared briefly but notoriously during Reconstruction, rose again after the 1915 premiere of D. W. Griffith's pioneer feature film *The Birth of a Nation.*

Perhaps, as historian M. William Lutholtz has remarked, the KKK's renewed popularity was a by-product of United States involvement in World War I. "America now had to be protected from the 'evil' Germans and a host of others: Catholics, Jews, Socialists, blacks, and union leaders ... Membership in the Klan was one way for Americans at home to help win the war in Europe." The November 11, 1918, armistice left many Americans "still spoiling for action. With no one left to fight, the nation's aggression turned inward." More than four million white workers walked off the job, protesting a mass influx of cheap black labor from down south. A "red scare," triggered by fears of an imagined Bolshevik menace, swept the country.

The Ku Klux Klan, revitalized, began a rapid spread northward into such otherwise unlikely states as Maine, Ohio, Pennsylvania, New York, New Jersey—and, most of all, Indiana. Starting in Evansville, on the Kentucky line, they quickly covered the state, reaching even into Martinsville and nearby Bloomington.

Indiana presented a particularly fertile environment. The mass immigration of the late nineteenth and early twentieth centuries had affected the state relatively little: in 1900, only 5.6 percent of its population was foreign-born. "They"—the hordes of newcomers from Eastern Europe and elsewhere—were far off, as were the generally leftist "Bolshie" politics with which "they" were so often associated; and the distance suited many Hoosiers just fine. Any individual or organization able to ensure that things remained that way could count on broad Indiana acceptance. Perhaps the chief irony here lay in a parallel tradition, a stubborn Hoosier tolerance for the views of others, a rigidly "live and let live" credo. A man had a right to his opinions, it maintained, however abhorrent they might seem.

Still, Indiana remained a bastion of nativist sentiment and a Republican Party stronghold. The Democratic Party, strongly associated with labor unions, poor immigrants, and the politics of the Left, found little support in this state.[18]

Was young Carmichael aware of such realities? Probably: throughout his life he remained a staunch supporter of the GOP and its right-of-center politics. Various remarks recalled by family members and friends indicate a brand of casual anti-Semitism common in those early twentieth-century times. But if "Hogie" won even mild censure for his association with Bucktown black folks, he doesn't mention it. College towns, moreover, tended to foster their own insularity, and Indiana University took pride in at least a selective color-blindness: in 1893 it had been the first American college to field a football team with a black player, halfback Preston Eagleston.[19]

*　　　　　*　　　　　*

Though standard jazz histories tend to gloss over the years 1919 through 1921 as a fallow period between the public mania generated by the Original Dixieland Jazz Band and the first records by such seminal, Chicago-based recording units as King Oliver's Creole Jazz Band and the New Orleans Rhythm Kings, "hot music" was universally in ferment and to be heard everywhere. Dozens of records made in those years, most unreissued and obscure, show bands of both races determinedly breaking free of ragtime into a new, more relaxed kind of rhythm and phrasing.

Jazz was still an ensemble music: the idea of a coherent solo style, chordal and melodic variations on a popular song or other theme, still awaited its champions: Sidney Bechet, Louis Armstrong, Leon Roppolo, Bix Beiderbecke. But the sound of bands playing "hot" had cast its spell on young Americans everywhere: from city dance halls and ballrooms to college fraternity houses, they found in its abandoned energy a natural expression of their own feelings. "There was a wide world out there, with jobs to be found and work to be done that fitted, or didn't fit, our moods," said Carmichael. "Being young, we knew it couldn't bend or push us around the way it had our fathers. If we worried about the things to come in private, in public we played the clown."[20]

What rock-and-roll would be to a much later generation, hot jazz, however inchoate—and even in its more adulterated forms—was to the "flaming youth" of the 1920s. Their parents, in the main, barely tolerated it? Wonderful. Their teachers disapproved of it? Fine. Pastors and priests loathed it? So much the better.

"The records were beginning to come into the music stores by the boxfull," Carmichael writes, "and I had my head in a Victrola most of the time trying to pick up bits of this and that to add to our slim repertoire ... We heard Ted Lewis's records and got a 'burn' out of the clarinet and the double-brass background effect." Whether these records—by Lewis, Sweatman, the orchestras of such long-forgotten figures as Joseph C. Smith, the saxophone-playing "Six Brown Brothers," or the brand-new West Coast outfit of Paul Whiteman—were "authentic" jazz is irrelevant now. They supplied the songs, demonstrated the rhythm, all of it raw material for avid young musicians trying to do things their own way.[21]

Recording had emerged as a strong promotional arm of the music publishing business, and sheet music sales, accordingly, took off. A new fad, the word "blues" added willy-nilly to song titles, guaranteed brisk trade in the early 1920s. The Original Dixieland Jazz Band's "Clarinet Marmalade" became "Clarinet Marmalade Blues," and presumably sold that much better because of it. Indeed, Tom Delaney's 1921 "Jazz Me Blues" probably could have sold itself on its title alone: though in no way an authentic blues, in "jazz" and "blues" it had *two* current buzzwords, rich in twin connotations of sensuality and forbidden thrills.

Yet another ingredient, stirred vigorously into the mix, added potency to the new enthusiasm. As of April 2, 1918, Indiana had joined the growing ranks of "dry" states, in which no beverage with an alcohol content of more than 0.5 percent could be manufactured, sold, imported, or exported. Forbidden alcohol, hot music, youthful rebellion in the air: if you were just hitting twenty and in search of a world to call your own, it was made to order. "Hogie" and his schoolmates did what thousands all over America did: let out a whoop and jumped right in. A Rudy Wiedoeft guest solo on Joseph C. Smith's record of Irving Berlin's "Tell Me, Little Gypsy" was a major event. Mamie Smith's million-selling "Crazy Blues" seemed all the more desirable for being a "race" record, aimed at black record buyers and hard to find outside "Bucktown." Arrival of a new disc by Ray Miller's Black and White Melody Boys, the Louisiana Five, the Original Memphis Five, or dozens of other groups was newsworthy.[22]

✱   ✱   ✱

Local drummer Glen Woodward, who had played with the Indiana "Rainbow Division" Army band in France during the war, talked up the idea of booking Carmichael's little band for Thursday night Elks Club dances, and ultimately for university social events. Namesake "Red" Carmichael, whom the young pianist had first heard playing with Hube Hanna and Hank Wells, joined in on saxophone. Other occasional participants included drummer Bob Harris (who "would be tossing a drumstick in the air and chewing his tongue"), a store clerk named Parks ("an unreliable trombonist but a great exponent of whiz bang racy stories"), and cornetist van Osdol ("without the customary lip, but who sang a sweet tenor"). Over the 1919 Christmas holidays, they did their first Indiana "tour," playing dances in Terre Haute and nearby Brazil, then Sullivan and Vincennes further south.[23]

"Much to our surprise, we found that the corn liquor that came out of the coal mining district was passed around rather freely at these affairs in spite of prohibition, and that the orchestra was supposed to drink more than its share to keep pepped up," Carmichael writes. "We carried on in great style until numbness began to set in, but by that time the crowd was also full of the Christmas 'spirits,' so it didn't matter if my arms felt like lead pipes."[24]

And, after a taste of this, he reached the conclusion that

"the people throughout the country wanted jazz and liquor. People were restless—young boys and girls thought it smart to drink . . . We took up drinking as a more regular diet ourselves [and] it wasn't long before we judged people by their temperance—sober and conventional individuals were not very interesting—people who were not appreciative of jazz were equally uninteresting. The relative merits of various cigarette brands and stories about drinking-parties were everyday topics of conversation.[25]

Back in Bloomington, he played at parties in Bucktown, savoring the uninhibited dancing and other antics of his boyhood chum "Pee Wee" Johnson. At Grandma Robison's, he filed down the hammers of his mother's Armstrong piano to make the sound more brilliant, and all but ruined the treasured "Golden Oak" in the process. "I was the nuisance of the neighborhood," he later wrote, and there seems no reason to doubt him.[26]

He watched Kathryn Moore grow into a young woman before his eyes, and fell into jealous sulks when she dated other boys. "Dissipation set in, and the germ of it soon ate up most that remained of a good disposition I had brought [back] to Bloomington." It also affected his schoolwork, and at graduation time, in early summer of 1920, Hoagland Howard Carmichael found to his dismay that he was two credits short of the twenty-two required to get a diploma.

Grandma Robison had tried to keep the boy in line, but in that, at least, she'd been unequal to the task. Desperate now, Hoagland visited his parents in Indianapolis and "brought my books along and laid them on the old gait-legged [*sic*] table" with a plea to Lida to help him with his makeup assignments in English history. All right, she agreed—if he'd promise to reserve two hours a day, come what might, for schoolwork. "I've a lot of postage stamps saved up," she said, to mail the completed lessons to Bloomington. And besides, "I could use a little English History myself. Who was the king who chopped off all his wives' heads?"[27]

Nor did her task stop there. The boy would also have to pay off his debts, including one for three dollars at Ed Whetsell's Bloomington shoe store. Whetsell had turned for help to university registrar John Cravens, complaining that the young Carmichael, whose aspirations for himself appeared consistently to outstrip his means, "seems to treat all attempts at collection with the most serious contempt you can imagine." In a second letter, more than a week later, Whetsell reports: "The young Mr. Carmichael came in last evening and paid the account . . . and in so doing he manifested a spirit which should be discouraged in any young man."[28]

Schoolwork and debts, he got it all done, though "it was no secret to the family that I was more interested in 'Wang Wang Blues' and 'Margie' than I was in the Magna Charta [*sic*] and Queen Elizabeth." Still, his parentally assisted diligence paid off. In September 1920, Bloomington High School diploma in hand, Hoagland Howard Carmichael registered as a freshman at Indiana University and pledged the Beta Theta chapter of the Kappa Sigma fraternity.[29]

He later described that autumn as

a most happy event for everyone . . . each new face I met or saw was a smiling one . . . I too was smiling because the few years of drudgery and despair that preceded 1920 were somehow shaken off now and here was I, by the grace of God, rubbing shoulders with many other notables—those who had managed to finish high school in such troubled times . . .

Tall maples, hickories, and beeches stood out in stately relief against the vine-covered sanctuaries of learning. These buildings, arranged in a semicircle behind the soft greenery of September and the fiery foliage of late October, were not foreboding [*sic*] to the initiate. I saw them as not only steamheated havens of learning but as places I could hurry to through snow-packed pathways to say "hi" to someone—someone you liked or someone who seemed to have an eye for you and vice versa.[30]

However vaguely he may have realized it at the time, the most influential years of Hoagland Carmichael's young life were about to begin.

* IV *

Sunshine and Sock-Time

Mike Fritzel recognized an opportunity when he saw one. It arrived in the person of a guy from New Orleans, a young trumpet player named Paul Mares, who'd begun renting a room from Tommy Harrison, a cop Fritzel knew. The guy talked a good line, mostly about all the great musicians he'd worked with, friends from back home who were now jobbing around the Midwest, some of them on Mississippi excursion boats. If he could round up a few and form a band, he said, he could guarantee steady business for the club Fritzel spent his evenings managing.

Though skeptical, Mike paid attention: bands from down south, playing the kind of stuff people were calling "jazz," or "hot music," had been drawing crowds to Chicago nightspots since 1915, when Tom Brown's "Band From Dixieland" broke attendance records at Lamb's Café. Back in those days Fritzel had run the Arsonia, over on Madison, and after the Lamb's success had booked his share of hot little bands, even using some men from the riverboats. Now it was 1921, and he was in charge of the Friars' Inn, a basement cabaret at 343 South Wabash, at the corner of Van Buren, billed in its advertisements as the "Land of Bohemia Where Good Fellows Get Together." With Prohibition the law of the land, one still-reliable way to bring in customers was to have lively entertainment.

Okay, he said to Mares. Get me your band.

Fritzel may have been thinking about a quintet, the standard instrumentation for such groups. What Mares brought in was an eight-piecer: himself and three pals from New Orleans, plus four more guys from the farm belt that stretched from Ohio to Iowa. But what the hell: the band fee was ninety bucks a week. They could break it any way they wanted, all the same to him. And, too, he got his money's worth, working them six nights a week, long hours with few breaks. Sometimes vaudeville singer and dancer Bee Palmer, then at the apex of her national popularity as "the Shimmy Queen," sang with them.[1]

By early 1922 they were doing well. As the word got around, young musicians started hanging around the Friars'; anyone who aspired to play "hot" would turn up sooner or later to hear Mares, George Brunies, Leon Roppolo, and their associates, and occasionally even to sit in. Fritzel didn't mind, as long as the underage kids sat off to the side, kept quiet, and didn't interfere with the regular customers, known to include such figures as Dion O'Banion, gangland czar of Chicago's North Side.

Don Murray, a minister's son studying at Northwestern, sometimes brought along his tenor sax. George Johnson, another Chicagoan, also played tenor; Vic Moore and Bobby Conzelman were drummers; Jimmy Hartwell and Voltaire "Volly" De Faut played clarinet. Wilfred "Min" Leibrook, a tall boy from southern Ohio, brought his tuba; tough little "Murph" Steinberg, like Mares an admirer of Joe "King" Oliver, sometimes sat in on cornet. But most often the visitors were content to just listen, while the band steamed through "Farewell Blues" or "Tiger Rag," or Roppolo played ruminative, ghostly clarinet solos on such slow specialties as "Tin Roof Blues."

Chicago's hot music epicenter might have been the black South Side, but for the majority of young middle-class whites, barely past adolescence, the State Street cabarets and dance halls were *terra incognita*, to be explored only in groups, and after careful planning. Friars' Inn, by contrast, was downtown, easily reached by bus or on the frequent trains snaking around the Loop.

Elmer Schoebel, who played piano, composed, and organized what arrangements the band used, functioned as *de facto* leader, with Mares and Brunies as strong ensemble players; but the one most visitors listened to, and watched, was Roppolo. Don Murray recalled seeing him "riding high on his clarinet, with one foot braced high up on a pillar alongside the stand,

and so full of marijuana he could scarcely move out of his chair at the finish of a set." Even at that early stage, with the music still in transition from its ragtime origins, this distracted, hemp-smoking wraith of a man presented an aspect new and a little exotic—a soloist, unmistakably artistic and more than a little mysterious, an unlikely Kubla Khan inhabiting his own private Xanadu.[2]

News of these developments quickly reached Bloomington, greeted with special enthusiasm at the Kappa Sigma fraternity house. Through friends in Indianapolis, "Hoagie" (the spelling was evolving) had met George Johnson, who "kept talking about a new style of playing," something he called "sock-time." At first, Johnson just sang the licks, "peculiar sounds with a bug-eyed expression on his face"; once he laid hands on a saxophone, the demonstration began in earnest.

> George was doodling and it burned me up. What a swing it had! It was done smoothly, but with an occasional jerk to accent a beat here and there. He doodled arpeggii like those Batty DeMarcus played, but the rhythm was different ... George said only a few were doing it, and he spoke about the New Orleans Rhythm Kings, a band playing in Friar's [*sic*] Inn, Chicago ... The thought of what I might hear when an entire band was playing this stuff made me weak.[3]

Carmichael's pursuit of his studies was as dogged as his quest for music was ardent. He particularly remembered a summer resort job at Lake Manitou, in north central Indiana, with a band whose cornetist had been, for a while, the up-and-coming Red Nichols; the other men seemed quite taken with his account of "sock-time," a way of playing four steady, equally weighted beats to a bar that seemed lighter and smoother than what most other bands were doing.

Sometime in late April or early May of 1922, he and a friend, a Bloomington high school chum he identifies only as "Lucky," paid their first visit to the Friars' Inn.[4]

> I was in a panic by the time we had checked our hats. The clarinet player was wiggling in his seat in rhythm and playing a solo chorus of "Sensation Rag" in the doodle style George had taught me. Then the cornet player picked it up and blasted his notes in a jerky style

with the tone quality that was brassy and penetrating. The notes smacked me in the face and at unexpected moments; they went right on through my gizzard and dropped on the floor, making my feet jump. George [Johnson] sat moving up and down on his chair like a trained seal; Vic Moore laughed like an idiot and drummed the table top with his palms. This was the third big moment of my life, and I was so excited I couldn't see a thing that was going on—I only heard.[5]

Their attention turned briefly to a newcomer, a fair-haired kid, just short of six feet tall and wearing a belted overcoat and patent-leather shoes. "His eyes were peculiar and his silly little mouth fascinated me," says Carmichael. "His upper lip was red and he had a faint odor of gin on his breath. I learned that he had just come from a job, and it was the cornet that had reddened his lip. George introduced the boy as Bix Beiderbecke."[6]

Leon Beiderbecke was from Davenport, Iowa. His parents had enrolled him at Lake Forest Academy, north of Chicago, reportedly in hopes the school's rigorous discipline would promote greater attention to learning. Though only there since September, he'd already begun stealing out of his dormitory after lights-out, bound for Chicago hotspots. Carmichael later represented the meeting as a personal epiphany ("Mr. Stanley was about to meet Doctor Livingston"), but most indications are that he found the rather vague young man likable but otherwise unmemorable. Even his speaking voice, recollected in tranquility, was pleasant but "unimpressive."[7]

"You ought to hear that kid play," Johnson confided when Beiderbecke had departed. "He's going to be the nuts someday. He's got the ideas, but his lip's weak yet." Self-taught, the young Iowan had learned cornet by imitating the records of the Original Dixieland Jazz Band; in the absence of formal instruction he'd taken to using what brass players call a "dry embouchure," locking the mouthpiece in place through pressure on a dry upper lip, thereby curtailing his endurance and ability to play higher notes. Further evidence uncovered by Beiderbecke researcher Philip R. Evans indicates that Carmichael actually went to hear Beiderbecke play at a college dance not long after this encounter, and came away not particularly impressed.[8]

Nor, apparently, were the men of the Friars' Inn band. Bix, still learning, "kept pestering us to play 'Angry,' because it was the only one of our

numbers he knew at the time," Mares said later. Schoebel concurred: the
kid's attempts to sit in "didn't really work out with the group that well . . .
We'd let him sit in occasionally, but we didn't encourage him."[9]

At this point, "Hoagie" seemed more concerned with something Johnson
had mentioned in passing: news that Vic Moore had landed some work for
a group in Palm Beach, Florida, winter playground for New York society,
and wanted the young pianist along. What to do? He'd fought hard to get
into Indiana University, no less so to earn his place among "Pink" Cadou,
Wilbur Cook, Jack Bell, "Granny" Keller, Louie Mitchener, Stu Gorrell, and
the rest of the well-off, socially adept young men at Kappa Sig; they lived
together in a grand-looking white frame house, complete with four-column
facade, at 714 East Third Street, main artery of both town and campus—a
house which, by no little irony, Carmichael's own Grandpa Robison had
helped build. Among its signal advantages was its location, right around
the corner from the Book Nook. "You could shout from the Kappa Sig
building and nearly be heard at the Nook, they were so close" was the way
one IU alumnus put it.[10]

His studies were headed, if somewhat uncertainly, toward a career in
law—which Lida Carmichael averred was a better prospect for her son than
professional music. Life at the Book Nook, too, was more interesting by
the day, with intellectually accomplished upperclassmen accepting the skinny kid in a yellow slicker who jerked and bobbed at the piano like a man
with St. Vitus's dance.

But Palm Beach? A chance to play "sock-time" in real high society, with
musicians who knew what they were doing far better than he? Guys who
had sat night after night at the feet of Roppolo, Mares, bassist Steve Brown,
and the rest, soaking in the new sounds? Hard to resist, even if his mother
and Grandma Robison questioned the boy's common sense.

"It's the nuts place," Johnson told him. "Warm and sunshiny all the year
round. All the New York brokers go there for the winter to play around
and drink champagne. It costs a hundred bucks a day to stay at the leading
hotel. Vic's Dad will fix us up on rooms. There's an ocean down there, and
you can actually swim in it in the winter time. We'll play private house
parties and Vic says the rich girls are plenty hot looking. He says that people
just throw away their money."[11]

Hoagland Carmichael, pincher of pennies, son of a chronically impe-
cunious itinerant laborer, began law studies in autumn of 1922, trudging
gamely to class, doing his homework, fighting his fear of disappointing

parents and grandparents. But there are also parallel images, no less vivid: "Hoagie" visiting the Casino Gardens in Indianapolis to hear Charlie Davis's new band; "Hoagie" taking a coach train all the way east to Boston with the IU football team, only to wind up playing the piano in a downtown music-shop window to help raise return fare; "Hoagie" bereft when his Bloomington bandsmen deserted *en masse* to join Walt Stiner, a campus competitor. It was good, and exciting, to be part of the college world, living among the swells at Kappa Sig, on his way to a life beyond what Howard and Lida Carmichael had dared covet for their only son.

As he writes in *Jazzbanders*:

> Restlessness was spreading like a disease among musicians; many other jazz-bos were getting it [and] some drank heavily as a result; they continually wanted something, they didn't know what. When the music they played failed to satisfy, musicians became bored. They were beginning to traipse the country. Bands shifted quickly, and men changed bands quickly. This was the beginning of years of trail blazing of thousands of musicians' wives that was to put to shame the Gold Rush of '49. How these girls stood the life, I don't know.[12]

According to Indiana University files, Hoagland Carmichael withdrew from his law studies January 3, 1923, without completing even a single semester. He moved out of Kappa Sig and not long thereafter headed south to join Johnson and Vic Moore in sunny, seductive Palm Beach. Music and anticipated glamour may not have been the only forces driving his withdrawal. Correspondence between Carmichael and university bursar U. C. Smith, spanning the 1921–22 school year, shows unmistakably how much trouble the young man was having keeping up with tuition and school loan payments. In June his grades had been withheld, pending payment of fees and even such incidental expenses as library fines, a total of $26.45.

"It was absolutely impossible for me to pay my fee this last spring," he wrote to Smith on June 28, 1922. "Rather than quit school, I asked for extension of time and it was granted. My position is such now that I will be able to pay it before school opens next fall, probably within a month. I shall be at school next fall."[13]

But what of payment for the spring semester? Viewed in this light, the trip to Florida seems less a matter of choice than of necessity, a way to avoid the humiliation of spending five months with the family in Indianapolis, unable to meet school costs and probably working at some menial job, stockpiling his wages. Harry Orchard's diary entry for Tuesday, January 2, 1923, records his friend's departure accurately and poignantly:

> Hoagland Carmichael a very good friend of mine and a regular genius on the piano left today for Chicago. He is quitting school. From Chicago he will drive to Miami, Florida, where he will spend the rest of the winter playing piano. I don't believe he will ever return to school either here at Indiana University or anywhere else. I hope he will, for the musicians [*sic*] life is a hard one with little chance for advancement.[14]

"What a wonderful place it was!" Hoagy exclaims, describing his Florida arrival in *Jazzbanders*. "Superlatives were no good—we just said 'Hot damn! Ain't this swell!' and let it go at that."[15]

For the first few days they seem to have done little besides loaf in the sun. Moore, whose well-to-do family lived in the area, got them a party job at a mansion packed with priceless antiques, women to match, and "everything on the bar from gin to absinthe, and it wasn't the bath-tub variety, either." It's hard to suppress a smile when Hoagy declares, "This was pretty lively going for a small-town boy like me, but I managed to affect an air of indifference." Each quartet member walked away from this fairy-tale evening with twenty dollars in his pocket, worth close to two hundred dollars in today's currency.

Among the guests at another, similar, soiree was Irving Berlin, though none of that songwriter's several biographers places him in Florida at this time. According to Carmichael, he played his 1922 hit "Lady of the Evening," "with a feathery and uncertain feel of the ivories, but with lots of charm." If Berlin could do so well playing that badly, the young man recalled thinking, perhaps he should consider professional music after all.[16]

Vic Moore's family showed them around, picked up their expenses; but the drummer, good-looking in a moustachioed way popular among silent-film stars of the era, seemed more interested in boudoir than bandstand. "Come on, Vic, talk sense" was Johnson's exasperated outburst after a few weeks of sun-bleached inactivity. "Get your mind off the women for a minute, will you? Are you going to hustle us a job, or not?" Moore "only laughed," said Carmichael, and carried on wooing the girls.

"Tommy Bassett, a fiddler from Cornell University, was eager to learn the new style, so we took him on. Tommy had a brother in the little hamlet of Monticello, Fla. A wire for funds saved the day. The brother arranged a stage presentation of our outfit at the Monticello High School building, and placards were posted all over town to announce the arrival of the country's foremost Chicago jazz band."[17]

A Florida newspaper item of the time announces an appearance on radio station WKAH, West Palm Beach, by "Carmichael's All-Star Collegians, the popular Chicago jazz orchestra," and lists "Hogay" Carmichael, Johnson, and Bassett—but no Vic Moore. The drummer is given as L. Root Jr. More intriguing still, this and a second item report that the four-piece combination will "accompany the Miami Motor Club delegation" on an excursion to Havana, sailing Thursday, March 15, supplying music on shipboard and in the Cuban capital. The fourth member becomes *Albert* Root Jr., this time playing banjo. After the trip, the band will "join the Keith's Vaudeville circuit," playing their first date in West Palm Beach. Again, Vic Moore's name is absent.[18]

Did they actually go to Cuba? Carmichael is silent on the matter, reporting only a later trip, which resulted in his rhumba "One Night in Havana." But he vouchsafes that the Monticello job was the group's last in Florida; shortly thereafter, the Indiana exile forsook his dreams of eternal sunshine and headed for home—only to discover that his Bloomington pal "Lucky," who played some fiddle and had been his Baedecker on that first visit to the Friars' Inn, "had died in Chicago. He was brought home to Bloomington for burial, and the town-boy quartette of which Lucky had been a member sang at the services."[19]

Such early "town friends" disappear entirely from Carmichael's later memoirs. Neither *The Stardust Road* nor *Sometimes I Wonder* contains any trace of "Lucky," or of Larry Leonard, the aspiring writer at whose reported behest, and under whose guidance, Hoagy wrote *Jazzbanders* in New York in the early 1930s. Did these characters exist? Does their disappearance from Carmichael's later memoirs demonstrate a need to shrug off what he perceived as humble origins and refashion himself through his law studies, his fraternity brothers, the Book Nook, and, still later, his growing ambition in music?

He moved back into the Kappa Sig house that fall and was soon caught up again in extracurricular musical life. In his absence, bands led by Hanna and Stiner had dominated the campus social scene, with periodic appearances by Curtis Hitch's Happy Harmonists and the popular Miami Lucky

Seven. Best of all, Kappa Sig roommate Wilbur Cook had helped hire the famed Benson Orchestra of Chicago, with Frank Trumbauer featured on C-melody saxophone, to play at the April 6 Junior Prom.

Things soon settled back into routine, with "Hoagie" (the spelling still fluctuated) attending law classes more or less regularly, playing dances with pickup groups, reveling in the companionable nonsense of fraternity life. "Musicians," he reflected, "are good buddies, but seldom real friends . . . [yet] I was conscious of a real love for every one of these [Kappa Sig] boys."[20]

Chicago was abuzz with hot music, the best of it on the South Side. King Oliver's Creole Jazz Band, with "Little Louis" Armstrong on second cornet and the Dodds brothers, Johnny (clarinet) and Warren "Baby" (drums), was packing in white crowds at the Lincoln Gardens. Doc Cook's big show band at Paddy Harmon's Dreamland had New Orleans emigrés Jimmie Noone on clarinet and Freddie Keppard on trumpet. Bands led by Carroll Dickerson, Erskine Tate, and Sammy Stewart included such authentic jazz soloists as reedmen Buster Bailey and Omer Simeon and cornetist George Mitchell.

This was truly, as scholar James T. Maher has called it, "the great dance band city of the '20s." Ballrooms and dance halls were springing up all the time, bringing opportunities to hear new examples of hot music. Isham Jones's band at the College Inn had much-admired Louis Panico on trumpet; Elmer Schoebel had moved on to a remodeled, expanded Midway Gardens, building his new band along lines worked out with the Friars' Inn group. Sig Meyer's Druids, at White City amusement park, had up-and-coming talents "Muggsy" Spanier on cornet and Volly De Faut on clarinet.

Hot records were now available in plenty, thanks in part to Indiana's own Gennett label, a subsidiary of the respected Starr Piano Company of Richmond, hard on the Ohio state line. Gennett's romance with hot jazz had begun one night in mid-1922, when Fred Wiggins, managing the Starr showroom on South Wabash, dropped by the Friars' Inn, a few blocks down the street. Animated by what he heard, he induced his boss, Fred Gennett, to join him for an evening at the basement cabaret.

Their visit led to the first records by the "Friars Society Orchestra," known ever after as the New Orleans Rhythm Kings, and, not much later, others by the Oliver band, by pianist-composer Ferd "Jelly Roll" Morton, by Doc Cook's eleven-piece Dreamland Orchestra, by Schoebel's Midway Gardens outfit, by a much-improved Bix Beiderbecke (with George Johnson and Vic Moore in the band)—and, ultimately, by Hoagy Carmichael himself.

A verbal snapshot of the young man in 1923 will show more intensity than focus, colliding ideas about what direction to take in life. He's had doubts from the start about becoming a lawyer but, though clearly enchanted by hot music, has demonstrated little sign of extraordinary pianistic skills. He's thought a bit about writing songs, particularly after being underimpressed by Irving Berlin at that Florida party, but even those thoughts have as yet taken no palpable form.

He meanwhile hacks away at his torts, plays for dances, carouses with fellow Kappa Sigs, drinks more than he should. But Hoagland Carmichael still differs little from thousands of flaming youths of the early 1920s; he remains *tabula rasa*, uninscribed, inchoate, ripe for inspiration—something to bestow direction and purpose on his life.

And sure enough, as if in response to a perceived need, it is about to arrive.

✳ V ✳

Monk

William Ernest Moenkhaus, born in Bloomington June 30, 1902, was a child of two cultures. His father, a professor of physiology at Indiana University, spoke German and French, spent summers traveling on the European continent, and remained convinced of the innate superiority of European education to any homegrown American equivalent. He made no secret of his intention that both his sons, once old enough, pursue their secondary studies in Germany.

The mid-1914 "Guns of August," opening salvos of World War I, found Professor Moenkhaus in Freiburg, on the edge of the Black Forest, where he had enrolled twelve-year-old William Ernest in a highly recommended *Gymnasium*, or preparatory school. Exact events after that are not clear, but the boy soon transferred to a school in neutral Switzerland, the father returning to Indiana.

Young William stayed two years, reading widely, concentrating on music studies, while the "Great War" roared and swirled around neutral Switzerland like some nightmare tornado. When, in 1917, President Woodrow Wilson reluctantly brought the United States into the conflict, Professor Moenkhaus agreed it was time for his elder son to come home. William, age fifteen, embarked for New York aboard the Holland-America liner *Ryndam*.

He entered Bloomington High School, at the same time beginning study with university faculty members in piano, cello, and composition. His musical gifts, obvious from early childhood, bloomed rapidly, and by September 12, 1921, when he matriculated at the university, he seemed headed for a brilliant career.[1]

From his first day on campus he attracted attention. Just short of six feet tall, a bony 140 pounds, he presented a wraith-like appearance, with a pallor best described as spectral; his emaciated aspect and oblique, often aphoristic way of expressing himself further enhanced an air of mystery. Here, surely, was a preternatural being, privy to realms of thought and experience denied ordinary mortals. Had he been lame from birth, like Lord Byron? Or was his chronic, foot-dragging limp the result of some mysterious injury sustained, as some said, on the icebound high slopes of the Alps? Everyone had a theory, but no one seemed to know. No one asked.[2]

The first time Hoagland Carmichael set eyes on him he seemed

undoubtedly the homeliest man with intellect in the world. His long face was pasty white, out of which bold, staring eyes and yellow teeth laughed at you with sneering insolence. The big hands that hung at his sides or propped a chin that invariably needed a shave were long-fingered and clammy. They looked dead; the finger-nails were long and blue. His clothes were unkempt, colorless things that hung on him and lent to the disgraceful disorder of his waxy hair and things generally.[3]

More puzzling still, this strangely brilliant young man seemed to exist in two parallel incarnations. There was the scholarly William (or "Bill") Moenkhaus, all *gravitas* and high seriousness, winner of the university's prestigious Grace Porterfield Polk music scholarship for 1924. "He was of the pure lineage of Bach and Mozart," said Phillip Rice, editor of the student literary magazine *The Vagabond*. "He lived in a world of melody and counterpoint, and for the most part he lived alone . . . it seemed to me that his compositions showed exquisite feeling kept under fine intellectual control."[4]

Moenkhaus's works, among them a *Two-Voice Invention* and a *Fantasia* for solo piano, had won praise at recitals. "No trivial expression ever entered into one of his own creations, but there was a strong reaction toward a formal purity" was the comment of B. Winfred Merrill, dean of the IU Music School. "His work was singularly exact and painstakingly executed."

He saw Moenkhaus as potentially "a composer of prominence, his native gift being coupled with unusual capacity and the ability to follow through."[5]

Living within, and alongside, that Moenkhaus was a second, both more obvious and infinitely subtler. Understanding its nature means reaching back to the young man's school days in Switzerland and experiencing, if vicariously, the wave of artistic revolt that swept Europe just prior to, and during, the "Great War."

In early 1916, the poet, actor, and sometime musician Hugo Ball, a German living in exile in Zürich, began meeting with a circle of friends at the Holländische Meierei Café in the Spiegelgasse, in the Swiss city's oldest quarter. Together they talked café owner Jan Ephraim into converting his *Stube* to a cabaret, to attract intellectuals with discussions and creative "artistic entertainments." Renamed the Cabaret Voltaire, it opened February 1 and quickly became a rendezvous for artists, writers, and musicians.

Driving the often fevered discussions was a shared sense of disillusionment: destruction and death, corruption and deceit, had devoured all the great expectations and high hopes for a new century that had informed their childhoods. What good, then, were traditionally ordered systems of art, language, meaning—even social organization—if all was ultimately chaos? Before long the Voltaire, with Ball and his friends Marcel Janco, Richard Huelsenbeck, Hans Arp, and Romanian-born Tristan Tzara at its center, had become a forum where intellectuals could vent their anger and despair at the absurdity of their times. Arp's oft-quoted description, in "Dadaland," evokes the off-center, often fevered, gaiety of the Voltaire:

> On the stage of a gaudy, motley, overcrowded tavern there are several weird and peculiar figures representing Tzara, Janco, Ball, Huelsenbeck, Madame [Emmy] Hennings, and your humble servant. Total pandemonium. The people around us are shouting, laughing, and gesticulating . . . Huelsenbeck is banging away nonstop on the great drum, with Ball accompanying him on the piano, pale as a chalky ghost.[6]

This "playground for crazy emotions," and the nihilistic philosophy driving it, soon burgeoned into a movement, spreading to other European cultural centers and as far as New York City. Ball himself reportedly coined the name "Dada-ismus," from a slang word for "nonsense" he'd found in a French-German dictionary. In 1918, Tzara issued his *Dada Manifesto*: though intended as a plea for peace, it also defines the entire idea—and leads, inexorably, to the emergence of surrealism in 1920s France. Tzara urges

> abolition of logic ... abolition of memory ... abolition of prophets ... Nothing is more delightful than to confuse and upset people. People one doesn't like. What's the use of giving them explanations that are merely food for curiosity? The truth is that people love nothing but themselves and their little possessions, their income, their dog.

Elsewhere he asks,

> What good did the theories of the philosophers do us? Did they help us to take a single step forward or backward? What is forward, what is backward?" What we want now is spontaneity ... because everything that issues freely from ourselves, without the intervention of speculative ideas, represents us.[7]

However young, William Ernest Moenkhaus has to have been aware of such resonant ideas and the shock waves spreading outward from them. Though it's hard to tell how much the young Indiana boy, studying in his Swiss *Gymnasium*, witnessed and absorbed, proximity, curiosity, and impressionable youth suggest that Ball and his friends had worked their seductions. With ardor and no little enthusiasm, he adopted the alternative persona of "Wolfgang Beethoven Bunkhaus"—reverential in its implicit tribute to two admired composers, appropriately Dadaistic in its German-language pun on his surname, itself an idiomatic variant on *Mönchshaus*, or "monastic dwelling."[8]

In this context the Book Nook's metamorphosis from simple hangout to scene of overheated discussion and spontaneous, often outrageous behavior (with hot jazz as both soundtrack and counterpoint) makes it seem a middle-American adaptation of the Cabaret Voltaire spirit. In the October 1924 issue of *The Vagabond*, his pseudonymous "Wolfgang Beethoven Bunkhaus" makes his campus literary debut, with a brief poem titled "Rhapsody in Mud":

> Men, hanging on grape-vines
> Shaving long rows of hogs

Men, trying to sing like umbrellas
Men, with brooms in their ears.

Hogs, seeking far and wide
For long lost suits of underwear
Hogs eating buckets!!!
Hogs screaming with laughter at the farmer's beard.

But when it rains
The earth, alas, is covered with mud
Then neither men nor hogs
Can sing or laugh. . . . [9]

The consistent theme is what Brecht, in the *Threepenny Opera*, calls *Die Unzulänglichkeit des menschlichen Strebens*, the futility of all human endeavor: we seek, yearn, prostrate ourselves before whatever deity seems worth propitiating—only to fall victim to inexorable laws of mortality and human fallibility.

Pieces by "Bunkhaus"—verse, plays (sometimes under the homophonous alternative "Lena Gedunkhaus"), treatises on nonsensically arcane subjects—began appearing regularly. Admiring fellow-students emulated the Bunkhaus-Gedunkhaus brand of erudite whimsy, sometimes quite cleverly— if too often missing the deadly serious undertone.[10]

It was to the "pure Bunkhaus" that readers turned with seemingly inexhaustible, "what'll he come up with next?" curiosity. Sample titles:

Abe Blooters, the Four-Legged Buzzard, or, Why Not Kill Aunt Hally?

Thanksgiving Come but Once a Dozen

A Snake in the Gravy, or, the Hissing Mortgage

Granville Unthanks Merger, or Why Hate Celery?

Flat Sage, or 13,000 Bucks in the Hole

Princess Bureau, Her Love and Creamery

Cups Down Feltment, or, Whose Color Is Your Sweater Now?

All abound in oblique language, regular (usually punning) references to multilingual idiom, lampoons of everyday situations and conversation, private jokes and improbable exchanges—echoing Tzara's view that the absurd should hold no terrors because, seen objectively, life itself seemed absurd. To his admiring fellow-students the writer was "Monk," who, in Hoagy's words, "made straight A's in a bored sort of way," all while declaring that "only peasants take pleasure in good marks."

> As his writings progressed, he became the founder and chief spokes-man of a campus cult which he named the Bent Eagles . . . Through his Dada and surrealistic nonsensical writings, he became a campus character in the eyes of most people. And to some, a fabulous literary figure in the mood of Ezra Pound.[11]

In 1923 Angelika Poolitsan, tired of the pressures of running her departed husband's affairs, leased the Book Nook and its property to a cousin, Peter Costas, and his brothers George and Harry. "Under the Costas' manage-ment," says one reminiscence, "the Nook was a haven for book-weary stu-dents, often found there late at night, guzzling 10-cent Cokes and devouring 15-cent ham sandwiches. Some discussed the day's events, while others sim-ply sat back drawing on their pipes as they listened to fellow-student Hoagy Carmichael hammering away at the battered piano in the corner."[12]

The Book Nook itself, says Carmichael, was "a randy temple smelling of socks, wet slickers, vanilla flavoring, face powder, and unread books. Its dim light, its scarred walls, its marked-up booths, and unsteady tables made campus history." He tells of "Bunkhaus" and friends pelting one another with empty grapefruit rinds, stroking the creamy surfaces of meringue pies or throwing them, face down, on the floor, "just to hear the sound"; carry-ing on ear-splitting, explosively monosyllabic exchanges peppered with such made-up words as "blooters!" and "hutches!"—usually at volumes calcu-lated to make life unendurable for the Nook's more sedate customers; deliberately issuing convoluted orders for impossibly complex meals, driv-ing both proprietor Costas and short-order cook "Klondike" Tucker (Car-michael's pal of Dunn's Meadow boyhood Saturdays) into transports of apoplexy.[13]

One typical jape resulted in an item in a Prom-day *Scandal Sheet*, under the headline "BOOK NOOK DEMOLISHED: Disciples of Bent Eagle Wreck Ancient Establishment." According to the text, "Hoagie Carmichael opened hostilities with a cornet solo," which resulted in "the crashing of cups, saucers, spoons and other foreign (Greek) matter," forcing the Costas brothers to take refuge across the street.[14]

It is easy to understand why this atmosphere, dominated by "Bunk-haus's" appearance, fey manner, and obvious intellectual powers, drew so many acolytes. Association with him meant immediate and unmistakable rejection of the everyday, prosaic norms of American middle-class life, as depicted in Sinclair Lewis's *Babbitt*. Published in 1922, the year of the Tzara "Lecture" and of Moenkhaus's enrollment at Indiana University, the novel both defined and challenged those norms, while introducing a new word, embodying them, into the popular lexicon.

College students of the early 1920s knew Sinclair Lewis's books and recognized in them a world their parents had espoused and were trying to pass on to them. "Bunkhaus" and the Bent Eagles represented escape; it wasn't necessary to understand the revolution then transforming European literature and art, just being present was enough. Certainly Carmichael's descriptions of his entry into the Nook's inner circle betray no hint of a greater awareness.

All the same, his meeting and friendship with Moenkhaus would prove fateful, and not only for him. In the mind of "Monk," New World liberation stepped not to the 2/4 cadence of the *Radetsky-Marsch* but to the 4/4 "sock-time" beat of hot jazz: surely, when Tzara proclaimed, "Nothing is more delightful than to confuse and upset people," he could just as well have had this new, gloriously anarchic music in mind.

Carmichael was immersed in it; lived and breathed it. To watch him, pale and intense in a yellow slicker, bobbing and jerking like a marionette at the keyboard, was to behold a man possessed by a purity of expression wholly consonant with the "manifesto" of Cabaret Voltaire days. It takes no great leap of imagination to see him as a Hugo Ball figure in Moenkhaus's mind, pounding away as the high-spirited japery of this midwestern "playground for crazy emotions" guggled and plashed around him.

Hoagy, meanwhile, also was making himself felt in campus dance music circles. He "got groups together on the slightest pretext," says historian Duncan Schiedt, "and when he wasn't himself playing, made it to everyone else's dances. He didn't let the lack of the price of admission stop him— he was sometimes to be seen hanging from a tree limb, listening to the music through an open window." Here, surely, is the essence of what the Dadaists had meant by "absolute and unquestionable faith in every god that is the immediate product of spontaneity." Even unaware, Carmichael was probably as much an avatar for Moenkhaus as this illustriously emaciated guru was for him.[15]

But "Bunkhaus" found his truest foil in another. Howard Warren "Wad" Allen came from Washington, Indiana, southwest of Bloomington, and had entered the university in 1921. At first he played violin, then added C-melody sax, and was soon working dance jobs with Walt Stiner's little campus outfit. More widely read than most of his fellow-zealots, Allen knew a bit about movements in art; he'd read about the 1913 New York Armory Show and Marcel Duchamp's *Nude Descending a Staircase* and was hungry for more. His verbal felicity, later to prove invaluable in the fields of advertising and newspaper reporting, proved his ticket of admission to the Book Nook crowd.[16]

Carmichael preserves the moment at which "Monk" and "Wad" discovered one another. Seated in the Poolitsans' Greek Candy Kitchen on Bloomington's main square, down in the dumps after having spent money he didn't have on a broken-down old car, Moenkhaus is astonished when the newcomer intuits his disgust "with life in general . . . by making silly sounds . . . [that were] soothing like the broken song of a mother to her child." They are soon convulsed with laughter, bellowing such nonsense phrases as "Smoke bush!" and "Moon cheese!" at one another, while others gawp. "Life had been boring a moment before, but now it was much better," Hoagy writes. "Why take it so seriously? Why not tear down everything that Man had accomplished? Why go in the same old rut?" The two laughed

> not together, but at each other. Their laughs were a little unreal, and this was a new sensation. Monk's laugh was coarse and raspy. He wound it up with a wail like that of a dying coyote. This completely unraveled Wad's spinal column. They grew weak and sat down in the middle of the street, saying, "Three dollars" at each other.[17]

Carmichael understands that Allen and Moenkhaus are kindred spirits and enjoys watching the sparks fly. At one point, for example, the two decide to pool their resources and go into a bizarre, short-lived taxi business—surely a curious echo for Hoagy, given his father's failed cab enterprise on these same Bloomington streets.

Hoagy's own friendship with Moenkhaus was of a somewhat different order. To the "half-educated man," as he called himself in those days, Monk was "a surrealistic intellectual, who looked at the world through a glass that threw it into a hopeless distortion . . . Wise and foolish, sane and crazy, lovable and laughable. Perhaps too sane."[18]

He notes the degree to which his hot music mania interested Moenkhaus and seems to have instinctively understood the privileged place it could grant him. Newly dubbed "Hogwash McCorkle" by Moenkhaus, he was welcomed to the inner circle. Monk, in his turn, pitched himself immediately into campus dance band activity, sometimes putting his cello to bizarre uses, more often supplying harrumphing bass notes on a battered sousaphone, in a manner both uninhibited and haphazard.

When, in late 1925, Hoagy handpicked his "Collegians" to play campus dances, Wad Allen was the saxophonist, but Monk was not in the personnel. Perhaps that was just as well, Carmichael reflected later, "because I had spasms every time I saw him blow a bass horn, and like as not he would have filled in a break by yelling 'chicken' instead of 'hot-cha!' "[19]

Moenkhaus continued to write for *The Vagabond*, sometimes as "Bunkhaus" or "Gedunkhaus," occasionally as "Oscar Humidor Martin" or "Roland McFeeters." Beginning with 1924's "Rhapsody in Mud," he'd almost single-handedly transformed a good, if conservative, campus literary quarterly into a congeries of new styles and ideas. Wad Allen, too, appears, writing in a style best described as *faux*-Bunkhaus—most often as "Tod Owlin," but sometimes as "Sir Polonius Panurge," a whimsically appropriate blend of Shakespeare and Rabelais.

"McCorkle" is cited frequently as a manic, occasionally demented, Ariel, "Owlin" as a no less deranged Boswell to the proceedings. Even after Phil Rice, under whose editorial stewardship "Bunkhaus" had first seen print, departed for Oxford University on a Rhodes Scholarship, *The Vagabond* continued serving up regular helpings of Moenkhaus—and readers clamored for more.

"Owlin's" mock interview with the great one, published in the mid-1926 *Vagabond*, was predictably droll—and yielded one of several mock aphorisms by which "Wolfgang" was to become known. The scene is a darkened chamber in some mysterious, unnamed hilltop building. Bunkhaus lies on a bier, face a "waxen mask." Slowly, deliberately, he recounts his life, a convoluted tale of crows, Indians, hogs—and finally, summoned out of the mist-shrouded shadows and bathed in an eerie greenish glow, a "queer, noiseless procession of strange appearing cows."

[Bunkhaus] mounted the largest of these cows, which kneeled in silence to receive its burden, and with a last majestic jesture [*sic*] he beckoned this mad train to move off on its journey. And as it dis-

appeared into the darkness of the night a low chant touched my ear.
It was the one immortal line of this great poet,
ONE BY ONE A COW GOES BY.[20]

The piece, with its subsequently oft-repeated closing line, prompted Rice, still getting *The Vagabond* by mail at Balliol College, Oxford, to declare Moenkhaus one of the "original men of his century. His type of originality consists of a style in which the ridiculous is made so true to good literary form, that some of his poems and plays have disturbed the mental equilibrium of local English professors, who seek to extort some meaning from the weird passages."[21]

Affectionate reminiscences of Moenkhaus words and deeds saturate Hoagy Carmichael's memoirs. The *Vagabond* writings, carefully preserved and filed in the Indiana University Archives, still make entertaining and imaginative, if occasionally sophomoric, reading. That he was a force, persuasive and pervasive, in the lives of those around him is beyond question.

But far less documentation remains of Moenkhaus outside his role as cynosure at the Book Nook. His classical music reviews for the *Indiana Daily Student*, written under his own name, are clear, erudite, sober, and insightful, the very antithesis of his nonsense writing. He played regularly in a string trio—cello and two violins—alongside fellow-student Alexander Isaac "Ike" Bercovitz, also a member of a campus dance band, the Crimson Serenaders.[22]

Moenkhaus also "had ideas about modern music in spite of his steeped interest in the classics," according to a 1931 Bloomington newspaper item. "But in the field of discussion, perhaps, he was best known. Nothing delighted him as much as a surrounding of congenial associates, a cup of coffee and an empty hour or two to talk about the college, his friends, metaphysics, the future—any subject which might be introduced."[23]

"Bunkhaus," then, may be familiar, beloved, public; but William Moenkhaus remains something of an enigma. If he shared his thoughts on himself and the world with anyone—Allen, for example—posterity has kept no record. Carmichael takes a stab at analysis in *Jazzbanders*, suggesting that "because of his physical handicaps he had not entered into the same spirit of college life that the rest of us had.

"Yet he craved associations and recognition that his first two years of college had not given him. He knew in his own mind that he was far superior in intellect to most of the students, and class work bored him. He had plenty of girl friends, proof of his intellectual strength, but a spirit of rebellion against the conventional routine of living had warped his soul."[24]

Not surprisingly, given the differences in their backgrounds, upbringings, and world-views, Carmichael misses a key point. Scarcely out of his Bloomington boyhood, Moenkhaus had found himself first in Germany, then in Switzerland, surrounded by war, ideological strife, intellectual ferment, and a preoccupation with existential issues quite alien to anything he had known.

In those long-ago years, heartland America lay very far from *Mittel-Europa* conceptually, philosophically, intellectually—even in the social conventions of day-to-day life. The distance, and its meaning, animate Booth Tarkington's 1905 *The Conquest of Canaan,* in which once-impoverished ugly duckling Ariel Tabor returns to her Indiana hometown after seven years abroad, a woman of style and worldly beauty; Tarkington, entranced by the contrast, makes much of the ease with which her sure, steady gaze levels the snobbery that had blighted her childhood.

> That people turned to look at her may not have been altogether a novelty: a girl who had learned to appear unconscious of the Continental stare, the following gaze of the boulevards, the frank glances of the Costanza in Rome, was not ill-equipped to face Main Street, Canaan, even as it was today.[25]

When Hoagy speaks of the "spirit of college life," it is that of an *American* college of those years; Moenkhaus had tasted a different spirit, as embodied in the Voltaire and all the other locations where European students generated intense, often portentous, debate and discussion. The life of the Book Nook seems less a matter of how (in Hoagy's words) "Monk discovered how to gain the recognition of his fellow-students" than how he adapted an aspect of his European years to a comparable, if necessarily different, situation in Bloomington.[26]

Ordinarily, his matriculation would have guaranteed graduation in 1926 with a bachelor's degree. But by the beginning of that year it was obvious that, in common with "Hogwash" and other Book Nookers, he was determined to take his time. Little wonder that in his IU Permanent Personnel Record he mentions that he expects to graduate in 1950. In a precise, backward-leaning hand, he gives his condition of health as "poor" and certifies that he's studying for a bachelor of music, with a minor in German. The only musical instrument he lists himself as playing is "bass horn": no mention of the piano, the cello, or the compositions which since 1924 had been winning praise from his teachers. The date, like so much else on the document, is of course a whimsical exaggeration; but the intention to remain a student for as long as it suits him is unmistakable.

✻   ✻   ✻

"A one-hour course, Hygiene, has prevented William 'Bill' Moenkhaus, approximately class of '26, local salesman, bass-player or musician—he does not play a cornet—[and] poet, from receiving his A.B. degree," according to the *Indiana Daily Student*, "and after two years he has returned to Indiana and is doing advanced work in the music school."[27]

The hygiene part, at least, seems to have been accurate. But there is nothing to indicate an absence from Bloomington during the academic years 1926–27 or '27–'28. On the contrary, life for the Bent Eagles had never been more riotous: student drinking, chronic even in those Prohibition days, had become a major headache for university administrators. College men and women seemed to be "tying one on" everywhere: in dormitories, fraternity houses, public gathering places—even in the sacred precincts of the Student Building.

When Dean of Men Charles E. Edmondson and Dean of Women Agnes E. Wells finally decided it was time to crack down on student alcohol, they found an easy target in the Book Nook. On May 13, 1927—Friday the thirteenth—the brothers Costas stood solemnly in the dock at Bloomington district court, charged with permitting liquor to be consumed on their premises and "operating a public nuisance." Students, noisily indignant, shouted catcalls from the spectator seats; several times during the six-day hearing Judge Herbert A. Rundell threatened to clear the courtroom if order were not restored.

The "trial" often veered close to farce. According to one account, "one state witness testified that he had seen beer brought into the Nook, but the defense witnesses, mostly students, insisted that they had seen no drinking. They did admit that they had noticed intoxicated people in the establishment." On it went, with some—public-spirited souls, one and all—telling dark tales of Cokes spiked with gin, others issuing ardently innocent denials.

Finally tiring of the whole circus, Judge Rundell found the three brothers guilty, recommending a five-hundred-dollar fine—and, for Pete Costas, a thirty-day suspended sentence.[28]

Rather than end the affair, the judge's verdict inaugurated a new round of japery. Less than two weeks later, on Thursday, June 2, the Book Nook held its "First Annual Commencement." Some said Monk's failure to pass the hygiene course had prompted fellow–Bent Eagles to ensure him a "graduation," but other versions credit Pete Costas with "the idea of a graduation from the social life of IU, complete with speakers, program, faculty representation, and diplomas." Either way, it constituted a none-too-subtle thumbing of collective noses at the "trial" and everything it represented.[29]

A photo of the opening parade shows Carmichael and friends, resplendent in bathrobes and striped fezzes, blasting away on cornets, trumpets, and clarinets as they march along Third Street, about to turn up Indiana Avenue toward the Nook. Costas, introduced as "President of the College of Arts and Appliances," presented the degrees, and an estimated thousand people watched as Moenkhaus, a dead fish grasped in his left hand, solemnly accepted a D.D.—Doctor of Discords—degree from the "President."[30]

*   *   *

In 1929, William Ernest Moenkhaus finally took a bachelor of music, in composition and with high distinction, from Indiana University. He performed his own *Sonata in G* at his senior recital that spring, along with the first movement of a *Sonata in C, Lullaby,* and the whimsically titled *S.I.T.G.* (commemorating the Book Nook nonsense phrase "Snake in the Gravy").

By then, "Hoagie" Carmichael was out in the world, reputation on the rise, playing piano and writing songs. Wad Allen had begun working as a reporter for the Anderson, Indiana, *Herald,* contemplating New York and a career in advertising. Though they all stayed in touch, sometimes got together to laugh and carry on as of old, the all-important *Lehrjahre* were over for them all.

Moenkhaus moved on to the Detroit Conservatory, where he studied piano with Professor William Middelschulte, set to work on his first symphony, and in late 1930 joined the faculty as an instructor in composition. All the same, comic plays and poems by "Bunkhaus" continued to appear in *The Vagabond.*

If Moenkhaus's imagination was healthy, his body, never strong, was not. With almost endearing oversimplification, one account noted "he was so intent upon making a success of his work at Detroit that he weakened his physical condition by long hours of study." During a Christmas visit to his family, he took sick with what may have been a ruptured stomach ulcer; hospitalized, he rallied briefly. But he was more desperately ill than anyone had suspected. At 6:10 A.M. on Saturday, January 17, 1931, William Ernest Moenkhaus died at Indianapolis Metropolitan Hospital. He was twenty-eight.

Even at so long a historical remove, it's clear that his was a brilliant and original talent, which realized only a fraction of its potential. Wad Allen, writing from Anderson, suggested that the man he called his "best friend" was still

> too young to have made a name for himself, but had he lived on, his work would have established his name throughout America . . . When Moenkhaus sat at the piano, his hands bending on the keys, there was no man in the world like him. His playing echoed the genius of the great masters of composition and yet his work was original. Had Moenkhaus been given to this decade, rather than die at the age of twenty-eight, we would all know more about the inspiration of music.[31]

Dean B. Winfred Merrill, who had taught him composition and played with him in numerous concert trios, elegized Moenkhaus as "a joyous and whimsical soul, one of the most lovable I have known." "Moenkhaus, I suspect, would not have welcomed death," said Phil Rice, at whose urging "Bunkhaus" had begun writing for *The Vagabond*. "For one thing he had his first symphony to polish. If he had known death was coming he would probably have met it with an arpeggio [or] as Bunkhaus—with a quip."[32]

"Monk never liked the scheme of things in this life," Carmichael writes, "so he left it, and I believe his strange expressions were a form of protest." But he makes little further attempt to assess Moenkhaus's effect on him, preferring to remember the fun, the youthful escapades of the Book Nook crowd, his friend's fascination with hot jazz. The rest of it, he hints, may simply have been beyond anyone's capacity to understand; but the zaniness of the "Bunkhaus" plays and poems, the spontaneous buffoonery, the eccentric behavior—all had resonated strongly, if intuitively, within him.[33]

For Hoagy's emergent consciousness, both Moenkhaus and the equally short-lived Bix Beiderbecke were muses, divine emissaries whose sensibilities helped shape his own. Both men crossed his path at a maximally impressionable time: if Bix's effect was more explicit, the subtler effect of Moenkhaus was no less powerful.[34]

"Bunkhaus" himself supplies fitting requiem for all of it: the bright promise of youth; the unforgiving alliance of time and mortality; the shadowed inevitability of what lies in store. Like Hoagy Carmichael, William Ernest Moenkhaus lies buried in Bloomington's Rose Hill cemetery; and, like his friend of long ago, he remains as quick, and as vital, a force as ever he was in life.[35]

> The years have pants! Yon
> Helmet of the sunburn gone,
> Lingering odors of the dead
> Who yesterday the wigwam fed.
>
> 'Tis not the grave of Hermann Burt
> Whose life was like an ugly wart,
> Fold up the trumpet which he drove
> And pour the music in the stove!
>
> 'Twas his to live and now to die.
> Who remembers not the pie
> That each and every evening went
> Into a mouth that now lies bent?
>
> A tear or two, then from us sweep
> The memories of men who sleep.
> Long live the drunken alphabet!
> The time for us has not come—YET.[36]

⁎ VI ⁎

Bix

⁑

It's Tuesday, May 6, 1924, and in Richmond, Indiana, in a single-story, gray wooden building by a spur of the Chesapeake and Ohio railroad line, Ezra Wickemeyer completes one last check of his recording equipment. In the next room, plainly visible through an aperture in the dividing wall, seven young men are setting up musical instruments. The cornet player, a pleasant, sandy-haired lad, flashes him a smile. Nearly ready.

Even in the context of 1924 this seems an unlikely place to record music. The "studio"—Wickemeyer has to laugh when he hears people call it that— is no more than 125 feet by 30. Floor-length draperies, and even an old rug hung on the wall, represent a forlorn attempt to deaden the room sound.

Still, day after day, the musicians keep arriving. Groups large and small, it's all the same as they blow, bow, and strum into the large end of two megaphone-shaped horns, which carry the sound through a crystal to a recording stylus that cuts a groove into a spinning carnauba wax disc an inch and a half thick. Placement of musicians is important: louder instruments stand farther away, lest they knock the delicate cutting stylus out of its groove.

Located in the gorge of the nearby Whitewater River, the studio—an outbuilding of the prestigious Starr Piano Company—is hot, unventilated, perpetually humid. Small electric fans mounted on wall shelves do little more than move the fetid air around a bit. Now and then activity comes to an abrupt halt, as a freight car rumbles by on the siding or a full train thunders through on the main line, atop a ridge only fifty yards away.

Starr made records here throughout the 1920s for release on its Gennett label, named for the family that had founded the company, and quite a few of them made a kind of history. The band from the Friars' Inn had brought its New Orleans music here in 1922 for the first of three sessions. Cornetist Joe "King" Oliver had turned up twice with his Creole Jazz Band. Countless other groups, many with neither name nor fame, made the long drive out the National Road, or came west from Ohio, to record their best numbers in this airless room.

Nor was it all band music. Former secretary of state William Jennings Bryan had stood in front of these very horns to repeat his 1896 "Cross of Gold" speech. Folksinger Wendell Hall had warbled his "It Ain't Gonna Rain No Mo' " right here and had taken a test pressing to the Victor Company, which promptly signed him. As long as prospective recording artists could pay for the time and use of facilities, they could record in Gennett's unprepossessing building.

This morning in May 1924 belongs to a band calling itself the "Wolverine Orchestra of Chicago." Wickemeyer had first recorded them in February, when they'd done four titles, only two of which were balanced well enough for issue. This time, surer of themselves, they knew better how to set up, with the cornet player back near the sousaphone, and the clarinet and saxophone off a bit to the sides.

They worked first through Walter Donaldson's new song, "Oh, Baby!" then moved on to a hot one that Charlie Davis, the Indianapolis bandleader, had been touting. Davis had named it "Copenhagen"—a reference, it turned out, not to the capital of far-away Denmark, but to a brand of chawin' tobacco favored by his tuba player. The young men got through that one just fine, even if the banjo player suddenly decided to play guitar, necessitating some shuffling around of chairs.

Next up was something new. A young guy down at the university in Bloomington had put this one together, the cornetist said. Hadn't written it down: he could neither read nor write music, really. But they'd been playing fraternity house dates he'd booked for them, and he'd worked this thing out on the piano at a campus hangout called the Book Nook.

Title? Wickemeyer asked.

Somebody laughed. The Bloomington fella—they called him "Hoagie"—had wanted to call it "Free Wheeling," but the guys in the band didn't like that much. As a matter of fact, the cornet player said, it reminded him more of riverboats on the Mississippi near Davenport, in Iowa, where he'd grown up. To the banjo player it had a kind of "shuffle" feel. Okay, then: call it "Riverboat Shuffle."

And it is as "Riverboat Shuffle" that Hoagland Howard Carmichael's maiden effort as a composer of popular melodies makes its appearance. Understanding that moment requires backing up just a few weeks. George Johnson, the tenor sax player with whom "Hoagie" had undertaken his ill-fated Florida trip just a year before, sent a wire. "I'm playing in a new band with Bix," it said. "We've worked out some hot stuff, and it sounds great. Need jobs. Can you help?"

After a breaking-in period around Hamilton, Ohio, they'd worked short stretches in Chicago and Cincinnati and done a few Indiana dates for Charlie Davis. Bloomington seemed a natural next step—and Carmichael didn't disappoint them. Johnson was his pal, after all, a true believer. He knew some of the other guys, too—especially genial, girl-crazy Vic Moore on drums. And, above all, there was Bix Beiderbecke on cornet.

"Bix had sounded good to me in Chicago, but he wasn't finished," Carmichael recalled. "I knew that he had improved from what George had told me, and I realized . . . that I had had only one desire for weeks, and that was to hear Bix. Somehow I rather dreaded to see him take his horn out of its case; I had confidence in him because of what I [had] heard him play in Chicago, but for some reason or other I wanted it to be super-special this time."[1]

They arrived on Friday, April 25, to play the IU Boosters Club spring dance. They'd be commuting, playing in Bloomington, staying in Indianapolis—and if things got too late, they could sleep on couches at the Kappa Sig house. Accordingly, Kappa Sig was their first destination.

Carmichael had good cause to remember the occasion. He was by then the not-always-proud owner of the "Open Job," a dilapidated 1915 Ford that "had been stripped down until there was nothing left but the chassis, [and] a high front seat." A wooden box, mounted at the rear, bore witness to a prior owner's use of the Ford as a delivery vehicle.

"The Open Job" was one of the first stripped-down college cars in the middle west. I never allowed her unlovely sides to be marred by any wisecracks, and I kept the oil level up so she responded gratefully every time I flipped the crank by breaking into a bone-shaking roar. As she had a large crack in the motor block, I never put in water for short trips.[2]

On this of all days, the car decided to act up. He'd tried to crank it, "jump to one side and get into it all in one operation, I missed the last and most important step and watched the old boat go down the driveway and head for the college campus under full power." Someone, fortunately, jumped on board before the car picked up much speed—but it was close. George Johnson, vastly amused, introduced its owner to the band as "Barney Oldfield," premier auto racing driver of the day.[3]

As "Hoagie" tells it, the Wolverines warmed up at Kappa Sig House, jamming on King Oliver's "Dippermouth Blues," with Carmichael replacing co-leader Dick Voynow at the piano. "Every nerve in my body began to tingle. My hands shook, and I experienced the same sort of feeling I had when I heard Jordan's colored orchestra four years before. Then I saw Bix get out his cornet and Jimmy [Hartwell, clarinet] told him to take the break in the middle of the chorus. He did. Bix played just four notes and that wound up the afternoon party."[4]

Carmichael's reaction, appearing in slightly different form in all his memoirs, reflects the zealot whose exaggerated passions and deranged behavior at the piano had so amused his friend Moenkhaus. It's been cited countless times as typical of fellow-musicians and hot music enthusiasts hearing Bix for the first time.

> The notes weren't blown—they were hit, like a mallet hits a chime, and his tone had a richness that can only come from the heart. I rose violently from the piano bench and fell, exhausted, on to a davenport. He had completely ruined me. That sounds idiotic, but it is the truth.[5]

Any attempt to reconstruct the scene in imagination stumbles badly at the image of Hoagy in a transport of ecstasy, bolting from the keyboard and swooning on a nearby sofa. A bit stagy, even for a moment of musical inspiration. Still, there's no denying that the ringing quality of Beiderbecke's tone, and the beauty of his note choices, strongly affected those who heard him. Bix's intuitive creativity astonished the "half-educated man" in much the way Moenkhaus's intellectual power and depth had astonished him. In both cases, as with Reg DuValle and Batty DeMarcus before them, there was a moment of epiphany, of revelation, carrying him to a new and higher level of awareness.

Rather more helpful is Carmichael's description of Bix playing the cornet, as told to documentary filmmaker Brigitte Berman in 1975. "He never had any show or display, wasn't a showoff in any way. Never handled his horn like other horn players do, you know, [waving it] up in the air and all that stuff when he was hitting a beautiful phrase. No: he kept it right down here [pointed at the floor] where he liked it, and where he could hear it and love it, and he'd forget about whoever was listening or anything else."[6]

The Wolverines played five weekends of dances at Indiana University. There is little indication what they did in between, though it's safe to assume that they spent a good part of their time on the IU campus. Hoagy, meanwhile, was carrying a fourteen-hour course load that spring, which must have severely curtailed his weekday availability.

Lida Carmichael provides an odd and disturbing counterpoint to her son's euphoria. In an April 25 letter, she informs university registrar John Cravens that her daughter Georgia has graduated from high school and completed courses in shorthand and typing, and would now like to enter IU as a freshman. As usual, money is short. The family can raise enough for tuition and books, if Cravens can help by placing her in a part-time job "in the office or some place about the university."

Warming to her subject, she writes, "It makes me bitter at times to think we cannot give our children the advantages, that seems [*sic*] so easy for other parents: but if they must acquire an education through their own efforts, mostly, I have the one consolation of knowing that it will at least make real men and women of them, or I hope so. Anything earned or fought for means so much more to people." Her efforts were in vain. As Georgia makes clear in her own later correspondence with Cravens, lack of money has forced her to abandon hopes of attending IU for the autumn semester. She promises to enroll at midterm "without any further parley on the subject."[7]

Even more troubling is a letter from university bursar U. C. Smith, dated April 30 and mailed to Hoagy at the Kappa Sig house. "The limit under the rules for non-payment of fees closes this week," it states. "I shall notify the Dean on Monday that all delinquent students are automatically withdrawn from the University on failure to comply with the rules."[8]

Again, as so many times before, lack of money is making things difficult for the Carmichael family. It all raises an unspoken, but tantalizing, question. Since the start of the 1923–24 school year, "Carmichael's Collegians" had played at nearly forty school social functions, and perhaps more off campus. Presumably these had been paid engagements. What has happened to the money? Why is Hoagy unable to help his sister begin school at IU, or even keep up with his own fees?

His memoirs, meanwhile, overflow with giddy depictions of this time: Bix and his friends jamming on "Clarinet Marmalade" or "Farewell Blues" at frat house dances; the Wolverines and Hoagy's own Collegians driving around campus in the rain, serenading sorority houses from the back of an open truck; Bix, supine on the floor of the Kappa Sigma parlor, absorbed in a record of Stravinsky's *The Firebird*. "Why don't you write music, Hoagy?" Beiderbecke reportedly asked during one of these idylls. Carmichael had no convincing answer—but he started to think about it.[9]

His campus popularity rising, he was inducted around this time into the prestigious Sphinx Club; then came a widely coveted invitation to a second circle, a

> secret organization that had been outlawed long before by the school authorities. Qualifications for both societies were good fellowship, a collegiate air, and a slightly tarnished character. in other words, if you should ask them, the members were "real guys." Some considered the organization snobbish in effect. Nevertheless, there was hardly a lad at school who wouldn't have given his right arm to be asked to membership . . . I found out that as a whole the (secret) society ran to football players, campus politicians and violators of the Volstead [prohibition] act.[10]

But Bix's question, however casual, resounded in his mind:

> Before the Wolverines had come to town, as it were, I had heard Zez Confrey's "Kitten on the Keys" and learned to play it by ear from the record. This was a sensational composition, and a new treatment in piano style. It occurred to me that I might compose something, too. The Book Nook piano was my work bench, and I gave it a fit one day in an effort to construct a masterpiece. When I got up I had composed a thing that had all the ear-marks [sic] of a piano solo, but

I was somewhat disappointed that it wasn't fancier. I was pleased, nevertheless, because I had composed something that I could call my own.[11]

He unveiled the "masterpiece" to Bix and the others at a Kappa Sig jam session—and, to his surprise, they seemed to enjoy it. "The verse was screwy and different, while the chorus was actually a thirty-two measure blues. The main theme of the piece offered the possibility of four breaks. This was a new idea, and [pianist-leader] Dick Voynow suggested that the band learn it and record it for Gennett."[12]

All of which brings the band, minus Carmichael, to the little room at Richmond, awaiting Ezra Wickemeyer's "start" signal. "Free Wheeling," a.k.a. "Riverboat Shuffle," is indeed a pleasant jazz band number: a four-bar introduction brings on a sixteen-bar verse in A-minor, in miniature AABA form. That opens into a thirty-two-bar chorus in F-major, with four ad-lib "breaks"—two-bar interruptions in the rhythm—adding pizzazz.

Given Carmichael's inability to write down his ideas, it's not surprising that the melody of the chorus is vague, at times little more than a sketch. The chord sequence is similar to that used by Jelly Roll Morton in the final, or "blowing," strain of his coincidentally titled "Wolverine Blues." It also occurs with minor variations in two other Morton numbers, "Shreveport Stomp" and, note values halved, "Mister Jelly Lord." With minor adjustments, the same pattern underpins such later popular songs as "I Can't Give You Anything but Love" (1928) and "Pennies From Heaven" (1934).[13]

In the hot music world of 1924, "Riverboat Shuffle" is a fresh addition, and the Wolverines give it spirited treatment. Beiderbecke's cornet chorus is poised but a bit innocent, the figure in bar 4 (repeated in bars 8 and 20) reflecting the vo-do-do-de-o spirit of the times. But he's already fitting his phrases together with tongue-and-groove precision.

"Riverboat Shuffle" soon became a staple of the white jazz band repertoire, both because of the series of solo "breaks" (the earlier "Jazz Me Blues" employs a similar device) and because of its close association with Bix. He recorded it twice: his second version, done in 1927 with a group led by Frank Trumbauer, is an acknowledged career highlight. There, too, the melody is vague, at best approximate.

But though bright and serviceable, "Riverboat Shuffle" shows little sign of heralding an innovative songwriting talent. Not as structurally ambitious as "Wolverine Blues," as melodically engaging as "Shreveport," or as insinuating as "Mister Jelly Lord," it is significant mostly in marking Hoagy Carmichael's transition in his own mind from piano-playing college student to "composer."

As he puts it in *Jazzbanders*, "I listened patiently and quietly. I wasn't thrilled—I was pleased, that was all—so much so that it made me sort of sad. I felt like crying over my little brain-child as a proud parent might cry at Thelma's graduation exercises. It was a swell record.

"And that," he adds endearingly, "is how to break into the song-writing business."[14]

His own Collegians, meanwhile, had taken on enough polish to land jobs playing for school events—often, to Carmichael's dismay, on the same nights when the Wolverines were working elsewhere on campus. If Art Baker, on trumpet, was primarily a "straight" man, Wad Allen proved himself a strong "hot" improviser on C-melody sax. Marshall "Bridge" Abrams was the violinist, Billy Little the banjoist, and Kappa Sigma fraternity brother Chet Decker the drummer.

Whatever its skills, the sextet gave its leader "three of the happiest years of my life. Only once during these years was there a quarrel among us, and on this occasion every man tried to take the blame for it, and offered to let the others kick him square in the pants for being such a heel. This quarrel left us heavy-hearted and with faces as long and sad as a cocker spaniel's."[15]

According to Indiana University archival records, Carmichael's Collegians played at least fifty advertised dates around Bloomington during academic year 1924–25 and even more in 1925–26. At times they appear to have averaged between three and five a week (often two per day), including fraternity and sorority dances, theatre engagements, Charleston contests, jazz band "battles," football games, and other campus events.[16]

Nor were they alone. Among other groups booked to play social functions during the same period were the university's own Crimson Serenaders, Charlie Davis's band, Hitch's Happy Harmonists, the Miami Lucky Seven, the Gold and Black Collegians from DePauw, and countless other regional groups, as well as the nationally known bands of Isham Jones, Ray Miller, Arnold Johnson, Paul Biese, and Jean Goldkette. Cornetist Johnny Bayersdorffer brought his group up from New Orleans, and trumpeter Louis Panico turned up with a Chicago unit. Paul Whiteman appeared with his full orchestra for an April 17, 1925, reprise of his famed Aeolian Hall concert, complete to George Gershwin's *Rhapsody in Blue*, with bandsman Harry Perella featured at the piano.

Among the numerous John Held Jr. cartoons depicting collegiate life in the 1920s is one bearing the title *The Girl Who Fainted at the Fraternity House Dance*. The lady herself lies on the floor, head cradled in the lap of her tuxedo-clad date; every other young man in the room hastens to proffer his own hip flask as the band, over by the fireplace, toots blithely and imperturbably on. Imagination need not leap far to visualize Carmichael's Collegians—or Bix and the Wolverines—in the role.

Though more than three years Bix's senior, Carmichael felt as much the acolyte in his presence as he had felt with Moenkhaus. When Bix sat down at the piano in the Book Nook, or at Kappa Sig House, and worked through his dreamy, neo-impressionist keyboard inventions, it was as an often unwitting teacher to "Hoagie's" avid pupil. Ironically, before Beiderbecke's arrival in Bloomington, the pupil hadn't even been aware his friend played the piano. The following passage from *Jazzbanders* provides a deliciously visual evocation of the young Iowan at the keyboard:

> He could play only parts of Ravel's compositions because his execution was not so good. It was a terrible thing to watch. His fingers were stiff and they invariably went the opposite direction from that which was expected. Bix didn't copy Ravel, but I recognized a slight similarity in style in the phrases he used either at the piano or on the cornet.

"Bix used the cornet merely as a means of expressing his musical ideas," Carmichael adds in a handwritten note. "He was a composer and inventor at heart. I should say that some of the finest contributions to American music are his interpretative cornet passages and his piano scores."[17]

More revealing still is his evocation of an obviously bibulous evening listening to records of *The Firebird* and other modern classics. They talk casually about ballet, about composing, about Stravinsky, Prokofiev, Rimsky-Korsakov. It's the conversation of two very young men, equal parts frivolity and high seriousness: for Hoagland Carmichael it also heralds a sea-change, a brand-new way of looking at himself.

"We lay there and listened," he writes in *Sometimes I Wonder*.

The music filled us both, I sensed, with terrible longing, dreadful urges, wonderful desires. Coupled with white mule liquor, it was strangely moving. It made us very close and it made us lonely, too, but with a feeling of release, a feeling of elation and ecstasy. You don't forget such a mood. They only come a few times in a lifetime.[18]

On Friday, May 23, 1924, the Wolverines wound up their Bloomington spring season by playing an "open dance" at the Student Building auditorium, sponsored by the Women's Self-Government Association. Charlie Davis, meanwhile, had come through with steady work—a way, as it happened, of extricating himself from an embarrassing situation. He'd agreed to play for Otto Wray and Gar Davis at their Rainbow Casino Gardens, on the White River northwest of Indianapolis; but that was before Charlie's pal Harry Page weighed in with a better-paying season at the Fairview Hotel, on Lake Manitou.

Davis juggled his options. His band and the Wolverines had played in separate rooms for the Butler College Prom that April, and he'd heard Bix and friends heat up the crowd. Now he had to convince Otto and Gar that this young group, brand-new rage of the college circuit, could pack their place. At length they took him at his word and hired the band (billed as the "Charlie Davis Wolverines") to do six nights a week on the Gardens' Rainbow Terrace, with a major promotional push.

The first weekend did capacity business, everything the managers had hoped; the collegiate audience turned out in force, Hoagy Carmichael among them.

The dance floor was surrounded by large umbrella effects, under which chairs and tables were placed, and it looked straight up at the moon from the highest bank of White River. The orchestra played on a tiered platform under dim lights. The picture of smartly dressed boys and beautiful girls in big straw hats and long flowing dresses, moving to the rhythm of the band, was a sight to see. These people danced because they loved it; they moved about silently, listening intently to every wicked note and beat of the music . . . The band was really at its best when they played low and dirty, but when Bix cocked his head to one side and popped his eyes it was a signal for a shower of beautiful notes that led the band into an explosive ending and sent the dancers to the tables with their panties on fire.[19]

He and Bix spent a few happy intermissions in a quiet corner, singing and doodling "Riverboat Shuffle," or one of the other hot numbers, at each other. "I'd doodle the melody while Bix pumped bass and imitated cymbal licks."

But their euphoria was short-lived. As Duncan Schiedt notes, the Wolverines' hot repertoire "was not really suitable to the Casino Gardens. The sedate, money-spending [older] crowd came, listened, and did not return." The band lasted just short of four weeks before Charlie Davis arranged for a local group to replace them.[20]

This 1924 Indiana idyll marks the period of closest association between Hoagy Carmichael and Bix Beiderbecke. There would be periodic reunions after that, including several record dates together. But this was the foundation of the friendship—and of the lifelong impact that Beiderbecke was to make on the pianist and neophyte composer. At this point the Wolverines wander off, first to Chicago, then to New York and Florida, and ultimately out of sight altogether. Bix leaves to pursue his own destiny—but his path will cross Hoagy Carmichael's soon again.[21]

At some point during Beiderbecke's Bloomington weeks, says Carmichael, "an insane desire overcame me. I wanted to play a cornet, and I wanted to play it badly. Literally, I did—that is, I played it very badly. The band director of the university gave me a cornet and I blew it with all my might. I was impatient and blew my lip to a piece of raw beefsteak in five minutes. I blew everybody out of the house, too." He taught himself the notes by comparing them with the piano keyboard, much as Bix had done at the start.

> I carried the horn around with me as though it were a baby, and each night I put it away in its velvet-lined cradle. Before long, everybody in the fraternity house was ready to throw me out, bag and baggage. They hid the cornet, repeatedly. One day I located it in the living-room chandelier.[22]

Some confusion attends the birth of this dalliance with the horn. He suggests it was early to mid-1924, though an affidavit on file at Indiana University, issued by the "Department of Military Science and Practice" and dated July 28, 1925, attests that

> I, Hoagland Carmichael, a musician in Indiana University, hold myself personally responsible for one cornet assigned to me this date to be used during the summer in practice, looking toward membership in

the University Military Band. I agree to return the cornet in good shape to the Military Department prior to the opening of college in September or to pay in full for any damage to same or for loss of same.[23]

Still, there is no doubt that by the night of January 25, 1925, when Hoagy and Bix drove the National Road toward Richmond, Carmichael had been toiling at the cornet for some time. It's therefore reasonable to view his 1925 summer rental as an attempt to transfer efforts to an instrument of higher quality, and in presumably better condition, than what he'd been using.

Fraternity brothers and Book Nook habitués spared no effort to discourage their friend's apparently none-too-skillful efforts on the horn. An item in the *Indiana Daily Student*, under the headline "Science Curbs Hogwash M'Corkle's Cornet," describes how

> his eyes and cheeks were bulged and his massive [??] body was writhing to the rhythm of the horrible blurbs emanating from the muzzle of the instrument. Six scientifically minded youths filed into the room silently and stood in solemn and sinister poses. Hogwash M'Corkle raised his eyes and continued blowing. Then—at a signal—the six produced lemons and sucked them. Hogwash's jaws began to ache and his lips puckered. A faint wheeze was all that came from the horn.[24]

No matter that the lemon-sucking remedy is a particularly stubborn bit of mythology with no basis in fact. The point is that Carmichael's cornet efforts, however industrious, found little favor among friends—or, alas, fellow-musicians. With wry self-deprecation, he describes bringing the horn along to an end-of-semester dance job "with the intention of showing them a thing or two. I showed 'em, and had difficulty collecting the money for the engagement as a result."[25]

He took to practicing outdoors, usually in sparsely populated areas. He even took a quartet job with himself on cornet, though he "knew I couldn't cut it." Sure enough, he quickly blew his lip out, and finished the evening at the piano. "To this day," he comments in all three memoirs, "I firmly believe that the cornet was my instrument." He means it: in a later handwritten memorandum, he comments,

> I'm truly sorry that I had not had proper training on cornet when younger. If so I could have been playing like Bix within a year after

our meeting, and I think many more melodies and ideas for jazz development and for instrumental compositions would have followed. In some ways the piano is inadequate. Bix composed as he played cornet, but nothing that you'd put down on paper as an entity—a complete composition.[26]

By this time Hoagy had heard plenty of hot music: he'd been to the Friars' Inn, heard Oliver and Armstrong at the Lincoln Gardens, bought all the records as they appeared. But Bix, even if incomplete, offered something different from all of them, a new approach to lyricism and melodic organization. Arguably, Carmichael filters his recollections of 1924 Bix through perception of his friend at maturity: the exhilarating solos with the Goldkette and Whiteman orchestras, the style-defining OKeh records with his own groups and under Frank Trumbauer's leadership.

But his choruses on such Wolverines titles as "I Need Some Pettin'" and "Royal Garden Blues," recorded for Gennett on June 20, already display felicity, structural logic—and, perhaps above all, signs of a complexity, a *layering*, of emotional response typical of European music but brand-new to jazz. Both Armstrong and Sidney Bechet, emerging around this time, were playing solos with high intensity and soaring emotional arcs, in content and effect not unlike grand opera arias. Such bravura statements were clear, direct, emotionally uncomplicated. Roppolo, with the Friars' Inn band, had hinted at darker, more complex utterances; now here was Beiderbecke, emotionally stratified, even his most exultant moments imbued with some ambiguously bittersweet yearning.

Bix and Moenkhaus, affecting Carmichael at approximately the same time, seem two complementary entities, able between them to shape their skinny, souped-up admirer as no formal studies ever could. And—little wonder—those two seem to have recognized, and taken to, one another from the start.

The friendship . . . between Monk and Bix endured to the end. Bix, the inarticulate kid, who played the wonderful horn. Monk, the surrealistic intellectual, who looked at the world through a glass that threw it into a hopeless distortion. Bix, the lone wolf, shy, silent. Monk, the campus character, who had a phrase for anything. They were friends. They understood.[27]

Moenkhaus, a man of intellect and deep musical scholarship, responds profoundly to the intuitional wonders of hot jazz; Beiderbecke, the intuitive musician, spends his leisure hours absorbing the intricacies of *Petroushka* and *The Firebird.* No accident, really, that they meet—and enjoy one another—in the surrealist precincts of the Book Nook. When Carmichael reads a satiric "Bunkhaus" creation aloud to Bix, the latter's instincts tell him how to respond: "I am not a swan," he declares with wholly appropriate ambiguity. In Hoagy's later recollection it was "the only inanity he could think of at the moment . . . [which] was to become a byword between us in the years to come . . . He tried to say with those strange words all the things he couldn't say, and for us he was successful."[28]

But even that doesn't tell quite the whole story, says Hoagy:

> It is his gentleness that is lost in the legends, his ability to charm, to hold friends, to make one feel that it was still possible to know and need—and be known and needed by—another human being.[29]

> When Bix opened up his soul to me that [first] day, I learned and experienced one of life's innermost secrets to happiness—pleasure that it had taken a whole lifetime of living and conduct to achieve.[30]

Bix stopped off in Indianapolis en route home in early December. He'd quit the Wolverines, he said, spent just short of two months in Detroit with Jean Goldkette's orchestra, made a record—and washed out. Go home and learn to read music better, Goldkette had told him kindly but firmly. He and Hoagy double-dated, dancing to Charlie Davis's band at the Severin Roof Garden. Then he was off, homeward bound.

He resurfaced toward the end of January: he'd been in touch with Wickemeyer and Fred Wiggins, he said, and arranged to record four titles for Gennett with five other guys, all but one from Goldkette's band. Would Hoagy like to come along? The answer was a foregone conclusion: the "Open Job" had died its natural death, and a reasonably solvent Carmichael had plunked down just short of four hundred dollars for a brand-new Ford, with "every gadget put on it that the salesman had to offer, including five balloon tires . . . The new car cut quite a figure around the [Bloomington] public square while the paint held its gloss, and I was very proud of it."[31]

Seated grandly at the wheel, Carmichael called for his friend in Indi-anapolis on Sunday evening, January 25. The session was scheduled for Monday morning, said Bix, so let's spend the night having some fun; we can get in the back door of the Ohio Theatre. Stealing in after the custodian had departed, they took their places at two grand pianos in the orchestra pit. "There, alone, we banged out chorus after chorus of 'Royal Garden Blues,' each chorus a new interpretation and a bigger burn than the one before. First one would play the bass chords while the other played the hot licks, then we'd reverse the process. It was great fun but we finally wore out, and left town as scheduled."[32]

Out along the National Road they went. Halfway to Richmond they stopped, high on the sheer adrenaline of the moment, and Bix reached for his cornet. "I happened to remember that my weird looking horn was in the back of the car," says Carmichael. Solemnly, they exchanged A's. "Bix suggested 'Way Down Yonder in New Orleans.' This was a lucky break for me; I knew it pretty well and managed to keep up a rhythmic lead while Bix laid it out for the farmers. I was in my glory. This kept up until every hound dog within three miles was on its ear." Bix's comment: "Hoagy, you weren't bad."[33]

They arrived at Gennett's frame building early, and after a time the rest showed up—Tommy Dorsey, Don Murray, pianist Paul Mertz, and a De-troit drummer named Tom Gargano. They'd brought plenty of hooch: De-troit, after all, was only a mile across the river from Windsor, Ontario, and Canada had no Eighteenth Amendment or Volstead Act to prohibit sale of liquor.

Of four numbers scheduled for that day they finished only two, Bix's own original, "Davenport Blues," which wasn't a blues at all, and the ODJB's "Toddlin' Blues," which was. By the time banjoist Howard "Howdy" Quick-sell showed up, the booze had taken its toll: they stumbled through three takes each on the other two numbers, never got them right, and called it quits. Ezra Wickemeyer, regarding the scene through the glass, just shrug-ged: these had been what the company called "test records," with the per-formers footing their own expenses. Production cost the company next to nothing. If only two titles out of four saw issue, no one was out of pocket except the musicians—and they were obviously too blotto to care.

"Driving back in a bone-chilling snowstorm, Bix nearly froze to death in his sleep," says Carmichael. "I asked myself, where are you going, Hoagland?

Hot jazz, hot trumpet, music, blues, stomps aren't for you as a career. The law is noble, the law is fat with rewards. That's where a man, a lawyer, finds security and position."[34]

But what of music? Music didn't just dry up and blow away at the mention of something as imposing, as substantial, as the law. When, many years later, Carmichael turned out (with Frank Loesser) a hit song containing the lines

> You better listen to your maw and someday practice the law,
> And then you'll be a real success[35]

he could well have been thinking of this moment. Do the responsible thing. Get your law degree and hang out a shingle. Play your music for fun, maybe, on weekends, alongside others who had taken the high road. But whatever you do, don't listen to the siren song: don't throw away everything for the sake of so evanescent, so insubstantial and ultimately frustrating, a pursuit as music. No fit life for a gentleman, they used to say: certainly no fit life for anyone with any sense.

But music, like some opportunistic bacillus, has a way of sneaking into the bloodstream and quietly just swimming along, awaiting its moment. Whatever had been set in motion by Reg DuValle, by Batty DeMarcus, by the Jordan Orchestra, and nurtured at the Friars' Inn, at the Lincoln Gardens, and during the magic evenings listening to Bix, was not going to disappear. At some not-too-deep level of his mind, Hoagland Carmichael knew that. Knew, too, that "Riverboat Shuffle," whatever its virtues, had helped him turn a corner.

"You don't write melodies," he said in reflection, "you find them. They lie there on the keys waiting for you to find them. They have always been there. If you find the beginning of a good song, and if your fingers do not stray, the melody should come out of hiding in a short time."[36]

* * *

One morning, en route to class, "Hoagie" stops in at the Book Nook. There, at the old upright, is a friend named Mack McCarthy. Mack plays pretty well, and Carmichael lingers awhile to listen. At length, McCarthy looks inquiringly at him: hey, Hoag, am I hogging the keys? Want a shot at it?

A melody, extraordinary and unique, is about to come out of hiding.

* VII *

Washboard Blues

Carmichael takes his place at the Book Nook piano. Come on out, melody; don't be shy. I know you're in there somewhere.

> In my efforts to imitate Mack, I struck a most peculiar strain; it was new, and different ... When I had finished the main theme, I discovered it was only seventeen measures, a thing almost unheard of in composition. Then I composed an interlude and a peculiar chanting theme ... Now all that was necessary was an introduction.[1]

One of the questions most frequently asked of composers, and least often answered satisfactorily, is one of the simplest: what's the process? How do you, does anybody, write a great song? Are melodies indeed "found" rather than created? Or are they slowly, painstakingly, hewn, phrase by phrase, bar by bar, out of the rock face of imagination?

In later years, Hoagy embellished his description of this moment almost beyond recognition, interpolating conversational exchanges drawn shamelessly from the realm of fiction. The scene begins to read like a Hollywood screenplay: "There, by George! I've got it!" the composer exclaims, as a complaisant muse bends forward to touch him, ever so gently, on the shoulder.

The piece that emerged was an instrumental in three sections. An eight-bar introductory strain, its arpeggiated cadence a little reminiscent of "Riverboat Shuffle," leads to the main theme, indeed seventeen bars long. A four-bar interlude brings on the third strain, a standard twelve-bar blues.

His first telling, in his early memoir *Jazzbanders*, is typical. Just fooling around with chord shapes, going where the melody leads him, stumbling across—finding—an idea. A seventeen-bar chorus? Why not? *Sounds* right, doesn't it?

HOAGY: "What does it sound like, Mack?"
MACK: "Sounds like washing clothes."
HOAGY: "Sure. That chant part's got a rhythm like rubbing clothes up and down a washboard. Can't you hear that colored mammy singin' to herself?"
MACK: "Name it 'Washboard Blues.' "
HOAGY: "That's it! 'Washboard Blues.' "

Slow dissolve . . .

He works on it some more, gets it about where he wants it, begins playing it for friends. Larry Leonard, his writing familiar, likes it. Harry Hostetter, Bloomington friend and neighbor since childhood, opines that it "ain't so bad."

That, especially, means a lot. "Harry's attitude toward me, in some ways, was that of a tolerant father," Carmichael writes. "Harry the tough guy, ex-Navy, [had] been a lot of places, seen a lot of things . . . He lived music and yet he didn't play himself. Its expression was in the work of others, me in particular, for if I showed signs of inertia he was there to goad me into working." If Harry liked it, it must be pretty good.[2]

Hoagy played his "Washboard" song for Evansville pianist Curtis Hitch, in town to play a college date with his band, the Happy Harmonists. They were sounding more and more like the Wolverines, especially because Fred Rollison, on cornet, was nuts about Bix. They'd been making records for Gennett since mid-1923 and had a date coming up.

The leader himself was smart, musically savvy. When Hoagy played the new tune he was intrigued—but realistic about his own ability to do it justice. "I could no more have played that stuff than the man in the moon," he told Duncan Schiedt. So why not bring the composer along to Richmond and have *him* play the piano part, rehearsing the band while he was at it?[3]

And on Tuesday, May 19, 1925, that's just what happened. Moenkhaus, musically trained, was pressed into service Monday to write out a coherent lead sheet, while Hoagy cobbled together a second number, which he called "Boneyard Shuffle" as a follow-up to "Riverboat." The band had spent most of a day running down the two, yet "I was as nervous as an old-time fiddler in anticipation of my first recording." Sure, he'd stood by watching while Bix and the guys from Detroit played and drank themselves into insensibility that January. Even knocked back a few himself. But this was different. Now it was he, Hoagland Howard Carmichael himself—law student, piano player, and aspiring composer—sitting in front of the two funny-looking horns, while Ezra Wickemeyer tweaked and adjusted his equipment behind the plate glass.[4]

They addressed "Boneyard" first. Wickemeyer liked it, Hoagy recalled, "because it was hotsy-totsy. Everything had to be hot in those days." But that does the number insufficient justice: it's an excellent, often ingenious, piece of work, considerably more adventuresome than "Riverboat." Taken at a brisk $\bignote = 206$, it breaks down as follows:

Introduction (band): 4 bars

A = Theme (cornet): 8 + 4 + 4 (insert) + 4 (cadence)

Interlude: 4

B = Verse (band): 16

A = Theme (tenor sax): 20 (as above), but introduces 4-bar segments with 2-bar figure borrowed from "Eccentric Rag"

C = Secondary theme: 32 (clarinet 16 over Charleston rhythm, cornet 8 bridge, clarinet 8)

A = Theme (piano): 20, as above

A = Theme (band): 20, as above

The piece bristles with little "modernistic" touches: whole-tone scales, unexpected chordal turns, irregular thematic structures—even an elision: bringing in the "C," or secondary, theme a bar early, foreshortening the tenor sax solo. Not surprisingly, Hoagy's piano chording sounds in spots like that of Bix on the Wolverines record of "Big Boy."

As a hot specialty, "Boneyard Shuffle" is an innovation, a great leap ahead of its predecessor; little in the output of either white or black bands of 1925 compares with its way of making the unconventional seem perfectly natural. Taken alone it might have been enough to announce this Indiana college boy as a talent to watch. But it's unlucky enough to be paired, on this day, with an even more ambitious, ultimately much greater, invention.

Wickemeyer has had his doubts about "Washboard Blues" right from the start, especially the slow ($\bf{\downarrow} = 120$) tempo. Worse yet, after listening to them run it down, the technician abandons his nest of pulleys, weights, and cranks to inform Hitch and companions that the performance is some twenty seconds short of Gennett's new, slightly longer, standard playing time. An eternity.

Hitch, unruffled, doesn't miss a beat. "Hoagy will put in a piano solo," he says. Carmichael looks as though someone has punched him in the gut. Oh he will, will he? "Sure, Hoagy will put in a piano solo for you. Hasn't got time to run down to the corner and buy one. He'll make one for you here. He makes three or four every morning before breakfast. Nothing to it."[5]

The musicians file out for a smoke, leaving the composer to his panicked thoughts. In his own various accounts, he thinks about everything he can—about Lida and her golden oak piano; Cyclone wandering all over creation in search of a steady job; sparkling-eyed little sister Joanne, dead so soon; Bix and Monk; *The Firebird*.

And by the time they return he's got something. A bit of the blues, some double-time stuff—and, in bars 5 and 6, an elegaic little phrase he'd someday extract for use in another, even better known, song. Twenty-two seconds by the clock. Drop it in at midstream, and voilà! They've got themselves a record.

Listening to a test pressing, says Carmichael, was one of the strangest experiences of his life.

> The tune caught me under the chin from the first note, and I could hardly hold myself from shouting my enthusiasm long enough to hear the record through. Then the piano solo came through the horn. I didn't recognize a note of it. Actually, it was like hearing myself play and being another person at the same time...At the end of the record, all of us let out a war whoop and danced ring around Rosie.[6]

A photograph of the band, presumably taken before recording began, tells its own story: the musicians are relaxed, with Fred Rollison leaning carelessly against the piano and drummer Earl "Buddy" McDowell puffing on his pipe. Hitch—steady, avuncular—sits at the bass end of the piano, smiling broadly. Perched beside him on the bench, natty but solemn in bow tie and white V-neck Joe College sweater, is Hoagland Carmichael. "Don't you guys understand?" he seems to be thinking. "This is *serious!*"

"Washboard Blues" is not yet quite a finished work: the text, the story-line, that will lift it presently to imperishability, is yet to come. But the beginning is here, a composition of charm, ingenuity, and a melodic purity that establishes it midway between country and city, folksong and vaude-ville, on a piece of musical turf all its own.

Sometime not long after that day, wise Harry Hostetter wrapped a press-ing of "Washboard Blues" in a towel and drove down to Bedford, to see a guy he knew. Fred Callahan made his living cutting gravestones and wrote sometimes very good poetry on his own time. History has no account of what was said: Carmichael wasn't present, and neither Hostetter nor Cal-lahan left a memoir. Taking his cue from Hoagy's thoughts about a world-weary black woman washing clothes, the stonecutter fashioned words—deep, profoundly, sadly evocative ones—and in so doing lent "Washboard Blues" shape and dimension. Gave it life.

In one deft stroke, its opening line achieves the goal of all fine writing: to establish time, place, setting, mood, emotion—and a sense of impending, inescapable despondency.

> Mornin' comes with cloudy skies and rain;
> Mah po' back is broke with pain.

The words track the music, making a scene-setter of Carmichael's eight-bar introduction. Gray morning comes, and the melody ascends scalewise, only to stall at the prospect of "cloudy skies and rain." The phrase repeats, this time in an expression of dismay culminating in the phrase "broke with pain," the melody moving up an octave to emphasize the word "pain." Then, in the first of several tumbling cries of sheer frustration, the exclamation:

> My man's sleepin', I'se a-scrubbin';
> Chillun weepin', I'se a-rubbin';
> Pain a-creepin', clothes a-tubbin'
> Washboard Blues.

It develops apace, gathering intensity in a mounting threnody of wear-iness and despair, each phrase deepening the power of expression. When the singer, with a resigned shrug, declares,

> Up to de washin' soap, down to de water once
> mo',
> Head down low—
> Head low,

the second "head low" adds a grieving poignancy to the scene.

Carmichael's melody is no less rich. The midsection of his "Up to de washin' soap" strain, beginning on bar 9, runs five bars: the melody groups five three-note phrases, each landing at a different place in its bar. The ear, detecting nothing asymmetrical, accepts the anomaly—largely because the final note extends through a fifth bar. This is a practice used widely by folk and blues performers to let a phrase "breathe" before moving on—and that is exactly the effect here.[7]

"Washboard Blues," chorus (17 bars), 1925

Callahan's original typescript, on file at Indiana University, repeats the introduction with a new text; but it adds little, merely restating the senti-

ments expressed at the outset and impeding the dramatic flow. With editorial instincts which were to serve him well, Carmichael expunges it, moving instead right to the interlude. It's a pause, a sigh, as the singer mops
her brow and reflects on her fate:

> Never get me gone from here,
> Scrubbin' dirty clothes all year.

Then, with an energy born of desperation, she attacks the clothes. This
section could only be a blues, drawing on all the majesty and emotive depth
programmed into that most enduring and extraordinary of forms.

Hoagy's twenty-second piano solo works here as a small elegy, a close-
focus look at the emotional landscape "Washboard Blues" has charted, before the scene-setting introduction returns, with a new text, to carry the
thought forward:

> Washin' in a shanty on de shore;
> River swingin' on by de door;
> Hear de river lowly callin',
> I'm a shiver, night a'fallin'
> Hear de river lowly moanin'
> Washboard Blues.[8]

The "Up to de washin' soap" melody reappears, again with a new lyric.
Broader, more general this time, it brings a premonition of tragedy, as the
singer looks at the river: eternal, heedless, implacable, it is symbol and
vehicle of her daily toil and the hopelessness of her life. And, perhaps for
the first time, she sees it as salvation, bringer of surcease and an end to her
troubles:

> Goin' to de rivah, goin' down to de rivah
>   some day,
> Hurry day, hurry.
> Goin' to de rivah, goin' down to de rivah
>   some day,
> Throw myself away (on mah po' soul).

Keep rubbin', keep scrubbin',
Keep tubbin', keep drubbin'
Old dirty clothes.

Goin to de rivah, goin' down to de rivah
   some day,
Hurry day, hurry day. Hurry day.
Hurry.

And there it ends. Even as recorded by Hitch and friends, its text not yet in place, this piece is something new. Not merely for any specific melodic or harmonic departure from popular music norms: what distinguishes "Washboard Blues," and seems to have been only dimly understood at the time, is its eloquence as musical narrative. It sets a scene, introduces character and situation, tells a story. There is not an unnecessary or superfluous bar or phrase, not a hint of condescension or minstrelsy, in its depiction of a day in the life of a poverty-stricken black woman, a woman stripped of everything save her abiding dignity.[9]

To put the importance of "Washboard Blues" in sharper focus it is useful to review, briefly, the popular song field of 1925 and early 1926. Among the most prominent Tin Pan Alley contributions: "Dinah"; "Collegiate"; "Five Foot Two, Eyes of Blue"; "I Never Knew"; "If You Knew Susie"; "Keep Smiling at Trouble"; "Sleepy Time Gal"; "Tea for Two"; "Sweet Georgia Brown"; "Yes Sir, That's My Baby." From the Broadway elite came "Manhattan" (Rodgers and Hart), "Poor Little Rich Girl" (Coward), "Remember" (Berlin), and "Sweet and Low Down" (Gershwin).

Good songs all, some destined to be honored standards. But not one among them approaches the complexity, narrative arc, or casual ingenuity of "Washboard Blues." Beyond argument, Callahan's text carries echoes of Bert Williams and his poignant "Nobody":

When life seems full of clouds and rain,
And I am full of nothin' but pain,
Who soothes my thumpin', bumpin' brain
Nobody![10]

Williams had recorded that song well before 1911, and his Columbia record, nationally distributed, had found its way into many homes, black and white. Callahan surely knew it: the "cloudy skies and rain" reference may even be an act of homage, intentional or inadvertent. But it in no way lessens the power or originality of his "Washboard Blues" lyric.[11]

✢   ✢   ✢

By the end of the first semester Carmichael had all the credits he needed for a law degree. Sooner or later he was going to have to face the future. But for the moment, the band was playing almost nonstop, sometimes with Violet Deckard along to sing or demonstrate that athletic new dance, the Charleston. "No need to tell you about these boys," a September 1925 advertisement in the *Indiana Daily Student* boasted. "They are known all over the state." They appeared regularly at Bloomington's Indiana Theatre; at Cascades Park; for such student events as the November 17 "Table Waiters' Ball," at the Sigma Nu house, in which fraternity dishwashers, table waiters, stewards, and others would "take a night off to disport themselves . . . No co-ed will know which white-jacketed waiter she will 'draw' until her arrival"; the November 21 "Blanket Hop," sponsored during Homecoming Weekend by the journalistic fraternity Sigma Delta Chi; for myriad other fraternity dances and—especially—Charleston contests.

Three such events, at the Indiana Theatre on January 12, 13, and 16, 1926 (music by Carmichael and friends), were "open to all white persons between the ages of 14 and 99," according to an advertisement in the *Indiana Daily Student*. Miss Virginia Singleton, a professional dancing instructor, presented her "jazz interpretation" of the Charleston. January 19 and 20 brought a "Colored Charleston Contest: now that the white Charleston dancers have had their innings, the colored dancers will be given an opportunity to compete for prizes." That gives some pause: a social hierarchy imposed on a traditional black dance, introduced to the general (i.e., white) public by a black entertainer (Elisabeth Welch), to a song by a black musician (pianist James P. Johnson), in an all-black Broadway revue (*Runnin' Wild*, 1923)? The irony is exquisite.[12]

Black or white, the Charleston was the fashion of the day. The usual voices condemned its perceived sensuousness and calisthenic abandon, its lack of decorum; hinted grimly at its probable effect on the manners of the young and ultimate damage to healthy family life. Clergymen inveighed against its destructive effect on morality—especially in reaction to news that young ladies, arriving at dances, were repairing to the powder room to doff their girdles for freer ease of movement. On February 13, 1926, the *Daily Student* reported that twenty-six campus organizations had banned the Charleston altogether—though admittedly as m··ch in fear of structural damage to buildings as to the moral health of the young.

Defense, at least in Bloomington, came from an unexpected quarter: none other than the respected Professor William Moenkhaus, father of Hoagy's friend "Monk." His observations on the physiology of the Charleston and other popular dances, delivered at a Rotary Club luncheon, were duly reported in the *Daily Student*:

> Although we do not like the new dances and are grouchy about the various activities of the younger generation, yet they are as natural [as] for a dog to gambol on the green . . . A fly, after reaching maturity, unlike a human, makes no effort to prolong its life and doesn't try to mold into its life's organization the younger generation as does man.[13]

Carmichael's Collegians, caught up in the craze along with such competing units as the Crimson Serenaders, rode the crest of the Charleston wave. Sometime that winter, flush with success, Hoagy wrote to Ezra Wickemeyer about coming over to Richmond to record a couple of titles for Gennett. The band had been together three years, after all, and all the regular work had conferred more than a little polish. What better time to take on the terrors of Wickemeyer's two recording horns?

Only the philosophical Bill Moenkhaus, invoking Kant, wondered at the wisdom of such a gesture. "If you remember your band," he said, "all your life you'll think it was wonderful. If you have a record of it you may play the record someday and think you weren't so good."[14]

All the same, on Tuesday, February 2, 1926, during midterms, Carmichael's Collegians headed for Richmond. On the schedule were "my latest efforts at composing": a signature piece later recorded as the "Wedding Waltz" (or "One Last Kiss") and a stomp, punningly titled "Watch Your Hornin'."[15]

But the old paneled room by the railroad spur had changed: the two megaphone-like horns were gone, supplanted by the primitive microphones of Gennett's brand-new "Electrobeam" recording apparatus. Tentatively at first, not quite convinced, the band recorded "Watch Your Hornin' " and listened to the playback. A bit muddy, but surprisingly good. Then they tackled the waltz. "Tears came to our eyes as we all listened to it, full-grown men sniffing back sobs for a last, last time," Carmichael writes. "Every note was an individual thing, a part of the man who played it, and that man a friend."[16]

But the new equipment, or the technician's inexperience in working with it, let them down. During first attempts to make pressings the master was damaged beyond repair—or so went the story—and "three years of musical sweat and friendship melted away into a blob of twisted copper." In a heartfelt postscript, he notes that it "was a sad lot that gathered at the hotel for our farewell dinner."[17]

Indiana University records show that Hoagy's band carried on playing dates on and off campus right through commencement, at the beginning of June. Mid-April, in fact, brought a highlight: back in December, he'd had a letter from Bix, touting the group Trumbauer was leading at the Arcadia Ballroom, in St. Louis. "Absolutely the hottest band in the country," it was "panicking the town." Couldn't "Hogey" rustle up some spring work for them in Bloomington? Carmichael, forever the acolyte, came through, getting the band—with Bix, Tram, and Pee Wee Russell—booked for the 1926 Junior Prom, Friday night, April 16.[18]

"That entire college thought with a beat!" an enthusiastic Trumbauer noted in his diary. "They knew their music—and what dancing! In all of my years in the music business, I have never found a school so sharp. We literally knocked each other out—the school and the band!"[19]

Bloomington diarist Harry Orchard, indefatigable as ever, describes in detail how he, "Hogie," and their pals drank some gin brewed up in the Carmichael bathtub (apparently by Carmichael *Père*); who was in their party (Virginia Tonalier, Hoagy's date, couldn't make it); what they talked about; how Harry Hostetter, whom they met outside the hall, kept raving that Bix sounded "like he is pounding out the notes with a little velvet covered hammer." After the dance, Hoagy went off somewhere with Beiderbecke, and "when the band left town after the dance Hoagy went with them."[20]

Not for long. On April 24, the Collegians are advertised as playing a dance at the local Masonic Temple. And on May 10 and 11 they meet the DePauw Old Black and Gold Collegians in a two-day "battle of music" at the Indiana Theatre—after a showing of *The Volga Boatman*, starring a pre-Hopalong Cassidy William Boyd. "No prizes are awarded," the *Daily Student* comments, and "no one is benefitting by the amount of applause given either organization; [it's] just a friendly affair all the way through."[21]

The band's last advertised Indiana Theatre date was Thursday, May 27,

1926, just before final exams. After that, under balmy summer skies, Hoagy Carmichael turned his new Ford south and set out again for Florida. The great Land Boom was at its peak: if there was a *'me to go, this was it. Historian Mark Sullivan captures the phenomenon well:

> All of America's gold rushes, all her oil booms, and all her free-land stampedes dwindled by comparison with the torrent of migration pouring into Florida during the early fall months of 1925. If Ponce de Leon's Fountain of Youth had just been found, it could hardly have attracted a greater multitude. Motor roads throughout Florida were crowded with cars from every state in the Union, while added streams of humanity arrived by steamship, by train, and afoot. Roadsides were dotted with tent colonies of tourists and fortune-seekers.[22]

The population of Miami, on the state's southeast coast, had ballooned from 10,000 at the turn of the century to 150,000 by 1925, with plans for another million in the decade to come. All over the state, lots great and small were going fast and cheap. "In Miami especially . . . the buying and selling of land was the paramount industry, organized on mass production lines."[23]

Stuart Gorrell, a Carmichael friend and Kappa Sigma brother, had moved there. Cyclone Carmichael, hearing about offers of double pay for hard work, snapped up Lida and the two girls and headed south. The pay was indeed good, he found—but again "they had to live in a shack. No houses for rent. And no piano but, by God, Dad owned an automobile, the worst worn-out heap of tin shavings you ever saw."[24]

Stu Gorrell wrote a letter, touting Miami as "the Magic City of moola, hip flasks and dough, the land of palms, the whacky [sic] metropolis . . . It's warm and swimmy here, crazy as a laughing farm . . . Come on down, Hoagy boy, and be a lawyer among the grapefruits and the 'gaters. I'll be waiting on a corner for you, smoking a dollar seegar."[25]

In the mountains he ran into some weather and drove through torrential rain lost in reverie, head abuzz with thoughts of past, present, and many possible futures. His father, equal parts impulse and naiveté, forever questing, uprooting wife and family in search of—what? Monk, Wad, and the gang at the Nook. Stu, Wilbur Cook, Pink Cadou, and the rest of the Kappa Sig gang. His early crush Kate Moore, who'd gone off and married handsome Art Baker, trumpet player with the Collegians.

"Yes, it was the end," he mused as the Ford bumped along. "I must put jazz behind me forever."

A couple of days and a couple of mishaps later, he rolled into Washington, D.C., and found Hank Wells, who had gone to work for the Department of Commerce but still played great piano and fiddle. "Hank was as enthusiastic over music as ever, and we had a session of it at his house," Carmichael notes a bit wryly, "two days after I had put jazz behind me forever."[26]

Then, perhaps on impulse—and perhaps after a bit of practical talk from once-upon-a-time mentor Wells—he took a detour north to New York. Batty DeMarcus was working at the fashionable Club Mirador and took it over for what he called "a meet Hoagy Carmichael party . . . I had been telling everybody about this different type musician and composer from Indiana for about six or seven years . . . Just about everyone capable of understanding Hoagy's potential was on hand at the Mirador that night. I played a couple of one-steps (his and Reggie DuValle's) with Hoagy to get him warmed up."

There were laugh-a-minute reunions with Johnny Johnson and other Indiana pals, some jamming with Red Nichols and pianist Arthur Schutt—and, thanks to Batty, an appointment with the grand poo-bah of Tin Pan Alley publishing, Irving Mills, who had published "Riverboat Shuffle" in 1925.

Mills lit a cigar, heard his nervous, brown-haired visitor out, and agreed to publish "Washboard," as he'd published "Riverboat Shuffle," cutting himself in on the royalties by adding his name to the composer credits. Then, said Carmichael, he made an offer: stay, kid, and I'll pay you a salary to write songs for me and record them for the labels I control. You got talent, boy, and New York likes talent. You're gonna go places, and I'm the one that can make sure it happens.[27]

Hoagy, Florida breeze blowing balmily through his mind, turned the offer down. Sorry, Mr. Mills, but "New York doesn't look wholesome to me. No trees, no leisure. Faces I don't understand." He promised to think about it, said his goodbyes, and turned the Ford back south.[28]

✻   ✻   ✻

According to the Florida Board of Bar Examiners, Hoagland Howard Carmichael applied in April 1926 for permission to take the Sunshine State's bar exam two months hence, indicating that he'd already found a position, in the collections department of a Palm Beach office run by M. D. (for Murray Dubois) Carmichael—no relation—who had graduated from Indiana University Law School in 1908.

Indiana music friends kept showing up: Vic Moore was around, romancing the society set and playing drums when the urge took him; cousin Hugh "Percy" Campbell, forever the rolling stone, arrived full of talk about a dream job in Fort Lauderdale; Stu Gorrell was doing fine at the *Miami Herald*, shortly to take over the city desk; another Kappa Sig, Wilbur Cook, already practicing law, offered to share "a dingy green basement apartment," splitting the ninety-dollar monthly rent. Hoagy grabbed it.

> I got fifty dollars a month as a clerk, and anything extra I could pick up on my own, free to choose among mule-kicking cases, collecting bad debts, shotgun weddings, orange grove escrows, wife beating, fishing contracts, land assessments, incorporating of fine companies by men with earnest smiles and no assets. Things went along first-rate.[29]

From all indications, the "other Carmichael" was a fair boss, and the newcomer did well, pulling in good money during his first two months. "Cookie was an excellent lawyer, and my constant association with him was of material benefit and an inspiration for me to keep up the law work. Music seldom entered my head, and I was glad that I wasn't one of the jazz hounds stranded at Palm Beach and Miami. When Arnold Johnson's band and Gene Fosdick's outfit came to play at the hotels, I played piano a few times, but that was all."[30]

The land boom began slackening, sending thousands of fortune-seekers scurrying back up north. Hoagy and "Cookie" had no trouble grabbing a roomy apartment that had cost $350 only weeks before and was now going for $65. A couple of "jazz hounds," ex-Wolverine Jimmy Hartwell and Indiana drummer Leo "Taz" Walters, landed a ten-day cruise on the S.S. *Sunflower*, calling at Nassau and Havana; Taz's drums hadn't yet arrived, so Hoagy borrowed Vic Moore's set, which wasn't getting much use during its owner's nocturnal pilgrimages from gambling casino to boudoir.

Then trouble struck. The ship's purser, a Frenchman with what later generations would come to call an "attitude," balked when he saw Walters, a hunchback, heading for the gangplank. Words were exchanged—and Taz stormed off, leaving both job and drums on the pier. The booking agent promptly offered the job to Carmichael,

> and although I had never played drums in my life, I accepted in anticipation of a wonderful tropical cruise. I put up a pretty good bluff as a drummer, and played piano during the afternoons for the captain of the ship while he took tea with the ladies. The purser was about as popular with the ladies as a snake—I had taken special care to inform most of them of the incident that accounted for my presence.[31]

The trip lived up to expectations. "We filled the three days we spent in Havana with every adventure imaginable," some of which Carmichael recounts in detail in his memoirs. He was especially taken with the roadhouse bands, whose "rhumba music knocked me cold, particularly the drum beats. Cuban drummers are usually Jamaicans, and the way they use their hands is nobody's business." There was also a girl named Carmita, who was "the real McCoy, and I returned to West Palm Beach with fond memories of Cuba."[32]

The way Hoagy tells it, a combination of his Cuban adventure, the lure of hot music, and simple homesickness for Indiana had eroded his interest in practicing law. The turning point, he says, came one sunny afternoon as he sat in the office; to his ears, faintly but umistakably, came a familiar melody. "I jumped up, shaking like a yearling maiden at the barrier. 'That's *Washboard Blues!* My *Washboard!*' I hollered . . . It was a record of *Washboard Blues* that I hadn't known had been made. By Red Nichols. I bought it—the only copy in the shop." After that, he says, his law-practicing days were numbered.[33]

It makes a fine yarn; but fact, dry and uncompromising, places the emphasis a bit differently. A letter from the Florida Board of Bar Examiners states, in part, "Hoagland Howard Carmichael was unsuccessful in his attempt to pass the June, 1926, Florida Bar Examination. From our records it would appear that Hoagland Howard Carmichael had no further contact with the admitting authorities of the Bar of Florida."[34]

Nichols first recorded "Washboard Blues," for Brunswick, moreover, on December 8, 1926, months after these events allegedly took place. Its "B" side, "Boneyard Shuffle," is from a December 20 session. Factoring in the production delay occasioned by the year-end holidays, it's unlikely that the disc saw release before late January 1927.

In *Jazzbanders*, Carmichael writes of having gone home for a vacation during the autumn 1926 football season, and with that as a reference point it's easy to read between the lines.

> While I was home rippin' her up, M. D. Carmichael pulled his purse strings tighter than ever (Lord knows they were tight enough), and the world lost a promising young attorney. The fact that my belongings were in West Palm Beach made no difference to him. I returned and stuck it out for a while, but the spirit was gone. I played in a ten-cent dance hall for two months to make ends meet and returned to Indianapolis to give the law one more chance.[35]

In other words, he'd been fired. Doubtless his failure to pass the bar had long since made clear to M. D. Carmichael and others that, for all the young man's obvious sincerity, his true strengths did not lie in torts and suits. If he failed the exam in June, it's possible that he remained some weeks thereafter, working out his notice. Perhaps he did go back to Bloomington during football season—but it is unlikely he still had the job by then. And, too, where was his family? Were Cyclone and Lida still living in Florida, or had they returned to Indiana?

After all the work and sacrifice that had gone into getting him into Indiana University, all the time spent in law studies, to be so ignominiously dismissed must have been humiliating, particularly in front of his mother and grandmother. An educated guess says he indeed visited Bloomington in late 1926 without telling anyone he'd been sacked, returned to Florida, and worked the dance hall piano job to make the rent—all while deciding what to do next.

As noted, Nichols's "Washboard Blues" record appeared early in 1927. In January or early February Hoagy wrote to the cornetist:

> It has given me the kick of my life to see my beloved brain children *Washboard Blues* and *Boneyard Shuffle* on opposite sides of the Brunswick record by the great Nichols...
>
> I am planning on leaving this tin-eared rendezvous of hunted bank

presidents and screw drivers' union for points north on April 3. I'm about broke and will, of course, need a good steer.

I don't think there is a thing in Indiana. I would like to keep at the law but times are too bad to have a young kid like me playing hoppity-hop on the glass-topped desks for 50 a month.

But the thing that interests me most is writing tunes.[36]

Having saved face, he describes a couple of numbers he's written (one of them obviously the "Tiger Rag" spinoff that will presently be "March of the Hoodlums") and solicits Nichols's interest. He's looking ahead, appearing to reconcile himself to a career in "writing tunes."

There is no reason to doubt that he came home as planned, at the beginning of April, and moved right into the new, larger, Kappa Sigma house at 1503 East Third Street. The IU campus was still a welcoming place, where he felt comfortable and secure. Settling back into life as a senior fraternity brother, booking bands, playing hot music, hanging out with Monk and the rest of the gang at the Book Nook, could make Florida seem distant, unreal.

He's clearly present for the Costas brothers' "trial" in May and—cornet in hand—plays a major role in the Book Nook "commencement" of June 2.

✻   ✻   ✻

At this point an unimpeachably reliable witness enters the picture. Charles "Bud" Dant, nine years Hoagy Carmichael's junior, had grown up in Indianapolis, attended Manual Training High School, and taken early to the cornet. By his graduation in mid-1925 he was good enough to go on the road as part of a little band backing a vaudeville troupe.

An industrious lad, he'd spent his spare time teaching himself to read music, learning harmony and transposition and rudimentary arranging. Coming home in spring of 1926, he fell in with a group of young local musicians and began working around Indiana, and sometime later that year they landed a job in Bloomington, playing for a sorority dance.

"Hoagy was on campus at that time," said Dant. "He was playing a dance at Kappa Sig and sent word for us to come on over after our dance, which was [probably] about eleven o'clock. Bring the whole band. I took everybody except the bass sax player, a Bloomington guy who didn't feel like walking all that way—something like three-quarters of a mile—with that big horn.

"In front of the house he had this big open truck, with heavy sides. He had the Book Nook's former player piano on that truck, painted kelly green. Had the guts torn out of the player-piano mechanism, and a piece of chicken wire across. 'Get on,' he says. 'We're goin' for a serenade, and we're gonna jam.' "[37]

They got rolling, with Hoagy at the piano. "I just got back from Havana," he told the eighteen-year-old cornetist, "and wrote a new-type song. It's a tango." What he started to play, and sing, was a lilting melody with decided Latin-American inflections and a lyric that went:

> Just one night in old Havana
> Under the Cuban skies;
> Just one girl in old Havana,
> Starlit Cuban eyes.[38]

"So Hoagy says, 'Bud, here's another good tune we can jam with.' I said, 'What's the title?' and he says, 'It doesn't have a title. It's just a jam tune.' And he starts playing it at a medium tempo. I said to the guys, 'At least it starts on a four [sub-dominant] chord, and that makes it a little different.'

"He wasn't playing much melody. All he had was the opening phrase, an arpeggiated thing, kind of attractive. We jammed it for about fifteen minutes, and got pretty good at it, though I didn't think too much of it— and I don't think we were [always] with Hoagy. When we were playing we couldn't hear him too much."

They finished the serenade, and Dant ran for the night bus back to Indianapolis, ending his association with the nervous, often morose, Hoagland Carmichael, at least for a while. But "I really dug him. He was an altogether different man when he was playing the piano—so happy and so intense, animated."

The number they jammed that night? Eyes bright, a knowing smile playing across his still-handsome face, Charles "Bud" Dant began whistling an immediately recognizable tune—the melody which, very shortly after these events, will come to be known as "Star Dust."

∗ *VIII* ∗

Stardust Melody

"For a while there"—Bud Dant's eyes took on an almost mischievous twinkle as he uttered the words—"I didn't want anything more to do with Hoagy Carmichael, ever."

He paused, letting the thought sink in. "He, Hoagy, kept calling me on the phone, every morning at seven. He says, 'Bud, you gotta come down to Bloomington.' And I'd listen awhile to him, and then say, 'Hoagy, good bye,' and hang up. He was a pest."

At ninety-one, comfortable on the verandah of his hillside home over-looking palm trees and ocean just outside Kailua-Kona, Hawaii, Charles "Bud" Dant remembered it all with undimmed clarity. His association with a young, wired, Hoagy Carmichael may have lain three-quarters of a century behind him, but it could just as well have been the day before yesterday.[1]

It was 1927, and Hoagy was home from Florida after a first, faltering attempt to practice law. He'd plunged right back into campus activities, playing piano and contracting bands for dances and other social events; he'd even helped book the Jean Goldkette Victor Recording Orchestra for the 1927 Junior Prom. Bix was there, and Frank Trumbauer, with New Orleans–born Steve Brown, anchor of the Friars' Inn band, on bass; beside him sat Chauncey Morehouse, whose drumming had powered Paul Specht's Georgians earlier in the decade. Bill Challis, a saxophonist from Pennsylvania, had built a library full of hot music arrangements, showcasing Bix and the others.

But things in Bloomington had changed since Hoagy's student days. Rival campus bands, once rare, now proliferated, attracting the best young musicians with jobs and good money. Many of these were trained players, able to read *and* take hot choruses: Hoagy might be energetically adept on the hot jazz end of things, but his reading was still haphazard, his method of "arranging" strictly hit-or-miss. If he was going to compete, he'd have to expand his reach, pull off a couple of real coups.

"He knew I could read, and knew harmony, and had taught myself to arrange," said Dant, fingering his handmade Benge cornet. "One morning Hoagy called me." He'd lined up a job for a sextet at a ballroom in New York; banjo and drums were already in place, and they needed two saxophones, a pianist, and a cornet player. Dant was mildly interested—until Carmichael broke the news that he himself wouldn't be along ("can't get away") and suggested they save money by taking only one sax player.[2]

In the end, just three of them—Bud, saxophonist Harold Keating, and pianist Bob McCuen—went to New York and ran smack into trouble. Hoagy had neglected to inform them, or just didn't know, that musicians' union rules designated them a "traveling band," prohibiting them from picking up local men to fill out their personnel. They wired for Frank Ballman, another Indianapolis friend, but by the time he arrived the job had folded and they were stranded.

It took them all summer—a job here, a job there—to raise train fare to get home. Once back in Indianapolis, Dant picked up ready work and was soon rehearsing with local leader Laurence "Connie" Connaughton for an autumn opening at the brand-new Indiana Roof Ballroom. Hoagy Carmichael? No thanks.

Carmichael, it turned out, had truly been unable to go east, but not for whatever reason he'd given Dant. Contrary to his declared intention of giving up the law, he'd joined the Indianapolis firm of Bingham, Mendenhall & Bingham, applied to take the Indiana bar exam, and been admitted to practice on November 4, 1927. His first duties, he said in a letter, were to "go to various places in the state and try to settle [automobile] damage claims for 10 cents on the dollar."[3]

He was also busy with new musical connections, introducing himself to Emil Seidel, Arkansas-born leader of the band at the Apollo Theatre. An accomplished pianist, Seidel had emerged as a serious rival to Charlie Davis, whose band was a fixture over at the competing Ohio. He'd formed his personnel with men both versatile and quick, able to read arrangements *and* turn in respectable "hot" solos. When Carmichael showed up one night at the Apollo with ideas for three new songs, the band had little trouble understanding what he had in mind.

One of these was the "jam tune" Hoagy had shown Bud Dant at the Book Nook piano during the sorority serenade a year earlier. By this time it had a name: just call it "Star Dust," said Carmichael. "I didn't much like the title," Dant confessed. "But *he* did—and it was his tune, after all."[4]

The history of this melody is now so encrusted in myth, much of it the composer's own creation, that any attempt to establish the facts seems almost disrespectful. Carmichael's memoirs weave an elaborate tapestry of lyrical reminiscence: jilted by Kathryn Moore (he calls her "Dorothy Kelly"), he sits watching the "little stars climb"—and lo! inspiration strikes. Here's a representative passage from *Sometimes I Wonder*:

> I sat down on the spooning wall at the edge of the campus, and all the things that the town and the University and the friends meant flooded through my mind in a sentimental [*sic*] banal but powerful, gulping of the past gone, of time consumed, of pleasures still in memory . . . Most people have room for *all* their loves and maybe I didn't seem to. Perhaps music was my only real love.[5]

The Stardust Road lays it on with even thicker brushstrokes:

> It was a hot night, sweet with the death of summer and the hint and promise of fall. A waiting night, a night marking time, the end of a season. The stars were bright, close to me, and the North Star Hung low over the trees . . . I looked up at the sky and whistled *Stardust*.[6]

Thus inspired, he dashes for the Book Nook, bangs on the door, implores Pete Costas to let him work it out at the piano—and grateful posterity knows the rest.

But no: not quite. He indeed seems to have worked out details of the melody on several pianos, perhaps including the one at the Book Nook. He finished it, he says in a private memo, on an old grand—location unspecified—with loose tuning pegs, bought for $125 and later sent to a junkyard. "Never had a fine piano," he added later. "[That's] rather sad and also rather unforgivable . . . So many bad pianos played on that it seemed normal to play on anything [that was] just adequate. [I] liked uprights better anyway: [my] hands fit them better."[7]

Possible clarification comes from Ernie Pyle, his fame as a celebrated World War II correspondent still far ahead; during Hoagy's student days Pyle was a journalism major at IU, writing for the *Indiana Daily Student*. In a 1936 reminiscence, he reports that Hoagy worked out "Star Dust" at the Pyle family's Indianapolis home. "I'd like to tell you about the evening he wrote it," Pyle declares, "but he asked me not to, because he says that the public likes to think these sweet songs are conceived under moonlight, amid roses and soft breezes." Hoagy himself later told a columnist that he'd worked out part of the melody at the Book Nook "and finished it at home in Indianapolis."[8]

As for love won and lost, hear Kathryn Moore Baker, remembering these events many years later. "I'll say what all the politicians do: 'no comment.' " Hoagy had dated her for a while, she said, but once she'd set eyes on Art Baker, who played trumpet in Carmichael's Collegians, that was all over. "I would never have considered marrying Hoagy Carmichael," she said. "I wasn't in love with him." But she did remember him humming phrases— well before 1926, she said—that may have found their way into the melody of "Star Dust." Violet Deckard Gardner, who sang on jobs with the Collegians between late 1925 and early 1926, also spoke of Hoagy's fascination with his fragmentary, so far unnamed, melody.[9]

In the alley behind the Apollo Theatre, Carmichael held music "conferences," said Dick Kent, who played alto and second piano with Seidel and did most of the band's formal arranging. He went over "every phrase, harmony, and nuance" with Kent, fellow reedman Gene Woods, and trumpeter Byron Smart, "humming solo parts and suggesting voicings until they all got the picture."[10]

He set up a record date at Gennett for Monday, October 31, firing off a letter (on Bingham, Mendenhall & Bingham stationery) to an old friend, Toledo banjo and guitar player Harry "Buzz" Wernert:

SURPRISE?

Dear Harry:

How about it boy can you pack up that skillet of yours and drop down to Richmond, Ind., on the 31st of Oct. or can you? If you can I don't see why you can't. I've got the recording date all set for then and am having a slave right [*sic*] some orchestrations so the rest of the braves can learn the ballyhoo and pick up the throbs . . . I want you to play the git there. They'll figure out a hot stretch for you so if you could come to Indianapolis on the 30th it would be duck slick . . . Going to make about 4–5 numbers.

He gives 3037 North Graceland, his parents' home in Indianapolis, as his return address.

The Jean Goldkette Victor Recording Orchestra, meanwhile, had succumbed to its inflated payroll and dwindling work schedule. After a brief fling with an all-star New York band led by Adrian Rollini, Bix Beiderbecke and Frank Trumbauer set out for Indianapolis, to join the popular orchestra of Paul Whiteman.

Hoagy couldn't believe it. Bix and Tram, here? Tommy and Jimmy Dorsey too, all as part of the most popular orchestra in the land? He got back in touch with Gennett and scheduled another, earlier, session for Friday, October 28, then visited the Whiteman musicians at their hotel, hired the Dorseys and others for the date—and dispatched a telegram to Buzz Wernert:

WIRE ME YOU CAN BE HERE BY THURSDAY EVENING TO RECORD FRIDAY AM DOING THIS BECAUSE I AM EXPECTING BIX AND TROMBAUER [sic] TO BE HERE THEN STOP THE DORSEY BOSY [sic] ARE HERE AND FRIDAY IS THE ONLY DAY THEY WILL BE AVAILABLE STOP BUT PREPARE TO RECORD MONDAY ALSO[11]

With friend Larry Leonard in tow, Hoagy came backstage at the Indiana Theatre Thursday night to pick up a couple of arrangements Bill Challis had sketched out for the next day. Bix and Trumbauer took them to meet the "King of Jazz" himself.

I'll always admire him for the warm reception he gave Larry and me. He took us in and told us his favorite stories. I liked him right off the bat. Then he told me what he thought of my scratchy Gennett record of "Washboard Blues." Larry told Paul about the stone cutter's lyrics, and we went to a piano to have a rendition . . . I did "Washboard Blues" the best my squeaky voice could do it. Paul looked at me and said: "You're coming to Chicago next week to make a concert record of that thing with me, and you're going to sing it, you screwy guy."[12]

Friday's Gennett date included the Dorseys, trumpeter Bob Mayhew, and several other Whiteman musicians, plus Buzz Wernert and the young Indiana cornetist Andy Secrest. The two numbers are tidy, well played: first, a decorously organized Challis sketch on "One Night in Havana," the "tango" Hoagy had played and sung for Bud Dant. Second came "The Waltz Supreme." Despite the presence of some able jazz soloists, there is not a trace of hot music on either title. Were Beiderbecke and Trumbauer in attendance at this date, as Hoagy promised in his telegram to Wernert? All sources are mute. Even indefatigable Bix researcher Philip R. Evans has nothing to say.[13]

Whiteman's orchestra left town Saturday morning, and Hoagy, with Monday's recording session on his mind, went to see Seidel. The band had a Sunday evening show and would have to drive out to Richmond right afterwards, make the three titles, then get back in time for a one P.M. Monday matinee. Close, but not impossible.

As saxophonist Maury Bennett remembered, they drove all night, arriving at dawn. "In those days the drive from Indianapolis to Richmond was quite a trip. There were no good roads, and cars didn't go as fast. We started recording at six in the morning. I don't believe we even had a runthrough."[14]

The session opened with another Carmichael creation, a stomp called "Friday Night," based on some generic chord patterns, a somewhat vague melody line—and a surprise. Out came Hoagy's beat-up cornet, its owner providing an avid hot counterline to Byron Smart's lead. "I remember this record well," Smart recalled. "Hoagy had never played this cornet part before, and as we cut the master he stepped up behind me and played it." Coming midway in the performance, the cornet duet is both abandoned and surprisingly well executed; Carmichael is clearly audible, punching out a middle register complement to the other man's more ambitious flights. Buzz Wernert, playing a four-string guitar, gets a bit of solo space along the way.[15]

Then it was time for "Star Dust." "The first we'd heard of it was the evening before," said Maury Bennett. "Didn't even know who was gonna take the second chorus. It was a pretty ragged performance, mainly because there was no adequate preparation or rehearsal. Hoagy hadn't yet written the number down on paper, and it wasn't orchestrated. In fact, I don't think he was too sure himself about how he wanted it played."[16]

More than a little nonsense has been written about this first "Star Dust": described, variously and erroneously, as a "ragtime piece" or "stomp," it is in fact just what Bud Dant remembered: a medium-tempo ($\rfloor$ = 136) jazz composition whose shape and overall flavor are heavily indebted to Beiderbecke's phrasing. Byron Smart enhances this aspect by playing the verse on trumpet in a heraldic, Bix-like manner, tonguing most of his notes. Gene Woods sets out the melody on alto, backed prominently by Wernert's guitar (which gets into some chordal trouble in bar 22 of the issued take).[17]

A lead sheet submitted for copyright January 5, 1928, is in D-major and obviously an exact, if amateurishly rendered, transcription of Woods's alto statement on the record. It differs greatly from later published accounts: the verse, for example, opens not on the tonic, but the supertonic; its harmonic underpinning is not the tonic but the richer relative minor.

It all lends strong credence to Bud Dant's contention that even Hoagy had only an approximate idea of how he wanted his tune to go. Though the lead sheet is recognizably in his hand, it seems likely, given his limited technical skills at this early point, that he had help from Dick Kent, with whom he'd worked out the routine used on the record.

Structurally the melody is a standard thirty-two bars, in ABAC form; but its essence lies in a phrase-building technique found often in Bix's solos. A brief phrase of one or two bars is set out, followed by a similar companion phrase, expanding or complementing it; a third phrase then sums up, often incorporating material from the first two.

A typical example of this method occurs at the opening of Beiderbecke's much-admired chorus on "Singin' the Blues":

"Singin' the Blues," Bix Beiderbecke cornet solo (first 4 bars), 1927

Even Bix's very first record, a February 18, 1924, account of "Jazz Me Blues," includes the following:

"Jazz Me Blues," Bix Beiderbecke cornet colo (bars 5–8), 1924

It's an unusual way for a hot improviser to phrase; more common by far is the seriate phrasing most often found in jazz improvisation, in which one phrase suggests another, building cumulatively to a climax.

Beiderbecke reportedly called his system of paired or otherwise conjoined companion phrases "correlated phrasing." It surfaces as a compositional device mostly at slow to medium tempos; many Bix solos on record, especially at faster tempos, show little sign of such phrase-building. But it's not hard to imagine Hoagy Carmichael, as a fledgling composer dazzled by Bix, seizing on it as a way of constructing songs.

The high spot of "Star Dust's" first recorded performance is Hoagy's own full-chorus piano solo, its chordal devices clearly echoing Bix's fascination with the Impressionists and such "moderns" as Igor Stravinsky—and his admiration for the now almost forgotten American composer Eastwood Lane.

Less a jazz improvisation (it is rhythmically static) than a melodic paraphrase, it generally follows the song's harmonies, freely interpolating parallel ninth chords, tone clusters, and whole-tone scale passages. The solo appears here in a transcription by the respected arranger-pianist Sivert "Sy" Johnson. Bars 9–12 are particularly characteristic.

"Star Dust," Hoagy Carmichael piano solo (33 bars), 1927

Considerable evidence, including an unissued take of this performance and various later Carmichael recordings, indicates that these thirty-
three bars were far from a random improvisation, but as lovingly worked
out—whether at the Book Nook piano or in Indianapolis is ultimately
irrelevant—as the "Star Dust" melody itself.[18]

So, too, the first eight bars of the arranged final chorus, developed
as a clarinet line, again paraphrasing the melody in the manner of a jazz
solo:

"Star Dust," band arrangement (8 bars), 1927

Several other records of "Star Dust" made between 1927 and 1930 use this format, with minor variations. Yet there's something in this first performance that arrests attention: a sense of moment, something more important going on than just a pop melody. Popular songs are relatively slender vessels, and it's perhaps dangerous to imbue them with significance beyond their capacity. But this "Star Dust" (notably the Carmichael piano solo), considered alongside "Washboard Blues," suggests a musical landscape alive with possibility and evocative potential.

What to call it? American "art song?" "Folk melody?" "Tone poem?" None of these quite catches the idea. Both "Washboard" and "Star Dust" are a form of musical portraiture, strong elicitations of time, scene, even character. That Hoagy Carmichael appears to have come to this intuitively is a small wonder; that he perceived only dimly what he'd found is to be expected.[19]

Most startling of all is that this idiosyncratic melody, so unlike either Broadway or Tin Pan Alley songs, should have become the quintessential American standard, surpassing the best of Rodgers, Kern, Porter, and Berlin, and even such beloved evergreens as "Body and Soul." Like them, it is a love song—but with a difference, and not only because its roots are in jazz: various tunes by both Duke Ellington and Harold Arlen share that distinction. It deals with love and loss; but those are the themes, if expressed in different ways, of such disparate items as Porter's "Begin the Beguine" and Berlin's "Remember." Even such Tin Pan Alley trifles as the 1927 "Blue River" offer fond remembrances of departed love.

But "Star Dust" stands alone. The most plausible, if elusive, explanation for its eternal popularity rests in some combination of young Carmichael's heartland upbringing, Bix's uniquely bardic sensibility, and the unself-conscious emotional directness that characterizes much non-urban American popular music. Overall, it is perhaps closer in flavor and content to the songs of Willard Robison, and even the earlier Stephen Collins Foster.[20]

Third item on that Halloween day Gennett schedule in 1927 was another bright-tempo ($\downarrow$ = 108) original, recorded as a trio by Woods, Wernert, and Carmichael under the title "When Baby Sleeps." From the opening phrase of the verse, it's obvious that this is what will shortly become "Rockin' Chair." Again, it's in D-major. "Hoagy had a penchant for the key of D," said saxophonist and campus friend Wally Wilson. "We couldn't play 'Stardust' or 'Rockin' Chair in that crazy key. I rewrote them in C. 'Stardust' finally came out in D♭, of course."[21]

Coming out of the verse, Gene Woods plays an eight-bar transition passage, then heads into the chorus. It's hard to tell at first what he means to play, but by bars 9–11 he's locked into the now-familiar "Rockin' Chair" melody. They're treating it as a hot number, and it's not quite working: even Carmichael's piano solo seems perched uncomfortably between rhythm and reverie. Toward the end, with Woods once again on the theme, Hoagy scats half a chorus before returning to the piano for an introspective finale. Clearly, "When Baby Sleeps" is a work-in-progress, awaiting retooling, adjustment of tempo and mood. These will shortly be forthcoming, along with a new title and appropriate lyric.

✻   ✻   ✻

Paul Whiteman, meanwhile, kept his promise. His manager, Jimmy Gillespie, wired Hoagy that on Friday, November 18, the orchestra would be recording a Bill Challis concert arrangement of "Washboard Blues" at Victor's Chicago studio, for release on a twelve-inch record. The composer was to sing and play the piano—including the twenty-two-second interlude he'd used on the Hitch record.

At first he apparently balked, even phoning his friend Robbie Robinson, who had sung with a campus band led by drummer George "Dixie" Highway, begging him to come along and sing "Washboard" in his stead. Terrified at the thought, Robinson hastily refused, leaving Hoagy with no option but to borrow the forty-dollar fare and board a Monon Line train for Chicago. Once there, he headed for the Uptown Theatre, at Broadway and Lawrence, where the Whiteman orchestra was appearing nightly, and where his old trumpet-playing pal Art Baker was now assistant manager. Again and again, Carmichael and Challis rehearsed "Washboard," with Bing Crosby, the designated understudy, hovering on the periphery—just, he recalled, in case.[22]

"I was so nervous I ruined a half-dozen master records and the best of a double-time trio arrangement," Carmichael writes. "Finally we got a master that was approved." Victor's files for the session list no breakdowns or ruined performances; but two takes issued over the years betray enough nervousness to lend some credibility to his account.[23]

The Whiteman orchestra, personnel cut to twelve pieces, plays a meditative introduction, making way for Hoagy's piano interlude before stating the main theme. Carmichael then sings the song to his own accompaniment, Challis bringing in the ensemble discreetly in the blues section. Regionally accented, with an engagingly reedy, nasal quality (Carmichael himself called it "flatsy through the nose"), his is anything but a conventional singing voice. He has problems with breath control, phrasing, pitch— just about every technical aspect of singing. But the sound nevertheless arrests attention: personal, conversational, it draws a listener easily into its small, clearly defined world. Like Crosby, Carmichael the vocalist would never have been possible without the assistance of the microphone: rather than requiring him to project, it listens to him, assisting and encouraging.

A "dixieland" front line of Bix (in his record debut as a Whiteman sideman) and the Dorsey brothers knocks off a second instrumental interlude, a double-time reading of the "Up to de washin' soap" strain, before Hoagy returns to reprise both introduction and chorus. Even if the interpolation disrupts the elegiac mood somewhat, this "Washboard" is an effective, affecting experience. Challis's problem was identical to what had faced Hoagy at the Gennett date: without the instrumental diversion the performance would have timed out exactly twenty-two seconds too short to fill a twelve-inch record.

*　　　　*　　　　*

In late 1927, relieved of the financial burden of his now-defunct Victor Recording Orchestra, Jean Goldkette was free to concentrate on his Detroit-based booking agency. Business was thriving, and his investment in Mc-Kinney's Cotton Pickers, now led by Don Redman, was beginning to pay dividends. When an engagement at the Pla-Mor ballroom in Kansas City came in, Goldkette made a shrewd move: he picked up the Indiana Royal Peacocks, a band regionally popular since the early '20s, augmenting their personnel with a few other top men active in the Midwest. The trumpet section, for example, now boasted lead man Nat Natoli and two improvising soloists in Andy Secrest, from Muncie, and Stirling Bose, from Alabama, both of them Bix admirers. As second pianist and occasional vocalist, Goldkette took on Hoagy Carmichael.

The Peacocks knew Hoagy, had socialized with him earlier that year, while they were working at the Trianon Ballroom in Fort Lauderdale and "Hoagmichael" was allegedly still practicing law in Palm Beach. They were happy to have him aboard, especially as most of the main piano duties fell to the more experienced Harry Bason. As a musical wild card, Hoagy could concentrate on an occasional hot chorus (Bason, though adept at ragtime, was no jazzman) and sing specialty numbers.

They were a polished band, as four titles recorded for Victor that December (supervised by Leroy Shield, who had done the "Washboard" date) demonstrate. An all-too-brief Secrest-Bose solo exchange on "Here Comes the Show Boat" lifts things nicely, and Bose's muted obbligato to Hoagy's vocal on "So Tired" has more than once been mistaken by collectors and discographers for Beiderbecke himself. Carmichael sings "My Ohio Home" in what seems, inexplicably and ill-advisedly, an attempt to reproduce the side-of-mouth inflections of a Chicago mobster.

Seeing membership in this band as an opportunity to learn how to put music down on paper, he enlisted saxophonist Raymond "Pink" Porter as a tutor. "Pink explained to me what the notes on the staff meant and their relationship to the orchestral pattern," he wrote. Why was a written C for trumpet really a piano B♭? Why did a guitar part sound an octave below written? Porter explained it all, and with admirable patience.[24]

Pink also helped him fashion a lyric to "One Night in Havana," and he got the band to play it, along with an adaptation of the Gennett "Star Dust" arrangement; Carmichael's input is unmistakable in a couple of Bix-like scored brass passages in "So Tired" and "My Ohio Home." A recorded Christmas-greeting disc sent by Porter to his family introduces "the incomparable Hoagy Carmichael, the master of the piano," and makes clear that they were all having a grand time.

For this, at least, they couldn't have chosen a better place than Kansas City, thanks to the rough-and-tumble administration of Tom Pendergast. "I'm the boss," he was widely quoted as proclaiming. "I know all the angles. I know how to select ward captains and how to get to the poor and how to deliver the vote." And that's just what he did. By the late 1920s he controlled the town, including a big piece of its bootlegging action. As Ross Russell remarks:

> Saloons and later, as the value of entertainment was understood, cab-arets were built at an increasing rate until Kansas City boasted the greatest concentration of them in America, one for every taste and pocketbook, many of them with live music. "If you want to see some sin," columnist Edward Morrow wrote in the Omaha *World-Herald*, after a visit to Pendergast's town, "forget about Paris and go to Kansas City."[25]

The Pla-Mor, on Main Street, was a prime location, and though—unlike most of the hot venues along Eighteenth Street—it catered to a whites-only clientele, many major bands of both races worked there. It was an early headquarters for Andy Kirk's Clouds of Joy, featuring the gifted Mary Lou Williams as pianist and arranger.[26]

For all the fun and good music, Hoagy's stay with this Goldkette band didn't last long. "The Pla-Mor ballroom didn't make any too much money during the winter," he explains, "and [Goldkette's manager] Charlie Horvath let me go to cut expenses, because I was the least necessary in the outfit. I pulled out for Indianapolis with a little dough saved up with the intention of organizing a band of my own."[27]

In a later statement to Indiana historian Duncan Schiedt he says he "quit because I couldn't read the piano arrangements and the type stuff they were playing required it. Too much to learn by ear." Carmichael expanded on the theme in a 1957 memo to designated biographer Ralph Hancock. "I was not keeping up betimes as a pianist. For lack of technique [I] doubt that I could [even] be called a pianist. I merely had style and some 'drive,' and had been innovative. It was not long before I knew that I was being out-classed as a band pianist and even as a soloist. Since [I] couldn't sight-read, I could not fit into a big travelling band. I was a one-step, sock-time Chicago jazz stylist with an inventive mind for melody and strange improvisations—hence the composing field."[28]

"Think I am leaving Goldkette Sunday," he wrote to reedman, bandleader, and fellow-Hoosier Gene Fosdick. "How about work? Have tuxedo. Double elephant. Have nickel-plated parlor cornet. Am a number one. Want $200, will work cheap. Oh yes, I play hot sock cymbal."[29]

En route home he stopped off in Detroit and spoke personally to Gold-kette, who gave him much the same advice he'd given Beiderbecke in late 1924: go home and study music, polish your technical skills, improve your reading. Become more versatile on your instrument. Hoagy took the advice to heart—at least for the time being. Under the headline "Popular Hoosier Composer Is Learning to Read Music," the *Indianapolis News* announced that although Carmichael " 'knows the notes' for slow reading, and for writing, he has never mastered the art of playing the piano from music, but plays chiefly by ear."[30]

Before leaving Detroit Hoagy spent an evening at the Graystone Ballroom listening to Don Redman and gave him a copy of "Star Dust"—presumably both a lead sheet and a pressing of the Seidel record. The saxophonist liked it, promising to arrange it for McKinney's Cotton Pickers.[31]

Back in Bloomington and still, in his own mind, the "half-educated man," he made a show of studying music—but was soon distracted by "a beautiful, exciting blonde named Virginia Tonalier. [I was quite] the man of the world—went to her class and introduced myself." At one point, he reports, he visited her at her parents' home, but it apparently came to nothing. "I was not very successful with girls," he reports. "I seem[ed] immature and [was] too slight looking." Anyway, he was "not terribly in-terested either, because music [was] still predominant." His unrequited crush on Kathryn Moore, the idealized "Dorothy Kelly," had lasted longest. But that, too, dissolved with time.[32]

He was meanwhile, disquietingly, back pretty much where he'd started. "It seemed so foolish to be back in Bloomington at the old game again," he writes, "but I'd made up my mind to learn arranging, and this was my opportunity." One of his first moves was to get back in touch with Bud Dant, who was somewhat less than thrilled to hear his voice on the phone. "He says, 'Bud, you gotta come down to Bloomington. We got a band down here—couple guys you know, and they need somebody who can teach 'em reading and stuff.' He even started talking about getting me to enroll in the University as a freshman."[33]

By now reestablished in Indianapolis dance band circles, Dant had no interest in Bloomington, less in going to college—and least of all in having anything at all to do with Hoagy Carmichael. But his parents, their curiosity aroused, were intrigued: who *was* this "Hoagy" character, and what did he want? Why was he phoning every day so early in the morning? The young cornetist, exasperated, finally blurted it out:

"He wants me to come down to school."

"Well, why don't you do that?" his parents asked.

"He's a nut!" came the heated reply. "He's out of his mind. He sent me to New York and it almost ruined me. He's just bad news."

Still, Mr. and Mrs. Dant rather fancied the idea of their boy as a college student and kept after him: "We were a poor family, and I couldn't go to college—besides, I didn't *want* to. But finally I gave in. I called [Hoagy], and said, 'Okay. I'll come and get your band started. But I won't go to school.'

"I came down, and he met me at the bus," said Dant. They rehearsed, and "right away I could see that there were problems. And right away he pledged me to Kappa Sig[ma]: I didn't even know what he was doing. Here I wasn't even a student, and he was pledging me to a fraternity! I wound up staying there.

"He had to have me no matter what, because I was the only guy he knew that could write [music]." Why not enroll? Carmichael kept asking him. You can study music, keep living here, and play with us. "We rehearsed every night for a week . . . During the days he'd take me down to the [Book] Nook and buy my lunch." And more often than not he'd start talking about "Star Dust." He'd even written out a lyric of sorts, he said. Couldn't Dant write an arrangement?

"I said, 'Hoagy, I haven't played that tune since that night we played it. I'd never played the melody before. I don't know the melody or anything. Play it for me.' And you know what he did? He played me his chorus, his jazz chorus, his paraphrase on the melody. But not the melody itself." Finally Bud— if only to lay the matter to rest—agreed to write an arrangement.[34]

It went on like that for a while, Hoagy importuning, Bud first declining, then reluctantly giving in, resistance waning. Finally—and later he wondered whether he'd been the patsy in another elaborate Carmichael con job—the Kappa Sig senior committee let him know he couldn't go on staying at the house without officially joining the fraternity and matriculating at the university. With more than a fair share of convincing from his parents, Charles "Bud" Dant registered for preliminary courses in music education.[35]

That also meant induction into the still-active rituals of the Book Nook. But Dant, once he'd decided to enter school, was determined to excel: between studying and rehearsing, he said, there was little time for hanging around and socializing. Hoagy, meanwhile, hooked up with Amos Ostot, whose piano strengths seem to have been more decorative than rhythmic, and through whom he now had access to a wider circle of good campus musicians. Perhaps not quite coincidentally, many of them wound up pledging to Kappa Sig.

"Friend Hoagy," Don Redman wrote on March 7, 1928, " 'Stardust' is going great and everybody likes it." In the same letter he promised to send Hoagy an arrangement, not yet completed, of "Too Tight"—presumably the blues recorded by the great New Orleans clarinetist Johnny Dodds in 1926.[36]

The Whiteman and Nichols "Washboard Blues" records had sold well; the Seidel "Star Dust," while not a big seller, had also been widely heard. Bix and Trumbauer's OKeh record of "Riverboat Shuffle" was being talked up as definitive; Nichols had recorded it at a slower tempo for Brunswick, spotlighting Pee Wee Russell in an outstanding (and rather Bix-like) clarinet chorus. The former Book Nook piano-thumper was beginning to matter— and now, in approaching Fred Wiggins about making some new records for Gennett, he was fully confident that the label's manager would take him seriously.

They booked a date for Wednesday, May 2, 1928, and Hoagy began putting together his idea of an Indiana collegiate dream band. Dant, by now deep in his IU music ed studies, would do most of the cornet work— though Hoagy also brought along his sixteen-year-old cousin, Fred "Yah" Murray, to fill in second parts. Arnold Habbe, banjo on Hitch's "Washboard" date, was on this one, too. Jack Drummond was generally considered the best bass player in Indianapolis, and Harold Keating, who had been with Dant on the ill-fated New York trip, was on tenor and clarinet. Fellow–Bent Eagle and Kappa Sig frat brother Ed Wolfe was a down-home "hot fiddle" soloist, Andy Van Sickle a steady and reliable drummer.

But the band's major figure, whose playing on this date wound up lifting the results to something extraordinary, was a nineteen-year-old alto saxophonist named Kerval Chauncey Goodwin. Born March 6, 1909, in Brownstown, not far from Bedford, he'd first gone to DePauw, majoring in music and playing both alto and trumpet in campus groups. Hoagy and Habbe had driven over to hear him, coming away sufficiently impressed to talk him into transferring to IU. "In my opinion Goodwin was tops," Habbe wrote to Duncan Schiedt. "I rate him with F[rank] Trumbauer. He never repeated a chorus, he was a master of harmony, and his tempo was perfect."[37]

Hoagy and his eight musicians recorded seven titles on that May Wednesday. Only two were issued, but a total of six survive. Easily the most stirring of these, and an extraordinary performance by almost any standard, is Carmichael's own "March of the Hoodlums," equal parts dixieland march à la "Tiger Rag" (which it resembles) and fight song (which it later became). They take it fast ($\mathord{\text{\musFlat}} = 140$), in a style that can only be described, without trace of obloquy, as "1920s collegiate manic," a heedless exuberance which proclaims quite eloquently what it must have been like to be young, boundlessly optimistic, and crazy in love with playing hot music.

It dashes gaily along, picking up momentum with each bar, Keating (on clarinet), Dant, and Wolfe contributing spirited bits. But Goodwin's full-chorus alto solo, bursting out of a *tutti* passage like a thoroughbred out of the gate, is the one that counts. Based on the "Tiger Rag" changes, it owes much to Jimmy Dorsey's well-known display piece (showcased on such records as "Sensation Stomp" with Whiteman and "That's No Bargain" with Red Nichols). It energizes the rhythm section, and they career through a musical roller-coaster ride until a single Van Sickle rimshot brings them to an abrupt halt. Then, in Schiedt's vivid description, "the final chorus, with everybody pumping furiously, pauses only for a mad piano break, then closes with a three-part harmonic phrase which is drawn out like molten glass."[38]

Shelton Brooks's "Walkin' the Dog," though not quite up to the same voltage level, is confidently played. Goodwin, opening over band stop-chords, shows absorption of both Dorsey and the more whimsical Trumbauer. Habbe appears to be playing guitar behind Wolfe's fiddle solo, but once the ensemble gets rolling he drops out briefly, only to come charging back on banjo, momentarily overbalancing Gennett's rather primitive electrical recording equipment.

From then on Hoagy is the whole show. Out comes the old cornet for sixteen bars (tone and embouchure might leave a bit to be desired, but the conception is on target), and bookending some over-the-top scatting within two reflective piano excerpts from Edward MacDowell's *To a Wild Rose*. Hoagy later adjudged his cornet effort "not too bad unless you are a lover of good tone and the proper handling of the brass . . . This recording ended my youthful desire to play a cornet. It left me with a sore lip and head noises." In the end, then, it was common sense, not science, that had curbed Hogwash M'Corkle's cornet.[39]

And there things might have remained—had test pressings of four unreleased titles not turned up among Carmichael's effects at Indiana University. Inevitably, perhaps, the May 2 date begins with another try at Hoagy's pet waltz, listed this time as "One Last Kiss," with Dant's solo cornet doing respectful justice to the pretty melody. Hoagy sings Pink Porter's lyric to "One Night in Havana," with only his own piano and Wolfe's violin as backing.

The other two are headier stuff. Dant opens "Shimme-Sha-Wabble" with a deftly turned blues before the band sets out the melody of the chorus, skipping the minor-key verse of Spencer Williams's 1917 classic. Hoagy's piano chorus is full of impressionistic conceits he could have lifted from one of Bix's late-night musings. After some serviceable Keating clarinet comes a surprise: a cornet chorus by young Murray, punchy and rhythmically secure. "Chance" Goodwin, as he preferred to be called, takes over, bright-toned and fluent, to carry things into a final, upbeat ensemble. "[Fred] was a good little cornet player," said Dant. "But he played like I did—strictly [mouthpiece] pressure. Couldn't play high notes." (Five years later Murray appeared on another Carmichael record date, his otherwise ebullient performance compromised by embouchure problems.)[40]

Almost as interesting is "Smile," a 1928 effort by "I'm Comin' Virginia" composer Donald Heywood, and also recorded by Whiteman's orchestra with Bix. Indeed, Dant's opening verse statement has more than a little of Beiderbecke's lilting delivery. Wolfe sets out the melody, Hoagy seems to treat his piano chorus as an elegy to the homiletic thoughts embraced by melody and lyrics:

> Smile when you are weary,
> Smile when you are blue ...

After an ensemble verse and a brief, Trumbauer-like Goodwin solo, Hoagy "talks" the lyric, with embellishments, in minstrel-show black dialect. The band takes it home in the manner of the Bix-Trumbauer OKeh records of the time.

Ironically, the only item missing from the Indiana University cache is the day's final title, a version of "Star Dust," performed by Carmichael and

Wolfe, and featuring the composer singing lyrics he'd devised that winter. Hoagy had a test pressing for years, Dant recalled, and played it regularly for his California guests; Hoagy Bix Carmichael, too, remembered hearing it often.

Dant recounted the lyric for Duncan Schiedt:

> Stardust melody, you hold a charm
> Through the lonely years;
> Stardust strain, beautiful refrain
> I hear you ringing in my ears.
> But the world goes by, paying no attention to you;
> To me you're everything in life and love
> I know, 'deed it's so;
> (Vocal "doodling" for eight bars)
> Oh, stardust strain, in my heart you will remain,
> Stardust melody, I love you heart and soul I do-o-o
> 'Deed I do.[41]

(The lyric, again, fits the melody as played by Gene Woods on the 1927 Gennett record and as transcribed on the 1928 lead sheet submitted for copyright. It does not conform to the later, published version of the song.)

More fascinating still is a comment made by saxophonist Wally Wilson. After graduation from IU, Wilson went to medical school at the University of Southern California, taking with him a handful of arrangements he'd received from Carmichael as part of a swap. He and pianist Bill Miller (not the same man who later distinguished himself with Red Norvo and Frank Sinatra) soon started up a USC campus dance band. "Whenever we played 'Stardust' we would get several requests from dancers to, 'Play it again, Sam!' So we did." One night, he said, they played it five times in the same evening, each time by request.

He found himself unable to get the melody off his mind. One night, he said, he awoke during a nightmare, and before going back to sleep scrawled notes for a lyric. "By the light of the next day it still looked pretty good, so I continued to work on it." The result rambles somewhat, but its opening few lines are worth quoting:

> I sometimes wonder why I spend my time
> Dreaming of a song.

A melody

That haunts my reverie . . . [42]

Wilson's lyric, unlike Hoagy's own, incorporates a one-note pickup to the melody. Mitchell Parish's lyric, added in 1929, expanded it to three and drew freely on elements in both earlier texts.

Even in this unfinished state, "Star Dust" is obviously a song about a song—a genre relatively rare in American popular music. There had been such songs before: Irving Berlin's 1909 "That Mesmerizing Mendelssohn Tune" (about the great German composer's famed *Spring Song*) is one example among many. But none had been a *major* song about a song—particularly a song that didn't actually exist. This was new.

What Carmichael and his 1928 Collegians laid down that day was hot music all right, but substantially different in texture and attitude from what was being made in the cities: miles removed from the easy intensity of the black bands; not half as slick as the records Nichols, Mole, and their cronies were turning out in New York; not as punchy as the crowd-the-beat stuff the young white Chicagoans were playing. It's also a lot less thoughtful than the Bix-and-Tram collaborations: like them, this hot music takes its time—but it weaves a far less complex emotional tapestry, never losing its sunny, indefatigable optimism. The "half-educated man," acolyte no longer, is on his way at last—but to where?

* IX *

Big Town Blues

*I had a drive that I call my Hoosier heritage, and the desire to make something
of my life, something solid and respectable. Yet I was usually in conflict
with that dreamer inside me.*

—HOAGY CARMICHAEL, *Sometimes I Wonder*, 1965

The 1928 Book Nook "commencement" came and went, bigger and more elaborately choreographed than its predecessor. The old gang was still in attendance: Wad Allen, introduced as the "out-of-town speaker," arrived in stovepipe hat and frock coat, a live white hen under his arm. Carmichael remembered his speech as "a marvelous thing . . . inspiring, yet completely senseless; as insanely futile as a Bent Eagle's notion of posterity."

Bill Moenkhaus and hot fiddler Ed Wolfe presented a solemnly magisterial appearance as "Ya-Lord" and "Ya-Lady" Bent Eagle, clad in long black robes and giant white eagle wings and riding along on a wheeled contraption that could have sprung from the mind of Salvador Dalí, René Magritte, or another of their Surrealist colleagues. Carmichael, Bud Dant, and the rest, bathrobe-clad, marched and played.[1]

But there was among them a sense—unspoken, disquieting—of glancing fondly back; that the time for such carryings-on, in their lives at least, had passed.

Summer brought the usual resort jobs. For a while, Dant and Ostot were working at Lake James, in northeast Indiana near the Michigan line. Hoagy, Ed Wolfe, and some other friends were at Lake Gage, not far away. But for Hoagy, at least, the unease he'd felt at being back in Bloomington didn't pass:

124

school days were over, yet here he was still playing dance dates with musicians he'd known as a student. Hadn't he written and published songs, recorded with Paul Whiteman and Bix, been offered a position in New York City? What was he doing negotiating with the management of the Columbia Club of Indianapolis to supply a band for the fall and winter seasons?

Founded in 1888 as an organization of prominent Republicans, the Columbia had boasted such members as James Whitcomb Riley, former president Benjamin Harrison, future Hollywood censorship czar William Harrison "Will" Hays, and dozens of Indiana's most powerful movers and shakers. Its stately second headquarters, architecturally blending English Tudor and early French Renaissance styles, opened in 1925 facing Monument Circle, the very heart of the city of Indianapolis. According to one particularly breathless newspaper account:

> The main entrance leads to a long, cool, dim corridor, paneled to a high ceiling with walnut rubbed to a dull satin finish. Great wrought-iron lanterns, similar to those which hang outside the doorway, are suspended from the ceiling of the hall. To the right as one enters ... [is] a curving marble stairway with a balustrade of gold and black metalwork.

Features of the third-floor main dining room, where the Carmichael ensemble was contracted to play, included a "plaster beamed ceiling, beautifully ornamented in color ... [P]laster friezes of viking ships are set over the doorways." Additionally, "austere marble floors were warmed by broad-striped woven wallhangings and carved walnut and tapestry chairs."[2]

The Columbia job came through Paul Driscol, who played respectable trumpet and had been at DePauw with Chauncey Goodwin. Graduating in 1927, he'd signed on as the club's official contractor, promptly booking Goodwin (on trumpet, which he played almost as well as saxophone) and some other school pals, including reedman Ed Beauchamp. As the latter's tales of the band's offstand behavior make clear, a certain collegiate zaniness was by no means confined to Carmichael, Moenkhaus, and their Bloomington circle.[3]

Among Indianapolis musicians a job at the Columbia, especially in the third-floor dining room, was considered nice going—as long as you knew how to keep the volume down during dinner, and no tempos too peppy for comfortable dancing afterwards, please. The club, after all, was private, members-only, its clientele well heeled and definitely older-generation in its tastes. Not exactly a forum for the kind of hot jazz Hoagy and his associates had been serving up for the college set.

Carmichael drew his men from various IU bands, a few local pros filling out the parts. Though he played piano solos now and then, he seems to have spent most of his time out front with a conductor's baton while local pianist Don Bye played the ensembles. The book included a handful of McKinney's Cotton Pickers arrangements, courtesy of Don Redman, and now—thanks to Pink Porter's Kansas City tutorials—Hoagy was also arranging, after a fashion. He "could hear a new tune," said bassist Charles Dowling, "go down to the music store, and overnight have an arrangement worked out. He wasn't able to put everything down correctly, but he knew what he wanted." Lead trumpeter Ray Conolly agreed: "Hoagy's arrangements would like as not be just a string of notes—all eighth notes—with no attention to time, interval or anything. He would explain orally what he wanted to get across and Warren Carr would finish it up from there." Trombonist Carr, an IU Crimson Serenaders alumnus, arranged some ballads for the group.

The leader's penchant for hot music and the patrons' steadfastly conservative resistance to it made a collision inevitable, and in later years various musicians opined that the job probably was doomed from the start. "Once in awhile Hoagy would feel the need to let off steam and he would call for a jazz tune as everyone was enjoying his roast beef and steak," Conolly recalled. Each time, he "expected to be called up before the Manager and members of the House Committee the next day; occasionally he was."[4]

"Oh, it must have been tough on that crowd," Conolly told Duncan Schiedt in 1960. "People as old as I am now would sit over their dinner, all hunched down, and scowl at the band." Now and then, he said, Hoagy would produce his cornet from some hiding place and let fly with a spirited—if not always accurate—hot solo. Finally Warren Carr removed the instrument's mouthpiece crook and hid it in the band room, solving that problem at least temporarily.[5]

Drummer Bob Vollmer recalled a night in January 1929 when Colonel Charles A. Lindbergh, visiting Indianapolis for the day, was a dinner guest at the Columbia. "Lindbergh . . . had come back from that [1927 transatlantic solo] flight and was a celebrity everywhere," he said. "Clark Aiken, the Club manager, brought him around to introduce him to everybody, and he shook hands sort of half-heartedly. Aiken introduced Hoag, and said, 'This is Mr. Carmichael, our orchestra leader.' Lindbergh went 'Un-h-h.'

And Hoag got mad and said, 'Un-h-h to you, too!' . . . I'll never forget that."
Saxophonist George Harper: "Hoag finally went over to [Lindbergh's] table
and asked if he'd like a request played. Lindbergh shook his head and said
no, so Hoag came back and we went into something wild." After that, all
agreed, the band's days at the Columbia were numbered.[6]

But they "had real finesse—a unique sound," said Hoagy. "Very little
drive, but it had my personality in it." So believing, he touted the group
to Leroy Shield, the Victor recording director who had supervised, and been
so admiring of, Whiteman's "Washboard Blues" session.[7]

On Tuesday, February 19, 1929, the eleven men assembled at Victor's
Chicago studios. Driscol, no hot soloist, bowed out for the occasion, ceding
his chair to young "Andy" Anderson, then doing an Army hitch at nearby
Fort Harrison. Wolfe played third sax and doubled violin. Contract singer
Frank Sylvano came in to do a vocal on "One Night in Havana."

But things didn't quite jell, and none of the seven titles they made was
released at the time. On the basis of five selections that have since turned
up (and subsequently been issued), balance doesn't seem to have been the
problem. Though the musicians play capably, both "March of the Hoodlums" and "Walkin' the Dog" seem self-conscious, earthbound, especially
compared with the Gennett versions. Something, some spark, is missing,
the band's apparent self-consciousness acting as a governor on its creative
engines. Even Goodwin, reproducing almost verbatim his "Hoodlums" alto
chorus, sounds almost calculating.

"Sittin' and Whittlin'," a *faux*-hillbilly number thrown in by Shield,
comes off better than might have been expected, with some rhythmic ensemble work and a "character" vocal by Carmichael. Another reading of
"One Night in Havana" suffers both from Sylvano's piping vocal and a
pedestrian arrangement. "We all tried too hard" was Hoagy's assessment.
"If I had really worked at it, and had known a bit more about instrumental
voicing, I think we might have developed into the first swing band . . . I
had the licks, as the Gennett date proved."[8]

The day's best moment, he said, was a version of "Sweet Lorraine," just
published by Mills. Shield kept a test pressing; but years later, when Victor
considered finally releasing it, neither pressing nor parts could be found.
"That one could be issued today and prove very interesting to the jazzo-
philes," said Hoagy. "My chord structure was way out, if I do say so."[9]

Disappointments aside, this Victor session did indeed produce one Carmichael highlight, all the more easily overlooked for not having been

released at the time. In the sixteen months since the Gennett "Star Dust" date, the piece called "When Baby Sleeps" had evolved at last into final and lasting form as "Rockin' Chair." Ironically, he said. "Writing 'Stardust' and 'Rockin' Chair' didn't seem terribly important or great discoveries [at the time]. It seemed only normal. I wrote the lyric to 'Rockin' Chair' while Mother sat in the room, and tried it out on her first. She, too, was not overly impressed."[10]

Stories vary as to the inspiration for "Rockin' Chair." Was it an old black woman known as "Granny" Campbell, living on the outskirts of Bucktown, who could always be counted on for high-quality corn-mash liquor? Another old Bloomington character, a man, who supplied home-brew beer? In a way it doesn't matter: as Hoagy later told an interviewer, "Rockin' Chair" forms a kind of sequel to "Washboard Blues." His own lyric seems to pick up just where Fred Callahan's "Washboard" text leaves off, in a spirit of quiet resignation. The verse (not sung on this record) even supplies a riverbank setting:[11]

> Moonlight on Swanee's muddy shore
> By my door.
> Music I've often heard before,
> Hear't no more.
> Years have slipped away and left me longin'
> For the days of happiness I'll see no more.

The speaker is old, infirm, waiting for the inevitable deliverance only death can bring. Nowhere to go, nothing to do but take a sip of gin now and then and "do my gallivantin'/In this old Rockin' Chair." Hoagy's lyric, as he sings it here, is still a work-in-progress, and some telling imagery is still to make its appearance: the line about "grabbin' " at flies has not yet replaced the "gallivantin'," and dear old Aunt Harriet has yet to arrive on the scene. The bridge, or middle section, as sung here, draws instead on a somewhat arcane piece of bodeful folk imagery:

> The old hound dog is howlin'
> You know what that means ...

But even on this first outing the idea is firmly in place: as with "Washboard Blues," "Rockin' Chair" tells a story, depicts scene and character, and foreshadows a sense of inevitable outcome. And, like "Washboard," it is a song about the realities of life far from city sophistication or Broadway artifice.

Often through the years, "Rockin' Chair" has seen service as a piece of quasi-minstrel "material," usually with a second, comedic voice added as a foil for the singer. In this form it has served many performers well, most notably Louis Armstrong and trombonist Jack Teagarden, who made it a perennially entertaining set piece. But such treatment all too often sacrifices the powerful subtext of fond, stoic resignation and the redeeming power of faith.

Mildred Bailey, who made the song her own at the start of the '30s, explored this dimension in several recorded "Rockin' Chair" interpretations. Among latter-day vocalists, Barbara Lea has brought even more subtly nuanced understanding to her performances. "To me, this song is nowhere near as dark a vision as 'Washboard Blues,' " she said recently. "There's a big loneliness in 'Washboard,' a sense of isolation and bleakness and desperation. But the person in 'Rockin' Chair'—it can be either a woman or man—has had a lot of family and friends and acquaintances pass through her life, a very full life.

"This vision is also leavened with a sense of humor: 'Fetch me that gin, son, 'fore I tan your hide.' An inner liveliness there, affectionate: she isn't *really* going to tan the boy's hide, is she? She's making a little joke. To me, this is a moment of reconciliation, and—yes—of expression of faith, acceptance."[12]

For a while, after the Columbia Club job ended, the band played dates around Indiana and Ohio with a slightly different personnel, but even that wasn't to last. Nor, coincidentally, was Carmichael's latest flirtation with law practice. After much consideration, Bingham, Mendenhall & Bingham decided to let him go. "The truth is, he was fired," said Nikki Schofield, longtime librarian of the firm, known in later years as Bingham, Summers, Welsh & Spilman. She quoted partner Claude Spilman saying that "in the afternoons, [Hoagy] would be at the Columbia Club playing the piano instead of doing his legal work." Meredith Bingham, widow of the man who had hired Carmichael, called it "a very friendly ending. There was no hostility involved. But I think perhaps he and they agreed that he was more of a musician than a lawyer, and that maybe he should go toward music and leave the firm."[13]

Carmichael, too, accepted it philosophically. "Yes, the law was a wrong guess," he remarked in a 1950s reminiscence. "A few years of practice revealed that the profession held forth many prospects to which my timid soul was not clearly [suited] and fewer hopes for constructive attainment that would satisfy my ego."[14]

✢   ✢   ✢

Whither next? With both the Columbia Club and the Bingham job behind him, there seemed little point in hanging around Indianapolis or returning to Bloomington. New York? Probably, inevitably—but the thought was still daunting. His dilemma seemed insoluble—until at some point a thought occurred: sound had come to the hitherto silent movie industry, and with it a need for music. The studios were beginning to make musicals, featuring such stars as Maurice Chevalier and Jeanette MacDonald, and that meant work for composers and arrangers. Irving Berlin, Cole Porter, Nacio Herb Brown, Richard Whiting, and others had begun writing for pictures. Why not Hoagland Carmichael?

"I put part of my little bank account into National City Bank stock . . . drew the rest, and was away to set Hollywood on fire," he writes. He went "with high hopes and a stack of compositions. Everyone said I'd return, discouraged and disillusioned . . . I didn't see that any disillusionment could harm me. If so, I felt it might be a man's coming of age. I bought a ticket west."[15]

Kappa Sigma brother Chuck Chamberlain (father of actor Richard) was there to meet the train, help the newcomer find a car and a place to stay; then Hoagy began making the rounds—only to find out that "I had made the gross mistake of not being sent for, and particularly from New York . . . Indiana was no-go in Hollywood, and I was unsuccessful in landing anything."[16]

Then, in mid-June, the picture brightened when Paul Whiteman's orchestra arrived in Los Angeles to begin work on Universal's all-color musical, *King of Jazz*. Hoagy was suddenly among friends: Frank Trumbauer, Min Leibrook, who had played tuba with the Wolverines; Bing Crosby and his fellow Rhythm Boys, Al Rinker and Harry Barris. Clarinetist Irving "Izzy" Friedman was from Indiana, and old pal Andy Secrest was in the trumpet section.[17]

And, too, there was Bix. He'd been sick with pneumonia and spent the winter at home in Davenport recuperating. He now walked with a slight limp, and there was talk of serious injuries sustained in some kind of brawl in New York—though no one seemed willing to talk about it. He'd put on weight, grown a little moustache, looked puffy and pale. He'd begun chain-smoking, and the drinking hadn't stopped; it was all beginning to affect his reliability. "He was sick and tired," Hoagy writes, "and losing his grip on the cornet. At rehearsals, he fumbled through his music like a little boy and sat by himself." In taking on Secrest, Whiteman had hired a capable bandsman who could also step in if necessary and deliver convincing hot solos in the Beiderbecke manner. As Carmichael read it, the presence of the young Indiana cornetist only made things worse: "I honestly believe that Bix developed an inferiority complex when Andy joined the band; needlessly, because no one could ever take his place as a horn-tooter."[18]

It proved an enjoyable, if not immediately productive, summer idyll. "I met a few celebrities, a few others who became celebs later," he wrote. "Occasionally I'd drive up to Beverly Hills, just to see if I could catch a glimpse of Clara Bow." Old Indiana associates kept turning up, among them Larry Leonard, Harry Hostetter, and even Batty DeMarcus. There were parties with the Whiteman musicians, including one particularly memorable evening at the palatial home of actor Richard Barthelmess. And, in a move that was to have far-reaching consequences, Al Rinker introduced Hoagy to his sister Mildred.[19]

Born in Tekoa, Washington, she'd worked as a song demonstrator in a five-and-dime store and been married awhile to a man named Bailey before hooking on to the Fanchon and Marco stage revue. She'd arrived in Los Angeles in 1925 and done some radio singing, but steady work was scarce—until in 1929 her brother and other Whiteman bandsmen contrived a situation, a party, at which their boss could hear her sing. Enchanted, he hired her on the spot, and as Mildred Bailey she became the first full-time female band singer, just as fellow-Washingtonian Bing Crosby had become the first regular male band vocalist—also with "Pops" Whiteman—two years earlier.

Chronically overweight, tart-tongued, short of temper, she sang in a high, rounded voice, phrasing with a clarity and delicacy few could match. Hoagy, who had shared keyboard duties at the party with Roy Bargy and Lennie Hayton, took to her at once. At some point during these California weeks he played and sang "Rockin' Chair" for her: she loved it, learned it, and soon became inseparably associated with it. To generations of popular music fans, Mildred Bailey would forever be "the Rockin' Chair Lady."

Hoagy got an apartment with Secrest and soon hunted up an old piano. "I spent a lot of time at the upright playing and thinking out tunes," he writes. One product of those sessions was something he called "San Francisco Blues," which begins:

> It's a song of a very unfortunate color[ed] man
> Who got 'rested down in old Hong Kong . . .

On his original worksheets—two pieces of Columbia Club stationery—he also plays with the rhyming possibilities of "Shanghai" and "Singapore," before opting for "Hong Kong."

For example:

> I need someone to find me
> In fancy dreams and then
> Leave Shanghai far behind me
> For happiness once again . . . [20]

It took "San Francisco Blues" a decade to achieve publication and lasting popularity as "Hong Kong Blues." But its genesis is here, in 1929, and in common with everything else Hoagy Carmichael had written up till then, it sounds like nothing else in popular music. Its melody line could have been part of an improvisation played on a horn. Certainly there is no resemblance to such bits of period *chinoiserie* as "Singapore Sorrows," "Chong (He Come From Hong Kong)," "Broken Idol," and even the more lasting "Limehouse Blues" of 1924.

With Labor Day approaching, and Universal showing no sign of a satisfactory shooting script, Whiteman decided to head back east. Hoagy, sick of knocking on Hollywood doors, had also made up his mind to go—especially after Trumbauer and Eddie Lang expressed interest in recording a couple of his numbers. When the Whiteman "Old Gold Special" train pulled out, it was with a five-foot eight-inch, 120-pound stowaway on board. He shared berths with Crosby and Secrest and spent many daytime hours hiding out in the men's toilet as the gold-painted train sped across the Rockies and on to the great plains.[21]

For an Indiana boy, arrival in New York in late summer of 1929 must have been an intimidating experience. The West Side Highway and Chrysler Building were going up, with plans in the works for an even taller structure, to be called the Empire State Building, at the corner of Fifth Avenue and 34th Street. The piers of the giant new George Washington Bridge, spanning the Husdon River far uptown, were taking shape.

"I liked the twenties at the end there, when it all came to a witch's boil," he has written. "And I feared it, too. It was too rich for my country boy blood. Follies girls and [cartoonist] Peter Arno faces on the yachts on Great South Bay, some jazzmen playing *Hold That Tiger* on deck, and Templar roadsters, Packard and Jordan convertibles parked on the dock."[22]

He hit town in the middle of a savage heat wave. Stu Gorrell was sharing an apartment on Horatio Street, in Greenwich Village, with some other Indiana alumni and offered the newcomer a spare room. Hoagy remembered it as "a cold and bare cubby-hole where trash was stacked and in which we figured that at least twenty old men had died during the hundred years the house had existed. I wasn't liking New York fast, but I stuck it out."[23]

Within a few weeks Gorrell had found new digs, across the East River in Jackson Heights, Queens. Hoagy came along—and ran right into some more Hoosiers: Harry Shackelford, Hube Hanna—by this time out of music altogether and working for Goodyear—and Shackelford's cousin Marjorie, whom he dated.

There were late-night expeditions to Harlem, listening to Duke Ellington's band at the Cotton Club and Charlie Johnson's at Ed Smalls' Paradise; to pianist Willie "the Lion" Smith at Pod's and Jerry's; and to Luis Russell's supercharged ten-piecer at the Saratoga Club, built around a nucleus of New Orleans soloists. Ellington, especially, impressed him:

> The Duke had color in his arrangements that Don [Redman] hadn't approached. He had transformed the ugly picture that most people have of jazz into a beautiful, black silhouette of fantastic figures and moods. That's why his "Mood Indigo" and "Black and Tan Fantasy" are so individual. I doubt that the present-day notion of jazz will ever be made more interesting than what Ellington has achieved.[24]

He also finally went to talk business with Irving Mills. For openers, the publisher scheduled a record date for Friday, September 20, with two more to follow in November and January—all for the purpose of recording numbers Hoagy Carmichael had written or would shortly produce. Eddie Lang and a group of Whiteman musicians booked a date at OKeh for October 5, to record "March of the Hoodlums" and another tune Hoagy had sketched out in California, "What Kind o' Man Is You," to feature Mildred Bailey. A Trumbauer session five days later would record a a new "modernistic" Carmichael instrumental, "Manhattan Rag," featuring Secrest in a solo originally intended for Bix.

But the cautious Indiana boy in him was not yet converted. Sometime during this period he wrote to Hugh Niven, the Indianapolis National City Bank officer who had advised him to invest in bank stock before his departure for California. He thanked Niven for the advice, assured him that he'd urged friends to invest—then sprang a surprise:

> I have realized for some time that I shall drop this music racket for good, particularly when I get all out of it that I can hustle without using guns. The time has arrived and I am very interested in the financial business and I think I can make good at it. I read it and follow it the best I can. You probably know that I have an L.L.D. degree tucked away in a dresser someplace and with 29 years under my belt I believe I am seasoned enough to know what it is all about as a beginner at least. I want a business, a clientele, and something that I can build up. What have you to offer? What have you to suggest?[25]

The letter requests an answer by return mail and ends with a postscript: "Am making some Brunswick records of some of my tunes of mine [*sic*] tomorrow and that ends it." At some point during these uncertain weeks he apparently returned to the Indiana capital for a few days and looked up some old friends, including Harry Orchard, who duly noted it in his diary. Carmichael remembered that trip as "foolish, except to rid my mind definitely of ever living in Ind[iana]."[26]

His letter to Niven mentions that "Bud Bollinger of the Cleveland office arranged that his kid brother should come to New York and go to the Nat. City headquarters and go to school, so to speak, in preparation for a position as a bond salesman . . . might I have the same possibility thru [*sic*] a recommendation or what have you?"[27]

Here he was in New York, flush with the prospect of having his songs published and recorded, and still wracked with doubt, still not trusting either the music business or his own ability to make his way in it. Events of the weeks that followed only deepened his misgivings.

The big bull market had peaked, and Carmichael's National City Bank shares were riding high; sell now, said his broker, and he sold. He rein-vested—and within a few days, on "Black Tuesday," the bottom fell out of the stock market. Among the $15 billion of investors' money that disap-peared into the abyss between then and the end of 1929 was a good chunk of Hoagland Carmichael's carefully hoarded savings.

Even the music business that had seemed so promising now looked tarnished. "Everybody was talking about Guy Lombardo and Rudy Vallee," he writes.

> I listened to their radio programs and tore my hair when people told me this was wonderful music." Jazz was dying and at a fast clip. The stock market crash had sent millions of jazzbos to the ranks of the unemployed. Radio programs turned to entertainment for the people who sat at home and grieved over their financial losses . . . I was doing recording work with Irving Mills, but it wasn't enough to keep the wolf away.[28]

He started looking around, indignantly comparing the inflated salaries of Wall Street executives, whose overconfidence had brought on the dis-aster, with the pittances paid to musicians "who had studied for years and were professional artists." Reading the fine print of his publishing contract, he realized that almost every clause favored the publisher, while committing Mills to almost nothing; discovered that there was effectively no way even of determining how many copies of a given song the publisher had sold. Very quickly, the young Hoosier came to understand why such prominent music business figures as Victor Herbert and John Philip Sousa had labored and lobbied so hard in setting up the American Society of Composers, Authors, and Publishers, known by its acronym ASCAP. With it came on-going realization of the frequency with which the financial interests of com-posers and authors collided with those of their publishers.

Hugh Niven wrote back, expressing regret: no job. Undeterred, Car-michael kept looking. Through Harry Shackelford and a new friend, fellow-IU alumnus Bill Shattuck, he found a position at S. W. Strauss and Co., one of New York's leading investment houses, where he remembered "spending most of my time answering the frantic telephone calls of elderly ladies, who seemed to blame me personally for the depreciation of their bonds." Among his fellow-employees at Strauss was Bostonian songwriter Johnny Green, who had written "Coquette" and sold it to the Lombardo brothers, but had not yet broken through with "Body and Soul." Hoagy described the job as "tough, but [it] gave me good experience about finances."[29]

Harry Orchard, visiting around the time, noted that his friend "had a private office and a secretary and was dictating letters to people who were writing in asking for their money. They were not going to get any of it back. Hoagy in his answers to them was letting them down as gently as possible."[30]

In the last month of 1929, with a tremulous Hoagy Carmichael at his side singing the "boy" part, Louis Armstrong recorded "Rockin' Chair" at OKeh's Union Square studios. "Those blubbering strange sounds he made at the mike in front of my face tickled me to the marrow," Hoagy recalled. "Jack Teagarden was there to lend encouragement, though he didn't play on the date."[31]

In hot music circles (if not yet for a public only dimly aware of his genius), Armstrong was the man of the hour. He'd played and sung "Ain't Misbehavin'" in *Connie's Hot Chocolates* on Broadway and had begun occasionally fronting Luis Russell's band at theatre dates. That July, a gathering of New York's top white musicians had honored him at a banquet, presenting him with a pocket watch on which was engraved "To Louis Armstrong, World's Greatest Cornetist, from the Musicians of New York."

To have the World's Greatest Cornetist play and sing one of your songs on record—why, that might just mean you'd arrived, made it to the big time. It didn't feel that way to Hoagy Carmichael, now rooming with Bill Shattuck in what he called "an old, creaky walk-up" at 113½ East 31st Street, between Park and Lexington avenues. Its chief attraction was a grand piano, and according to an Indiana news clipping of the time:

> From an apartment on East Thirty-first Street in the evenings comes a strange, discordant exercising of the keys of a grand piano, and it is so wierd [sic] and good that the neighborhood turns out on its tiny porches and stands outside on the sidewalk to listen. Hoagie Carmichael, of Bloomington, Ind., is at work.[32]

Evenings, weekends, days off, he kept "finding" tunes at the old grand. "Why don't you write a song about Georgia?" Frank Trumbauer said to him one day. "Nobody ever lost money writing songs about the South." And one night, at Harry Shackelford's place in Jackson Heights, he did just that. Unlike "Washboard Blues" and "Rockin' Chair," the new melody had no programmatic element: it was a song, simple and straightforward. Stu Gorrell, never far away, lent a hand with the lyric, and got credit for it when the song was published. They called it "Georgia on My Mind."

From the first bars, music and words strike an elegaic tone. Perhaps intentionally, the lyric is ambiguous: is the Georgia of the singer's thoughts and longings simply a place, or is the apostrophe also to a person? The verse sets up this duality:

> Melodies bring memories that linger in my heart,
> Make me think of Georgia, why did we ever part?
> Some sweet day when blossoms fall and all the world's a song,
> I'll go back to Georgia, 'cause that's where I belong.[33]

The song continues in this vein and can be read either way. The melody, as with all else Carmichael has written to date, spills off the page like a hot chorus—a Bix chorus. Not only is the "correlated" phrasing of the first eight bars readily apparent, but the half-step downward shift from tonic to E7 in bar 5 is a particularly subtle move. Conventional practice would have shifted to a generic VI (D7 in this key)—as Ray Charles did in his 1960 hit record—or some form of diminished chord, incorporating at least three of the same notes found in the E7. Carmichael's choice of the E7 is not based on any lack of theoretical knowledge: all three options fall easily within any jazz pianist's harmonic vocabulary. Instead, it seems impelled by a keen aesthetic intuition, yielding the choice most expressive of the song's lyric content.[34]

"Georgia on My Mind" (8 bars, 1–8), 1930

"If anyone is a true jazz composer," said tenor saxophonist Bud Freeman, "we'd have to call Hoagy a true jazz composer, because his tunes seem to carry their own improvisation . . . his songs seem to improvise themselves, in that they are based on true jazz phrases." George Gershwin, said Freeman, "wrote lovely melodies like 'Summertime' . . . but when a jazz musician plays 'Summertime' he feels a *need* to improvise around it, in order to express something he feels. But a Hoagy tune has the improvisation already in it, and there is no *need* to add to it."[35]

The song also introduces a concept that will permeate, and come to characterize, many Carmichael songs. Hinted at in "Rockin' Chair," it can be called the idea of home, a place where wandering ceases and the heart comes to rest. It need not be any specific place—Hoagy Carmichael had never set foot in Georgia when he wrote "Georgia on My Mind"—but it must be what thought and emotion perceive as home. The little boy gazing out over the Montana mountains, dreaming of smokestacks in far-off Bloomington, had come of age and crystallized the feelings of those early years in music and words.

A lucky, and unanticipated, break helped shape "Georgia's" ultimate destiny. Leroy Shield, supervising Hoagy's unsuccessful Chicago record date, had been intrigued by "Rockin' Chair" and passed it on to a friend of his named Ralph Peer. Like Shield, Peer had a reputation for recognizing and recording talent. Back in 1917, as a Manhattan-based artists-and-repertoire man, he'd tried to interest the Columbia Graphophone Co. in a five-piece band then causing a nightly riot at Reisenweber's Restaurant. He'd even gone so far as to record two numbers, which the company duly issued but did not bother to promote. The rival Victor Talking Machine Co., perhaps more attuned to popular taste, inherited the Original Dixieland Jazz Band.

It was Peer who, in 1924 and 1925, took mobile recording equipment to New Orleans to record a series of that city's best jazz bands, black and white, *in situ*, a coup for the feisty young OKeh label. Throughout the decade he did much the same with scores of regional blues and "hillbilly" artists.

By 1929 he was with Victor, for whom he recorded at least two groundbreaking, racially mixed bands: Eddie Condon's Hot Shots (teaming Jack Teagarden and pianist Joe Sullivan with some top-of-the-line Harlem men) and the Jones-Collins Astoria Hot Eight, from New Orleans. On clarinet in the latter group was Sidney Arodin, whose path would shortly cross Hoagy Carmichael's in a mutually beneficial way.

All this experience had convinced Ralph Peer that a potential market existed for songs by up-and-coming young musicians, talents outside the New York Tin Pan Alley or Broadway mainstreams. The result was Peer's Southern Music Co., first tenant in the Brill Building, at Broadway and 49th Street; in early 1930 Hoagy signed with them, terminating his contract with Mills. Southern published "Rockin' Chair," and it was to Peer that Hoagy came with "Georgia on My Mind."[36]

Mills, meanwhile, still owned a clutch of Carmichael songs, including "Star Dust." Mitchell Parish, a young southerner working for the publisher as a staff lyricist, had fashioned a text, incorporating various ideas of his own and Hoagy's, and including Wally Wilson's opening line.

The company published the result in 1929. "There was no one special approach," Parish said in 1985. "Sometimes we were both together at the piano. We sometimes met at random, just ran into each other. Just singers and writers, gossiping and talking shop, latest news on songs, exchanging views. Whatever we decided to do, the publisher was always the last to hear."[37]

Two separate Mills bands, one of them with the composer himself at the piano, had recorded instrumental versions of the song for Brunswick; Don Redman, leading McKinney's Cotton Pickers, had done one for OKeh with blues guitarist Lonnie Johnson added as a guest soloist. All were based, in one way or another, on the same loosely organized arrangement Seidel's men had used at the 1927 Gennett session.[38]

On May 16, 1930, came a major shift in use of Hoagy's melody, when the dance orchestra of Isham Jones recorded the newly published "Star Dust" as an instrumental. Himself an accomplished songwriter ("I'll See You in My Dreams," "It Had to Be You"), Jones had heard McKinney's Cotton Pickers play the song and spotted it at once as a potential hit. According to James Breyley, soon to become Jones's manager, the leader immediately went to work with his violinist Victor Young, rearranging "Star Dust" as a romantic ballad.[39]

It's a matter of custom to credit his recorded performance, with violin solo by Young, as the first to slow Hoagy's tune to ballad tempo, but this is not the case: that honor belongs to the first of the two Mills records, made November 8, 1928. Jones's 1930 tempo, at $\bullet = 125$, is considerably *faster* than the Mills.

What makes the Jones record significant is its conception. Where Mills's musicians are still thinking of "Star Dust" within the context of its jazz origins, Young's arrangement recasts it in a sentimental mode, with legato phrasing, a touch of rubato, and an emotional stance owing nothing to hot jazz. Other recording artists, including singing bandleader Will Osborne, quickly followed suit.

The treatment worked, and the song caught on immediately. Bands started playing it on the radio, and newsman Walter Winchell, an early fan, began touting it in his columns and on the air. Usually it was little more than a one-line mention of "the lad who composed the memorable 'Star Dust,' " tossed off in passing. But that was enough: millions read and listened to Winchell's machine-gun patter—and tended to remember what he said.

Still, more than a year went by before verse and chorus of "Star Dust" got their first vocal exposure on record, in an August 19, 1931, Brunswick performance by—no surprise, given his nascent popularity at the time—Bing Crosby. His reading is ardent in his best 1931 manner, and in the published key of C, taking him repeatedly to a high written E, almost into tenor range. Interestingly, he sings the first bar of the verse not as published, beginning on the tonic (in this case C), but as Carmichael first conceived and wrote it, beginning on the supertonic (or D). Though a small difference, it reflects what must have been a familiarity with the song stemming directly from its composer.

Bing's is an affecting performance—rather more so than the more casual, if more smoothly sung, Decca remake of May 22, 1939 (which drops the key a minor third to A). At times in the 1931 version it is easy, and right, to imagine the singer kneeling beside the garden wall portrayed in the lyric, absorbed in a reverie of passion and regret for a love won and lost.

✻   ✻   ✻

Arguably this New York period, beginning in late 1929, was the most productive of Hoagland Carmichael's career. Riven by doubt, caught between a need for security and the lure of songwriting, convinced that hot jazz as he knew it was dying, he nevertheless was turning out songs, some of them superb, as quickly as he could get them on paper. "Let's face it," he wrote, "New York is a great big, beautiful and exciting place even in the eyes of the poor and lonely, and the greatest monument to mankind. It is actually the hub of the world, and strangely enough it has a far greater hold on me than the whole state of Indiana." New York, he says, "made practically everything possible that has happened in the United States. You have to have a New York in order to make hit songs. Might have been physically impossible otherwise."[40]

He embraced his New York life with enthusiasm, and the songs show it. "What Kind o' Man Is You," as sung on Eddie Lang's OKeh date by Mildred Bailey, is naturally rhythmic in a way that illustrates Bud Freeman's comment that Hoagy's melodies are "based on true jazz phrases." The first four bars of the chorus, with their Bix-like "correlated" phrases, make the point even more emphatically:

"What Kind o' Man Is You?" (bars 1–4), 1929

Andy Secrest emphasizes the flavor with a strongly Bix-like opening cornet melody statement, and Bailey's vocal demonstrates disarming ease with the beat. "High and Dry" and "Harvey," recorded on Mills dates, are lightweights—though the latter, an indictment of the kind of "swell fellow" parents invariably single out to their wayward children as models of good behavior, is never less than entertaining.[41]

Carmichael recycled "March of the Hoodlums" twice on 1929 records, though neither version comes up to the excitement level of the number's first Indiana performance; "Manhattan Rag" is a medium-tempo instrumental which, a year earlier, would have been a natural for Bix: in its melodic lines, flavor, phrase construction, choice of notes, it's as much a composed Beiderbecke solo as the original version of "Star Dust." "Barbaric," highlight of the December 1929 Mills date, is an instrumental in two contrasting episodes: the first a chordally simple thirty-two-bar stomp, the second a bluesy theme shortly to reemerge, with lyrics, as an independent song, "In the Still of the Night."

"My Sweet" seems to have been written expressly for Louis Armstrong. The trumpeter recorded it on April 5, 1930, and his remains the only American record, its label crediting Stu Gorrell as co-composer. Apparently never published, the song has disappeared entirely, leaving only a penciled band arrangement in Carmichael's hand, without lead sheet. Armstrong takes enough liberty with both melody and lyric to thwart any attempt to discern their original form.[42]

He accorded similar treatment to "Star Dust" on November 4, 1931, in one of his most impassioned vocal and trumpet performances. Fletcher Henderson had recorded the song that March in a Bill Challis arrangement saturated with Beiderbecke flavor, Rex Stewart paying solo homage to his friend and fellow-cornetist. Victor Young recorded a twelve-inch "concert" orchestral version for the same label, with harmonically imaginative vocal interjections from the three Boswell Sisters. Carmichael later listed it as among his favorite versions of the song.

The Armstrong record, available in two takes, is a singular, and incomparable, event. Using only the chorus, and based on a doctored version of the published "stock" orchestration, it consists of three choruses, bookended by an eight-bar intro and four-bar coda, all at a swiftly moving ♩ = 131, closer to Carmichael's original conception.[43]

Neither the tempo nor the mewling of a scrappy, out-of-tune saxophone section can diminish the might and majesty of Armstrong's performance. It is an aria, trumpet and vocal proceeding from the same broadly operatic conception, at once a transfiguration of Carmichael's melody and a reaffirmation of its hot jazz origins. Armstrong's feat is all the more astonishing for having been achieved twice: both issued takes of "Star Dust," full of variety even within the same overall structure, carry the same supernal splendor.

It does no disservice to two exemplary trumpet choruses to suggest that the performance's most startling feature lies in the vocal. Through an alchemy that was his alone, Armstrong attenuates, foreshortens, extends and compresses, words and entire phrases, sometimes almost into incomprehensibility—only to emerge with a dramatic impact far greater and more immediate than Parish's lyric, however manifold its virtues, could ever have dreamt of attaining.

How does he do it? There is no fully satisfying, sufficiently concrete, explanation. At best, specific moments can be studied: the ascending phrase "baby you KNOW," in bar 13 of take −2, lends weight and force to the singer's realization of love grasped and lost—subsequently reinforced by a closing, repeated, "Oh memory, oh memory" at vocal's end. But even such examples fail to explain *why* this "Star Dust" works as powerfully, and as imperishably, as it does. In the end, as is forever the case with transcendental music, it simply has to be experienced—and savored.[44]

✻   ✻   ✻

Presumably armed with recommendations from Shield and Peer, Hoagy landed a Victor record date, scheduled for Wednesday, May 21, 1930, at Manhattan's acoustically resonant Liederkranz Hall. Given a free hand to pick his musicians, he went for top men, including Joe Venuti, Eddie Lang, Tommy Dorsey, Bud Freeman, Gene Krupa, and Benny Goodman. At the insistence of Victor executive Loren Watson, the personnel also included trumpeter James "Bubber" Miley, who had played a major role in shaping the "jungle" sound of the Duke Ellington orchestra. Ellington had fired Miley in early 1929, and Watson had apparently made the trumpeter's welfare an almost personal matter since then: no Miley, no date, he told Hoagy.[45]

Miley dominates the first chorus of "Rockin' Chair," using his plunger in an aggressive way that seems uncomfortably suited to the song's gently wistful mood. Bix turns in eight contemplative bars later on, before Miley returns for a swaggering ending. Beiderbecke gets a better shot on "Barnacle Bill, the Sailor," given a high-spirited going-over by Hoagy and his musicians.

Bix had returned to New York in April, rested and optimistic, brimful of plans to organize and tour with his own band. Though nervous about recording, he tackled Carmichael's second Victor session, held at Victor's West 24th Street studio, on Monday, September 15, with bright determination. The other musicians were old friends, and solidly all in his corner: Venuti, Lang, Freeman, Jimmy Dorsey, drummer Chauncey Morehouse, and trumpeter Ray Lodwig from Goldkette days; former Wolverine Min Leibrook was on bass sax.

Sure enough, it is a relaxed, lively Bix who carries the opening and ensemble rideout on the pop tune "Bessie Couldn't Help It." "I really wish I'd given him more," Hoagy told the author. "I'm sorry now, because when he did play he was the old Bix, beautiful, as if nothing had ever happened. And just listen to that rideout on 'Bessie': you can hear what a lift he gave the band."[46]

"Georgia on My Mind," recorded here for the first time, seems to underscore Hoagy's regret at not allocating a more prominent role to Beiderbecke. Following a Carmichael vocal, Ray Lodwig states the melody in a mute, "nanny-goat" vibrato very prominent. It's an anomaly, in that Venuti and Teagarden, following him, play brief but effective hot solos. Could this sixteen bars have been intended for Bix? As it is, he does the last eight bars of the final chorus, and does them beautifully, ending with a poignant little coda.

This apparent remission was not to last. The touring plans fell through, and Bix blacked out during a solo on the Camel Pleasure Hour show. Shaken, he headed home again to his family in Davenport, Iowa. Then, in the first weeks of 1931, came the news that Bill Moenkhaus had died at twenty-eight. "I'm going to die any day now," Monk had told Hoagy once—and, prescient to the end, he'd been right. The carefree days in Bloomington, days of Bent Eagles and Book Nooks, open jobs and nonsense verses, suddenly seemed long ago and very far away.

Bix got back in February, checking into the 44th Street Hotel, a midtown domicile popular with musicians. He spent most days in his room, sometimes reading poetry. Hoagy, working at the S. W. Strauss office on Fifth Avenue, dropped by when he could. "Once, a maid asked me if Bix was sick. She said he didn't get out of bed for days. I could tell when I saw him that he wasn't eating enough. Sometimes he seemed lonesome; other times, I got the impression that he never wanted to see anyone. Occasionally we'd sing and doodle some of the old tunes, but it wasn't the same, and I'd leave the hotel with the feeling that it was a rather hopeless situation, and it wouldn't be long until he was gone."[47]

And it wasn't. On August 6, in a tiny apartment in Sunnyside, Queens, Leon Beiderbecke succumbed to pneumonia and general bodily failure. Like Monk, he was but twenty-eight. Wad Allen called Hoagy with the news. "Bix died," he said, in an exchange that would resound through the rest of their lives. No, he didn't, came Hoagy's stricken reply. "I can hear him . . . I can hear him fine from here . . . I guess he didn't die, then."[48]

The loss was bitter and lasting: but by the time both these bright young men died, their pivotal moments in the fledgling songwriter's life had passed. Together they had set him on his way, conferring perceptions, tastes, standards, that had shaped him and would go on shaping him.

Now, beyond doubt or denial, he was on his own.

The Carmichael family, 1905. Clockwise from top: Hoagland, Lida, Georgia, Howard.

Joanne Carmichael in 1918, just weeks before her death. (ARCHIVES OF TRADITIONAL MUSIC, INDIANA UNIVERSITY [ATM])

Martha Claire Carmichael, an early portrait. (HOAGY BIX CARMICHAEL COLLECTION [HBC])

Georgia Carmichael, c. 1930. (ATM)

Lida and "Cyclone" Carmichael share a lighthearted moment, 1928. (ATM)

Above: Jam session at the
Book Nook, Hoagy at
the piano, c. 1922. (ATM)

Right: Bradford "Batty"
De Marcus at French
Lick, Indiana, c. 1919–20.
(DUNCAN SCHIEDT COL-
LECTION [DSC])

The "half-educated man" on an Indiana University tennis court, c. 1924. (DSC)

William Moenkhaus at Indiana University, c. 1924. (INDIANA UNIVERSITY ARCHIVES [IUA])

Hoagy "at liberty" in Palm Beach, 1923.
(ATM)

Two of the Wolverines—Bix and saxophonist George Johnson, summer 1924—
flanked by Dick Voynow, Jimmy Hartwell, and drummer Vic Berton. (DSC)

On a Monday morning in January, 1925: Bix and his Rhythm Jugglers record for Gennett, with Hoagy present. (RICHARD M. SUDHALTER COLLECTION [RMS])

An intense Carmichael with Fred Hitch's Happy Harmonists, recording "Washboard Blues" and "Boneyard Shuffle" for Gennett, May 19, 1925. (DSC)

Section of Kappa Sigma Fraternity group portrait, c. 1924, with Carmichael directly in front of column. (ATM)

The band that recorded "Star Dust." L. to r.: Dick Kent, Gene Woods (saxes), Emil Seidel (leader), Byron Smart (trumpet), Maury Bennett (sax), Oscar Rosberg (trombone), Don Kimmel (banjo, not on recording), Cliff Williams (drums), Paul Brown (bass). (DSC)

Above: Book Nook 1927 "Commencement" parade. Hoagy on cornet, with Chauncey Goodwin and Bud Dant playing brasses immediately behind him. (DSC)

Right: A solemn young lawyer in the making, c. 1929. (ATM)

Socializing in Fort Lauderdale with the Indiana Royal Peacocks, early 1927. Third from left: trumpeter Andy Secrest (later to replace Bix in Paul Whiteman's orchestra). (DSC)

A reunion with
Paul Whiteman,
c. 1940. (ATM)

Lida Carmichael (right) and Ma Robison listening to "Young Hoag" on the radio, c. 1938. (ATM)

Hoagy and Ruth, c. 1936. (ATM)

Feeling no pain: The Mercers and the Carmichaels, Palm Springs, 1938. (ATM)

Preparing "Star Dust" for presentation on Tommy Dorsey's radio show, March 1, 1939. (RMS)

A gathering of star songwriters, c. 1941. Left to right: Al Dubin, Lorenz Hart, Mack Gordon, Hoagy, Leo Robin, Harry Revel, Harry Warren. (RMS)

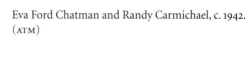

Eva Ford Chatman and Randy Carmichael, c. 1942. (ATM)

With Lida and the irreplaceable Buddy Cole, 1950s. (ATM)

Broadcasting for CBS, 1940s. Buddy Cole at rear. (ATM)

Four old jazz pals in action, 1940. Left to right: Hoagy, Jack Teagarden, trumpeter Wingy Manone, Johnny Mercer. (RMS)

Five tennis stars on the golf course, 1940s. Left to right: Pancho Segura, Don Budge, Hoagy, Tony Trabert, Pancho Gonzales. (ATM)

Autographing ARA records, 1945–46. (ATM)

Coming of Age

Hoagland Carmichael now admitted what he'd known all along: whatever happened, he was destined to make his living as a songwriter. If no single event had determined it, the deaths of Monk and Bix, following so closely on one another, seemed to place a full stop at the end of any thought of doing anything else.

"There was a kind of desperate urgency that took over all of us in the early 1930s," he wrote. "Everyone who could tried to shut out personal loss, the depression, and carry on as if the era were to last a thousand years. It was a hell of a time to be part of; not a place for a jazz composer to be trapped in. But there I was."[1]

Sidney Arodin was in town, playing at what Hoagy recalled as "a little joint on West 56th Street," and Carmichael went to listen. The New Orleans clarinetist was featuring a thoughtful little tune of his own making, sixteen bars with a tag, beginning on the chord of the sixth, in the manner of "There'll Be Some Changes Made" or "Ballin' the Jack."

A wanderer who had visited New York several times during the 1920s and even recorded there, Arodin had won wide respect among colleagues for his records with Abbie Brunies's Halfway House Orchestra and other major Crescent City groups. Ralph Peer had recorded him for Victor in

1929, with a mixed group under trumpeter Lee Collins, and couldn't stop singing his praises.

He'd barnstormed throughout the South and Southwest, where saxophonists Eddie Miller and Drew Page, among others, heard him play his number; it was ripe for conversion into a song, Carmichael thought, told him so, and found Arodin more than willing: they worked on it one afternoon, Hoagy suggesting a few minor adjustments to the melody and adding a verse, then outfitting the whole thing with a lyric.[2]

Carmichael recorded the result, as "Lazy River," for Victor on November 20, 1930, backed by the Dorseys, Freeman, and Venuti, with Ray Lodwig and Mannie Klein on trumpets. The melody, opening on what can only be described as an arpeggiated, Bix-like hot lick, does indeed sound like a converted instrumental solo; Hoagy's lyric is yet another ode to that mythic place where a wanderer can rest under a leafy bough and watch life's cares float away on fluffy cumulus clouds:

> Up a lazy river by the old mill run,
> That lazy lazy river in the noonday sun.
> Linger in the shade of a kind old tree,
> Throw away your troubles, dream a dream with me...

The reference to a "kind old tree" is particularly fetching—and, for a popular lyric, imaginative. William Zinsser, in a keenly observed 1994 article, calls Hoagy's "Lazy River" text "a perfect product of the innocent America [Carmichael] grew up in—a classic of escapism . . . For good measure, the lyric has a generous helping of words beginning with *l*, those well-known inducers of languor and lassitude. We get five *lazy*'s, one *linger*, one *loaf*, and one *love*. If the song had a second chorus, a lark would sing a lullaby."[3]

The "Lazy River" session also included a Carmichael curiosity, unissued at the time, listed in Victor's files as "Papa's Gone Bye Bye Blues (Jewish-Boy Blues)." As "Jew-Boy Blues," it had been around since 1925, first sung in public by Violet Deckard on a January 5, 1926, Bloomington job with Carmichael's Collegians. Such lines as "Isidore, I'm telling you" and references to "rocking little Abie's cradle" mark this as Hoagy's attempt at a Jewish "character" song in the early Irving Berlin manner, a "my man's gone and left me" lament with an ethnic spin.[4]

The strongest feature of "Jewish-Boy Blues" is its melody, clearly an effort to capture the Yiddish flavor also sought by fellow-Hoosier Cole Porter in such songs as "My Heart Belongs to Daddy"—and done more successfully by Carmichael himself in the later "Baltimore Oriole." The verse, in fact, makes a good approach to the cantorial "cry" of Ashkenazi Jewish tradition—only to be thwarted in this performance by Jimmy Dorsey's rather impersonal reading.

By early 1932 Hoagy had left S. W. Strauss and joined Ralph Peer's company, Southern Music, as a staff writer in "a rather shabby deal—no dough—but they were a new firm and I thought Ralph Peer was a good businessman. He was, and he profited much more out of the deal than I."[5]

Perhaps. But he also kept his employee generating quality songs. Hoagy came up with "Come Easy, Go Easy, Love," an unbuttoned, upbeat paean to what a later age would term "avoidance of commitment" in sexual relationships. His lyricist was trombonist and sometime songwriter Sunny Clapp. The composer's vocal on the first record, made under Clapp's leadership, is engagingly manic, bookended by good solos from alto sax, trombone, and two distinctly different trumpeters.[6]

Still, as far as Hoagy was concerned, such records seemed a kind of requiem. "I was tiring of jazz," he writes, "and I could see that other musicians were tiring of it as well. The boys were losing their enthusiasm for the hot stuff, and many of them, such as the Dorsey boys, Miff Mole, Carl Kress and Phil Napoleon joined radio staff orchestras to play programs of every description. No more hot licks, no more thrills—into the [orchestra] pits!"

As he heard it, radio sponsors were now—literally—calling the tune, "with the result that music lost much of the rich spontaneity and color it had in the days when the record business was booming. Even songs were being constructed in a monotonous pattern to satisfy the musical tastes of the average radio audience."

The final pages of *Jazzbanders* are full of such pessimistic utterances. "The romance of jazz was gone," he declares, going on to report that "the stars of the pioneering days were fading to stardust." Hot music insiders might gather at Plunkett's, the Onyx, or some other midtown watering hole to trade jokes and stories, but "the jazzbandia days were turning to history, and I wondered when a new crop of jazzbanders would arrive to carry on. How would they play? What would they strive to give an unappreciative public? What could they invent? Would there be another Bix Beiderbecke among them? Another Bill Moenkhaus?"[7]

There, at last, lies the key to such eschatological ruminations. What

Hoagy mourns here is not the death of hot music at all: that survived, flourished, for many years thereafter. His elegy is to his own youth, to the sense of wonder bestowed only in the first golden moments of discovery. Hoagland Carmichael would never again be a music-crazy youngster, bug-eyed as he listened to Howard Jordan's Louisville orchestra, to Reggie DuValle, to Hube Hanna or Batty DeMarcus—or swooning on a couch at the first notes tumbling from Bix Beiderbecke's cornet.

❊   ❊   ❊

He moved again, this time to East 57th Street. Ever self-conscious about his appearance and slight build, he began paying serious attention to his clothes. On one occasion he and Shattuck ordered full evening dress suits in midnight blue. "We went all the way: tails, white gloves, top hats, canes, the white tie, and even if we could not afford it, a flower, a white one, of course, in our buttonholes." They turned up that way at parties, on excursions to Harlem nightspots, even occasionally to the opera, "young men on the town, fresh and full of juices; even the [nineteen-]thirties didn't scare us."[8]

He especially sought out any style that would make him appear larger than his five feet, eight inches:

> I went to one of the best tailors in New York, on Fifth Avenue. I had them make me a double-breasted suit with a narrow lapel, not the wide peaked lapel that everybody else was wearing all over town; an innovation of having the overlap only four inches wide instead of the customary six or seven. This made me look taller; most of the boys were looking shorter with those fat short coats.[9]

Wad Allen, newly married, arrived in New York, and—thanks to fellow-Hoosier George Wellbaum—promptly found a job in the advertising department of the New Jersey Bell Telephone Company. Other Indiana friends followed, lured even in those dark Depression years by the promise of the big city. There were parties, double and triple dates with various girlfriends of choice, evenings of reminiscence about people and good times past, and, invariably, too much drinking. Adventures uptown usually also involved Shattuck, Shackelford (whose cousin Marjorie was Hoagy's current steady date), Burns and Lazelle Rafferty, Harry Hostetter, and other Indiana expatriates. Harry Orchard, in town on one of his frequent visits, told of accompanying Hoagy on an outing to a Westchester golf course. En route back, their cab stopped for a red light. "A young colored fellow was standing at [sic] the sidewalk near where our taxi stopped and he slowly started whistling the opening notes to Hoagy's song 'Star Dust.' Hoagy was sitting at my left in the taxi and hearing his song he grabbed my left arm in a fierce clench, saying 'I've got it! I've got it!' "[10]

Hoagy's enjoyment of city life, with all its temptations, is obvious and infectious. A song lyric idea, dashed off at about this time and preserved, unused, among his papers, puts it succinctly:

> Just gin agin, gin agin,
> Here I am drinking bathtub gin agin.
> I came to this here party thinking it would be worthwhile,
> But High and Dry and Gordon's seem to be the only style.
>
> It's gin agin, gin agin,
> It's Saturday night and I'll get tight agin.
> I had visions of red Burgundy,
> Of bubbling Champagne; but
> Here it is agin—just gin agin.[11]

He kept turning out songs. "Charlie Two-Step," though a trifle, had its moment with a witty record by the singing Boswell Sisters. Hoagy and veteran lyricist Jo Trent set words to the brooding second strain of "Barbaric," and the Casa Loma Orchestra recorded it as "In the Still of the Night," along with a concert arrangement of "Washboard Blues," featuring an expressive Connee Boswell vocal. Trent was also the lyricist for "Sing It Way Down Low," a blues-saturated number whose opening phrase brings to mind Fats Waller's 1928 "Willow Tree."

Throughout this period especially, Carmichael's love of black musical and vocal idioms is explicit and proudly displayed. A newspaper article of the time hails him as a "young man with the moaning rhythm of the Mississippi levees in his brain." Another identifies him as a "Negro blues composer." A feature in the *Indianapolis Sunday Star* discloses that his "favorite hangout is the Cotton Club" and names his three favorite musicians as Louis Armstrong, Don Redman, and Duke Ellington, whom he regards as "the king of jazz in the United States."[12]

Among the better Carmichael efforts for 1932 is "Daybreak," reflective and elegaic even in its opening phrases. Each of the song's three eight-bar episodes begins in minor and works its way gradually to a major cadence, as if light were dispelling the last moments of darkness. Each eight bars combines two four-bar sections, each with a separate thematic identity. Parsed according to theme, it could be expressed as AB, AB², CB³.

"Daybreak" (bars 1–8), 1932

An ambitious and unusual song, "Daybreak" was recorded only twice that year, first as part of a two-sided "Dance Medley of Hoagy Carmichael Compositions" commissioned by Peer and issued by Victor as a ten-inch, two-sided experimental 33⅓ rpm long-play record, again by Paul White-man's orchestra, with a fervent vocal by jazzman Red McKenzie.

❖   ❖   ❖

As that and "Lazy River" attest, Hoagy's lyric-writing skills had come a long way, though he often seemed at pains to minimize the achievement. His text for "Rockin' Chair" shows a growing skill at evocation; a yellowed typescript for "Georgia on My Mind," moreover, makes clear that though Stu Gorrell got the credit, Carmichael's was the major contribution to the text. Jo Trent's typed worksheet for "Sing It Way Down Low" (at first "Play It Way Down Low") bears many changes in Carmichael's hand, determining the form in which it went to the publisher.

The composer's papers, on file at his beloved Indiana University, include dozens of other handwritten and typed lyric worksheets, some of them instantly recognizable blueprints for well-known Carmichael songs. Many more remain just ideas, unrealized and unpublished: some are ephemeral, disposable, others good enough to have been developed into potentially excellent form.

One outstanding 1932 item is "New Orleans," celebrating another southern locale its composer had never visited. Built on the same chord sequence that underpins the bridge, or middle section, of such standards as "You Took Advantage of Me" and "Wrap Your Troubles in Dreams," it is a jazzman's melody in its shape and note choices, a sixteen-bar improvisation.

But as performed briskly on record by Bennie Moten's Kansas City band ($\downhalfnote$ = 124) and even faster by the Casa Loma Orchestra ($\downhalfnote$ = 132), it seems awkward, its sing-songy, dotted-eighth-and-sixteenth-note melody marching along with dismaying rigidity. Neither Ben Webster's rubato tenor sax solo on the Moten record nor Gene Gifford's rich scoring on the Casa Loma succeeds entirely in breaking the rhythmic lockstep.

The tempo, though all but required for dancing in 1932, was demonstrably wrong for this melody and may account for the song's failure to catch on until 1938, when the composer found his own solution: singing "New Orleans" in a recorded duet with Scottish "Highland Harlequin" Ella Logan, he slowed it down to a more leisurely $\downhalfnote$ = 96, allowing the words to elasticize the melody. That has since been the convention, producing heartfelt, even slower-tempo, records by many jazz stylists, among them—memorably—cornetist Bobby Hackett and trombone master Jack Teagarden.[13]

Especially tantalizing among the collected lyric sheets are those produced by other minds, other typewriters—but heavily edited, emended, even reinvented in Hoagy's own hand. Mute yet eloquent, they help explain why

Carmichael songs, written over nearly five decades with lyricists of differing perspectives and abilities, convey so recognizably consistent a "Carmichael sensibility." From the start, in a pattern that would recur throughout his life and in contexts far removed from songwriting, Carmichael had to be involved intimately and directly in everything he did.

Yet his lyric writing remained the most private side of his musical life. He seldom discussed it, called little attention to it, willingly ceded credit to his collaborators—or, as in the case of Stu Gorrell, just friends who happened to be around to help out. He encouraged no comparison of his skills with those of the elite he often called "the big boys"—Lorenz Hart, Ira Gershwin, Cole Porter, and, above all, Johnny Mercer.

Born in Savannah, ten years Carmichael's junior, John Herndon Mercer had arrived in New York in 1927, crazy for hot music—especially as played by Bix and Tram—and dreaming about a career on the stage. When the latter showed no sign of materializing he turned to songwriting, placing a maiden effort called "Out of Breath (and Scared to Death of You)" in a 1930 *Garrick Gaieties* revue. Among his other early endeavors was the light-hearted "Would'ja for a Big Red Apple?" Its opening lines are a harbinger of things to come:

> Greater men than I have sought your favor,
> But you merely glance at them and grin,
> You spurn the vermin,
> Who offer ermine and just a bit of sin.

The four-part play with the "in" endings, interlocked with the pairing—effective in its incongruity—of first-syllable "vermin" and "ermine" within, suggests a subtle ear, a sense of the relative weights and connotations of words.

In later years no one could quite remember how, or exactly when, Mercer and Carmichael met: Hoagy thought the intermediary was a "professional manager" at Southern Music, or perhaps a song-plugger. Mercer himself remembered a man named Eddie Wood, a friend of Peer house arranger Archie Bleyer, whose "Business in F," an instrumental in the question-and-answer Casa Loma style, had been widely played and recorded. Trumbauer, who featured Mercer's agitated scat singing on an April 1932 record date, may have mentioned Carmichael.

Whatever the circumstances, Mercer's reaction was immediate and enthusiastic. "I leapt at the chance to write with Hoagy," he wrote in an unpublished autobiography. "He proved an understanding, sympathetic friend and teacher . . . When I say teacher, I mean just that; he broadened my ability with his knowledge and experience." Later in the same manuscript, however, he reveals that the "teacher" often proved a stern taskmaster. "He is such a gifted lyric writer on his own, that I felt intimidated much of the time and tightened up too much to do my best work."[14]

Hoagy, for his part, remembered "a young, bouncy butterball of a man from Georgia. He hadn't had a song hit, but I could tell that he could write . . . [and] I was impressed by his personality."[15]

They hit it off and agreed to try collaborating. A first effort, "After Twelve O'Clock," with lyrics credited to a pseudonymous "Joe Moore" (the initials give it away) appeared and disappeared in short order. "Thanksgivin'," celebrating the wonders of newfound love, fared a bit better, especially after a spirited Casa Loma record.[16]

Mercer, meanwhile, entered one of the weekly "Youth of America" contests held at NBC's Times Square studio, the former New Amsterdam Roof Theatre. Sponsored by Pontiac automobiles and hosted by Paul Whiteman, it was basically a radio talent search, each week's winner getting a shot at performing with Whiteman's orchestra. With Bleyer at the piano, the twenty-three-year-old Georgian sang two songs, and Whiteman, ever astute, took note: by early 1934 John Mercer was earning seventy-five dollars a week as a staff songwriter and "hot" vocalist for the "King of Jazz."[17]

As show business folklore has it, the Carmichael-Mercer partnership went into gear one afternoon in 1933 when the Georgia boy climbed the stairs to the Indiana boy's apartment and announced that he felt like writing a song he wanted to call "Lazybones." The idea seemed straightforward enough: an older, wiser figure (father, mother, grandparent, uncle, aunt) remonstrates, affectionately, with a lad who'd rather while the days away in idleness than do a lick of work.[18]

Hoagy ever after declared that they knocked out the song in twenty minutes. "Just now wrote 'Lazybones,' " he says in a letter to an unidentified journalist. "All of a sudden like. That's when they're best." Mercer's own account, recollected in tranquility and just a bit more plausible, testifies that "Hoagy . . . suffered through long months of waiting until I came up with the lyrics of 'Thanksgiving,' and finally, 'Lazybones.' "[19]

The dialect used in "Lazybones" makes clear that the boy they depict is black, thereby tapping into an issue that has complicated recent attempts to deal with songs of this period. Some, listening today, find such portrayals patronizing, grounded in a racial stereotype now considered demeaning. Various scholars and historians have expressed mild discomfort, others angry condemnation: Roger Hewitt, for example, accuses Carmichael (and, by extension, Mercer) of "cultural reproduction of racism." More than a few latter-day performers, as conscious as politicians of their constituencies, have tiptoed carefully around "Lazybones" in scheduling Mercer and Carmichael programs.[20]

Such thinking seems rooted in the premise that social and political attitudes of the present can be applied freely in judgment of the past. A contrary viewpoint, expressed by historian Barbara Tuchman and others, suggests that "[t]o understand the choices open to people of another time, one must limit one's self to what they knew: see the past in its own clothes, as it were, not in ours."[21]

Beyond dispute, some of the lyrics *do* employ racial stereotypes. Hoagy's 1933 "Old Man Harlem," listing radio crooner Rudy Vallee as lyricist, refers to uptown nightlife as a (benignly) corrupting influence. "Lazybones," its melody derived from a phrase in Hoagy's "Washboard Blues" piano interlude, became controversial largely through Mercer's words—though, as postmodernist New York scholar Krin Gabbard reminds us, "Carmichael certainly did not disown them."[22]

"It was the coin of the day, the way people talked," said Hoagy Bix Carmichael. "It was part of our world. Nobody *likes* it . . . But the lyrics weren't meant to be in any way deprecating, or 'dissing' anybody . . . Today, when people jump on a couple of those tunes—and I know they do— because of the lyric, I think they have to consider the context, the years, and above all the way other black people felt about my father. It wasn't 'Here comes Hoagy with another one of those Stepin Fetchit songs of his.' It was 'Hey, Hoag, whatcha got?' "[23]

Newspaper columnist Carl Rowan, black and southern born, summed it up best. "As a boy of eight in Tennessee," he said in 1976, "wading barefoot in a creek looking under rocks for crawfish, I learned about 'the work ethic' from Johnny Mercer. I truly believed he was telling me something when I sang lines from his 'Lazybones' . . . Now, it seems, Americans learn about the work ethic only from politicians who seek power by berating welfare recipients."[24]

Changing political fashion later forced the transformation of the "color[ed] man" of "Hong Kong Blues" into a "Memphis man," and the "little colored boy" of a later collaboration with Mercer into a "little Harlem boy" and ultimately the all but meaningless "swingin' little boy." As late as 1999 a prominent operatic soprano refused to sing "Washboard Blues" in an all-Carmichael concert program because it was a "dialect song."

If the young scamp of "Lazybones" *is* black, what of it? Does Mercer's lyric endorse, even for a moment, any notion that *all* black youngsters are layabouts? Certainly not. Similarly, it is hardly demeaning to identify the narrator of "Rockin' Chair" or "Washboard Blues" as a black man or woman; resignation and reminiscence, suffering and despair, are universal. Race, in this context, is less a political statement than a simple identification, not meant to carry social baggage.

Typically, Carmichael's melody for "Lazybones" begins like a jazz improvisation:

"Lazybones" (bars 1–4), 1933

He makes affectionate use of the word "lazybones" in his own lyric to "Snowball," which precedes the effort with Mercer and may have in some way inspired it. Sung by an obviously black father to his "baby boy," it's a tender little lullaby without a trace of condescension:

> Snowball, my honey, don't you melt away,
> 'Cause daddy likes those dark brown eyes.
> Snowball, my honey, smile at me each day,
> 'Cause daddy likes those dark brown eyes.
> You're my only sweetheart, little chocolate bar,
> I'll eat you up some day.
> Your two hands and feet are just as black as tar,
> But don't you cry. Why, say:
> The good Lord said he used an apple dumplin'
> To make your head; you know that's really sumpin'.
> Snowball, my honey, don't you melt away,
> 'Cause daddy likes those dark brown eyes.

Louis Armstrong, who premiered many Carmichael songs in his concerts and records of the 1930s, recorded "Snowball" first, affectionately, in January of 1933. Mildred Bailey, recording it eight months later (three months after doing "Lazybones"), paints a vivid portrait of parental love. A week later Carmichael himself did it for Victor, along with "Lazybones." These two performances were among his best on record so far, vocals confident and convincing, alternately chiding and consoling. Even his intonation was improving. His piano backing, deft and assured, had far outdistanced the wavering featherduster touch he remembered from his early Florida encounter with Irving Berlin.

For all that, "Snowball" remains unperformed today, consigned to an artistic no-man's-land created by retrospective political judgment.

*   *   *

That summer, and a now-regular flow of song royalties, brought Hoagy what he later called "a two-bit, six-week tour of Europe," in company with Marge Everson, Bill Shattuck, and Shattuck's girlfriend of the time. His passport, still intact, bears entry stamps for England, France, Switzerland, Italy, and a few more exotic destinations, among them Hungary and Romania. From his own accounts, the Indiana boy had the time of his life. "In Budapest," he writes, "we walked into the best night club, the New York Café, dressed up to the teeth and as we entered the orch[estra] was playing 'March of the Hoodlums.' Didn't know the song was out . . . Heard one clarinetist in Budapest who would have been great in this country. That was all. But was impressed by young people's interest in jazz. More than this country maybe."[25]

Arriving home, he found to his astonishment that "Lazybones" had ridden to success in what a later age would have called a "media blitz." Walter Winchell was plugging it relentlessly in print and on the air. From coast to coast, stores had affixed the name "Lazybones" to everything from sport shoes to patio furniture: Franklin Simon, one of Fifth Avenue's classiest shopping destinations, was proclaiming itself "first to present LAZY BONES, our exclusive nightgown and bed jacket set." Cartoonists were using the term to chide Washington for laggardly implementation of various New Deal programs.

A nineteen-year-old Kentucky medical student named Charles Foster

Egolf made momentary headlines by claiming to be the real composer of "Lazybones"—until a letter from Ralph Peer to his hometown newspaper deflated his case. United Press reported from Germany that Adolf Hitler's new Nazi regime, dismayed at the growing popularity of what it considered a "Nigger song," had banned "Lazybones" because it "encourages idleness and does not conform to Nazi ideals."

According to Peer, "Lazybones" was selling fifteen thousand sheet music copies a day and being sung regularly on the radio by the likes of Kate Smith and Rudy Vallee. "Johnny and I were made," says Carmichael—but adds that, however musically compatible the two might have been, their partnership had already hit some bumps: "We didn't get along so well . . . I guess the main trouble was [that] I considered him my helper. I got most [of the] credit because of [my] established name."[26]

In a later memo, he admits to thinking "that I was more informed and more worldly-wise than Johnny, being older. I don't think he liked or took it in the right spirit. [I] am sure now that my conception of property rights and values was unfortunate." Mercer, in his unpublished autobiography, takes a rather mellower view: "Have you ever had a tough teacher whom you appreciated later? That's how it was to write with Hoagy."[27]

Carmichael mentions a meeting under the auspices of ASCAP, then barely a decade old, implying some dispute between himself and Mercer over "Lazybones." He'd always considered himself a fair man, he says, adding rather cryptically that "maybe fairness went both ways in my mind." Slightly clearer is a passage in *Sometimes I Wonder*, in which he confesses, "The conventional rules of conduct, even in business dealings, I'd throw aside when the going got tough or when I got overanxious . . . I needed to make money in those early years. It was the tangible reward we were judged by. Young men mistake rewards for progress. I did."[28]

"Lazybones" won a $2,500 ASCAP Special Dividend Award for 1933, selling a whopping 350,000 copies in three months. Exhilarated, they split it fifty-fifty. But for a while at least, the Carmichael-Mercer relationship, to borrow Hoagy's word, "drifted," and "our next efforts were not so good." Surely such efforts as "Down t' Uncle Bill's" and "Old Skipper" do not rank high among either man's accomplishments. Meanwhile, Hoagy's own "In the Churchyard," an attempt to recycle the melody of the luckless "One Night in Havana," fell flat (even with radio plugs from ever-loyal Paul Whiteman), as did "Give Me Tonight," based on a Gypsy melody he'd heard in Europe, with a lyric by British bandleader Lew Stone. "Poor Old Joe" never quite got off the ground, even helped by a spirited Fletcher Henderson record.

A reunion with Mitchell Parish, who had done so well by him with "Star Dust," yielded "One Morning in May," cited by the composer ever after as his (and his mother's) favorite among his own songs. Its melody spans sixty-four hymn-like bars, its long notes and wide intervals reminiscent of such Jerome Kern theatre masterpieces as "Make Believe." From its opening phrase,

"One Morning in May" (bars 1–4), 1933

it invokes and evokes customs and flavors of times past, the more leisurely pace of old-fashioned courtship. Music and lyric are matched perfectly, Parish's imagery amplifying and illuminating Hoagy's expansive melody. When the bridge, for example, tells us of "Kisses that came with the flame of springtime," the melody line, appropriately, soars up a major sixth:

"One Morning in May" (bars 33–40), 1933

As Alec Wilder comments in *American Popular Song*, "Were Carmichael's name not on the cover, I'd be puzzled as to which theatre writer had composed it ... [and] would not be surprised to learn that [it] had been written to be the 'big ballad' for a show which never materialized. It's a beauty."[29]

The composer shared that view. "I was highly pleased, and then I knew that I might have something pretty big as a melody, a big melody that could have gone into a big show," he said in a radio interview. Not long after writing the song, he dropped in at a midtown musicians' hangout, perhaps Jimmy Plunkett's, and cornered Mildred Bailey and Roy Bargy, both of them members of Paul Whiteman's orchestra. "Hoag, you got something real nice there" was the pianist's immediate response to the new tune.[30]

Carmichael went to Chicago to record "One Morning" with a quintet of old Indiana pals: Andy Van Sickle, on drums, and cousin Fred "Yah" Murray, on trumpet, had played on the 1928 "March of the Hoodlums" session at Gennett, and celebratory libations flowed freely. Perhaps a bit too freely: a couple of bourbons apparently went right to Murray's embouchure, and in Hoagy's words, "his lips went flabby." Perhaps ill-advisedly, they take "One Morning in May" as a jazz instrumental—and Murray does seem to be struggling.[31]

The session opener was something Hoagy had devised in 1928, a jam tune based on an unconventional descending chord pattern. Hoagy called it "Judy"—though Wad Allen, tickled by its "weird" chord movement, had nicknamed it "Birdseed." The band plays it crisply, and Carmichael's half-chorus piano solo blends unusual voicings with some rolling, almost Earl Hines–like, left-hand figures. But the record was never issued, presumably because Elvan "Fuzzy" Combs, on alto sax, is overbalanced throughout. "Judy" had to wait another five months before being published and recorded in New York, with a fetching lyric by Sammy Lerner, perhaps best known for "Is It True What They Say About Dixie?"

"Judy" also enjoys two sidelong distinctions. According to most accounts, its title helped prompt young Frances "Baby" Gumm, hoping for a career in the movies, to change her name to Judy Garland. It is also what a teenage Ella Fitzgerald was singing in a talent contest at Harlem's Apollo Theatre, imitating the style of Connee Boswell, when Benny Carter heard her and started talking her up to other Harlem bandleaders. Chick Webb soon took her on, starting her along her road to stardom.

❖   ❖   ❖

Alongside the songwriting, another aspect of Hoagy Carmichael's talent had surfaced. Paul Summers, a Kappa Sig brother who later worked for Jim Bingham's Indianapolis law firm, caught an early glimpse of it. In New York for an ASCAP meeting, he found the lawyer-turned-songwriter in "golf clothes (knickers) in his stocking feet, and with score sheets of music on or around the piano, ashtrays filled with burned-out cigarettes, and dishes evidencing 3 or 4 meals without washing . . . working on a semi-classic number to be entered in some Boston music competition."[32]

Carmichael set great store by this piece, which he'd titled *Phrases*; and that may be the ideal name for its series of rhythmic piano figures, over an ostinato bass falling somewhere between boogie-woogie and a *faux*–American Indian rhythm. Here and there, especially in a developed middle strain, there are passages briefly reminiscent of Bix's *Flashes*—as if Hoagy were momentarily remembering his departed friend. In a 1933 letter to Cincinnati fan Tom Adler, Carmichael calls the piece "my attempt at a new style of jazz. No set melody—just a group of phrases and a heavy background rhythm such as in the Bolero."[33]

Paul Whiteman took an interest, commissioning arranger Carroll Huxley to prepare *Phrases* to be played by the full Whiteman instrumentation. The name was changed, first to *Bolero*, then finally to *Cosmics*. All three titles are found on surviving orchestral parts, indicating that the relabelings may have gone on during rehearsals. Huxley's score, moreover, includes the notation to "write two piano parts"—indicating the possibility that Carmichael was to join regular pianist Roy Bargy in performing the work. A simplified orchestral tympani part also bears the composer's name, presumably as an auxiliary player.[34]

The degree to which Hoagy Carmichael cared about this "serious" piece emerges from Paul Summers's recollection: "Prior to my visit [he] had made a soft record of the composition. It had been criticized by a prominent critic (Deems Taylor, as I remember). As I sat listening he went to the record player and as the record was played he explained the motif of the number, indicating the parts needing the change. Then he went back to the piano and . . . interposed the changes worked out."[35]

According to Carmichael, Whiteman scheduled *Phrases* for a Carnegie Hall concert. If the Summers visit was in mid- to late 1932 the reference could be to the fifth "Experiment in Modern Music," given at Carnegie January 25, 1933. If the visit was later, the concert was perhaps the sixth, at first intended for Carnegie Hall presentation on December 15, 1933, but later moved to the Metropolitan Opera House. Whichever the case, *Cosmics* was dropped at the last minute, premiered instead at one of Whiteman's new Sunday evening concerts in the Cascade Room of the Biltmore Hotel. The composer gives no hint of what must have been substantial disappointment.[36]

Nor was the experimentation suggested in this piece an isolated effort. Three acetate discs, recorded close to this time and later found among Carmichael's effects, find him at the piano, probing territory even farther beyond that of the popular songs. Labeled *Echo[es] of the Opera*, his more or less continuous musical free-association contains few explicitly rhythmic passages, instead allowing expansive thematic material to rise from the pianistics. A musical reverie, an anomaly for the Hoagland Carmichael of 1933–34, it bespeaks the influence of the French Impressionists, and frequently the broader pianistic approach of Sergei Rachmaninoff, so beloved of Hollywood film-score composers.[37]

✻   ✻   ✻

Whatever popularity "Lazybones" may have achieved, the Carmichael-Mercer partnership enjoyed its first full flowering and showed the breadth of its potential in another, slightly later song. "Moon Country" appeared in early 1934 and is in every sense a union of two compatible and complementary sensibilities. A hymn to home, it casts a longing glance back at an age already vanishing when Hoagland Carmichael and John Mercer were boys, and an America still largely agrarian in character. The Industrial Revolution had not yet touched this imaginary landscape or its people. No matter that the composer had grown up in Indiana, the lyricist in Georgia, or that the lyric refers to a "sycamore heaven back South," a heaven that may never have existed in this form for either man. This idealized Elysium transcends geography and hard reality; it is what singer Barbara Lea, a faithful interpreter of both writers, wisely calls "generic home," immune to time or despoilment.

"Change is the enemy of everything really worth cherishing," the New England writer Howard Phillips Lovecraft wrote to a friend at almost exactly the same time. "It is the remover of landmarks, the destroyer of all which is homelike and comforting, and the constant symbol and reminder of decay and death. It is change which makes one old before his time by snatching away everything he has known, and substituting a new environment to which he can never become adjusted."[38]

Lovecraft's words précis the thought behind "Moon Country" almost exactly. From its very first line,

> I know where the peach trees bear a harvest
> All the year 'round,

every image in Mercer's lyric evokes some idealized home. The gray mare grazes peacefully, and the land affords both sustenance and contentment. Moonlight through the pines, lazy river flowing serenely by. A rocking chair, emblem of solace and peace of mind, waiting on some shady verandah, as an old hymn, played on the parlor piano, wafts across a breeze at dusk. The apple pie tastes good beyond words, as it must have done when Grandma Robison served it to a lonely little boy returning to Bloomington from exile in wintry Montana.

"Moon Country" cemented a musical partnership unlike any American popular music had yet seen. The two men sensed in one another a longing for an idealized America outside the burgeoning cities—a pastoral place in which even romantic love, so often cast as the *sine qua non* of popular song, played no unduly inflated role. Hoagy's music, said Mercer, "is just American. It's home stuff. It sounds like the South, like Indiana, like any other place we used to know." Meredith Willson, another songwriter in tune with the rhythms and cadences of Middle America, called it "our folk music of tomorrow."[39]

Both Carmichael and Mercer, of course, went on to write successfully with other collaborators, and Mercer's adaptability and eloquence soon proclaimed him a poet laureate among American lyricists. But it is hard to resist Indiana historian Duncan Schiedt when he reflects, "It would be interesting to see the output of these two men had they remained full partners in music, in the manner of Rodgers and Hart, or the Gershwins."[40]

Carmichael agreed. With guidance and diligent work, he wrote, "Johnny and I could have flooded the market with hit songs. We were atune and I knew he 'knew' and he knew I 'knew.' But the chips didn't fall right. Probably my fault because I didn't handle them gently."

A brief passage excised from the final manuscript of *Sometimes I Wonder* puts that remark in better focus: "When we wrote *Moon Country*, there was a question in my mind as to who wrote what. I had done most of the writing, as I recalled it. When it came time to make up the contract I said to Ralph Peer, the publisher: 'I think this is the way it should be divied [*sic*] up, I should get so much for what I did and Johnny should get so much for what he did.' "[41]

"Moon Country" remains a musical still-life, a captured moment, a summing-up; idealization and artifact, it resists age, mortality, attrition. For Hoagy Carmichael especially, it defines home, and he returned there— as he returned to his beloved Indiana—again and again for the rest of his days.

✳ *XI* ✳

Bread, Gravy, and Cream

Eva Ford replaced the telephone receiver and stood for a moment, lost in thought. A songwriter, newly discharged from Flowers Fifth Avenue Hospital, needed home care. One of her friends, a nurse, had been offered the job but couldn't take it. Would Eva fill in for her?

She'd come down to New York after graduation from high school in Cambridge, near Boston, to take up nursing, and this was definitely a nursing opportunity: she couldn't very well turn it down without at least giving it a chance.

Still, he was a single white man, living alone. Attending him would mean going to his East Side apartment every day, often working late hours. Her father, especially strict since her mother's death, was bound to view that as a breach of propriety for a carefully brought-up young black woman. Shaking off such misgivings, Eva took a bus downtown to Flowers, to discuss the case with resident physician Dr. Frank Borrelli.

"He was my sounding board," she said. "I'd talked to him about the nursing profession before. Right off, I said I didn't think my family would approve of this arrangement, but he said he'd talk to them—and he did. In the end they came to an understanding. I needed the money to help get my tuition to go to [nursing] school, so in the end I did it."[1]

So it happened that one late summer day in 1935, Eva Ford, age twenty, rang the doorbell at 121 East 52nd Street and met Hoagland Howard "Hoagy" Carmichael. A severe stomach ulcer had laid him up for a few days at Flowers and all but grounded him for the next few weeks. Writing in *Sometimes I Wonder*, Carmichael says his ailment "was called a heart attack by some, but may have been only indigestion," after eating at a Swedish restaurant with visiting Indiana friend Hank Wells. Proximate cause, perhaps, but ulcers don't happen overnight. A more likely diagnosis, Eva suspected, was too much round-the-clock high living.[2]

Halfway between Park and Lexington, the flat was small but comfortable, a second-floor walkup with high ceilings, marble fireplace, a terrace—and, in the center, a grand piano. Sheet music and records were stacked everywhere. In an unpublished first draft of *Sometimes I Wonder,* he refers to it as his "dream apartment," adding that "my friend Dick Huber moved in to help me pay for it, and it was wonderful for parties, for girls, for playing my tunes and other people's tunes. The girls were models and show girls, and we were young and human. And friendly, very friendly.

"I can't say it [was] all like in the books and movies of the period. First of all I was busy writing my tunes, and at parties I was usually at the piano, and there was in me this drive; and girls were only part of it. When it was the girl *or* the song, the song often won out."[3]

Eva's family was musical, and she knew Carmichael's name as the composer of "Star Dust." But all that was secondary to the patient himself, a small bundle of nervous energy, thin to the point of emaciation. Whatever you do, Borrelli had said, keep him still. Don't let him get up. Make sure he takes his medicine and observes a careful diet. No exertion. No coffee or cigarettes, and absolutely no liquor.

"He didn't like the idea of being sick, not one bit," she said. "Sickness was a dirty word to him, and I had my hands full keeping him out of trouble. He was very stubborn, especially about getting to the piano. There'd be a tune hummin' in his head, he'd say, and he just had to reach that piano: that's how he did his music. He might have been sick, but in his mind he was still working, had to get that music out. Sometimes the doctor would [come and] order him to stay in bed; and he'd say yes yes, wait till the doctor left, then get up and over to the piano, and [play] until he was satisfied—and then get all dizzy, and I'd have to help him back to the bed."[4]

Eva stood her ground: music or no music, this troublesome little man would have to behave, stay in bed. If not, there would be no more trips to the piano, and that was that. Nurse and patient quickly took each other's measure, developing a wary sort of mutual respect; and when it emerged that they shared a November 22 birthday, a bond was sealed which was to last the rest of their lives.

It took Eva only a few days to conclude that her charge must be someone special in his end of the music business. Friends phoning and dropping by at all hours included Louis Armstrong, Mildred Bailey and Red Norvo, Jimmy and Tommy Dorsey, George Gershwin—even the magisterial Duke Ellington, star of the Cotton Club.

Hoagy Carmichael had joined a songwriting elite, even being feted at one of the celebrity-studded Sunday evening parties hosted by Jules Glaenzer, a vice president of Cartier's. Aptly named (from a German word meaning "gleaming"), Glaenzer had run such end-of-weekend affairs since the 1920s, bringing together prominent people from entertainment, sport, art, politics, and high society, all amid impeccably luxurious surroundings. Frequent guests at his 417 Park Avenue home included Gershwin, Charles Chaplin, Douglas Fairbanks, Jascha Heifetz, Maurice Chevalier, Noël Coward, Gertrude Lawrence, Paul Whiteman, Fred Astaire, and beloved Irish tenor John McCormack. To Gershwin, he was "one of the most famous hosts on two continents"—reference to the fact that Glaenzer maintained a sumptuous apartment in Paris and entertained there as well. As one Gershwin biographer put it, "Glaenzer collected celebrities the way others collected great works of art."[5]

Covering Hoagy's induction into the Glaenzer circle, society reporter Harry Evans reported that the newcomer played and sang several of his own songs, including "Star Dust" and "Washboard Blues," the latter "one of the most original blues songs ever written." He then went on to introduce "Judy" and "Moon Country," part of whose lyric Evans quotes inaccurately, and with no mention of Johnny Mercer.

"No person in the room was more interested in Hoagy's playing and singing than George Gershwin, nor was anyone more appreciative of his work," says the reporter. "Why a Hoosier should be able to capture the spirit of negro music so completely is difficult to understand." Gershwin, still immersed in what was shortly to become *Porgy and Bess*, had spent two months on Folly Island, off South Carolina, listening to and absorbing that same "spirit of negro music." "You've got it, Hoagy!" was his exultant reaction to Carmichael's performance. Hoagy quickly returned the compliment, asking Gershwin if he'd treat the gathering to excerpts from the still-unfinished *Porgy*. To general delight and astonishment he obliged, after having steadfastly refused to preview the work-in-progress for anyone else.[6]

Gershwin plays a uniquely contradictory role in Carmichael's life. In Hoagy's eyes he appeared to be everything the young Hoosier was not: musically trained, a flashily accomplished pianist, operating with equal ease as both songwriter and composer of "serious" music; and, into the bargain, a natural entertainer, relaxed and gregarious in playing for guests in even the most auspicious surroundings. In Gershwin's presence, Carmichael seemed unable to shrug off a nagging sense of inadequacy, not unlike what had haunted his friend Bix. Had all his good luck been just a fluke? Were his skills gimcrack, fraudulent? Would he someday, somehow, be found out, exposed as a charlatan and publicly shamed, suffering by contrast with Gershwin, so obviously the "real thing"?[7]

Sylvester Ahola, a skilled dance band trumpeter who worked alongside Beiderbecke in Adrian Rollini's 1927 band, remembered meeting his sectionmate and praising the cornetist's lyrical, ringing solos. To Ahola's astonishment, Bix (who knew no theory, read music haphazardly, and even conceived of his B♭ cornet in concert C) seemed embarrassed, averting his gaze and muttering, "Hell, I'm only a musical degenerate."[8]

Hoagy later affirmed that it took him years to accept his own talents, to stop being intimidated by the bravado and sophistication of others. "I'd say I've always been what you might call a runner," he said. "Run here, run there, run after this and run after that, and yes—running scared most of the time. [I was] scared, never sure, whether I could write a good song or not... Will it last? Or am I just one of the passing freaks, like flagpole sitters or channel swimmers?"[9]

In the end, in common with many gifted autodidacts, Hoagy drew strength from his faith in the correctness of intuition. Just as he *knew*—regardless why—the first four notes Bix played in his presence were what he'd been waiting to hear, he became equally confident, in the end, about his own musical utterances. Finally he acknowledged that "I was on my way and [knew that] practically any song I wrote would be published."[10]

Eva, meanwhile, saw to it that his convalescence went well. Even an anticipated crisis at Thanksgiving time was happily averted: she'd celebrated every year with the family, but despaired of getting away from her pint-sized charge—until her father, grasping the problem, arranged for a full turkey dinner, with trimmings, to be delivered to 121 East 52nd Street. "Every once in awhile they'd send Sunday dinner, too," said Eva. "Massachusetts people are old-fashioned that way, and they have to have Sunday dinner no matter what. After church you came home; the table was set, and you sat down and ate dinner."[11]

✻   ✻   ✻

One of the perquisites of success, Hoagy Carmichael had discovered, was access to beautiful and stylish women: models, actresses, socialites—those usually glimpsed only in the company of rich, powerful men. Hoagy, who by his own testimony had never had much luck with the opposite sex, took eagerly to this "fine, healthy, well-stacked lot." In *Sometimes I Wonder* and elsewhere, he speaks of double-dating with various friends, including Dick Huber and Bill Shattuck; for a while he dated Chicago radio actress Doris Gillen, then appearing on the daily soap opera *The Story of Mary Marlin*. Eva, ever discreet, confirmed only that there were indeed women—but otherwise disclaimed any specific knowledge.

Still, Carmichael was surprised one evening to answer the phone and find himself talking to a woman with a particularly melodious voice. "You probably won't remember me," she began, "but we met at a dance at the Kappa Sig house about six years ago. I'm Helen Meinardi." The name rang no bells, but he wasn't about to admit that. "Are you beautiful?" was his impulsive question. Yes, she said, thereby winning herself an invitation to the East 52nd Street apartment.

She was indeed lovely. Born in Chicago, daughter of a Presbyterian minister, Helen Meinardi had attended the Lucy Cobb Finishing School in Georgia and gone on to Indiana University. She'd heard Carmichael's Collegians play at a dance at Purdue, and at a party afterwards had sat next to Hoagy on the piano bench. She'd even heard Bix and the Wolverines, she said, playing a dance at Richmond under the auspices of Gennett Records.[12]

She'd spent time in California, determined to break into movies. The first time she visited the set of an MGM musical, she said, "they had an orchestra [and] . . . during some of the long waits [between shots] the orchestra would play and some of us would get up and dance . . . The director noticed my sister and me and asked what the step was that we were doing . . . I said it was the 'Hoosier Hop' because it was the way we danced in Indiana. Well, he sent for the producer and then he sent for the people from the music department, and the upshot of that was that the production number of the movie was to be called *The Hoosier Hop*—very exciting; we were walking on air when we went home."

Not for long. "How much did they pay you?" a family friend asked. Pay? They'd never thought of that—the idea that a studio might actually *pay* someone for an idea.

Back she headed the following day, determined to put her case to no less a personage than Irving Thalberg. At Metro in those days, getting to see Hollywood's boy wonder, vice president to MGM founder Louis B. Mayer, was considered just a bit tougher than climbing Mount Everest in shorts and tennis shoes. As Neal Gabler has put it, "Waiting to see Thalberg was an endurance test to which all MGM employees were regularly subjected." More than one prominent movieland figure cooled his heels for days before being ushered into Thalberg's office, where "it took only thirty seconds or so for the Thalberg charm and the Thalberg praise . . . to heal all wounds."[13]

High or low, insider or outsider, all Hollywood knew and revered Thalberg's quiet nature; his visionary, even idealistic, ideas about the cinema set him apart from Mayer, the brothers Warner, Harry Cohn, and the other studio pashas. He "had a theory that film was a form, an art form on its own and it shouldn't have to depend on books or anything else or any other kind of creative work, that things should be directly written for film."

After talking her way through the front gate, she spied a group of well-dressed men chatting, barged right up, and announced herself—and her intention of bearding the great Thalberg in his lair. After a stunned silence, a small, pale man detached himself from the group and turned to face her. "I'm Thalberg," he said with what looked like quiet amusement. "What can I do for you?" Unintimidated, she stated her case strongly and with a forthrightness that clearly intrigued Hollywood's "Little Prince." To her astonishment, she got paid, landed work writing dialogue for screenplays—and was even offered a screen test. The studio was looking for a certain kind of beauty, she was told, a younger woman to compete with Ann Harding, elegant leading lady of such box office hits as *Condemned, Devotion,* and the western *The Conquerors.*

Now, back in New York, she'd begun to pick up quality work as a radio scriptwriter. "Why don't you model?" a friend had suggested, and made an appointment for her with John Robert Powers. "Things went a lot easier for me because I was young and pretty, but [I] wasn't in the 'pretty business,' " she said. It took only one interview with Powers to get the model agency kingpin so intrigued by the girl's beauty, insouciance, and obvious intelligence that he phoned his friend MacLelland Barclay. "I have a real Barclay Girl for you," he told the illustrator. "You've got to see her."

Like Charles Dana Gibson before him, illustrator Barclay was best known for idealized, yet realistic, portraits of beautiful women. Where the "Gibson Girl"—hair upswept, chin lifted, expression slightly haughty—had left her mark on the century's first decades, and the flat-chested, bobbed-hair "flapper" on the 1920s, the "Barclay Girl" became the new American ideal for the early 1930s, "a combination of—not sophistication, but almost wholesomeness and sexiness," said Helen. "It's a wonderful combination, and he got it into everything."[14]

Dazzled by her good looks, obvious intelligence, and confident manner, Barclay put her to work at once—and, soon enough thereafter, asked her out socially. Before long they'd become, in the shorthand of the time, "an item."

And, ironically, it was "Mac" who first let her know Hoagy Carmichael was in town, and "Mac" who wanted to meet him. Did she know him? Sure, said Helen, and picked up the phone. At the back of her mind, she later confessed, was a personal, even professional, interest. A capable pianist herself, she'd thought now and then about writing a lyric or two for fellow-Hoosier Carmichael, whose songs had been all the rage back in Bloomington.

Naturally, the moment Hoagy set eyes on her he asked her out—a feint she deftly and smilingly parried by mentioning her romantic association with Barclay. And there things stood until late 1935, when Helen's mother died and kid sister Ruth came to New York to live with her. "I thought she ought to have her own friends who might be . . . well, to me there is always something sort of, always kind of wholesome about Indiana people; unlike other people, they can go to New York and live there for years and never get sophisticated. So I called [Hoag] and took her over to meet him."[15]

In *Sometimes I Wonder*, Carmichael says he met Ruth through her friend Annabelle Utter Graham, a fellow–Indiana alumna, who worked in the show at Billy Rose's Music Hall, recorded once with Benny Goodman's first band, and was an occasional George Gershwin date. But Helen Meinardi insisted categorically that it was she who introduced the couple. However it happened, there is no doubting that Hoagy the confirmed bachelor was much taken with the twenty-two-year-old "kid sister." Petite, viviacious, with large, soft brown eyes and a complexion that quickly revealed why her friends called her "Cream," she quite unhinged him. "I overdid it a bit," he confessed. "Managed to emulate a second-rate gangster" and poured her a straight shot of bourbon with a side-of-mouth "Down this one, sister."

Helen remembered it differently, and perhaps somewhat more plausibly. "He was at the piano," she said in 1996. "So Hoag said, 'Fix yourselves a drink, I'll be there in a minute,' because he'd hit a phrase on the piano and he was working on it. So he came over after a while—[but] all that didn't set very well with my sister. When we left she said, 'That's the rudest man I've ever met.' " Hoagy remembered that part, at least, the same way. "She thought me rude and rather uncouth," he said, and "I was."

In Hoagy Bix Carmichael's view that defined the real difference between the sisters: "Helen was the go-getter, the worker bee. My mother was the queen. It was that way all their lives."[16]

Helen laughed out loud at the memory of that long-ago moment. "It was just like a Hollywood movie: she couldn't stand him—and they fell in love, and surprised themselves and everybody else by getting married."[17]

They began keeping company. When Ann Graham, by this time Ruth's roommate at the Barbizon women's residence hotel, went to Europe with a show, Hoagy and Ruth spent even more time together and "became very fond of each other, the usual result, I am told, of being young and meeting often." He "admired her looks, walk, talk, wit, charm, vitality: I liked being with her, wanted to be with her when I wasn't, and I thought about her when I should have been working." But, he's also quick to add, he wasn't ready to contemplate marriage: Ruth "made me think of domestic life and I resented it a bit; I was having so much fun as a bachelor."[18]

Nevertheless, the nascent friendship soon developed into something deeper. Ruth "was quite a lady," said Eva. "Her father was a minister, and she'd been raised along those lines. She was staying at the Barbizon, and told me all about things that happened there—about all the rules, and the way the girls got around them. I liked her." Always clothes-conscious, Hoagy started showing even greater attention to his appearance, polishing and augmenting his social graces. Almost overnight, he began taking an interest in tennis. The couple was seen at El Morocco and "21" and turned up together at more than one of Glaenzer's soirees. Their circle of friends broadened steadily to include figures from the New York Social Register and café society. And everywhere they went, Hoagy would invariably gravitate to the piano.

"I've said it a million times and I'll say it again," said Helen. "There was nobody that could touch Hoagy entertaining in the living room. It was just great: [he had] a habit of picking out some babe at every party and having her come sit beside him—but it wasn't that: you wanted to hear him, is all. I know it's difficult for people today to realize that you didn't go to bed with a guy the minute you met him; it wasn't that way in those days. We were enjoying, truly enjoying, the music . . . He'd play into the morning hours, you know—and when you're young, sleeping is such a waste of time and you stayed out most of the night if you could."[19]

Born in Edison, Illinois, just outside Chicago, Ruth Mary Meinardi had followed her sister through Lucy Cobb, attended the University of Georgia, studied some art along the way. She, too, had sat for Barclay, who saw qualities in her quite different from her sister's pristine beauty. "Mac loved Mom's look," Hoagy Bix Carmichael confirmed. "She was, had the look of being, this little dreamer girl: you know, the world was a kind of fairy-tale place, and everything was going to work out. She communicated that. He used her on more than a few magazine covers, including the *Saturday Evening Post*."[20]

Ann Graham sent word from London that she had fallen for Count Nicholas "Nicky" Embricos, a young, Oxford-educated Greek shipping heir, and they planned to marry. Could Ruth come over for the wedding, to keep the bride-to-be company? Ann could even wangle her an invitation to the upcoming coronation of King Edward VIII. She went, leaving an unexpectedly bereft Hoagy Carmichael in New York. What was going on here? He hadn't counted on this. Why was he feeling this way, and where was it all leading? What should he do?

Somehow the idea of a vacation in Barbados came up: *Sometimes I Wonder* describes it as a jaunt with friend Bill Shattuck; in other accounts, Hoagy cables Ruth in London to meet him there, and she does. Beyond dispute is one fact: he took his opportunity where he found it. "Out in the moonlight he proposed," said Helen, "and they went inside, walking on cloud nine, into the [hotel] bar to toast this thing and told the bartender. He said congratulations—and immediately launched into this tale of woe about his own marital problems. Ruthie said she could just feel herself drooping, until they could politely get out of there."[21]

✣   ✣   ✣

Musically, too, 1935 was a year of transition in Carmichael's life. His was still a regular face at such West 52nd Street hangouts as the Famous Door, the Hickory House, the Yacht Club, and Joe Helbock's Onyx Club. But "Hogwash McCorkle" was now running along his own track, moving imperceptibly away from the world of jazz discovery he and Bix had shared in the '20s.[22]

In the two years since the success of "Lazybones," he'd emerged as a new kind of performer, a singer-pianist who specialized in presenting his own material. Singer-songwriters have become so central in current pop music that it's difficult to imagine a time when this was not the case. In the music world of 1933, songwriters wrote songs, instrumentalists played them, and singers sang them. The idea of three in one, a triple-threat performer who blended them all, was new, and still rare.

Willard Robison had played and sung songs of his own devising, among them "Peaceful Valley," "A Cottage for Sale," and "'Tain't So, Honey, 'Tain't So," on records and on his weekly *Deep River* radio program. Soft-voiced Gene Austin had crooned his "My Blue Heaven," to his own piano accompaniment, and racked up record sales in the millions. Yet none was a songwriter of Carmichael's consistency or scope, and none so immediately vivid a performer. Perhaps it was the jazz foundation, perhaps the Indiana twang: but people *noticed* Hoagy Carmichael, remembered him. The voice was so individual, so unmistakably *his*, as to appear inseparable from the songs themselves. Others might sing "Lazybones," sing it poignantly and well: but only the composer seemed able to make it sound so inevitable, an utterance lifted directly from life.

He often expressed surprise that so many responded so avidly to his singing. He sang, he once said, "the way a shaggy dog looks. I figure there is hair hanging on my voice. I have Wabash fog and sycamore twigs in my throat." Pete Martin, writing a Carmichael profile for the *Saturday Evening Post*, spoke of a voice "that sounds as if it were being strained through a rust-caked trombone instead of a human larynx." John Crosby, longtime radio reviewer for the *New York Herald-Tribune*, got perhaps closer in declaring that Carmichael sang "as if he were lying on a hammock, dressed in a warm sweater and his oldest flannels, on the verge of falling asleep."[23]

Nor, it must be said, was the singing universally adored by a generation brought up on Crosby, Austin, Russ Columbo, and even the confidential vocals of Rudy Vallee. "Your songs are grand, most of them," one radio listener wrote. "But *must you sing*?"[24]

For some, Hoagy's very emergence as a solo performer constituted a defection from the ranks of the "hot music" faithful. As a *Melody Maker* article put it, Carmichael's "recent tendency toward commercial numbers calls only for one comment: Hoagy has, alas, tired of jazz. The beauty of the old days, when music was comparatively independent of commercialism, is lost. Half his interest in music went, too, with the death of Bix."[25]

The 1935 songs do show Carmichael facing in several directions at once. He does both music and words for "Mister Bluebird," notable mainly as the first specimen in a musical aviary ultimately to include "Skylark" and "Baltimore Oriole." "My Introduction to Love," written with lyricist Irving ("Tea for Two") Caesar, adumbrates the broadly sentimental style of Rodgers and Hammerstein.

"Ballad in Blue" is both deeper and better. Though the published text is credited to Irving Kahal, best known for such items as "When I Take My Sugar to Tea" and "You Brought a New Kind of Love to Me," a lyric sheet for the chorus, written out in Carmichael's unmistakable hand and bearing evidence of work on imagery and rhyme, was found among his papers. Was Hoagy his own lyricist here, allocating *pro forma* credit to a partner? Did he write "Ballad in Blue" as an instrumental, adding a lyric afterward? Did Kahal write the words to the verse only, or any of the text at all? Did they work it out jointly, Carmichael taking down the result?

Taken as a body, Carmichael's lyric sheets seem to indicate a far greater role in putting words to his own songs than has been recognized. In the margins he's forever tinkering with the mechanics of meter, rhyme, metaphor, the weights and evocative properties of words and sounds. In many cases, what at first appear to be "dummy," or *pro tem,* lyrics wind up as published text. In all, there are strong hints of a talent comparable to those of Irving Berlin and Cole Porter, who achieved unique musical identities by writing both words and music for their songs.

"Ballad in Blue" is bold and unusual, the kind of song usually described as "ahead of its time"—most often a damn-with-faint-praise euphemism for something not easily accepted by the public. Its eight-bar verse, in minor mode, introduces a doleful, end-of-affair feeling "that hangs around the mem'ry of you," creating the darkest ambiance yet perceived in Carmichael's work. The sixteen-bar melody heads right into a thicket of flatted ninths (bar 1), flatted fifths (bar 2), chromaticism, and unusual intervals.

"Ballad in Blue" (bars 1–4), 1935

Each four-bar episode consists of three phrases, fitted together in a Beiderbecke-like tongue-and-groove manner. Hoagy's youthful mania for jazz may have departed, but his ties to Bix remain. When the melody in bar 14 lands squarely on a ninth it's a jazzman's choice: among other popular songwriters only Harold Arlen, former dance band pianist and "hot" vocalist, displays such note choices and affinity for the timbre and flavor of the blues. "New Orleans," also a sixteen-bar chorus, also begins in minor, but quickly opens out into the soft illumination of a major cadence; even "Daybreak" resolves in sunlight. "Ballad in Blue" remains shadowed throughout: only Carmichael's much later "Winter Moon" explores so tenebrous a world, and with such harmonic sophistication.

"Ballad in Blue" was recorded twice, both times by Benny Goodman, both times as an instrumental. On both of these, and on a third version, broadcast live from the Los Angeles Palomar Ballroom and later issued on record, he and his band read through Spud Murphy's *marcato* arrangement in an oddly perfunctory manner. The clarinetist's own solos on all three versions, almost identical, are little more than noodling, embellished melody statements.[26]

✻   ✻   ✻

Increasingly, Hoagy Carmichael's thoughts were fixed on his own future. What to do? Where to go next? Though living high and handsome in New York, he clearly stood no chance of breaking into the charmed circle of Broadway composers—in his own phrase, "the big boys." Unlike Porter or Gershwin, he had no background in musical theatre, and there is every indication that his sense of his own technical deficiencies inhibited any ambition he might have had in this direction. Tin Pan Alley? He'd seen enough of life in the Brill Building beehive to know that wasn't for him.

The most inviting option seemed the movies. German-born director Ernst Lubitsch had all but created the modern screen musical in 1929 with *The Love Parade*. Rouben Mamoulian, another European, adapted his mastery as a director of the musical stage to the needs of film, with often spectacular results. *Forty-Second Street* and *Gold Diggers of 1933* had proclaimed the arrival of Busby Berkeley, whose innovative use of the camera could turn masses of dancing chorus girls into extravagant geometries of motion. Dick Powell, who had sung with Indiana dance bands while Hoagy was in college, was now a major Hollywood attraction, as were operetta sweethearts Nelson Eddy and Jeanette MacDonald. Fred Astaire, a song-and-dance star since the 1920s, teamed up with dancer-comedienne Ginger Rogers for a series of box-office winners built around music by Berlin, Gershwin, and Jerome Kern. Even dramatic films were featuring songs.

The boom was on, and it was time for Hoagy Carmichael to be part of it, to partake of the sunshine and luxury. Visiting Hollywood in 1929, while Whiteman and his musicians were waiting to begin filming *King of Jazz*, he'd seen the new film capital as a land of promise, where a talented songwriter could reach untold millions of listeners, earn fabulous sums—all while living the easy, sunlit life that had haunted his boyhood dreams. The gates had been barred to him then, but they might not be barred now: "Star Dust," "Georgia," and the rest had turned the agitated young piano player into a respected songwriter, with the greater bargaining power that respect commanded.

Sometime early in 1935 he secured his release from Ralph Peer and signed with the Music Publishers Holding Corporation, a conglomerate of the old Harms, Witmark, and Remick music houses now operating as the New York branch of Warner Brothers. He'd start writing songs for Warner films and ultimately would be summoned to Hollywood to take his place among movie composers. But "when an opening to write songs in Hollwood came up," he added just a bit acidly, "they sent Johnny Mercer and left me at home to tend the store."[27]

Hoagy inaugurated his Warners association with a bright rhythm tune based on an engaging conceit: if staying too long in the sun could produce a sunburn, then why wouldn't a lover exposed to excessive moonlight get a "Moonburn"? Ed Heyman, whose words to "Body and Soul" had advanced him to the front rank in 1930, helped amplify the idea in a jaunty lyric: but, as usual, Heyman's typed sheet bears much evidence of Carmichael's editorial participation, including a completely rewritten verse and "Eddie's" scrawled note, "If you want to change the rhythm scheme a bit, okay—I'll go over it with you Monday." As published, the chorus of "Moonburn" is Heyman's, but the verse is pure Carmichael.[28]

"Dad was not exactly an easy guy," Hoagy Bix Carmichael said in confirmation. "He had a very clear idea of how things should happen. He had a way of going about his life, and it was different from a lot of people. He was very creative, and sometimes things other people did bothered him; I don't think he ever saw himself in his own mind as *interfering* with others— just helping out, making things better. And that most probably involved editing other people's lyrics, too."[29]

Copyrighted July 30, "Moonburn" soon found its way to Bing Crosby, who liked it enough to help get it into Hollywood's much-altered version of the Cole Porter stage hit *Anything Goes*—the first Carmichael song to be used in a Hollywood movie. Bing's Decca record, made that November with a backing including jazz piano great Joe Sullivan, is notable for its relaxed, easy swing. Other prominent artists, including the Casa Loma Orchestra, contract vocalist Chick Bullock, and a Decca house band featuring Bunny Berigan on trumpet, also recorded it.[30]

With Crosby's popularity at an all-time high, the song stood every chance of becoming a major hit. But just as *Anything Goes* was beginning to generate box-office revenue, Herman Starr, president of the Warner Holding Corporation, announced the company was abrogating its agreement with ASCAP. According to Starr, Warners controlled some forty thousand ASCAP songs, just short of a quarter of the society's catalogue; that should have translated into higher licensing fees. When ASCAP refused to consider such an arrangement, Starr pulled out, leaving six months of radio without a single Warners-owned song. "Warner's songwriters and publishers were the big losers," notes historian Thomas A. DeLong, "suffering greatly reduced earnings as their tunes, chiefly from current Warner musicals, were virtually forgotten on the air."[31]

Among the dispute's victims was "Moonburn," which, deprived of any airtime at all, failed to achieve its hoped-for place among Carmichael standards. "Consequently," fellow-Hoosier Ernie Pyle put in a column that July, "everything Hoagy writes goes on the shelf until this row blows over. He has turned out about 16 in the last six months. He thinks there are some hits among them."[32]

Ralph Peer, meanwhile, copyrighted the few Carmichael items he still had in house; but if "Maybe You Know What I Mean," "No Doggone Business," and "Swingin' on the Moon" were published at all, they dropped quickly from sight. "Bread and Gravy," also in this batch, might have been similarly forgotten but for a 1939 record by Ethel Waters.

After her success in Berlin's show *As Thousands Cheer,* Waters hit the road with a backup band led by her husband, trumpeter Eddie Mallory. They began recording together for Victor's Bluebird subsidiary in late 1938 and on August 15, 1939, did six titles, three of them Peer-controlled Car-michael songs. "Georgia on My Mind" and "Old Man Harlem" are nicely modulated performances; "Bread and Gravy" rather more than that. Peer had known the singer-actress since his days in "race" records, and his de-cision to hand her this unpublished Carmichael song was certainly an in-spired one. As Wilfrid Mellers notes in *Angels of the Night,* Waters imbues "Bread and Gravy" with "its own truth, poised between wit and pathos."[33]

Extending a world picture first glimpsed in "Washboard Blues" and "Rockin' Chair," Carmichael's "Bread and Gravy" lyric celebrates a hap-piness achieved after times of poverty and slender means, and sustained by faith. The protagonist is black, but the vision, the "message," applies to anyone struggling to keep his head up in Depression-era America. Hang on, it seems to say; work hard, and the good life will be yours. Is Carmichael thinking autobiographically? More than a few of the lines could have de-scribed his father's errant fortunes, his own hardscrabble boyhood, and the extraordinary course his life was now taking.

Words in italics represent changes made either by Carmichael or Waters, presumably for purposes of recording.

> Bread and gravy, lots of bread and gravy,
> Beans and bacon, lots of beans and bacon,
> No more lay-offs, (*No more frettin'*)
> Full-day pay-offs, (*Since I'm gettin'*)
> Lots of bread and gravy all the time.
>
> Peace and quiet, lots of peace and quiet,
> Friends and money, lots of friends and money,

No more ramblin',
Through with gamblin', (*scramblin'*)
Right up with the Joneses all the time.

Toward the end of 1935, Peer also took out a copyright for the waltz
Carmichael had tried to record in 1927 and 1928 and still treasured. It was
a timely move: not long after returning from Barbados, Hoagy announced
that he and "Cream" would be married on Saturday, March 14, 1936, at the
Fifth Avenue Presbyterian Church, where the Reverend Garrett Meinardi,
Ruth's late father, had once preached.

Helen Meinardi was more than a little perturbed by the news. No denying Hoag's talent, his special brand of charm, even the fact that he was
an Indiana boy, not without importance in this situation. But she couldn't
dodge a lingering suspicion that Ruth was getting married, above all, for
the sake of getting married, her way to avoid having to meet the world on
its own terms, standing or falling on her native strengths and abilities.
"Ruthie was the kind—unlike me, I was always going to be a writer or a
concert pianist, one of the two," Helen said. "She—well, there wasn't anything . . . In New York there was a school of design; I sent her to that, [but]
it didn't mean anything. I mean, if somebody isn't burning to do something, you can't do it for them. They've got to really care.

"So when she told me she was going to marry, because of her insecurity
. . . I just had the feeling that he was not—well, I said, 'Are you sure you
know what you're doing? Because I'm not sure Hoagy's right for you.' "
For one thing, she said, he was kind of odd about money, almost miserly
in unexpected places, yet heedlessly extravagant in others. The Carmichaels
had been "very poor," after all. "They didn't have indoor plumbing, and
it's easy to see why his view of money was what it was.

"I remember once he had some radio program and his mother was
on it and got paid for it, and by God, he let her pay him back for the
ticket to get there. Now that's quite foreign to some of us, but it's the
way he was . . . I mean, if you haven't come from the same background
it's kind of hard [to understand]. You try, but you approach things so
differently."

At first, she added, "he used to drive Ruthie crazy 'cause he never had
any money with him . . . so when she finally got him on this subject and
everything it was all at once the other way round, he was the one who
insisted on paying for things, [but] it didn't come naturally to him, that

sort of thing. The music world he was perfectly at home in, [but] the rest of it, I always felt, was an acquired taste."

He was also, she added, alarmingly and impenetrably self-centered. "I say that not as critically as it sounds . . . [but] he used to sometimes get up from the piano and wander out . . . he was off someplace in his head and didn't bother to tell anybody . . . You'll see kids going along the street and they seem to be in their own little world, whatever it is, they're humming something. Well, he always struck me as being off over there in his world, and it didn't make him, you know, the easiest person to get along with."

"But oh well, you know . . . So that was that." Ruth was obviously in no mood to hear or heed any such qualms, and her sister knew better than to press them. The marriage was going to go ahead.[34]

✻   ✻   ✻

It was an afternoon wedding, and as bride and groom approached the altar, Hoagy Carmichael finally got to use his little Indiana waltz in an ideal setting, beaming at the bride while singing his own words:

> Hand in hand, giving our love to this endeavor,
> Heart and soul, vowing this tryst will be forever.
> I take thee as mine, dear;
> Take me so as thine, dear.
> God hath said we may this day be wed.

Contemporary accounts of the reception afterward describe a confluence of Hoagland Carmichael's past and present—and, to those observant enough to notice, just a peep at his future. Best man Wad Allen, forever the Bent Eagle, hires a hansom cab, complete with walrus-moustachioed driver, to carry the newlyweds back to East 52nd Street. After Lida Carmichael knocks off "Maple Leaf Rag" at the piano, George Gershwin takes over to play his suite of *Porgy and Bess* songs. *Paterfamilias* Howard Carmichael, more than a bit in his cups, avers in a stage whisper that "your mother plays much better than that Gershwin feller," as Sherman Fairchild, a wealthy executive with a partiality for pianos and the people who play them, hovers nearby. George Welbaum, president of the Sons of Indiana alumni organization, makes party chitchat with Jules Glaenzer and publisher Condé Nast. Radio baritone Conrad Thibault sings, and Bill Shattuck keeps his home movie camera rolling—only to discover later that he's forgotten to remove the lens cover. Trumpeter Bunny Berigan takes the floor with a quintet including Bud Freeman on tenor sax, Joe Bushkin at the piano, and Dave Tough on drums. Lee Wiley, romantically linked with Berigan at the time, sings a few songs. Hoagy, of course, joins Bushkin for some four-hand byplay, while Eva Ford demonstrates "Truckin' " and other new Harlem dance crazes for the guests.[35]

There was even, Bushkin recalled, a moment of unintended comedy. As the horse-drawn cab pulled up to the church, "the cab driver got off on the left-hand side, and [while] Hoagy [was] waiting to help his bride out of the hansom cab, the horse just took off at a gallop, right down [Fifth] Avenue." Carmichael, in hot pursuit, managed to grab the reins and bring the runaway vehicle to a halt.[36]

Once the revels (including a star-spangled Harry Evans party at the Hotel Pierre) had abated, it didn't take the new Mrs. Carmichael long to find she had her work cut out for her. "I had been a bachelor a long time and lived the life of a modern musician," Hoagy writes. "Housebreaking me was a task and I was never fully domesticated . . . outwardly I was the shiny success, the well-tailored popular song writer, the crisp creases of New York styling hiding what was still in many ways the Indiana country boy on a lucky spree."[37]

Lucky spree or not, things seemed to be going his way. He'd written two new tunes for Louis Armstrong to use at Connie's Inn, and in May 1936 the trumpeter recorded both, though neither "Ev'ntide" nor "Lyin' to Myself" was published at the time. Stanley Adams, a partner in the Warner New York operation, supplied words for the latter, and for the next two years he and Carmichael worked under company auspices as a team. Some of their joint efforts are forgettable, among them "Pagan Star," "Papa Treetop Tall" (a kind of addendum to "Old Man Harlem," recounting the largely amorous exploits of "the King of Lenox Avenue"), and "Sing a Song of Nonsense," an ode to childhood pleasures based on an old nursery rhyme. "Two of You," a brooding, minor-mode exploration of an affair with a Jekyll-and-Hyde lover, is good work, deserving of wider attention. The bright "Sing Me a Swing Song" fared better, with lively records by Goodman, Wingy Manone, and Ella Fitzgerald, with Chick Webb's orchestra.[38]

Warner Brothers, meanwhile, came through at last with a contract, Hoagy's long-awaited shot at Hollywood. "I was wanted now, not just going out on hope," he wrote. "They were sending for me, on my terms, and the waste land would be milk and honey, caviar, palm trees—and even some day a place of our own." Hoagy and Ruth Carmichael, with Harvey III, a pet monkey they'd bought in Barbados, headed west, eyes full of a gleaming future beyond the Rockies.

Wealth, fame, and luxury awaited them. But dreams invariably come at a price, and in this case the cost would be considerable.

* XII *

Paradise Perceived

Hollywood in the 1930s? For a good general idea, said Edward G. Robinson, consider "the Holy Roman Empire or Germany prior to the unification and Bismarck."

"It consisted of seven duchies (Fox, MGM, Warner Brothers, Columbia, R.K.O., Paramount, United Artists), each reigned over by a feudal lord in battle with each other and yet bound together by their common interest, which was simply to get as much talent as possible and pay as little as possible for it. Or, if it served their purpose, to pay as *much* as possible for it."[1]

As the great actor's words imply, such an agglomeration of principalities was invariably autocratic, contentious, indefatigably devious. Politics among them, and among the powerful men who ruled them, often seemed drawn from the pages of Machiavelli:

A prince, therefore, must not mind incurring the charge of cruelty for the purpose of keeping his subjects united and faithful . . . one ought to be both feared and loved, but as it is difficult for the two to go together, it is much safer to be feared than loved, if one of the two has to be wanting. For it may be said of men in general that they are ungrateful, voluble, dissemblers, anxious to avoid danger, and covetous of gain; as long as you benefit them, they are entirely yours.[2]

As in any nation-state, each Hollywood duchy had its hierarchy, its pecking order. In their carpeted offices, masters of their small universes, sat the studio executives; mostly Jews of Eastern European origin, they'd fought free of old-world fetters to reach the United States, struggling up economic and social ladders to create a "dream factory," dispensing easy fantasy to the masses. They, and their satraps, controlled the product; controlled, most visibly, the contract players, grooming and pampering them like racehorses, even while keeping them under tight control.

When recorded sound came to the movies, the industry as usual attracted and hired those who would best serve its ends—writers, composers, arrangers, musicians—and paid at least some of them well, all the while practicing a degree of surveillance few of them had experienced and fewer yet could tolerate. In historian Neal Gabler's words, these included "playwrights and novelists and newspapermen and magazine journalists and college boys with fresh English degrees, many of them of indifferent talent, most of them attracted by the money and the promise of paradise."[3]

And paradise it must have seemed to many a transplanted newcomer from the East or Midwest—at least for a while. "I loved the hills back of Hollywood," playwright Jerome Chodorov said years later. "I loved the air, I loved the sunshine, and going to the beach was so easy and then I had a car for the first time in my life. You don't know what it is to live in a city where the jackhammer wasn't going."[4]

Before long each came to realize that he—or she, in the case of such luminaries as Algonquin Round Tabler Dorothy Parker—had bought into, and been bought by, a far less glamorous reality. Writers in the employ of the filmland duchies often seemed like battery hens, constantly pressed to produce, closely scrutinized and even punished if they didn't lay a certain number of eggs each day. The world at large might know them as Raymond Chandler, William Faulkner, Ring Lardner Jr., John O'Hara, F. Scott Fitzgerald, Ben Hecht; but in the writers' cubicles of the Hollywood studios they were hired hands with typewriters, all but anonymous, except when their names could help market a picture.

The same conditions applied to songwriters, their reputations mostly made and still rooted in New York. Some, such as lyricist Al Dubin, actually took gratefully to the regimented life. All the same to him, said his daughter, that such "songwriters had no celebrity status with either the public or the studios." Dubin, vastly overweight and given to near-mythic excesses of food, flesh, and alcohol, "wanted to live in California where he was close to the border towns of Tiajuana and Juarez, to the gambling spots and the brothels ... Why, he could be in the desert in a couple of hours and in snow-covered mountains a couple of hours after that. As far as Al was concerned, California had it all."[5]

Inevitably, some had an easier time than others: Cole Porter, whose great wealth afforded him total independence from studio largesse, reacted with detached amusement to the more outlandish of Hollywood's ways. "It's like living on the moon, isn't it?" was his mild reply to a reporter's "How do you like Hollywood?" Richard Rodgers, like Porter a scion of the Broadway stage, seemed more interested in the step-by-step techniques of filmmaking than in his life as a movie songwriter. He soon realized that, as far as such studio heads as Irving Thalberg were concerned, "we were all faceless, anonymous cogs. Whenever we were needed, all he had to do was press a button and we'd hop over to help turn the company's wheels."[6]

Unlike them, Hoagy Carmichael could not return to a Broadway welcome if working for movies failed to live up to expectations. He was one among dozens engaged to write songs to order, individual tunes to be inserted as needed into any film. Each duchy—each studio—had them on staff: Broadway veterans Dubin and Harry Warren were at Warners; Arthur Freed, Nacio Herb Brown, and lyricist E. Y. "Yip" Harburg at MGM; Mack Gordon and Harry Revel at Twentieth Century–Fox. Paramount's major songwriting team, Ralph Rainger and Leo Robin, had scored with "Please," "Here Lies Love," and "June in January," all major successes for Bing Crosby.

Here, then, was a trade-off, the first of many he was to make. His new one-year contract with Paramount, for a thousand dollars a week, offered security, a degree of comfort he'd never known—and which he'd soon invite his mother and sisters to share. In return, there was little choice but to accept the relative anonymity of Hollywood songwriting: when, in 1935, RKO's *Top Hat* scored a major box-office success, it was mainly as a vehicle for Fred Astaire and Ginger Rogers; though the score was one of Irving Berlin's best, *Top Hat* remained, in the public perception, a Fred-and-Ginger movie. A vast difference from Broadway, where *Face the Music* and *As Thousands Cheer* had been, emphatically, Irving Berlin shows.

Hollywood "was booming like a thousand wildcatters hitting oil at once," said Hoagy. "The frightening studio millionaires had all recovered from the depression in their rosewood suites and Cadillacs." Studio power "was naked and cruel. Some producers made and broke stars for a whim. Great palaces looted from Europe, loaded with art, held continual parties," all floating on "a strange idea that reality began in Pasadena and that the world needed the dream-boats made here in the hard white Hollywood sun." It might be a distorting-mirror land of Oz, golden Xanadu built of iron pyrite, but to Carmichael it also represented fulfillment of a promise, of a dream first dreamed in the front yard of a barren little house in wintry, far-off Montana.[7]

"I [had] retained my inner core of loneliness which diminished in time but didn't entirely disappear," he wrote. "And I lived away from the world most of the time in the cloaked enigma of the music man, bent over a piano probing for some secret voice." He could avoid engagement with popular culture, he said, "by the use of will power and firmness."

Ruth, well aware what kind of man she'd married, saw to it that the couple launched a full and vigorous social life. "My mother could go to a party," said Hoagy Bix Carmichael, "and in twelve minutes she knew nine people; they were all inviting her over, and Dad, too. She opened a lot of doors for Dad."[8]

In New York he'd socialized with jazz colleagues, with Indiana friends, even with Jules Glaenzer's circle of artists and musicians. But people out here seemed absorbed in the movies, and above all in themselves and their careers. Jazz acquaintances were few and far between. Even distances were greater: getting to and from an evening's entertainment often cost unanticipated time and effort. The left-wing political causes so dear to so many Hollywood hearts appealed little to him: actors, actresses, writers, and directors might contibute money, time, and emotional energy to President Franklin D. Roosevelt's New Deal, the loyalist side in the Spanish Civil War, or agrarian reform in the Soviet Union. But Hoagy Carmichael remained a staunch backer of the Republican Party.

"I mean, he *hated* Roosevelt," said Helen Meinardi, "with such a passion that he managed to blame Roosevelt for even the new design of the Lincoln car which he had looked at, and [seated in which] he couldn't see over the steering wheel. That was Roosevelt's fault, y'see." Given the choice, she added, Hoagy preferred to stay at home and work at his piano keyboard.[9]

And he was pulling in a thousand dollars a week for doing it. That was what the great F. Scott Fitzgerald, back in Hollywood for a third and final try at screenwriting, was making. More than a few songwriters he knew were earning a lot less. Still, he reasoned, an industry doing more than $400 million turnover a year, paying stars like Bing Crosby more than

$400,000 annually, could afford to shell out $52,000 a year for the guy who'd written "Star Dust" and "Georgia on My Mind," no? A bit bedazzled all the same, he got to work on his first project, a song for an upcoming screen adaptation of Thorne Smith's best-selling novel *Topper*.[10]

In the meantime, his New York songs were still bearing fruit. Louis Armstrong had been signed to appear in Paramount's *Every Day's a Holiday*, playing and singing "Jubilee," an upbeat Carmichael-Adams novelty, at the head of a street parade band. Decked out all in white, sporting a plumed helmet, he "accomplishes just what the filmmakers want," writes movie historian Donald Bogle. "His energy really can send viewers soaring. In the 'Jubilee' section of *Every Day's a Holiday*, the Negro seems a part of society, not wholly removed in a world of his own."[11]

Armstrong recorded "Jubilee" for Decca on January 12, 1938, backed by Luis Russell's orchestra, and his performance stands out for a great jazzman's ability to ennoble an otherwise pedestrian song through majesty of conception and execution. After making short (if enjoyable) work of Adams's generic "let's all have a good time" lyric, Louis points his Selmer trumpet at the heavens and, lofted atop Paul Barbarin's drumming, rides "Jubilee" into high orbit.

He spends one chorus paraphrasing the melody over band riffs, then intones complementary replies as Russell's horns punch out the melody in the second. Taking over at the bridge, he works to a final soaring, transcendent high concert F. The balance and wisdom of these seventy-four bars defy explanation or analysis: what divine intuition dictated that he hold the concert G in bar 26 of the final chorus (corresponding to the word "of" in the phrase "carnival of joy") for three and one half beats, rather than the gone-in-a-blink eighth note assigned to it by the lyric, before landing emphatically on the F for "joy?" Only a peerless aesthetic sense could have understood the effect of that move, one among many, on the emotional density of its phrase. The word "genius," so devalued in this age of inflated superlatives, surely finds its rightful application in such details.[12]

However compelling Armstrong's performance, "Jubilee" was not the year's most popular Carmichael-Adams effort. That distinction belongs to an even less likely candidate, an unassuming little song paying homage to Hoagy's boyhood, and particularly the grandmothers who had helped raise him during the lean years. An almost folkish melody, wedded to a lyric of unembarrassed sentimentality, it surfaced in *The Show Is On*, a revue that opened on Christmas Day 1936 at New York's Winter Garden Theatre under Vincente Minnelli's direction and featuring Bert Lahr and Beatrice Lillie.

The score created considerable advance buzz: new songs by Rodgers and Hart ("Rhythm"), Harold Arlen and "Yip" Harburg ("Song of the Woodman"), the brothers Gershwin ("By Strauss"), Herman Hupfeld ("Buy Yourself a Balloon"), Vernon Duke and Ted Fetter ("Now")—and, almost inconspicuously, "Little Old Lady," by Carmichael and Adams.

"As far as the ear could hear last night," Boston drama critic Elliot Norton wrote after seeing a tryout performance,

> *The Show Is On* is song-hitless, which is a defect but not a major flaw . . . Some one of the many songwriters who worked on the piece may coax a hit out of his inspiration in the next few days. Or it may be that a pretty piece called "Little Old Lady' " will catch fire and confound us.[13]

"Little Old Lady" did indeed catch fire, but in a decorous, long-cooking sort of way. Even now, after more than six decades, it appeals to surprising numbers of listeners. Adams's lyric—if it is fully his—abounds in nostalgic references to dress and manners of times past:

> Little old bonnet set in place,
> And a smile on your face,
> You're a perfect picture in your
> Lavender and lace.

Such images bear Carmichael's clear imprint. They are pure Indiana, reminiscent of such verse as "When Grandma Talks to Her Garden," by Hoosier newsman–folk poet William Herschell:

> When Grandma talks to her garden—Say,
> Eavesdroppers listen, then walk away;
> Never a word do they hear that means
> Motherly talk to her evergreens.

By 1937, those images, even the regard in which old age had once been held, seemed to be slipping from the public ken. "We were still coming out of the Depression," said scholar James T. Maher. "The whole world, remember, had gone to pieces, and people were really hungry to hang on to substantive images of the past, anything that gave them a sense of family and stability and place."[14]

In subject and appeal, "Little Old Lady" recalls such Frank Capra film landmarks as *Mr. Deeds Goes to Town* and *It's a Wonderful Life*, still able to charm even case-hardened audiences. The people who walk the streets of George Bailey's Bedford Falls, or the Mandrake Falls of Longfellow Deeds, survive mainly as archetypes, ideals. Selectively remembered, they incarnate a shared longing for simpler, by implication more humane, times; in that sense they are of a piece with the characters and scenes of "Moon Country," "Lazy River," "Rockin' Chair," and Carmichael's other home-and-hearth songs. "The life that is lived wholly in memory," Danish philosopher Søren Kierkegaard has said, is "the most perfect conceivable [;] the satisfactions of memory are richer than reality, and have a security no reality possesses."

But memory, novelist Lillian Smith replies, "has so little talent for photography, [that] it likes to paint pictures. Experience is not laid away in it like a snapshot, to be withdrawn at will, but is returned to us as a portrait painted in our own psychic colors, its form and pattern structured on that of our life." Because folk memory is idealized, its process of selective remembrance ever at work, it tends to thrust less benign aspects of times past into a deliberately unfocused middle distance. The halcyon past of a popular song, then, depends on a narrow and surprisingly fragile balance, in which the sunlit foreground scene stands out against a backdrop, explicit or implied, of darker things: of the knowledge that death ends every idyll; that human nature doesn't always function altruistically, or good necessarily trump evil; that time and change distort, then demolish, even the most delicately and carefully tinted of landscapes.[15]

When portraiture attempts to prevail against photography, its attention to detail at the expense of setting can upset the balance, plunging the entire scene into bathos. "Little Old Lady" exemplifies such a risk, in that its vision is of only a small situation or character, lifted out of any larger or more complex setting. Displayed on its own, it has no life to sustain it beyond "a little bit of business here, a little bit of business there." Finally, "Little Old Lady" appears, even if affectionately, to patronize its subject, a transgression absent from Carmichael's other "generic home" songs.

Other songwriters have worked with sentimental themes, with widely differing results. From its first bars, Irving Berlin's 1928 "How About Me?" sinks into leaden self-pity, beyond rescue even by a chord sequence closely paralleling that of George Gershwin's "The Man I Love"; Willard Robison, born and raised in Missouri, taps springs of collective memory in "Old Folks," his 1938 portrait of a beloved old small-town character. Lyricist Dedette Lee Hill avoids mawkishness by sketching in a wealth of contextual detail which, in those days, still included many who had fought for the Blue *and* the Gray, and who marched proudly in each year's Decoration Day parade.

"Old Folks," moreover, acknowledges the inevitability of death, a reality indispensable to both "Washboard Blues" and "Rockin' Chair"—and absent entirely from "Little Old Lady." "It certainly does what it sets out to do," Alec Wilder says of it in *American Popular Song.* "But old as I am, it makes me consider that perhaps everyone over, not thirty but seventy, may not be dead but certainly should never be the subject of a song."[16]

✳   ✳   ✳

Hoagy and Ruth, meanwhile, had settled comfortably into their California life; Helen, well established in the film community, had even managed to find them a home. She'd been dating writer John (*Teahouse of the August Moon*) Patrick, who'd been renting a Spanish-style ranch house in Brentwood with two young easterners, Henry Fonda and James Stewart. When Fonda, his divorce from actress Margaret Sullavan still fresh in memory, returned from a trip to England and announced he was getting married again, Patrick and Stewart started looking for less expensive digs. Hoagy and Helen agreed to split the costs, and the Carmichaels moved right in.

It had belonged to "some old movie director," she said. "Marvelous place: the driveway, the way it went in, left this baseball field there; it had tennis courts, [too,] and the bar was a western bar complete with slot machines that worked, and everything else—and these movies with characters I remember mother talking about." Tour buses took to stopping outside, she said, their guides identifying various famous and near-famous faces taking part in the Carmichaels' Sunday morning softball games. "Then we'd wind up in the bar later for poker, or there was tennis. It was like running a country club."[17]

Carmichael home movies, many shot in mid-1937, show them having just that sort of good time, romping at tennis, softball, archery, and in an assortment of swimming pools in Hollywood and Palm Springs, alongside recognizable movie stars; watching Seabiscuit run at Santa Anita track with comedian Oliver Hardy; speedboating with industrialist Sherman Fairchild; partying with a visiting Jules Glaenzer; wandering around William Randolph Hearst's own personal Xanadu, San Simeon, in company with an engagingly boyish Jimmy Stewart; sharing a summer afternoon's fun with Van Johnson.

Carmichael's efforts on the tennis court, marked by more intensity than grace, bespeak a dogged determination to master the game—and the social standing it confers. Eva Ford, who had come west with them, puts in a few lighthearted appearances. "We were just a few doors down from [Greta] Garbo," said Helen, "and Eva knew that Garbo took a walk early in the morning; poor Eva was bleary-eyed getting up early to try to run into Garbo, and never did."[18]

In one home movie sequence Hoagy drives up in his brand-new Ford convertible, climbs out, then stands on the running board, proudly stroking his acquisition as he might a Thoroughbred. Other familiar film faces flit in and out of the frame: athletic leading man and former football star Johnny Mack Brown; dramatic actor Paul Lukas; suave George Sanders, in top hat, tails, and boutonniere. Helen is a constant presence, at one point joining her sister and some other guests in some impromptu "Truckin'," as taught them by the redoubtable Eva.

It's all a long way from Bloomington—both the town of the Carmichael family's hard realities and the idealized home of young Hoagland's fantasies. Hollywood, he reflected,

> wasn't such a sinister town when I got to know it better ... It was the social scene now, exclusive parties, and name people; lots of name people, and I shall try not to list most of them. The columnists kept printing items about us, but I don't really regret that I didn't keep a full social scrap book. All I remember is that we were accepted, mainly because of Ruthie's charm, and in a few years' time were attending at least half of the big social events of the times. By 1950 there wasn't a movie star, producer, director, or columnist in town that we didn't know personally."[19]

Here, as elsewhere in his reflections on the period, is an almost palpable sense of satisfaction that the boy from the wrong side of an Indiana town has finally *arrived*, finally "made it," and is savoring every moment. For all his later protests that he didn't take his new affluence seriously, there is every indication that the opposite was true: the man who remarks that he "fitted in best with people who liked to be amused, enjoyed parties, played golf and tennis, and [then] had to get up in the morning to go to work" is disclosing perhaps far more than he knows.

Lost to sight, at least temporarily, is the world of thought and experience, imagination and endless disputation, first glimpsed through the bright, brief life of Bill Moenkhaus. Lost, too, the curiosity about art and classical music fostered by similarly short-lived Bix Beiderbecke. Had the onetime "half-educated man" found such easy solace among sleek people whose leisure lives were all golf, tennis, and parties, and who toiled away their days on the "dream factory" assembly line?

"It made a country-club setup for all of us," said Helen. "The drinking was at parties . . . You drank. Everybody did, and topic 'A' every morning was hangovers. I remember one morning Ruthie—I wish you could have known her then, she was more fun—she had this scarf tied around her head, the way gals do. And I said,'Look at our little peasant.' And she said, 'Peasant, hell—it's a sling for my hangover.' "[20]

❖ ❖ ❖

Before leaving New York Hoagy had collaborated with Helen on a song. "I was back [east] as usual," she said, "seeing shows and stuff." The Carmichaels had feted her with a small dinner party, during which "Hoag played all the new stuff he'd done since I'd last seen him, and one melody caught my ear. I thought it was just beautiful, and so he played it again, and said, 'Well, words are your racket, so give me a title. I can't even get a title.' So I said, 'April in My Heart,' and it fit—and then I was describing what I meant: 'There's snowflakes in the sky and geese are flyin' high/But there's April in my heart again . . .' "

"Well, I plunked right down at the piano—no more party for me—I was simply the guest of honor. People left, and we said goodbye, and they streamed out and the party was over, and at three in the morning we'd written 'April in My Heart,' and woke Ruthie up to see how she liked it."[21]

It is indeed a beautiful song, its arching melodic line faintly reminiscent of "One Morning in May," the lyric abounding with evocative images:

> There's frost in Central Park,
> At five it's almost dark,
> What's the difference when you've heard
> Love's sweet amen?

Hoagy—or Helen—even finds a way of working the word "stardust" into the verse, as part of a particularly fetching couplet:[22]

Frost to me is simply frozen stardust
From the heavens above . . .

"April in My Heart" created an almost immediate stir, friends and music business colleagues talking it up as potentially another "Star Dust." There were several good records, among them an excellent Teddy Wilson version with Benny Carter, Harry James, and a Billie Holiday vocal. At first, Paramount scheduled it for use in *Every Day's a Holiday,* alongside "Jubilee." Dropped from that film, it bounced first to *College Swing* and finally to a 1938 feature, *Say It in French,* starring former circus bareback rider Olympe Bradna and Welsh-born leading man Ray Milland.

For all that, and even through the efforts of such Hollywood names as June Allyson and Dick Powell—who had sung with bands in his native Indiana and known Hoagy there in the '20s—to talk it up in the film colony, "April in My Heart" failed to catch on. One reason may be the melody: as so often it's basically an instrumental line, built on intervals uncomfortable for easy singing, but lying more naturally on a horn, especially a Beiderbecke-style cornet.

Acute musical instinct seems to have impelled Billie Holiday, a singer with a relatively narrow vocal range, to flatten the song's hill-and-dale contours. This problem recurs in such later songs as the striking "Blue Orchids," so similar in spots to "April in My Heart" that one could have been written (or played) as a counterline to the other.[23]

"April in My Heart" (1937) and "Blue Orchids" (bars 1–4), 1939

Another, unpublished, 1937 Carmichael item is no less surprising. Identified on its manuscript copy only as "M'Lady," the melody—it has no lyric—reads like a preview of "Candy," credited to Joan Whitney, Alex Kramer, and Mack Gordon, and sung with great success on a 1944 record by Johnny Mercer. Like the later song, "M'Lady" begins on a major seventh, following a general descending chord pattern that within a decade would become common among partisans of the new jazz style called bebop.

✻   ✻   ✻

Only one event could trump the parties, ballgames, palatial houses, flashy cars, and movie stars in lending Hoagy's summer of '37 a truly fairy-tale quality. Adapting *Topper* for the screen, veteran director Hal Roach set one scene in an after-hours bistro: stars Cary Grant and Constance Bennett, out on the town, are unwilling to call it a night and wind up hanging around the piano, singing along, even dancing a bit, as—who else?—Hoagy Carmichael serenades them with his own "Old Man Moon."

When the manager, exasperated, puts a firm stop to things by slamming the upright's lid shut, Grant and Bennett buck-and-wing their way right out the door with a cheery "G'night, Hoagy." The song gets a reprise later in the film, sung by the Three Hits and a Miss. While serviceable, "Old Man Moon" seems less than memorable now—save for another insertion of the word "stardust" into a lyric.[24]

At this point Carmichael was writing with whatever lyricist the studio assigned him. For a while, during 1937, his collaborator was Ned Washington; though their "The Only Way to Fly" never left the ground, another effort did—a melody Hoagy apparently had dashed off during his last New York days for a screen adaptation of Shakespeare's *A Midsummer Night's Dream*, featuring fifteen-year-old Mickey Rooney as Puck. With Washington's lyric, it became "The Nearness of You," scheduled for inclusion in the Paramount feature *Romance in the Rough*. The film was never produced, and the song had to wait for republication in 1940 to win its place as a standard.[25]

Among the newer faces at Paramount was a brash young New Yorker named Frank Loesser. He'd teamed with Viennese-born Frederick Loewe on a now-forgotten trifle called "A Waltz Was Born in Vienna" and attracted some Tin Pan Alley notice with "Junk Man" and "I Wish I Were Twins," the latter popularized by Thomas "Fats" Waller. Son of a music teacher, younger brother of concert pianist and critic Arthur Loesser, he'd arrived in Hollywood around the same time as Carmichael, on a contract with Universal—only to be let go when the contract lapsed. Being out of work in New York was one thing: there was always a support network of family and friends to make the rough times a bit less rough. The young man might struggle, but he'd not starve.

To be adrift in Hollywood was quite another, far lonelier state, "akin," music historian Max Wilk has written, "to that of an Untouchable in far-off India." Salvation appeared in the person of fellow–New Yorker Burton Lane, who had just signed with Paramount and was shopping for a lyricist. Lane never forgot his first visit to his new partner:

> He lived on Sunset Boulevard. I had to walk about two hundred steps [up] from the street to get to his little apartment. I'd been there about five or ten minutes when Lynn, his first wife, asked me if I'd like to have dinner with them. I said no, I'd already eaten. She opened a can of [baked] beans—one can for the *both* of them—and an apple, which she sliced for their dessert. They were absolutely broke."[26]

Through Lane's intercession, Paramount signed Loesser—and quickly put him to work. He wrote "Moments Like This" with Lane, the witty "I Go for That" with Paul Whiteman orchestra alumnus Matty Malneck, and, for the movie *The Hurricane*, "The Moon of Manakoora," a collaboration with film veteran Alfred Newman. Then, in early 1938, the studio teamed him with Hoagy Carmichael.

"Frank was gifted and energetic," Carmichael wrote, "but he was very flighty at first in his choice of lyrics ... He had a tendency to want to write things 'way out.' This may be because he was so packed full of ideas then that he was overloaded." Carmichael's choice of adjectives here arrests attention. "Flighty?" "Way out?" Curious words from a songwriter who was himself for so many of his early years "way out" and on a cutting edge of his own—and who so often disclaimed any but the most superficial, utilitarian aspirations as a lyricist.[27]

Reminiscences of friends and other collaborators fill in the picture. For Burton Lane, Loesser was "a very difficult guy." Broadway producer Cy Feuer recalled a "very powerful temper ... He's the only guy I ever saw who would make his point by jumping with both feet off the ground! While yelling!" Feuer's partner, Ernie Martin, remembered Loesser as "strictly a city boy. Loved to quote [screenwriter] Nunnally Johnson, who said that if he had a place with green grass, he'd pave it." Other descriptions include "paranoid about people" and "hated to make commitments."

"It was a good thing that he worked with me for awhile" was Carmichael's rather dry observation. "I had a sobering Indiana effect on him." Whatever the specifics, it's clear that the city boy and the Hoosier did find common ground, and for a few years they turned out tunes together that audiences liked and remembered.[28]

Compared with some of Hoagy's earlier efforts, these are slight, unassuming songs. Two, "Heart and Soul" and "Small Fry," ride on that hoariest of chord patterns, the circular I-VI-II-V, widely known as "We want Cantor." Its simplicity, especially in the key of C, and the stepwise nature of Carmichael's melody, have guaranteed "Heart and Soul" (or at least most of it) a rather unconventional immortality. From coast to American coast, wherever there's a piano and a group of kids to gather around it, someone invariably starts the familiar shuffle vamp.

The bridge, melodically and harmonically the song's most original feature, is generally absent when young hands pound out "Heart and Soul," repeating the "A" section with mounting glee. Paramount slotted the song into a 1938 short subject, *A Song Is Born*—not to be confused with the 1948 feature film starring Benny Goodman, Louis Armstrong, Tommy Dorsey, and other major jazz figures. Many years later, Hoagy declared himself unimpressed with his own melody, but averred that it was nevertheless "a pretty good ballad."

"Small Fry," written at about the same time, is more intriguing. Also using the "We want Cantor" sequence, it's clearly intended as a successor to the still immensely popular "Lazybones"—but with a difference: Loesser's lyric, as published, presents none of the racial ambiguity that makes the earlier song so vivid, and, for some, controversial. The young scamp of "Small Fry" could be anybody's kid, white or black, getting into various forms of mischief when he ought to be in school.

That it didn't start out that way is obvious from Hoagy's and Loesser's lyric worksheet:

> Small Fry, papy's [*sic*] pickaninny,
> Small Fry, small and black and skinny,
> My, my, you're wet behind the ears
> Where did you get those Harlem town ideas?

The sheet is typewritten, then heavily edited in Carmichael's distinctive hand. Almost line by line, he works at expunging the racial theme—and in a wide right-hand margin writes out what is in effect the published version. At another point he interpolates the line "You better listen to your pa[w]/And learn to practice the law," then changes the "pa" to "ma" and the "learn to" to "someday." The reference is obvious, and not a little poignant.

"Small Fry" wound up in Paramount's *Sing You Sinners*, sung by Bing Crosby (and former saxophone player Fred MacMurray) to twelve-year-old Donald O'Connor, making his screen debut. Both tunes, and several others with Loesser including the engaging but unpublished "Wallpaper Roses," were freestanding efforts, written not to order but because songwriter or lyricist had come up with an idea. When Paramount finally gave Carmichael and Loesser a specific assignment, it was a tough one.

The Big Broadcast of 1938 had handed the studio a surprise hit in Robin and Rainger's "Thanks for the Memory," as sung by Bob Hope and Shirley Ross; a couple, now estranged, meet on an ocean liner and discover they're still in love, but remain unable to admit it to one another. The result, in Benny Green's apt phrase, is "one of the very few songs in the popular repertoire with claims to the status of a short story." Robin's lyric, which he continued to augment as years passed, is a narrative gem; it could have found no better interpreters than Hope and Ross, so expert at portraying strong emotions flowing beneath a nonchalant, bantering surface.

Realizing that "they had accidentally produced a highly profitable film which included a highly profitable song and [in Hope] a potentially highly profitable new star," said Green, the Paramount heads "now did what all studios did in those days whenever they had blundered into a moneymaking production. They produced it again." With a logic comprehensible only among the rulers of the seven duchies, they called the sequel *Thanks for the Memory*, but discarded their A-team's hit song. Instead, they tapped second-stringers Carmichael and Loesser for a follow-up, also to be sung by Hope and Ross.

"No two songwriters could ever have inherited a less rewarding job," said Green, "for however well they performed, their new song was doomed to unfavorable comparison with Robin and Rainger's small masterpiece." Yet somehow they pulled it off: "Two Sleepy People," like its predecessor, is "a flippant piece whose unspoken sentiments, delivered in an elusive compromise between talk and song, imply a passionate romantic attachment."[29]

But it also stands handsomely on its own, due in no small measure to Hoagy's melody. Where Rainger's foursquare theme parked solidly on the first and third beats of the bar, resisting even jazz phrasing, Hoagy's reads, as usual, like a Bix improvisation. It's easy to imagine the cornet setting out the tune at a comfortable $\quarternote = 92$, with Frank Trumbauer supplying a counterline and Adrian Rollini's bass saxophone loping along below.

Loesser's lyric, presumably with emendations by Carmichael, works its way into one potentially awkward spot—awkward, at least, in the morally sensitive climate of the time. Since 1930, the Hays Office, watchdog agency for Hollywood's rigorously self-enforced Production Code, had carefully scrutinized each film turned out by the "dream factory." Under the stewardship of Joseph I. Breen, successor to founder Will Hays, the office regularly "suggested" changes in scripts, even to deletion of entire scenes, in the interests of preserving public morality (or, during World War II, morale). Such songwriters as Cole Porter and Lorenz Hart, whose sexual innuendo and sense of *double-entendre* had delighted Broadway audiences, found themselves repeatedly in dispute with the guardians of movie morality, as well as the Roman Catholic Church's Legion of Decency.

According to Carmichael's worksheet, the bridge of "Two Sleepy People" read:

> I remember how we had to linger in the hall
> That's because your father didn't like my looks at all.
> Just to find a place to sit, we married in the fall,
> A very normal life
> A solid man and wife.

A "place *to sit*"? Surely another sort of repose was intended. In place of the awkward third line, Carmichael penciled in a possible substitute:

> Then we married to settle things for once and all . . .

Settle what? Certainly not a place "to sit." The intention is obvious: what the couple seeks, under her father's wary eye, is a chance to savor the delights of the flesh. In most cases, within the morality of the day, that meant getting married: so why not resolve, i.e., "settle," the issue directly? As finally used, the line employs lighthearted innuendo involving the word "nest," universally understood shorthand for "love nest," a conceit at once charming and easily read—and delivered by Hope with a slight, one might say pregnant, pause after the phrase "a bit of":

> Do you remember the reason that we married in the fall?
> To rent this little nest, and get a bit of rest.

Carmichael recorded "Two Sleepy People" that October 14 for Brunswick, on his first commercial date in more than four years. In many respects, this and a second session four days later, each yielding a pair of titles, are an index to both where Hoagy Carmichael has been and where he's headed. Each of the four performances tells an indispensable part of the story.

He sings "Two Sleepy People" as a duet with Ella Logan, backed by a studio group including Mannie Klein on trumpet, Abe Lincoln on trombone, and, on drums, a young Californian named Lindley Armstrong "Spike" Jones, shortly to find his own unique brand of fame. Like Carmichael, Glasgow-born Logan had made her first impact in jazz surroundings, recording in New York with Bud Freeman, Max Kaminsky, Adrian Rollini, Jimmy Dorsey, Benny Goodman, and guitarist George Van Eps within months of her arrival. Her Louis Armstrong–like phrasing on an extraordinary performance of "It Had to Be You," at a 1934 Rollini session, had impressed fellow-musicians.

But Ella Logan's gaze was set firmly on the movies, and early 1936 found her in Hollywood, with her five-year-old niece Annabelle Short—one day to make her own mark as Annie Ross—in tow. At the end of 1937 she recorded four titles for Brunswick under her own name, backed by several of the same musicians heard on the Carmichael session. All four, including debut performances of George Gershwin's last two songs, are strongly jazz-flavored, Logan swinging lightly and happily along, Scots burr lending an ingratiating edge to the lyrics.

By mid-1938 no news item about Ella Logan seemed complete without at least one descriptive phrase such as "Highland Harlequin," "Vocal Volcano of the Heather," or even "Loch Lomond Lass." Accordingly, her second and third Brunswick dates laid on the tartan touches pretty broadly, the jazz band backings increasingly at odds with the theatricality of the vocals.

"Two Sleepy People" betrays little of this: it's comfortable, affectionate, with Hoagy a far more assured vocalist than in 1934. So too "New Orleans," done October 18 at a leisurely tempo far more suited to melody and lyric than the various 1933 performances. The two singers, each en route to someplace new, are enjoying their common ground, and one another, thoroughly.

Hoagy Carmichael as artist-in-transition shows up most vividly on the two other titles. "Hong Kong Blues" was nearly a decade old, souvenir of his first, discouraging, California visit. The lyric, his own, rests on an unusual, even striking, conceit: a pianist, black, stranded far from home, gets hooked on opium in the backstreet warrens of Hong Kong. His need to feed his habit leaves him perpetually broke, playing piano in a dive, trying forlornly to raise his boat fare home. But he's never going to make it: he knows that and so, too, does the listener. Sweet opium has him in its clutches, and he's stuck for good.

That's the plot. Not that there weren't other "reefer" songs: far from it, as a casual review of "Minnie the Moocher," "Reefer Man," "Texas Tea Party," and others of the time will reveal. Carmichael's way of setting out his situation encapsulates the genre and transcends it. His opening phrases, melody and lyric, mimic perfectly the cadences of pidgin English:

"Hong Kong Blues" (intro and bars 1–4), 1939

Even the "very unfortunate" is functional, reminder that most Americans of these years knew little of the Far East. At best, the word "Chinese" conjured up either the sordid *demi-monde* of opium dens and white slavery portrayed in such songs as "Limehouse Blues," or movie detective Charlie Chan, as portrayed first by Swedish-born Warner Oland, then, after his death in 1938, by Sidney Toler. Both actors could be expected to use such phrases as "very unfortunate colored man" and "twenty years privilege" in the clipped, stilted manner reproduced by Carmichael in the opening lines of "Hong Kong Blues."

Is there another formulation in all popular music that says more, without actually *saying* it, than "kicked old Buddah's gong"? In four words, we learn that our hapless hero has got himself hooked on opium and run afoul of Oriental drug lords and, presumably, law-enforcement authorities as well. After a flurry of pidgin phrases in eighth and sixteenth notes, he lands squarely on the phrase "old Hong Kong," its three quarter notes set emphatically on the beat. He knows just where he is, and so do we.[30]

Though written in 4/4, the music has a quasi-Chinese, quite appropriate, *alla breve* feel: its first four bars, establishing place and situation, use a pentatonic scale—i.e., without chromatic steps and avoiding the Western subdominant (fourth) and leading-tone (seventh). Only when the ill-starred Tennessean begins "bobbin the pi-ano just to pay the price/Of a ticket to the land of the free," does the melody take on a jazzier, more Western flavor.

Lapsing into self-pity, he croons:

> I need somebody to love me,
> Need somebody to car[e]-ry me
> Home to San Francisco
> And bury my body there.

The word "care"—rhymed, principally, with "there"—also becomes the first syllable of "carry" (rhyming, in turn, with "bury"); such wordplay bespeaks a verbal sophistication all the more effective for being so unexpected. More of the same with "yen": the Indiana boy will be forgiven, in the context of the pre–World War II 1930s, for failing to realize that the yen as a unit of currency was Japanese, while China traded—officially, at least—in the yuan. Even that has its mitigations: in the first decades of the twentieth century, Hong Kong was Japan's key trade pivot for the rest of the Far East; yuan, yen, and Yankee dollars were traded interchangeably in Hong Kong, where everything was available to anyone who could raise the price.

More important here, "yen," in its other sense, derives specifically from a Chinese expression describing opium addiction. When the pianist says,

> Oh won't somebody believe
> I've a yen . . .
> To see that Bay again?

he's talking on at least two, perhaps even three, levels. His yen is, clearly, his thralldom to the drug; it's also his longing to go home; perhaps it also identifies a banknote or two in his pocket—but never enough to afford a ticket home.

Again, as with "Washboard Blues," this is the early, pre-Hollywood, narrative Carmichael at work, taking the listener from a strong opening description (much in the spirit of "Mornin' comes with cloudy skies and rain") through a vivid exposition of place and character, all in a neatly rendered story-song.

Whether or not he meant it as such, "Hong Kong Blues" constitutes a backward glance at another, musically rich, time of Hoagy's life. So, too—albeit in quite another way—does the fourth title from this pair of Brunswick dates, a conversion of "Riverboat Shuffle" from jazz band instrumental to popular song.

It must have seemed a good idea at the time. Because Mills still owned the copyright, a logical choice of lyricist seemed to be Mitchell Parish, who had dealt so sensitively with "Star Dust" and "One Morning in May," and, as expected, Parish turns in a thorough, workmanlike job; dispensing entirely with the sixteen-bar opening section, he concentrates instead on the longer "blowing" strain.

The title offers the first of many problems. What, exactly, is or was a "riverboat shuffle"? Originally, on that 1924 day in Richmond, Bix and his friends had bestowed the name only because they liked the sound the words made together, and the feelings evoked. But a popular song demanded something more explicit. For the purposes of 1938, a "riverboat shuffle" would have to be a kind of party, preferably one held on board a fondly remembered Mississippi excursion boat. An early draft of the lyric, again in Carmichael's hand, conjures the vision:

> Good people, you're invited tonight,
> To the Riverboat Shuffle.

Good people, there'll be dancing tonight,
   To the Riverboat Shuffle.
Your cares'll go floatin' away
   Down the Mississippi,
When you hear that two-piece swing band play,
   Banjo and piano.
Good people, there'll be lots of "oh gee,"
   At the Riverboat Shuffle,
Lots of gallavantin' on the good old Robert E. Lee,
   What a sight to see.
I'll teach you to shuffle it right,
Then I'll introduce you to my baby,
Just meet me at the Riverboat Shuffle tonight.

Then, whatever his reason, Carmichael (and it surely was he) began to tinker. The line about cares floating away down the Mississippi itself floats away, replaced by something about a "slide-pipe tooter"—even then a rather labored (and resoundingly "square") bit of quasi-musicianspeak meant to identify a trombone player. Also gone is the line about the two-piece swing combo, replaced by what seems a lame attempt at current slang— "freighter" to mean girlfriend, and "alligator" as a verb (?), roughly equivalent to the slightly later "dig."

Strangest of all is the phrase slotted into bars 15 and 16: "Mister Hawkins on the tenor." Hawkins? On a riverboat? Who, outside the relatively small circle of hot jazz initiates, would recognize the name of Coleman Hawkins, who—though born in St. Joseph, Missouri—had spent the 1920s and early '30s as a sideman in Fletcher Henderson's band, and been out of the country four years at the time of this record? And who, finally, is "Mama Dinah," who in the lyric's published version is going to "strut for the boys/In a roomful of noise"?

It's difficult now, and pointless, to conjecture who contributed what to this misbegotten undertaking. Suffice to say that it doesn't work, either as an updating of the original composition or as a freestanding popular song. At any tempo faster than a comfortable $\quarternote = 176$, moreover, the wordy lyric is all but incomprehensible, its rather obscure topical references flashing by too fast for a listener's mind to register. It is not without significance that when Jeffrey Sultanof began compiling material for the 1999 *Centennial Collection* of Carmichael songs, he printed not this version of "Riverboat

Shuffle" but the piano arrangement copyrighted by Mills in 1925 and re-published in 1939.

As historian and critic John McDonough put it in a 1999 interview, jazz "may have been [Carmichael's] roots but it didn't become his life. [Duke] Ellington remained in the jazz life and the jazz world, but Carmichael—he exercised other options . . . [He] left the jazz world behind him at a point in his career, and chose the route of the popular songwriter."[31]

As in 1924, the 1938 "Riverboat Shuffle" marked a divide, a watershed, in Hoagy Carmichael's career. But as events were soon to show, it was a divide of a quite different sort.

✳ XIII ✳

Quests Failed and Fulfilled

The American year 1939 opened on a note of cautious national optimism. War was again darkening Europe, and strong voices at home were urging the Roosevelt administration to stay out. With the nation clearly mending after nearly a decade of depression, there seemed time, and reason, to indulge in some high spirits.

In the words of historian Robert Kee, "the New Year seemed to be welcomed with a greater revelry than for some years past. In New York the emphasis of nearly all the many public and private parties in hotels and restaurants was on the theme of the New York World's Fair, 'Dawn of a New Day,' " scheduled to open in May. Following George Gershwin's death in mid-1937, his brother Ira and their friend Kay Swift had fused two of his unpublished melodies into a song of that name, quickly adopted as the fair's official march.[1]

A January 3 *New York Times* editorial caught the mood:

Even after such a year as 1938 which was once young and innocent as 1939 is now, there persists an unconquerable human conviction that the turn of the year is also the most auspicious moment in which to turn over a new leaf.

Certainly the sense of well-being found resonance in the daily life of Hoagy Carmichael. He'd arrived at, if not a pinnacle, at least a high plateau of success and had every reason to look about him with satisfaction.

His songs were doing well. "Little Old Lady," "Heart and Soul," and such established standards as "Lazybones" and "Rockin' Chair" were racking up steady sales. "Star Dust" shone on undimmed. At the movies, *Sing You Sinners* ("Small Fry") and *Thanks for the Memory* ("Two Sleepy People") held steady at the box office, as did *College Swing*, with Bob Hope, Betty Grable, Martha Raye, Burns and Allen, and other top stars kicking and strutting to a new Carmichael rhythm number. A long Paramount trailer showed Hoagy teaching avid alligators the "College Swing" dance step, based on the childhood game of pat-a-cake and requiring that partners tweak each other's noses.

Paramount had slotted Carmichael's "Kind'a Lonesome" into *St. Louis Blues*—despite its title a standard musical set aboard a Mississippi riverboat. Though the female lead was Dorothy Lamour (who had toured with Bud Dant in Herbie Kay's Indiana band and married the leader), the song featured Maxine Sullivan, who had swung the old Scottish air "Loch Lomond" into national popularity.

Even at home, destiny seemed to be smiling on Hoagy and Ruth, with the birth of their first child, a son. In a nod to a fondly remembered past, they named him Hoagy Bix.

Beiderbecke—his music more than his life—had been the inspiration for Dorothy Baker's *Young Man With a Horn*, one of 1938's best-selling novels. Now Broadway producer Jed Harris was in Los Angeles, reportly conferring with actor Burgess Meredith about a film adaptation of the book. As reported by band publicist and radio producer Herb Sanford, Carmichael had been approached as musical consultant.

Hoagy had meanwhile filmed a Paramount short as guest soloist with old pal Jack Teagarden's band, featuring "Small Fry" and "Lazybones," "Rockin' Chair" and "Washboard Blues" (their effectiveness compromised each time the camera cut away to scenes of rural black life), and a new item, "That's Right—I'm Wrong," plus "Two Sleepy People" and, as a finale, "Star Dust." Whether "conducting" the band, playing and singing, or trading quips with Big Tea, Hoagy seems stiff, ill at ease before the cameras. He's a bit more relaxed at the piano in a *Top Tunes* short subject, playing and singing "Rockin' Chair," "Lazybones," "Star Dust," and "Little Old

Lady." But overall, he's still the solemn collegian of the 1925 Hitch photo: "Hoagy Carmichael," who will presently become a familiar laid-back character in Hollywood movies, is still a work-in-progress.

In a move soon to have a profound effect on Carmichael's career, the New York–based Shubert organization had meanwhile contacted librettist Guy Bolton about purchasing American rights to produce a musical version of *Three Blind Mice*, a light comedy Bolton had written and staged in London's West End. Born in Britain of American parents, Bolton had made his U.S. reputation as co-librettist, with P. G. Wodehouse, for Jerome Kern's great Princess Theatre shows of post–World War I years. He'd worked with George Gershwin during the 1920s on *Oh, Kay* and *Lady Be Good*, and on various projects with Cole Porter and Rodgers and Hart, among others.

Though attributed to Bolton's wife Virginia de Lanty (under the pseudonym "Stephen Powys"), *Three Blind Mice* was widely understood to be Bolton's own work and seemed a natural for musical treatment: originally titled *The Gibson Girls*, its lighter-than-air storyline followed the exploits of Vivi (later Pamela), Rhoda, and Carrie Gibson, owners of a New Hampshire chicken farm, when they go south to Palm Beach looking for mates. In 1937, Twentieth Century–Fox had outbid two competitors and filmed it as a comedy vehicle for actress Loretta Young.[2]

January also brought what has to be the most storied of Carmichael songs. According to most accounts, a Carmichael friend, identity unknown, had noticed a short poem in *Life* magazine (not the Henry R. Luce illustrated weekly but its predecessor, a journal of humor and social commentary published from 1883 to 1936), copied it out, and passed it to Hoagy. Titled "Except Sometimes," and signed only with the initials "J.B.," it took the form of an elegy to a love savored and lost. Carmichael read it, apparently liked it, and filed it away.[3]

Sometime in 1938 it again fell under his gaze. In its original form, "Except Sometimes" conveys a nicely measured melancholy.

> I get along without you very well,
> Of course I do.
> Except the times a soft rain falls,
> And dripping off the trees recalls
> How you and I stood deep in mist

> One day far in the woods, and kissed.
> But now I get along without you—well,
> Of course I do.
>
> I really have forgotten you, I boast,
> Of course I have.
> Except when someone sings a strain
> Of song, then you are here again;
> Or laughs a way which is the same
> As yours; or when I hear your name.
> I really have forgotten you—almost.
> Of course I have.[4]

He began to rewrite it, rearranging key phrases and even entire thoughts. His penciled worksheets show the step-by-step transformation, as he discards obstructions (the consonant-heavy "boast," for example) and "listens" with eye and ear.

"J.B.'s" opening couplet remains in place. At first, Carmichael follows it with

> Except when soft rain falls
> And dripping from the trees recalls
> How we once stood deep in the woods and kissed . . .

He tries changing that to

> That day that we strolled through the woods and kissed . . .

only to reject it for

> That day we stood there in the woods and kissed . . .

He adjusts it to

> That day we stood in rain-soaked woods and kissed . . .

rounding out the thought with

... So tenderly.
... How sweet that was.
... So sweet to me.
...'Twas heavenly.
... Of course we did (echoing the "of course I do").
... But there I go.

Still, it doesn't quite work. The problem, he realizes, is the "woods-mist-kissed" imagery, too abrupt a sonic lurch from the gauzy tone of the opening couplet.

He tries modifying it, keeping the rain and the kiss, but introducing the more generalized, and emotionally denser, concept of love-as-refuge:

> The times that I found shelter in your kiss,
> Of course I did.

But a kiss, however rapturous, doesn't provide shelter—and that's what's keeping things earthbound. Its convergence of sibilants both hardens the texture and stays the forward momentum. At last he discards it, opting instead for the softer, open vowel-consonant blend of

> The thrill of being sheltered in your arms,

lending "of course I do" an appropriate, suitably ironic, finality.

Beyond doubt, an acute ear has made these decisions, its accuracy obvious in the completed lyric, an elegy of poignancy and surprising depth.

> I get along without you very well,
> Of course I do.
> Except when soft rains fall
> And drip from leaves, then I recall
> The thrill of being sheltered in your arms,
> Of course I do.
> But I get along without you very well.
>
> I've forgotten you just like I should,
> Of course I have.
> Except to hear your name,

> Or someone's laugh that is the same.
> Yes I've forgotten you just like I should.[5]

Continuing into the bridge, he introduces an element of self-reproach present in the original poem:

> What a guy, what a fool am I,
> To think my aching heart could kid the moon.
> What's in store? Should I phone once more?
> No—it's best that I stick to my tune.

In at least one respect, this text faintly echoes "Washboard Blues." Both songs are first-person musings, both in the mind of a woman; both begin with a strongly defined stance: where "Washboard's" narrator contemplates a day full of "cloudy skies and rain," this speaker begins in fond reflection— I get along without you very well, adding "of *course* I do" to shore up flagging resolve. The listener knows what the speaker won't admit: she does *not* get along without him very well. Not a bit.

Just as "Washboard's" middle, or blues, section drops its façade of resignation, allowing real emotions to break through, the release of "I Get Along" reveals that all so far has been bravado, self-deception. What's left? Just the final, touching admission that

> I get along without you very well,
> Of course I do.
> Except perhaps in spring—
> But I should never think of spring,
> For that would surely break my heart in two.

Like "Washboard Blues" before it, "I Get Along Without You Very Well" lies halfway between song and recitative, words and music ascending side-by-side along a finely calibrated emotional arc.

Surprisingly, an almost querulous Alec Wilder missed this fundamental point, instead (in *American Popular Song*) complaining of a lack of harmonic complexity and citing long stretches underpinned only by dominant harmony. Yet that is as it should be, Carmichael's instincts directing the focus inward: any attempt to dress the line in more sophisticated raiment would have drawn the listener's attention from content to structure, breaking a fragile inner continuum.

Writer Gene Lees, an accomplished and respected lyricist, has pronounced the song "a jewel"—not least because Carmichael has fashioned his melody from a completed text, rather than the reverse order more common among songwriters. One indication of how well the entire enterprise succeeds lies in the ease with which instrumentalists playing "I Get Along Without You Very Well" slip into the mood and content of the lyric, even when no singer is present. Wilder is quite right in ending his discussion with the admission, however grudging, that the song is "unlike any other popular song I know."[6]

✻　　　✻　　　✻

Once completed, "I Get Along Without You" was scheduled for immediate release—until attorneys for Famous Music delivered a piece of not-quite-welcome news. Carmichael's lyric had drawn heavily on a piece of published verse, which (in common with everything else that had appeared in the old *Life*) was still in copyright. "J.B." would have to be identified, found, and induced to allow publication of material first used in "Except Sometimes." That would involve either a waiver of any claim to proprietorship—unlikely in the circumstances—or a contractual arrangement granting the poet some form of credit and, presumably, a share in the royalties.

But where to look? How to find a writer, identified only by initials, whose work had appeared only once, more than fifteen years before? The answer, then as now, lay in media coverage, in a well-publicized search for the identity and whereabouts of the enigmatic "J.B."

Enter, in shirtsleeves and fedora hat, an unlikely hero: newsman Walter Winchell, who through his syndicated columns in William Randolph Hearst's *New York Daily Mirror* and fifteen-minute Sunday-night *Jergens Journal* NBC radio broadcasts reached an estimated fifty million Americans weekly.[7]

On Sunday, November 27, 1938, little more than a week after copyright was registered on the song, Winchell read the first of several items devoted to "J.B.":

Attention, poets and songwriters!
　　Hoagy Carmichael, whose songs you love, has a new positive hit—

but he cannot have it published. Not until the person who inspired the words communicates with him and agrees to become his collaborator . . . I hope that person is a listener now.

He lists some of Carmichael's past hits, quotes part of "Except Sometimes," and winds up with an exhortation:

If you wrote those lines in a poem, tell your Uncle Walter, who will tell his Uncle Hoagy, and you may become famous.[8]

A week later, during the part of the broadcast he calls "Oddities in the News," he remarks that the numerous responses to the search for the poet have created a new problem:

Hoagy wants to do the right thing by the man or woman who inspired [the song]. But . . . I never knew that one poem could have forty authors; at least forty people in as many states claim writing it, and I am afraid that these forty claimants will be terribly embarrassed when we find the real author.[9]

Weeks passed before Winchell again brought up the matter, this time in one of his *Daily Mirror* columns:

Hoagy still seeks the author to give him or her a share of the royalties. Many people claim it—but . . . we have a clipping of it signed by the initials "J.B." which appeared in *Life* magazine in 1922. H. Newman, publisher of *Judge,* who owns the material in the old *Life,* will get the royalties—until "J.B." is found.[10]

Finally, eight days later, he reported:

Well, we've found the lady who wrote that verse in the old *Life* (1922) at last! The verse which inspired Hoagy Carmichael's new love lilt. At least "Jane Brown" (it was signed "J.B.") claims authorship. She will rate 3¢ a copy on the ditty if her claim holds up.[11]

As events quickly revealed, this was less the end of the story than its beginning. "Jane Brown" was Mrs. Jane Brown Thompson, a widow, born in Bremen, Indiana, in 1867 and living in Philadelphia. She did not have a telephone, listened only seldom to the radio. Her husband William H. "Harry" Thompson, father of their three children, had died in early 1934 following a long illness.

According to British researcher Roger S. B. Hinsley, "Jane had literary aspirations all her adult life and had a number of poems and short stories published. All were of a fundamentally romantic nature, usually with amusing or cynical overtones."[12]

Neither a listener to the *Jergens Journal* nor a reader of the *New York Daily Mirror*, she'd been tracked down through the efforts of two retired *Life* magazine staffers. Through her attorney, she'd agreed to the proposed terms. The contract, on file in the archives of Famous Music Corp., is dated January 6, 1939. The title on the published sheet music was to read "I Get Along Without You Very Well (Except Sometimes)" and bear the inscription "Words inspired by a poem written by J.B. (?)"

As told by Carmichael, by Herb Sanford, and in countless newspaper stories, the song was to be premiered on Thursday, January 19, 1939, sung on network radio by Dick Powell. Jane Brown Thompson had been in poor health for some time and died of a thrombosis on Wednesday evening, January 18, twenty-four hours before she would have heard the Carmichael song she'd helped write. It's a poignant story, a journalist's dream, its ironic ending quite in keeping with the elegaic nature of both poem and finished lyric.

Perhaps too much in keeping. A brief item in Winchell's "On Broadway" column for Monday, December 26, 1938, reports that "Hoagy Carmichael's latest love lilt, 'I Get Along Without You Very Well,' will be introduced by Guy Lombardo's crew tonight." If this indeed happened, it raises obvious questions: had Jane Brown Thompson already been found, and a contract anticipated, as early as the day after Christmas? Did the Lombardo band in fact play the song? Was there a vocal? Was it broadcast, or simply featured during an evening's work at the Roosevelt Grill? If the Royal Canadians indeed broadcast the song, why did Jane Brown Thompson not hear it at that time? Have Carmichael, Sanford, and the rest simply dropped an inconvenient bit of information in the interests of a more colorful story?

Winchell, again, provides evidence, albeit circumstantial. In his column for January 20, 1939, he reports, "Dick Powell's version of Hoagy Carmichael's new torchant [*sic*] 'I Get Along Without You Very Well' was a new radio high spot." No mention of Mrs. Thompson, of the search, or of her death. If the Powell broadcast was indeed the premiere, and if the poet's death robbed her of so major a satisfaction only a day before the big moment, surely Winchell, ever alert to such stuff, would have made mention. But he remains silent.

✻ ✻ ✻

"I Get Along Without You Very Well" was on the playlist the evening of March 1 when Tommy Dorsey's orchestra broadcast live from the stage of the Lyric Theatre in Indianapolis. Hoagy was booked for a spot on the show—and insisted that the guest roster also include a second Carmichael.

"It seemed only fair and logical that my mother, who had done so much to inspire me musically, should have some fame of her own," he wrote in *Sometimes I Wonder*. "She was a very fine piano player, and in some other time and setting, with a different destiny, she could have become a star performer."

A feature in the *Indianapolis Star*, under the headline "Hoagy Carmichael Returns for Mother's Radio Debut," told the story. The band would contribute performances of various Carmichael hits, with the composer joining in at the piano for "Riverboat Shuffle." Lida would close the show with her specialty, Scott Joplin's *Maple Leaf Rag*, backed by Dorsey and his musicians. "She looked like an old pro," Hoagy wrote, "and if she had the butterflies in her stomach she didn't show it . . . Mother was taking it all as if it were coming to her, and in a way I am sure it was."[13]

"Mrs. Carmichael attacked with an enthusiasm and a confidence that would have been the envy of Fats Waller," producer Sanford noted. "Her head moved with the beat and the notes leaped out. The band's accompaniment was affectionate even in the crescendos."

According to a story in the next morning's *Star*, the "capacity audience that had gathered hours in advance whooped and hollered, whistled and clapped." That wasn't the half of it, said Sanford. "The audience was electrified. They hadn't expected anything like this. They thought we just wanted them to meet Hoagy's mother. The response was overwhelming. They cheered. They screamed. Some were even moved to tears. Mrs. Carmichael had stolen the show right out from under Tommy and Hoagy."[14]

✻ ✻ ✻

Herb Sanford figures more than tangentially in Carmichael's life during these months. They had been friends since the late 1920s, when Sanford was hanging out with Bix and the Dorseys, and playing piano in the Princeton Triangle Club jazz band alongside "Squirrel" Ashcraft, Bill Priestly, Frank Orvis, and Avery Sherry. He'd scheduled Carmichael to appear on one of Dorsey's regular Raleigh-Kool shows in mid-February, to help plug "I Get Along Without You Very Well." He'd even collaborated with Hoagy and Helen Meinardi on a song, "Manhattan in the Spring," published the following year.

At some point in early 1939, he writes, Hoagy turned up in his midtown Manhattan office with news of the *Young Man With a Horn* project. But as Sanford recalls it, the conversation was not about a movie but about a Broadway production, a dramatic play with music in which an actor would portray Bix onstage while an offstage trumpet player provided the horn bits. Hoagy had been named music consultant, he said, and was on the lookout for the right cornet player. He'd already put together a theme, a kind of Bix-like *Leitmotif*, to announce "Rick Martin," the Bix character of the Baker novel.

Calling it "Bix Lix" for short, he hummed it for Sanford at a medium, Beiderbecke-like tempo:

"Bix Lix" (4 bars), 1939

"I had some doubts about a production of 'Young Man With a Horn,' " Sanford writes, "for reasons having nothing to do with Hoagy, but I did want to hear more of that tune. The play was never produced, and the tune found a resting place in Hoagy's trunk."[15]

His account rings true, but the time seems wrong. Apart from the *Variety* and *Down Beat* items describing the Harris-Meredith movie plans, there is no evidence of a *Young Man With a Horn* stage project at this early point. But a feature story in the *New York Sunday News*, dated ten months later, on November 19, 1939, suggests that Sanford may have gotten his facts right and placed them at the wrong time.

Under the headline "World of Swing O.K. to Burgess Meredith," writer

Julia McCarthy describes the Cleveland-born actor rehearsing for the Bix role in a Broadway *Young Man With a Horn* production, even to the point of practicing the cornet in "his own rural retreat near New York City . . . so as to make the Beiderbeck [*sic*] impersonation practically perfect."

"I'm not good enough yet on the horn," he tells the reporter. "I don't know how we'll arrange that in the play." He goes on to explain that the play "isn't biographical, [but] follows the spirit of the man whose whole experience was wrapped up in his genius." There is no mention of Carmichael.[16]

Could this have been the play of which Hoagy spoke so glowingly to Sanford? Does the presence of Burgess Meredith in both projects provide a link between Jed Harris's plans for filming the story at New York's Astoria studios and the late-1939 news of a dramatic stage presentation? Harris is not mentioned in the latter report. Nor is Carmichael. Another decade would pass before *Young Man With a Horn* made it to the screen—with Hoagy Carmichael, in the most fully realized role of his screen career, playing "Smoke," a piano player who befriends the doomed, trumpet-playing Rick Martin.

The trail to the 1939 production quickly grows cold in all but two particulars: first, Burgess Meredith soon got to use his newfound skill with a trumpet in Hollywood's 1942 *Second Chorus,* casting him and Fred Astaire as two jazz hornmen (soundtrack solos by Bobby Hackett and Billy Butterfield), rivals for the favors of Paulette Goddard. Second, and of far greater importance, Hoagy's "Bix Lix" motif resurfaced in 1941, this time with a nonpareil Johnny Mercer lyric, as "Skylark," one of the most beloved of Carmichael ballads.

Carmichael hardly had time to reflect on such developments. Negotiations on Bolton's *Three Blind Mice* had reached contract stage, and in mid-1939 the Shubert Organization approached Hoagy and Johnny Mercer about composing words and music for the show, to be retitled *Three After Three*—reference to the three Gibson sisters and their quest for eligible bachelors.

In a letter to J. J. Shubert dated August 31, New York attorney Arthur Fishbein declares that he represents Carmichael and Mercer and inquires "whether or not a deal can be consummated" on the show. The Shubert office responds a week later, setting out contracts for both *Three Blind Mice* and a second production, identified as the *Ziegfeld Follies, 1939–1940 version.* The negotiation process consumes the month of September, with attorneys for both sides proposing and rejecting terms and conditions.

By the time the blizzard of paper let up, the *Ziegfeld Follies* idea apparently had been dropped, and *Three Blind Mice* (title subject to change) was going ahead. Mercer and Carmichael were contracted to supply a maximum of ten songs, constituting the entire score. Each would receive $500 [$5,752 in today's currency] upon signing, and 1.25 percent of the weekly box-office gross—a negotiated improvement over the 1 percent each first offered by Shubert. In addition, each would be entitled to approximately a quarter of any proceeds from movie sales, radio, television, condensation or tabloid publication, amateur or stock performances, or foreign options.[17]

Three After Three went into rehearsal during the first week of November. Its stars were to be Simone Simon, a French actress whose chief experience had been in films, and Mitzi Green, who had sung "My Funny Valentine," "Where or When," and "The Lady Is a Tramp" in Rodgers and Hart's 1937 Broadway hit *Babes in Arms*. In the strong supporting cast were veterans Frances Williams, Jack Whiting, and Mary Brian, former trombonist and band vocalist Art Jarrett, black comedian Stepin Fetchit, and a vocal quartet called the Martins, two of whose members were future songwriters Hugh Martin and Ralph Blane.

The show's break-in period, beginning late that month, took the form of a tour, playing New Haven, Boston, Philadelphia, Baltimore, Washington, Pittsburgh, Toronto, Chicago, St. Louis, and Detroit, sometimes for only a week at a time. Judging from press reaction, *Three After Three* was in trouble from the start. "The foundation is there," a New Haven reviewer remarked, "but it's going to require skill and plugging to build a hit show on it." The Carmichael-Mercer score was "not outstanding . . . The tendency of the lyrics is toward a mere rhyming of lines, rather than inspired wordage."

Elinor Hughes of the *Boston Herald,* by contrast, praised "some of the nicest songs of the new season: we expect to hear such numbers as 'Way Back in 1939 A.D.,' 'Wait Till You See Me in the Morning,' 'Everything Happens to Me,' and 'Ooh, What You Said' all over the place from now on. Hoagy Carmichael and Johnny Mercer can take bows for them, but in the meanwhile they'd better write a few more, as the second act seemed to consist mainly of reprises."

Donald Kirkley, writing in the *Baltimore Sun,* also found the songs "consistently bright and pleasing," but added that "one listens in vain for an outstanding hit." More of the same in Washington, with one writer describing Carmichael's music as "adequate" but offering "little chance to drop into the threnodic spirit" of "Star Dust." Most writers opined that *Three After Three* had potential but needed work, and the Shuberts agreed: a letter to Actors' Equity confirms that "a good part of the show is being rewritten and many new numbers [are] being added with a view to insuring a successful New York run."[18]

On to Pittsburgh, where one writer declared that "not in a long time has any musical been so generously blessed with microphone fodder, for practically every tune is out of Tin Pan Alley's top drawer." Yet again, "none of the tunes is the equal of Hoagy's 'Star Dust,' but Johnny [Mercer] did a pretty good job on the lyrics." For Toronto writer Karl Krug, the Mercer-Carmichael score "seldom lets you down."

Ashton Stevens of the *Chicago Herald-American*, who had won a kind of immortality in coining the phrase "sweetest music this side of heaven" for the band of Guy Lombardo, heard the *Three After Three* songs as "workmanlike" but nowhere near the achievement of "Star Dust." Others generally concurred, though to at least one writer Carmichael and Mercer "show unmistakable signs of crashing the Rodgers-Hart, Kern-Hammerstein-Cole Porter inner circle."[19]

That thought must have fallen sweetly on Hoagy's ears. Since his first days in New York he'd regarded the "inner circle" across what seemed an unbridgeable chasm. The Broadway "big boys," as he was heard more than once to call them, had everything he found lacking in himself: polish, sophistication, formal training in music. Above all, a level of respect that lifted them out of the music-for-hire status he still occupied as a Hollywood songwriter.

Music apart, most reviewers felt that the show had potential but that extensive doctoring was needed, particularly on Bolton's libretto. Simone Simon, who had made headlines some years before by publicly offering an amorous George Gershwin the key to her Hollywood mansion, generally failed to project her Gallic charm beyond the footlights. "She doesn't act much," said one writer, "she sings scarcely at all, she doesn't try to dance—all she really does is walk and flirt—and look."

At one point in the Chicago run, J. J. "Jake" Shubert, one of three brothers who had built the theatre empire bearing their name, paid a visit—and did not like what he saw. He had viewed the fledgling show during its New Haven tryouts and now had to admit that, for all the tinkering with the book, staging, costumes, and even additions to and deletions from the score, *Three After Three* hadn't improved significantly. "It was not a good show," says Shubert biographer Jerry Stagg. "Jake had his usual comments and suggestions and decided to change the title to *Walk With Music*—there was very little else that might help."[20]

They called time out. Rather than open in New York directly after Easter as originally scheduled, *Walk With Music* went back to the drawing board. Mlle. Simon departed, the part of Pamela Gibson going to the scintillating—and distinctly American-accented—Kitty Carlisle. The Martins left, replaced by the Modernaires, who had lately created a stir with Paul Whiteman's orchestra. "Give, Baby, Give," a non–Carmichael-Mercer song interpolated during the tour, was scrapped. Script doctors, including Parke Levy, Alan Lipscott, Rowland Leigh, and Guy Bolton himself, came and went. New scenery arrived, costumes were revamped and replaced. A tentative New York opening date of May 27 was announced, then set back a week. By then, according to press releases, Carmichael and Mercer had written four new songs for the score, retaining five of the originals.

At last, on Tuesday, June 4, *Walk With Music* opened at the Ethel Barrymore Theatre. The time for discussing possibility and potential, prediction and promise, was past. This was Broadway: *Walk With Music* had to deliver—or face the ignominy of empty houses, meager box-office returns, and a quick closing.

This time, as everyone had expected, the critics were not as indulgent as they'd been during the road tour. Brooks Atkinson set the tone in the *New York Times:* "The truth is that 'Three Blind Mice' hangs around the neck of 'Walk With Music' like a stricken albatross. If it were not for the original plot, with its mechanical complications, Hoagy Carmichael's music would seem gay and tingling, and an excellent cast of talented performers could dance on tip-toe straight through it." Hoagy, he added, "writes melody with dash and enthusiasm," singling out "Ooh, What You Said!" and the lilting "I Walk With Music" for special praise.[21]

For Richard Watts of the *New York Herald-Tribune*, Carmichael's score was "passably pleasant, but far from distinguished." Where Burns Mantle of the *New York Daily News* enjoyed its "pleasant lilt," the *Journal-American*'s John Anderson found it "runs in one ear and out of memory so quickly that it will take a snappy echo to capture all of it." John Mason

Brown of the *New York Post* sounded the death-knell: "There is one thing, however, the [historical] records do not make clear. That is why anyone, after closing [the show], should have believed in it to the extent of rewriting, recasting, and rechristening it to bring it in."[22]

Backstage, said Kitty Carlisle Hart, it was "a real big mess. Utter chaos. Everything was all mixed up: everybody connected with the show, I mean not the performers, seemed very—well, social. You could never pin them down to anything that was serious. My second-act costume arrived—I mean *arrived*—at the end of the first act. It had nice music. Also Mitzi, Betty [Lawford], and I got along very well, had a very nice time. But the rest? Badly directed, badly organized, and the producer—was it Ruth Selwyn?—didn't seem to have a very firm grip."[23]

Walk With Music lasted fifty-five performances before sinking. Though script and music still exist, it has not been performed since. Standard histories of Broadway in the prewar years, when they mention it at all, do so only briefly and in passing. Brooks McNamara, in his chronicle *The Shuberts of Broadway*, notes only that "the book, about three farm girls who seek their fortunes in West Palm Beach, was weak, and constant interpolations and changes weakened it even further."[24]

Looking back, Johnny Mercer summed it up well: "It was a nice, ineffectual show, out of date and just not vital enough to stand up to *Pal Joey* and the music that was being written then. 'Corny' is the word we would have used then—but not [for] Hoagy's tunes. They were ahead of their time, as usual."[25]

Hoagy himself has little to say. "We all liked the score but the show was too weak to give the songs much exposure. Jake Shubert got under my skin on a few occasions and most of us were disturbed anyway because we did not think enough thought and money was being put into the production."[26]

Would the *Walk With Music* score have fared better in a show with better organization and a stronger book? In all probability, yes. The songs, if not memorable, were tuneful enough, well-enough crafted, to have enjoyed lives independent of the show. "Ooh, What You Said" did nicely through records by the Glenn Miller and Bob Crosby orchestras, "The R(h)umba Jumps" via Woody Herman and Gene Krupa. "What'll They Think of Next?" and the first act finale, "Break It Up Cinderella," are catchy and rhythmic, and "Way Back in 1939 A.D." is a *faux*-medieval love serenade somewhat in the spirit of Rodgers and Hart's "Thou Swell."

All deserve better than the obscurity which has been their lot for more than sixty years.

And, too, the score offers one for the ages, the astonishing "I Walk With Music." This centerpiece ballad, sufficiently compelling to prompt Jake Shubert to retitle the show, spans forty bars (plus a sixteen-bar verse), gliding in 4/4 atop unsyncopated sequences of half and quarter notes. With its open intervals and spacious, lighter-than-air quality, it seems less typical of Carmichael than of Jerome Kern.

"I Walk With Music" (bars 1–16), 1940

Mention of Kern points up an intriguing parallel. *Very Warm for May*, with score by Kern and Oscar Hammerstein, had opened in Broadway in November of 1939, lasting only fifty-nine performances. The Kern-Hammerstein songs ("All in Fun," "Heaven in My Arms"), though engaging and well promoted, had failed to transcend an inept book and all but vanished with the show—with the memorable exception of "All the Things You Are." Also written in half and quarter notes over an unaccented 4/4, also virtually without syncopation, it shares even deeper affinities with "I Walk With Music" in working off a melodic line which constantly shifts tonal centers.[27]

In the Carmichael song, each eight-bar episode brings a modulation: as published, it begins in C-major, shifts effortlessly to A; then, respelling the C♯ (third step in an A-major chord) at the end of the passage as a D♭, it modulates to G♭ and thence back to C.

"I Walk With Music" (bars 17–31), 1940

So skilfully does Carmichael manage these bits of *trompe l'oreille* that the listener's ear, none the wiser, never loses its bearings.[28]

There is no question why "All the Things You Are" endured as a standard long after *Very Warm for May* was forgotten. But why has "I Walk With Music" failed to achieve comparable eminence? Beyond Carmichael devotees and a relatively small cadre of Broadway historians, it remains all but unrecognized.

The Broadway career of *Walk With Music* ended amid recrimination. Stepin Fetchit left the show without notice in Detroit, missing the last three performances. His part, the valet Chesterfield, was subsequently written out of the script. As early as March 29, the Shuberts registered formal complaint with Actors' Equity, demanding the comedian's suspension and repayment of $600, representing two weeks' salary [$7,000 in today's currency]. Shubert correspondence beginning in July discusses which of several participating organizations will assume responsibility for paying the cast, chorus, and crew for the duration of the short run. A letter to the Shuberts from an attorney representing Mercer and Carmichael lays claim to one of the songs, "Darn Clever These Chinee," dropped before New York and still unpublished, though copyrighted by the theatre organization.

"Soon after the opening," Hoagy writes,

> it appeared that one of our songs was not going to work out and in an impertinent manner Jake [Shubert] yelled at me, "Write another

song." I'd had it. I followed him up the aisle, took him by the coat lapels and shook him.

"Don't ever talk to me that way again," I said.

This bit perhaps explains why I was never invited to write another Broadway show.[29]

These events, or something like them, probably took place. But Carmichael's explanation seems more than a bit disingenuous: Broadway, after all, is a business. If a show succeeds and there is money to be made, personal relations among participants are of relatively little moment. Broadway lore abounds with stories of classic quarrels between producers and directors, leads and supporting cast members, impresarios and composers.

Here, as in any marketplace situation, the bottom line rules supreme. From most accounts, *Walk With Music* was doomed from the start, and J. J. Shubert, his money at risk, more than likely expressed himself tactlessly, even intemperately, to Carmichael.

It takes little second-guessing, moreover, to suppose that Shubert knew full well he was dealing with a newcomer to theatre composing. A Porter, Berlin, Kern, or Rodgers had long since mastered the art of deflecting such excesses with charm or self-possession. That Carmichael lacked comparable skills is hardly surprising: too much of himself, of his artistic self-respect, was riding on this score for diplomacy to enter the picture. Kitty Carlisle Hart, who witnessed and survived many such altercations, and some far worse, summed it up succinctly. Informed that Carmichael aspired to the stature and reputation only Broadway success could confer, she nodded enthusiastic agreement.

"He was right," she said. "That was a sign of having made it . . . When Moss [Hart] and I used to go to Hollywood, and he was writing those movies . . . I remember saying to him one day, 'Why don't we see any other [writers] around socially?' He said, 'There are very few, and they live across Wilshire Boulevard, on the other side, and not within Beverly Hills.' They were not considered *persona grata*, he said. Very few of them were. [But] there were [also] the New York writers—Irving Berlin, Cole, and the rest— and Moss was one of the chosen few. We used to go to dinner at Louis B. Mayer's, and stay at the Goldwyns', so it was really a compartmentalized society."

When a movie came out, it was "a Bing Crosby film, or somebody else's film—but never a Robin and Rainger film. Whereas on Broadway a Porter show was a Porter show, a Kern show was a Kern show, and so on." *Walk With Music*, had it succeeded, would have been "a Hoagy Carmichael–Johnny Mercer show," she said, "and that would have been the affirmation he wanted. Needed."[30]

Ira Gershwin, writing of his brother's dissatisfaction with composing for movies, has commented that the composer "wasn't so much a part of the songs as he would be in New York . . . There in New York George had always been consulted as to how the numbers should be done . . . Here it seemed the moment your contract ended . . . you were through. Then everything was left to the studio, to do whatever they wanted."[31]

Carmichael, it seemed, would have to heed a thought from one of his own song titles and get along without that New York brand of affirmation as well as possible.[32]

* XIV *

A Poke in His Pocket...

Americans responded to the December 7, 1941, Japanese attack on Pearl Harbor in intense, often personal, ways—but with an overall unity. The fractiousness that had tied up public debate over possible U.S. involvement in the century's second "foreign" war seemed to evaporate overnight. As *Time* magazine put it:

> The war came as a great relief, like a reverse earthquake, that in one terrible jerk shook everything disjointed, distorted, askew back into place. Japanese bombs had finally brought national unity to the U.S.[1]

From ballparks to boatyards to bandstands, Americans dropped whatever they were doing and signed up in their thousands to fight. Rumors of a possible Japanese invasion flashed up and down the West Coast of the United States. Air-raid sirens went off in San Francisco after someone reported seeing Japanese aircraft; another account, similarly unfounded, had Japanese carriers off the mouth of the Columbia River, on the Oregon-Washington border.

Blackouts, strictly enforced, became the rule. The annual Rose Bowl football game was hurriedly relocated from Pasadena to North Carolina.

Barbed-wire barricades sprang up on California beaches. Some locations had spotlights and even hastily installed anti-aircraft guns.[2]

Almost immediately, suspicion focused on the 110,000 Japanese living on the West Coast—the immigrant Issei and their children, the Nisei. Even so respected a figure as columnist Walter Lippman warned that "communication takes place between the enemy at sea and enemy agents on land . . . The Pacific Coast is officially a combat zone: some part of it may at any moment be a battlefield."[3]

How easy it would be, such thinking went, to recruit significant numbers of Japanese-Americans as a fifth column, to undermine the American cause from within. Pressure mounted to act against them, to preempt the threat from within by forcibly interning all West Coast Japanese in camps far from the coast.

And in the exclusive Holmby Hills section of Los Angeles, Philip K. Wrigley put his luxury home at 10281 Charing Cross Road up for sale. Son and heir to chewing gum magnate William P. Wrigley Jr., Philip shared the thoughts of many: if the Japanese could surprise, and all but destroy, the U.S. Pacific fleet at rest on a Sunday morning, how long would it be before they turned their gaze, and their guns, on California?

It didn't take his representatives long to find a customer in Hoagy Carmichael. Things were going well, and the composer—who had lived in a series of rented homes since his arrival in California—found little difficulty raising the reported $100,000 (about $1.15 million by today's valuation) asking price. A second son, born June 27, 1940, and named Randy Bob after actors Randolph Scott and Bob Montgomery, both good friends, had increased the family number to four. Eva Ford, more than ever a part of the Carmichael household, made it a quintet, with room to spare. They finally moved in toward the end of 1942.[4]

A U-shaped structure in the California ranch style popular at the time, and situated on a manicured three-acre plot, the house encircled an open-air, sun-washed patio and swimming pool. Every room opened onto this center area, the master bedroom onto a rose garden. Morning, noon, or evening, its rooms glowed with light. The two boys were housed in what was in effect a separate guest house, located at one end of the U-shape.

Nestled in a hilly area of West Los Angeles just off Sunset Boulevard at the western edge of Beverly Hills, Holmby Hills was becoming known as a Hollywood celebrity neighborhood. Among those who lived there at various times beginning in the 1940s were Bing Crosby, Lana Turner, Judy Garland,

Jennifer Jones, Freeman "Amos 'n' Andy" Gosden, Alan Ladd, producer Walter Wanger and his wife, actress Joan Bennett, songwriter Sammy Cahn, radio and TV host Art Linkletter, Humphrey Bogart and Lauren Bacall, and, later, Bill Cosby and *Playboy* founder Hugh Hefner. As A. M. Sperber and Eric Lax described it in their Bogart biography:

> Thick woods protect its large houses from view, and its plantings have the trimmed-but-rustic look that can be afforded only by the truly rich. The narrow winding streets are bordered by steep, wooded embankments that give the impression of country lanes.[5]

Hoagy Bix, growing up there, remembered "a wonderful, wonderful place—big lawn out in back, perfect for tent parties." And the Carmichaels gave their share. "Everybody gave parties," Randy Bob Carmichael confirmed. "Big parties . . . clowns and musicians and tents, and maids and caterers—a party for two hundred people would cost a hundred dollars; when you were making five thousand a week, that was nothing."[6]

"That was a great, great house," Hoagy Bix said. "Dad was not able to do that sort of thing in New York or Indiana . . . He needed, as he always called it, a poke—a few dollars in his pocket, which was something his family didn't have much of, and a nice house in the sunshine. And writing for the movies . . . gave him all of that."[7]

For Ruth, too, gaining the house in Holmby Hills was a pivotal event, culmination of an acculturation process that had been going on since their arrival in California. They had socialized frequently at celebrity homes and at that most legendary of Hollywood gathering spots, the Garden of Allah apartments, mixing with a crowd of transplanted easterners that included such figures as Robert Benchley, Dorothy Parker, and other members of what had been the Algonquin Round Table. One veteran quoted by Sperber and Lax even referred to the Garden in its heyday as "Algonquin West."

Professional good luck, meanwhile, kept smiling on Hoagy Carmichael. He reworked the theme he'd written for the failed production of *Young Man With a Horn* into thirty-two-bar AABA format and gave it to Johnny Mercer. After some time—a matter of weeks, months, or years, depending on the account—Mercer delivered; the "Bix Lix" theme had become "Skylark," a song that still stands as a Carmichael masterwork.

Perhaps its most memorable feature is the bridge, or middle section, which casually changes key to the dominant, then works its way logically back around to the tonic, or "home" key. There is not a phrase, not a moment, in which it resembles the bridge of any other popular song.

"Skylark" (bars 17–24), 1941

The lyric, too, has been extolled as a masterpiece, a unique expression of Mercer's endlessly varied talent. Yet here there is also strong indication of some creative involvement on Carmichael's part. A penciled worksheet in the composer's hand, found among his papers in Bloomington, contains what appears to be a preliminary draft for the text.

> Skylark—have you anything to say to me?
> Is it all the way it used to be,
> Over the meadow where we kissed
> Does there remain a golden mist?

It's as if the "mist-kissed" imagery he'd discarded from "I Get Along Without You Very Well" had lodged in his consciousness, awaiting development in another setting and passed on to Mercer.

To some degree, the bridge text is obviously still a work-in-progress:

> And in your lonely flight
> Haven't you heard the music of the night?
> (Haven't you heard it?)
> (Wonderful music)
> Soft as a lullaby, crazy as a loon,
> Sad as a gypsy serenading the moon . . .

"Dad was very laid back, very cool, very Indiana" was son Randy's assessment. "That's why he always gave his lyrics away to a lyricist, or to someone else. He could write the lyrics to all his songs . . . a guy comes up with an idea for a song, and bingo! Dad puts him on as the lyricist. That's the way he was."[8]

Tantalizing, but altogether too simplistic, too generalized, for this situation. It may well have been true with Stuart Gorrell and "Georgia on My Mind"; as has been illustrated, Mitchell Parish drew on both Carmichael's and Wally Wilson's drafts in creating a text for "Star Dust." But in Johnny Mercer, Carmichael was dealing with arguably the preeminent popular lyricist of his generation, a man of unique and unassailable gifts and seemingly limitless adaptability. The interaction, therefore, must be subtler, more complex.

Carmichael himself supplies a useful, if general, glimpse of his dealings with lyricists. In a 1957 memo, he reflects on the possibility that "my production could have been much greater if my conduct with collaborators had been much more congenial and 'leave it to you-ish . . .' I was quick with the notes, and I expected the other fellow to be quick with the words."[9]

The very fact that Hoagy was "quick with the notes" was enough to land him a special place in Johnny Mercer's esteem. The two men "had a special respect for each other," said Mercer's daughter, Amanda Mercer Neder, so lovingly celebrated in Mercer's 1942 song hit, "Mandy Is Two." "My Dad thought Hoagy was above everyone. He had this natural thing, very intuitive, that placed him above the others as far as Dad was concerned. They both had fast minds; things would go through my Dad 'click-click,' that fast, and if he thought of something he'd get on the phone and call Hoagy right away. They both had those kinds of fast minds. He got such a kick out of Hoagy. He'd say, 'How can a boy from Indiana write about the South?' They both got a kick out of that."[10]

Mercer himself adds that "Hoagy, whom I had had such a hard time writing words for in New York, was completely different in Hollywood. I had learned a lot, but he had softened up, too . . . He painted, cooked, and did all the things that have become such common hobbies with us all."[11]

With all that in mind, it takes no great leap of imagination to picture Carmichael giving Mercer the melody and, at sometime midway through the writing process, the lyricist contacting him, perhaps by phone, to read off what he's done so far; Hoagy copies it down, telling Mercer yes, he likes it, perhaps offers a suggestion or two, and exhorts him to keep going in that vein.

"Johnny would often check with his collaborators on a lyric on which he was working," said lyricist and Mercer biographer Gene Lees, a close friend. "He seemed to be plagued by doubt. In some instances he wrote two or even three versions of a lyric and submitted them to a composer. That, and Johnny's fondness for what I'd call 'bird songs' and bird imagery, convinces me that he called Hoagy during the writing process, just to check with him and be sure they were on the same wavelength."

Fellow-lyricist Alan Bergman agreed. "It just seems more likely to me that Hoagy sent him the melody, and that Johnny got in touch with him when the lyric was half-done, just to—well, run it by him, to make sure they were thinking along the same lines. That's the way it reads to me— as if Johnny had the idea more or less where he wanted it, and wanted to be sure Hoagy was in agreement."[12]

"Skylark" had no verse. Nor, perhaps, did it need one. From the moment of its appearance, in mid-1942, it was in almost constant demand. Glenn Miller recorded it, as did Dinah Shore, Helen Forrest with Harry James, and others. It spent nearly three months on *Your Hit Parade* and quickly became a popular standard.[13]

Another Carmichael-Mercer collaboration, appearing around the same time, carries forward a genre tradition popular since the mid-1930s. In it, the singer exhorts a previously "square" individual to "get hep" and embrace the delights of swing. A 1936 Sam Coslow effort, for example, asks "Mr. Paganini" to "play my rhapsody," and if the great maestro finds himself unable to do so, his only choice is to "swing it." Another item finds a highland bagpiper named MacPhearson "rehearsin' " to swing. Mercer's own excellent "Bob White" describes the efforts of a hopelessly "square" bird, whose songs are "off the cob," to get with the jive. The Carmichael-Mercer idea was more refined. An old music master sits alone, at a loss for ideas. Suddenly up jumps "a little colored boy" to tell him:

> You gotta jump it, Music Master,
> You gotta play that rhythm faster,
> You're never gonna get it played
> On the happy cat hit parade.

The young visitor describes a future full of jazz, swing "boogie-woogie and jive," and exhorts the Music Master to drop his old-fashioned ways and catch the trend. It's all great fun, and rides along on an engaging Carmichael melody, Mozartean when describing the Music Master, rhythmic when the lad takes over. "The Old Music Master" appears, sung by Dick Powell, in the 1943 comedy *True to Life*, alongside another Mercer collaboration, the upbeat "Mister Pollyanna" and Carmichael's own "There She Was," a straightforward love ballad, both sung by Powell and co-star Mary Martin.

❖   ❖   ❖

Among the Carmichaels' new Hollywood friends was at least one relatively unlikely figure. Three years Hoagy's senior, Howard Winchester Hawks was a native of Goshen, in northern Indiana, not far from the Michigan border. But the two men could as well have hailed from different galaxies: Hawks, scion of a prominent milling family, had come from money, done indifferently at several top-quality schools, and—in one friend's words, "just languished his way through his youth." By the end of World War I he was in California, where he easily gravitated to the fledgling movie industry, working as a behind-the-scenes handyman and general assistant to pioneer director Cecil B. DeMille.

It didn't take long for the "rich kid in Hollywood," as biographer Todd McCarthy identifies him, to absorb himself in the moviemaking process. He watched film after film, absorbing conventions of pacing, lighting, camera work, plot construction, the mechanics of storytelling. John Ford, then on the very threshold of success, particularly interested him.[14]

Through friendships with such figures as Victor Fleming (best known to latter-day audiences as the director who finished *The Wizard of Oz*), Paramount vice president Jesse Lasky, and, most of all, Irving Thalberg, he eventually found his way into making pictures, and by the end of the 1920s had done screenplays and begun directing. His was the hand guiding such now lost features as *The Road to Glory* (1926), *The Cradle Snatchers* (1927), *A Girl in Every Port* (1928), and *Trent's Last Case* (1929).

Hawks made the transition to all-sound in 1930 with *The Dawn Patrol* and finally found recognition in 1932 with *Scarface,* based loosely on the career and exploits of Chicago mobster Al Capone. By decade's end Hawks had consolidated his reputation with such box-office successes as *Twentieth Century, The Prizefighter and the Lady, Ceiling Zero* (still respected as one of the best of the early airplane pictures), and a remake of *The Road to Glory.*

His *Bringing Up Baby*, teaming a breezy Cary Grant with patrician beauty Katharine Hepburn, revealed a deft touch for fast-moving "screwball" comedy. In the words of critic Otis Ferguson, "I am happy to report that *Bringing Up Baby* is funny from the word go, that it has no other meaning to recommend it, nor therapeutic qualities, and that I wouldn't swap it for any three things of the current season." Grant turns up again in Hawks's dramatic *Only Angels Have Wings*, regarded by many film scholars as a defining moment in Hawks's directing career. Its characters are archetypal figures, idealized, delineated by their actions. For Ferguson, whose film criticism forms a key part of a small but impressive body of work, it demonstrates the director's ability to be "faultless in a sense of how to speed up a situation, or make it flexible and easy with the right emphasis, grouping, understatement."[15]

But overall, the 1940s represent the high noon of his career. Within a five-year span he turned out one winner after another. *His Girl Friday* was an adaptation of the Ben Hecht-Charles MacArthur newspaper play *The Front Page,* but with the character of reporter Hildy Johnson reconceived as a woman. In *Sergeant York*, Gary Cooper played the World War I rifleman hero with taciturn charm. *Ball of Fire* cast the same actor in a comedy about some professors defining slang, with surprisingly endearing results.

By the time Hawks went to work on *Air Force*, the country was at war, and its jingoistic sentiments sounded just the right notes for a public still smarting from the attack on Pearl Harbor.

All the while, Hawks was developing one pet project, and the key to it was Ernest Hemingway. In October 1939 he and his new wife Nancy Rae Gross—"Slim," more familiarly—drove cross-country, spent some time in New York, then continued on south to Florida. Hemingway was in Key West for a breather during the writing of *For Whom the Bell Tolls*. He and Hawks took to one another at once—due perhaps in some small measure to the writer's instant attraction to Mrs. Hawks, whom he took to addressing as "Miss Slimsky."[16]

What happened after that is unclear. In Hawks's own colorful—and self-serving—account, Hemingway sternly resisted Hawks's entreaties to come write material for him.

"I can make a movie out of the worst thing you ever wrote," Hawks has himself telling the author.

"What's the worst thing I ever wrote?" comes the rejoinder.

"That piece of junk called *To Have and Have Not*," counters Hawks. Some time, and ten thousand dollars later, Hawks had the rights to film Hemingway's novel of romance and intrigue in the Caribbean. Hemingway had written it in 1937 and thought little of it; he firmly declined to help with any adaptation process. Hawks, undeterred, went ahead, enlisting the help of another major American novelist, William Faulkner, on the script. "There wasn't *anything* in that picture that was in the book," the director boasted later, an assertion strongly and famously seconded by critic-novelist James Agee.[17]

It is hard to imagine what sort of movie *To Have and Have Not* would have been—if it had become a film at all—without the extraordinary success, in 1943, of another Hollywood effort, the singular *Casablanca*. Among other points, it made clear that a melodrama, with a love story at its core, could be set in an exotic locale on the fringes of the war then raging in Europe. At a stroke, it carried Humphrey Bogart from a string of tough-guy roles into a romantic, if rough-hewn, lead.

And, in the singing piano-player role played by Dooley Wilson, *Casablanca* set the stage for Hoagy Carmichael. In later years, newspaper feature writers—and Hoagy himself—went to imaginative lengths in retailing the circumstances of his casting. The factual record is rather more straightforward. The Hawkses and Carmichaels had become social friends, part of a circle which also included the Victor Flemings and actor Lee Bowman and his wife Helene. Hoagy and Ruth had been houseguests at the Hawkses' S-Bar-S Ranch, situated on a beautiful 105-acre plot facing Moraga Drive in the foothills of the Santa Monica Mountains. "I was rather fascinated with Hawks," Carmichael recalled in a conversation with Hawks biographer Todd McCarthy, "because I knew he had what you call class and understanding and intelligence . . . I was delighted we could be friends."[18]

According to a magazine profile by Pete Martin, Slim dropped in one day while Hoagy was on a stepladder helping the Carmichaels' gardener. "He hadn't shaved for two days," Martin quoted Ruth as saying.

> His corduroys were rolled up and his hair was down over his face. Slim took one look at him and said, "You ought to be in pictures." Her husband had already been thinking of Hoagy for the part of Cricket, a hot-piano player in a Martinique honky-tonk, for his next film, but up to that point Hawks's thinking had only got to the point of deciding, "Hoagy might be a good actor because he makes such screwy faces when he sings."[19]

Randy Carmichael's version is rather less colorful, but probably closer to fact. "My mother and Slim Hawks were friends, as you know," he said recently. "Slim happened to mention that Howard was working on this film and needed somebody for the piano-player role. The way I heard it, my mom said to her, 'Hell, if you're looking for a piano player, I'm married to one.' Howard may even have seen Dad perform at a party. Anyway, her aggressiveness on his behalf was the beginning of a film career for Dad."[20]

Hoagy was visiting New York, he said, when a cable arrived from Hawks asking him if he might test for the role of Cricket, the piano player. The test, according to McCarthy, was a scene already part of the script, in which Hoagy plays and sings his own "How Little We Know," with Hawks's discovery, teenaged actress Lauren Bacall, sitting nearby.

"I chewed on a match to help my jitters," Carmichael writes,

> and when the time came to shoot, I asked Howard if I could keep the match in my mouth." It was a very noisy night club set, and Mr. Hawks couldn't hear me in all the confusion. I thought he said "yes" and started the scene. By the time it was finished, Mr. Hawks decided to let it go through. So from then on, in addition to all his other

problems, he had my match to worry about. But he was kind—he
kept me from overacting.[21]

While undoubtedly true, the story doesn't begin to sum up the process
of transformation Carmichael underwent for this, his first real role in a
feature film. He'd appeared briefly, and unmemorably, in a student production while at IU; even his *Topper* singing-and-playing spot had amount-
ed to little more than a prelude. In the various Paramount shorts—*Top
Tunes, College Swing*, and the appearance with Teagarden's band—he'd
come across personably enough, but without sufficient ease in front of the
cameras to establish him as a vivid personality.

From various fragmentary accounts, and on the evidence of *To Have
and Have Not* itself, he appears to have set to work with single-minded
determination shaping the cinematic character henceforth to be known as
"Hoagy Carmichael." In their biography of Humphrey Bogart, Sperber and
Lax describe the actor's realization that Carmichael was "very, very serious"
about his screen work. Bogart, they write, found Hoagy

at his mirror one day, studying the lines around his eyes. Carmichael
had gone to bed early the night before and was now worried that the
wrinkles might not correspond with those of the previous day. Another time, he had come up with the idea of chewing on a match—
new to him, anyway, though not to the cast. The next day Bogart
handed him a box of multi-colored matches. They were actors'
"mood matches," Bogart solemnly assured him, color coded for use
with various frames of attitude.[22]

Carmichael himself leaves a deceptively casual mention of his transformation into a screen actor. After realizing that his role required more sitting
around the studio waiting than actually being in front of the cameras, he
declared: "I decided then and there that acting was the life for me. I had
earned a week's salary just by dressing up and smearing a little grease paint
on my nose and cheeks. It was certainly an easy living."[23]

Behind so seemingly casual an utterance was a foundation of simple
hard work in creating the laid-back, laconic, piano-playing sage who quickly
became "Hoagy Carmichael" in moviegoers' minds. His own Indiana youth
gave him plenty of precedent on which to draw. Beginning in the last years
of the nineteenth century, Indiana had enjoyed a flowering of vernacular

literature, particularly of the rustic or home-grown variety. In Merrill, Meigs & Company (later Bobbs-Merrill and still later Macmillan), moreover, Indianapolis boasted a major publishing house, able to carry Hoosier wisdom and ways far beyond state lines.

"Abe Martin," a crackerbarrel philosopher created by cartoonist-satirist Frank McKinney "Kin" Hubbard (1868–1930), had been a feature of the *Indianapolis News* since 1904. Tricked out in battered hat and baggy pants, puffing deliberately on a corncob pipe, "Abe" delivered rustic, understated commentaries on issues of the day. "If I was as humorous as Kin," an admiring Will Rogers once declared, "I would be one of the two funniest men in America."[24]

Before Hubbard there had been Indiana poet James Whitcomb Riley (1849–1916), on whose shoulders Hoagland Carmichael had ridden as a six-year-old, and whose genial dialect poems, usually attributed to "Benj. F. Johnson of Boone," blended what one commentator has called "simple sentimentality, a quaint whimsical kindliness, and cheerful philosophy."[25]

In later years Carmichael expressed his appreciation in an unpublished "Ode to Whitcomb Riley":

> You carried me in your tender way
> Along Lockerbie Street,
> To candy stores most every day
> Just giving me a treat.

Also appearing in the *News* were William Herschell's folksy but trenchant apothegms and such poems as the beloved "Ain't God Good to Indiana?" Another presence in Hoagy's formative years was Hoosier writer George Ade (1866–1944), whose 1899 *Fables in Slang* enjoyed a place of honor on every Indiana bookshelf—and still commands respect as a literary representation of common American speech around the turn of the twentieth century.

There is no hard evidence that Hoagy directly emulated such figures in synthesizing his movie persona. But it is not without significance that, in 1946, he showed his reverence for Herschell by setting "Ain't God Good to Indiana?" to music, and three years later did the same for Riley's "When the Frost Is on the Punkin'."

(Regional speech turns up frequently in lyrics to Carmichael songs, whether credited to him or to others. Examples abound: the phrase "mussity clothes" in "Washboard Blues"; the exclamation "Well, looky here" in "Lazybones"; most of "Small Fry," "Rockin' Chair," and "The Lamplighter's Serenade." In that context, Carmichael had been drawing on his Hoosier origins for a long time.)

The Carmichael character that emerged in *To Have and Have Not* belongs to this Indiana tradition. Cricket doesn't talk much: when he's not performing he listens and watches, delivering himself of an occasional piece of common-sense wisdom. Above all, he's relaxed. He takes his time. He's invented—synthesized—a persona, and its name is Hoagy Carmichael.[26]

"On the stage I'm a relaxed character," he declared in a 1964 interview, "but I *portray* that. And it's been successful." Hoagy Bix agreed. The screen Hoagy "was Dad, but it was a studied Carmichael, a Carmichael that he had perfected, really, and had decided, and knew, that it worked, and that people liked it. It wasn't very far off center for him, but with the few props he had, he knew he could play that part." A magazine article at the time put it more bluntly, referring to Carmichael as "a fierce, persnickety perfectionist, who drives himself to create."[27]

Carmichael's *To Have and Have Not* co-stars, especially Bogart, took notice. Hoagy, he averred, was a natural, to whom it all appeared to come easily, with no hint of hard work done away from the camera's eye. It seemed, he said, "a great deal easier, I assure you, than for me to sit down and write 'Stardust.' I don't like to have my chosen profession made to look quite so simple."[28]

Hawks biographer McCarthy notes that William Faulkner, whose relations with the director during filming were often tempestuous, nevertheless found time to visit the set whenever Carmichael was scheduled to do a scene. Three Carmichael songs, two of them already published, were to figure in the film: "Hong Kong Blues," a set piece featuring the composer surrounded by a nightclub audience; "Baltimore Oriole," a brooding melody in minor, with a lyric by Paul Francis Webster; and a Carmichael-Mercer collaboration, "How Little We Know," singled out as something Bacall could sing. According to Bacall, Hawks planned to use "Oriole" as a soundtrack theme each time the actress appeared onscreen. "He thought it would be marvelous if I could always be identified with it—appear on Bing Crosby's or Bob Hope's radio show, have the melody played, have me sing it, finally have me known as the 'Baltimore Oriole.' What a fantastic fantasy life Howard must have had! His was a glamorous, mysterious, tantalizing vision—but it wasn't me."[29]

The scheme came to nothing—not least because Bacall, whether through nerves or a lack of musical ability, proved unequal to the challenge of singing "Baltimore Oriole." The song, one of Carmichael's most evocative of the time, ended up as background music on the soundtrack. What Bacall *did* sing was "How Little We Know," in a low, engagingly husky voice.

Even there, in a song considerably less challenging than "Baltimore Oriole," there was doubt at first. "Her vocal training was coming along, but no one knew if she would sound good enough for her singing voice to be used . . . To find a singer whose voice would match up plausibly with Bacall's husky tones was not easy, and quite a few were tried." Hawks's final choice was teenager Andy Williams, who did indeed record a version for soundtrack use.[30]

But it is not his voice heard in the film. During shooting Bacall sang to a dead mike, with Hoagy miming his accompaniment on a silent piano. Listening to her, both he and Hawks came to the same conclusion: she was doing just fine. Let her try recording a take, with Hoagy at a real piano. She passed the test, and it is Bacall's voice heard in this scene from *To Have and Have Not*.

Onscreen, Hoagy comes across as never before. The nervousness is gone. He's relaxed, amiable, his dialogue paced for maximum effect. In the interplay with Bacall leading up to "How Little We Know," he begins playing the melody, sans accompaniment.

BACALL: What is that you're playing?
HOAGY: Did you say something?
BACALL: Yeah. What's the name of that tune?
HOAGY: It hasn't got any name yet. I just been foolin' around with the lyrics. And not so hot, either. Would you like to hear it?
BACALL: Sure.
HOAGY: (plays song, as Bacall hums)

Simple. But it plays naturally—mostly because Hoagy's "Did you say something?" slows down the pace, pulls attention to them and to the song that must follow. He delivers his lines almost casually, as if her question were interrupting a reverie.

Here, as in the songwriting process, Carmichael's participation exceeded the letter of what he'd been engaged to do. "Hawks told me that about three weeks into the shoot, Dad knocked on the door to his trailer, and here he had some changes in the script," said Hoagy Bix Carmichael. "Dad was just one of those fellows who just didn't know how to say no. He had 'improvements.' "[31]

(In an amusing, and perhaps symmetrically appropriate, postscript, Carmichael played Sam, the Dooley Wilson singing-pianist role, in a television adaptation of *Casablanca*, presented on the *Lux Video Theatre* during the mid-1950s. The series, which began on CBS and moved to NBC, also re-created *To Have and Have Not*, but there is no indication that Carmichael participated.)

Carmichael's initiation as a movie actor did not instantly transform his life. He began making records again, this time for Jack Kapp's Decca label. Most of the songs were such established favorites as "Old Man Harlem," "Judy," and "Hong Kong Blues." A 1942 reconception of "Star Dust" finds far more economical Carmichael piano and a vocal chorus that paraphrases the melody, smoothing its extremes of register to fit his singing range. He even whistles eight bars. Altogether it's a more wistful performance than any previous version, evidence of his own evolving concept of the song. "He was asked to play it a lot, at parties and things," said Hoagy Bix Carmichael. "When he acquiesced, which was most of the time, he'd never play a version that was his standard. He'd go for something different . . . never played it the same way . . . But that was Dad. He played with that song a lot when he played it in front of [other] people."[32]

All the while, Hoagy kept "finding" songs on the keyboard: in partnership with Frank Loesser he turned out the sentimental "We're the Couple in the Castle," the lighthearted "Katy-Did, Katy-Didn't," and "I'll Dance at Your Wedding (Honey Dear)" for *Mr. Bug Goes to Town* (later retitled *Hoppity Goes to Town*), an animated feature produced by Dave Fleischer, brother of *Betty Boop* creator Max Fleischer. "Can't Get Indiana off My Mind," written with Texas-born lyricist Robert DeLeon, found lasting popularity through a recording by singer Kate Smith, still riding high on her success with Irving Berlin's "God Bless America."

"I Should Have Known You Years Ago," with a lyric by Helen Meinardi, found its way into *Road Show*, along with three other items including "Calliope Jane," an unlikely charmer about a girl who makes calliope-like "toot-toot" sounds when she falls in love. Veteran lyricist Ray Gilbert joined him for "Drip Drop!," an off-beat rhythmic ode to parenthood. "Blue Orchids," with its particularly instrumental melody, turned out to be a minor hit, thanks to records by Glenn Miller and several other major bands, as well as Crosby-influenced crooner Dick Todd.

Perhaps the key Carmichael alliance of those early war years was with the young lyricist Paul Francis Webster. A native New Yorker, Webster had begun writing as a teenager, winning his first major recognition with "Got the Jitters," a rather frenetic evocation of Depression-era high finance. By the end of the 1930s he'd moved to Hollywood and was writing lyrics to such songs as "I Got It Bad (and That Ain't Good)" for the short-lived Duke Ellington musical *Jump for Joy.*

For Webster, working with Carmichael was a departure. "He was dapper, well-dressed, sophisticated—from a different gene pool than my family," said Guy Webster, the lyricist's son. "My father was like an English school-teacher, and Hoagy was—seemed—much more urbane, more worldly. I think I could say that the two of them weren't exactly sympathetic souls—personally, I mean. Hoagy—well, he was kind of aloof. But I also have to say they wrote some wonderful songs together. 'The Lamplighter's Serenade'—that was a major hit, and it put my Dad on the map."[33]

Like "Little Old Lady" before it, "The Lamplighter's Serenade" is an exercise in unabashed nostalgia. Set, according to the lyric, in 1893, it recalls a small-town American scene and the "old-fashioned gent" making his nightly rounds, lighting the gas lamps in the park and chatting amiably with friends and lovers along the way. Carmichael's sweet melody is a departure from the AABA form of many standard popular songs: its first, or "A," strain is stated only once before the release, or "B" section, creating an ABA structure, twenty-four bars long rather than the more common thirty-two. In historian John Edward Hasse's words, the song affords "a Norman Rockwell-like peek at a wholesome and innocent bygone era."[34]

"Baltimore Oriole" was neither sung nor clearly heard in *To Have and Have Not,* and that is regrettable. First published in 1942, it's totally in minor mode, never resolving—as do such earlier efforts as "New Orleans" and even the dark "Ballad in Blue"—to major. An early manuscript version of the melody, perhaps written as early as 1940, bears the title "Kantor Song," leading to the conclusion that Carmichael was having another try at capturing a "Jewish" sound—considerably more successful than the clumsy "Jew-Boy Blues" of 1925. Indeed, without the distraction of Webster's text, the melody weds a strongly cantorial flavor with a sensibility clearly drawn from the blues.

Based heavily on quarter-note triplets, the melody also has a natural swing that has made it a favorite of jazz instrumentalists and singers.

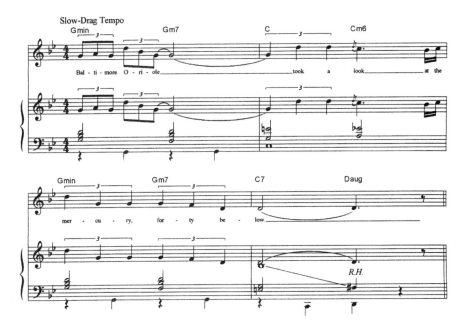

"Baltimore Oriole" (bars 1–4), 1942

Alec Wilder, writing in *American Popular Song,* stops just short of suggesting that Webster's lyric to "Baltimore Oriole," retailing the misadventures of an errant female bird, trivialized the song, preventing it from achieving wider currency, especially among popular singers. He does the lyric a disservice. As usual, the worksheet bears evidence of substantial Carmichael input, particularly in the stringing-together of adjectives in the phrase

> Forgivin' is easy,
> It's a woman-like, now-and-then-could-happen thing.

And, too, this must be the only song lyric in existence in which "Tangipaho(a)," the name of a river, town, and parish in northeastern Louisiana, appears. Even if Carmichael and Webster were merely looking for a southern place-name of four syllables to fit the rhythm of the lyric, they couldn't have made a more fortuitous, distinctively exotic, choice.

"Baltimore Oriole" did find its place on a movie soundtrack, and in 1944, the very year *To Have and Have Not* was released. The film was Universal's *The Ghost Catchers,* an Olsen and Johnson vehicle casting the veteran comedy duo as nightclub owners trying to help an old southern colonel (Walter Catlett) and his daughters, who have just moved into a haunted house. The singer was teenaged Gloria Jean, then being groomed as a successor to the studio's widely popular Deanna Durbin. Neither the movie nor Gloria Jean herself fulfilled Universal's hopes; *The Ghost Catchers* vanished nearly without trace, to be glimpsed now and then on late-night TV.

One lifelong champion of the song has been jazz vocalist Sheila Jordan. An intense performer known for highly complex, even surrealistic, treatments of standard material, Jordan found both music and lyrics a welcome challenge. "To me it's always been a voice-and-bass tune, wide open, with lots of breathing space," she said in a recent conversation.

"I never force any improv[isation] on it—you don't have to. It's already there, just laying [*sic*] where it is. How can you make a line like that any better? In a way it's a little like [Thelonious] Monk: it's simple yet it's hard. And the lyric. You know, a lot of people don't realize it, but there's a lot of humor behind that lyric. Usually, in most songs, it's the man that strays, the male, leaving the woman singin' the blues. In this one it's the female— 'no life for a lady, to be draggin' her feathers around in the snow.' I've been singing it since the mid-1950s, and I still get requests for it. Always will, I guess."[35]

❊   ❊   ❊

Hoagy Carmichael in the 1940s was a man bursting with plans and possibilities. A newspaper interview given during his June 1942 visit to Indianapolis—one of many to his home turf during the decade—announces that he "has written the story for a musical, titled 'Dream Street,' and has made tentative plans for producing it when he returns to the West Coast the last of this month." Russian-born Gregory Ratoff was to direct the independent production, and Hoagy would be assistant producer. Lyrics would be by Johnny Mercer and Frank Loesser. Carmichael would go on to New York, the article continued, to place two new songs, "Morning Glory" (lyric by Webster) and "Plain People."[36]

His newfound celebrity also propelled him into more exalted social company than ever before—and brought him face-to-face with Hollywood politics. A Republican Party supporter since his Indiana youth, he'd voted for Hoosier favorite (and fellow–IU graduate) Wendell Willkie in the 1940 presidential election and, as his sons have observed, had little good to say about

Franklin D. Roosevelt, the New Deal, and Democratic Party politics in general. "To Dad," Hoagy Bix has said, "FDR was a guy from a wealthy family who took other people's money—particularly his—and just gave it away."[37]

What distressed him far more, however, were Hollywood's left-leaning political views and what he saw as the too-pervasive influence of the American Communist Party. "The left-wing boys were pretty much in power," he notes, "and somehow I was always tangling with them." In the original, pre-edit typescript for *Sometimes I Wonder*, he remarks that Humphrey Bogart, for example, was "a bit confused politically in my opinion. He had a tendency at parties to be on the pink side in those days when it seemed to be fashionable to follow the far left line in Hollywood society. He shouted a tirade of abuse at my Republican stand one night at a big party. I invited him outside, coats off, fists up. I weighed 135, he 150. (He was not a tough man at all offscreen, in my opinion). My wife, Ruth, broke it up."

Attending another party with friends Lee and Helene Bowman, Hoagy "listened in astonishment . . . at the party-line conversation going on around the table . . . We who didn't join in felt like hicks in the corn fields. After many subversive-sounding monotones [*sic*], this whole group, minus us, moved to Ira Gershwin's house for conversation." Carmichael, it must be noted, stopped well short of allowing such differences, regardless how extreme, to goad him into intemperate action or utterance: his success had been too hard-won to be placed so easily at risk.[38]

After Pearl Harbor, he writes, "There was little I could do but give the world something to *hum*." He amplified on that theme in a 1942 interview with the *Los Angeles Times*. "I think everyone in the music world is conscious of the lack of an outstanding popular song in the present war," he said. "For some reason or other, nothing written so far has clicked. I believe it's because the tunes haven't gotten underneath the surface enough. Their treatment of the war has been too superficial. America is in a situation today that calls for a tune with real depth of sentiment. I think people are past the stage where they're impressed by songs that indulge merely in flag-waving or boasting of our national might."[39]

In common with Johnny Mercer ("G.I. Jive"), Irving Berlin ("This Is the Army, Mr. Jones," "Any Bonds Today?"), Frank Loesser ("Praise the Lord and Pass the Ammunition"), Jimmy McHugh ("Comin' In on a Wing and a Prayer"), and countless others, he turned out a clutch of songs aimed squarely at U.S. servicemen and their loved ones. "My Christmas Song for You," lyric credited to Webster, draws on much the same familiar, homey imagery that imbued Irving Berlin's 1942 "White Christmas" with the "real depth of sentiment" Hoagy had prescribed: jingle bells, "red stockings hung by glowing fires," village choirs singing carols.[40]

Several of his other wartime songs have worn surprisingly well. In "Don't Forget to Say 'No' Baby," a departing GI exhorts his sweetheart to remain faithful while he's serving Uncle Sam. "The Army of Hippocrates," written as a 6/8 march, is a heart-on-sleeve salute to Army doctors and nurses stationed at General Hospital No. 32 in Indianapolis. Among Carmichael's papers at Indiana University is a melodic sketch marked "Hitler Blues," which apparently never went beyond the manuscript stage.

An unusual take on the American home front comes in "Billy-a-Dick," a collaboration with Webster unpublished until 1990. In the lyric, the speaker imagines he (or she) is hearing someone upstairs practicing "hot licks" on a set of drums. Couldn't be Johnny, because he's "overseas we know not where," fighting the enemy. But every night, without fail, the drums seem to say:

> Billy-a-dick, billy-a-dick, tick, tack,
> When's that character comin' back?
> When's that kid in the G.I. lid
> Gonna choo-choo down the track?

The drumsticks lie where he left them, covered with dust. All the speaker can do is pray for the day when the young drummer comes back, and "we'll soon have a Japanese derby to beat like a cymbal on the music rack." "Billy-a-Dick," formerly only performed by its composer, enjoyed a burst of latter-day popularity when Bette Midler sang it in her 1991 World War II film, *For the Boys.*

No less unconventional is "The Cranky Old Yank (in a Clanky Old Tank)," for which Hoagy wrote both music and lyrics. By far the most jingoistic of his wartime songs, it bears passing resemblance to the Joe Bushkin–John DeVries "(There'll Be a) Hot Time in the Town of Berlin," but with more verbal dexterity:

> I'm a cranky old yank in a clanky old tank
> And I'm headed for a hullabaloo.

I'll be ridin' my tank through a Tokyo bank
Sure as I'm an Army buckaroo.

And when I set my khaki down in old Nagasaki
I'll be singin' like a wacky jackaroo,
And you can bet, by cracky, every Sukiyaki lackey
Will be lookin' mighty tacky when I do . . .

As Carmichael's lyric sheets make clear, the song's original conception placed the "Cranky Old Yank" not only in the Pacific but in the European and North African theatres as well. One sample lyric, unpublished, goes:

There's a cranky old yank in a clanky old tank,
And he's headin' down the African coast,
He's been ridin' his tank
Into old Casablanc'
Now it's just another Army post . . .

And brother, he went socco
When he hit Morocco,
With a lot of loyal Frenchmen for his host . . .

There were still other wartime songs: "Morning Glory," written with Webster, imbues a simple flower with strong patriotic overtones; "No More Toujours l'Amour," also known as "Eager Beaver," recounts a GI's romantic misadventures on a weekend furlough. Even more affecting is "Plain People," whose lyric—never finished—salutes the folks who are "peaceful to the core/But brother, when they're sore/Oh me! What a troublesome crew."[41]

Hoagy performed his songs in more than a hundred appearances at military installations, under the auspices of the United Service Organizations, or USO. He also got his first crack at regular mass exposure in mid-1944, when the Mutual radio network first aired *Tonight at Hoagy's*, a weekly half-hour show in prime time, broadcast Sunday evenings at 8:30 Pacific time. Social reporter Harry Evans, who had chronicled Hoagy's entry into the Jules Glaenzer circle in New York and was now the editor of *Family Circle* magazine, signed on to write the scripts.

"As I saw it," he told reporter Pete Martin, "the best way for him to achieve informality was by having the announcer appear to be a guest in

Hoagy's home. The trouble was, Hoagy has a very active imagination. Instead of being content to open the spot by saying 'Hello, folks,' he had radio ideas you couldn't have put across with eighty-five men and a boy."[42]

Some recordings of the shows survive, and they find Carmichael quite at home with a cast that includes actress-comedienne Ruby Dandridge, singer Loulie Jean Norman, and a studio band including violinist Joe Venuti and other jazz veterans. On trombone is Casa Loma Orchestra alumnus Pee Wee Hunt, who joins Hoagy for vocal duets on such favorites as "Lazybones" and "Small Fry."[43]

Sponsored at first by the Safeway supermarket chain (its president, Lingan A. Warren, was a Carmichael fan), *Tonight at Hoagy's* stayed on the air two years. When that ended he shifted seamlessly to NBC, as host of *Something New*, another weekly half-hour broadcast Mondays at 6:00 P.M. Pacific time. Unlike *Tonight at Hoagy's*, the new show hit the East Coast in mid-evening; audience response was national, immediate—and, as before, not always complimentary.

"You cannot sing for sour owl," one listener wrote. "Your voice has all the musical quality of a drum solo." Another, signing himself (or herself) "A pained radio fan," informed the composer that he sounded "like a sick jackass. When are you going to learn to sing?" Still another averred, "You are wrecking your program with your singing . . . who told you you could sing?"

Most of the surviving letters and cards are in this vein. But one, from a Los Angeles listener named Anne Webb, takes a more thoughtful approach, wishing him luck while declaring that "your singing is so delightfully awful that it is really very funny. There is a child-like quality about it that is very lovable."

Hoagy himself got into the spirit of things, disparagingly anointing himself "the Voiceless" (a reference to Frank Sinatra's then-current nickname, "the Voice") in a newspaper interview.[44]

Something New, as its title suggests, focused on discovery of new, young talent. Even the studio backup band, the Teenagers, was made up of youngsters between sixteen and nineteen—including, on tenor sax, future modern jazz star Warne Marsh. Like its predecessor, the show lasted about two years—and was succeeded by yet another, this time on CBS. The fifteen-minute *Hoagy Carmichael Show* went on the air at 5:30 P.M. Pacific time, Sunday, October 26, 1946. "I wrote the script," he recalled, "little simple things pretending that I was in my library working with my secretary and rehearsing new songs, some mine but mostly others."

In what was to be a major and lasting change, he brought in studio pianist Buddy Cole to do most of the accompaniments. Equally comfortable playing piano and organ, Illinois-born Cole had worked with several major bands, including Frank Trumbauer's 1939–40 unit, and become a fixture in radio and the movies, backing Bing Crosby, Phil Harris, and other personalities. In later years he was associated with Rosemary Clooney and Nat "King" Cole. His adaptability to any situation was legendary: as Hoagy put it, "He could even imitate *me* playing the piano, which has come in handy on occasion."[45]

      ✠   ✠   ✠

"Star Dust," meanwhile, like the "little stars" in its lyric, continued its steady climb to the topmost reaches of American popular song. Almost every major dance band of the day, including those of Tommy Dorsey, Benny Goodman, Will Bradley, Les Brown, Cab Calloway, Edgar Hayes, Jimmie Lunceford, and the Casa Loma Orchestra, had recorded it; leading jazz artists did as well, among them Louis Armstrong, pianists Art Tatum and Fats Waller, saxophonists Coleman Hawkins and Chu Berry, trumpeter Louis Prima, and bass sax pioneer–turned–vibraphonist Adrian Rollini. Even for those bands and soloists who didn't record it commercially, "Star Dust" was a standard repertoire item; a solo tenor saxophone performance by Ben Webster, recorded November 7, 1940, during a ballroom appearance in Fargo, North Dakota, by Duke Ellington's orchestra, is particularly eloquent.[46]

Even in this august company, two recorded performances stand out. On October 19, 1939, trombonist Jack Jenney accorded the song an interpretation unprecedented at the time: a series of improvisations in which the melody, while occasionally alluded to and paraphrased, is never explicitly stated. At another session little more than a week before, Coleman Hawkins had treated "Body and Soul" in similar fashion. While less well known than the Hawkins record, Jenney's performance is no less creative, no less startling in capturing, summing up, a melody's full evocative strength. Two masters, or "takes," of that performance were issued; the trombonist seems to approach each version as a fresh opportunity, with very little carried over.

His own band an economic failure, Jenney was in Artie Shaw's trombone section a year later for the clarinetist's own "Star Dust" record. Ever restless, Shaw had returned from his self-imposed Caribbean exile to front a large orchestra, including strings. From the arrangement, by Paul Whiteman veteran Lennie Hayton, to individual solos by Shaw, Jenney, and trumpeter Billy Butterfield, this "Star Dust" achieves a kind of perfection in both overall shape and individual details. Butterfield's silvery-toned opening melody statement has been a model for trumpeters ever since. Shaw's sixteen-bar solo, almost a composition in itself, makes stunning use of his instrument's uppermost register. Jenney's eight bars emerge as both digest and précis of his earlier record.

✻   ✻   ✻

Capitulation of the Axis forces in May and September of 1945 brought an end at last to World War II. Anxiety evaporated in the euphoria of reunion with returning fighting men. Joy and celebration, it seemed, were everywhere.

It all found a certain resonance in the life of Hoagland Carmichael. It's not hard to imagine him, the kid from Bloomington, the "half-educated man," once-upon-a-time jazz pianist and Bent Eagle, looking about him in quiet satisfaction; the songs, bathed in the glow of "Star Dust," already become, or becoming, popular American anthems; his marriage stable, the kids growing fast; a "poke" in his pocket and a house in the sun—all the trappings of a life he'd dreamed of all those nights on Fess Avenue, listening to the rich boys at their fraternity house revels, and never thought would be his.

And if, in proper Hollywood fashion, he just closed his eyes and wished hard enough—well, who was to say it might not go on, and on, forever?

✳ XV ✳

Movie Star

To *Have and Have Not* had shown Hollywood casting directors they had a bankable character actor in Hoagy Carmichael. Offers for new pictures began arriving at 10281 Charing Cross Road, always for—as Hoagy rather wryly put it—"the hound-dog-faced old musical philosopher noodling on the honky-tonk piano, saying to a tart with a heart of gold: 'He'll be back, honey. He's all man.' "[1]

As scholar Krin Gabbard sees it, that was a handicap. The Carmichael character stood forever outside the main action, and outside any romantic involvement, commenting but never participating. Gabbard calls it a "feminized" image, presumably meaning neutered, and compares it to Hollywood's desensualized casting of black male actors.[2]

In *The Best Years of Our Lives* (1946), Carmichael is Butch, piano-playing proprietor of a local bar, helping the three male leads adjust to civilian life after World War II. At one point he provides what Gabbard calls "music therapy" to Homer, a young sailor played by real-life D-Day veteran Harold Russell; with Butch's guidance, the young man uses the metal prostheses that have replaced his hands to play "Chop Sticks" at the piano—symbolic proof that anything is possible, given will and determination.

"He was so conscientious, so patient," Russell recalled. "I mean, teaching a guy without hands to play the piano is no small thing. But he was so quick and sincere about it. Knew just how he wanted to go about it. Did a marvelous job. In fact, I was amazed at how well he got me to do with it—all thanks to his ability to teach."[3]

Here, again, Hoagy's absorption in his task quickly exceeded the role's requirements: "I devised an attachment, which was made in the machine shop, that would enable [Russell] to grasp a golf club and hit the ball. I had hoped that this episode could be brought into the picture but it never made it." That, said Hoagy Bix, "was Dad. He wasn't trying to interfere, or overstep. He was a perfectionist: when it came to his work he was a man with a purpose. His creativity, and his conscientiousness, just wouldn't quit."[4]

In later years Carmichael enjoyed telling friends how director William Wyler found him one day coaching Russell on definitely non-musical aspects of his role. "Hey, Carmichael!" Wyler roared across the set. "What the hell do you think you're doing? I'm the only one around here who talks to the actors!" Assuming what he called his innocent Hoosier voice, Hoagy would explain, "I wasn't doin' anything. Just tryin' to help this young fella, who'd never acted before. Just tryin' to give him a few tips, just kinda relaxin' him, y'know."[5]

The Best Years of Our Lives swept the 1946 Academy Awards, taking Oscars for production, direction (William Wyler), performances (Russell and Fredric March), screenplay (Robert E. Sherwood), editing (Daniel Mandell), and musical score (Hugo Friedhofer). Hoagy confessed to a flush of pride when Samuel Goldwyn announced his name at the presentation ceremony—even if it was as "Hugo Carmichael."

Night Song (1947) cast him as Chick, a clarinet(!!)-playing bandleader who abandons music to help a blind pianist-composer played by *Best Years of Our Lives* co-star Dana Andrews. His most generous scene is a protracted gin rummy game with the grandmotherly, and quite winning, Ethel Barrymore. In *Johnny Angel* (1945), he's a cab driver to George Raft's lead; in *Canyon Passage* (1946), he's Hy Linnet, local "character" and homespun philosopher. The roles may have seemed casual, even incidental, to audiences and reviewers, but each was, for Carmichael, the product of thought and hard work. "One of the ways to be a success in a movie, if you are not a great actor, is to have a gimmick that people will notice," he writes in *Sometimes I Wonder*. For *Johnny Angel*, his "gimmick" was a child's toy, a small propeller mounted on a stick, which whirled when he rubbed the stick with a second stick. Later, in *The Las Vegas Story*, it was a croupier's trick of holding two silver dollars, flipping one over the top of the other with thumb and forefinger.

He'd become aware of the "gimmick," he said, after watching Raft years before in *Scarface*, casually flipping a nickel—a trick developed to cover that actor's nervousness before the cameras. Vincent Price, Hoagy's co-star in *The Las Vegas Story*, complained during shooting that Carmichael's dollar-flipping was stealing scenes from him, just as Raft had stolen them from Paul Muni two decades before.

In each movie appearance Hoagy managed to sing and/or play at least one of his songs. In *The Best Years of Our Lives* it was "Lazy River"; in *Night Song*, the entertaining but undistinguished "Who Killed 'Er (Who Killed the Black Widder)." In one *Johnny Angel* scene he's seated at the piano, back to the camera. Over his shoulder he sings what was shortly to become one of his anthems, a nostalgic paean to bygone days much in the spirit of "Lazy River" and "Moon Country."

His penciled manuscript identifies it only as "Lullaby." But soon after Hoagy delivered the melody to Paul Webster it became "Memphis in June," melody and lyric recalling an earlier, pre-Hollywood Carmichael. When played at a comfortable $\sqrt{} = 80$, the melodic line immediately evokes Bix, particularly in its substitution of a D♭7 chord for the more common G7+5 in bar 3:[6]

"Memphis in June" (bars 1–4), 1945

It's a device especially common in the music of the French Impressionists and in the arranging of such 1920s jazz figures as Bill Challis, Fud Livingston, and Arthur Schutt. The only major change is to introduce with the G, now the eleventh of the substitute chord, a new richness of coloration.

"I was just a little kid, but I remember the day he wrote it," said Randy Carmichael. "He comes into the house, he's standing at the piano—not sitting, but standing—playing it, and keeps putting those tags on at the end and can't finish, because he's getting so excited. He makes his way through the whole tune and breaks out in this uproarious laughter, because he'd made it all the way through without falling down or cracking up."[7]

The lyric abounds in what William Zinsser calls "magical words," their imagery reaching us "not only through the eye, ear, and nose but through two even more powerful transmitters: memory and longing." We see a shady verandah, smell cousin Amanda's rhubarb pie, hear the old clock ticking as Granny, in her rockin' chair, watches the neighbor folk passing in their finery. Evocative touches are everywhere: the sky is "Sunday blue"; sweet oleander is "blowing perfume in the air"; the moon doesn't simply rise—it *jumps* up. As singer Barbara Lea has said, even if the song is ostensibly about Memphis, "it could be anywhere, any place in memory and longing, any place that is home."[8]

✻   ✻   ✻

Hoagy, meanwhile, was thoroughly enjoying his movie celebrity. According to Hollywood gossip columnist Sheilah Graham, RKO was looking for a vehicle in which he could "sing, act, play the piano and make love to the heroine." With mock indignation, Hoagy himself averred he'd "never taken such a ribbing before in my life... When I gave up practicing law to take up songwriting, my friends and acquaintances let it go with a simple, 'He's nuts' or 'smart guy,' depending on their tastes or their success with the law."

"But when I took on the acting role in pictures, I suddenly became the target for ribs and wisecracks. The worst of it is, I didn't always know when I was being ribbed." Most of his fan mail, he told Sheilah Graham, "is from young girls." Sure enough, the columnist reported, "it seems Frank Sinatra has a rival in Hoagy. In fact, some of the maidens expressed themselves as preferring Carmichael to Sinatra."[9]

Magazine writers sought him out for interviews, their articles appearing under such titles as "Melancholy Minstrel," "Starduster," and "Star-Dust Troubadour." At one point he captured headlines by suggesting a return to an earlier, less rangy version of "The Star-Spangled Banner" because in its modern form the melody had too many high notes and wide intervals. In a *Down Beat* magazine piece, he advised aspiring tunesmiths:

Sit down and write a dozen songs. Get yourself all worked up over them (that shouldn't be hard to do) ... then sit down to some serious writing ... talent isn't enough; you've got to work and work and work. And if you're lucky your song might catch public favor.[10]

Such attention came as nourishment to the nervous young man from Bloomington, welcome redress for *Walk With Music* and whatever other disappointments he might have encountered along life's way. "You know, Hoag," Lida Carmichael wrote to her son, "the admiration and publicity and adulation you receive from people should compensate you for a lot of other things." In the same letter she chides him gently for living beyond his means, reminding him that "living where you do is like Mrs. Jones keeping up with her neighbor."[11]

Amid all this he began talking seriously with Mark Saxton, an editor at Rinehart and Co., about an autobiography. More than ten years, and many changes, had passed since he laid *Jazzbanders* aside, adding a wealth of new experience on which to draw. Yet the new memoir returned to the early Indiana years, the Book Nook, Moenkhaus, and the Bent Eagles. And, most of all, Bix. Published in 1946, *The Stardust Road* begins and ends with Beiderbecke's death, a pivotal moment which frames the story. The writing is recognizably Hoagy's own, the voice familiar from the songs: elegiac, lyrical, lilting gently in the purple dusk of twilight time.

Here, for example, is Carmichael riding along in his stripped-down Model T, the "Open Job," in early 1924, the cornetist at his side:

The good spring air, soft and cool in motion, blows the fumes from our heads. It blows away the hangover and it blows away the night before, the music, the things we strove to put into words.

Just a couple of average boys tooling down Indiana Avenue in an old open Ford, our minds pleasantly unoccupied, well pleased to be alive, surveying with appreciation the familiar scenes of a small-town Sunday morning. The people coming from church, content and unafraid, dressed in their best, at peace with their world as we are with ours.[12]

The real-life Carmichael might be living in California luxury, acting in movies, throwing star-studded parties, playing singles at the West Side Tennis Club with Don Budge and Tony Trabert (ultimately becoming its president)—but not in the 143 pages of *The Stardust Road*. In that microcosm he's still the "half-educated man," living in a selectively remembered past aglow with hot music, and full of wonders revealed by Moenkhaus and Bix, Harry Hostetter and Wad Allen.

Some counted that a shortcoming. Calling the book a "chronicle of fact and near fiction," Laurie Henshaw complained in Britain's *Melody Maker* that "bearing in mind Hoagy's colorful life and the abundant material that must have been available, the book is . . . something of a disappointment."[13]

Henshaw couldn't have known it, but *The Stardust Road* had clearly defined the contradictory forces driving Hoagland Carmichael. Secure in the sun, he finds refuge in twilit memory, portraying his formative years as he wants them perceived, right down to details of casual conversations he could never have recalled verbatim. Not that the book is a falsehood, or even (*pace*, Henshaw) a work of fiction. Carmichael the memoirist is Carmichael the portraitist, reconfiguring and blending the facts in a gentle watercolor wash. As he admits in the text:

> I write from a memory of the events that made the firmest impressions upon me, more or less in the order of their remembrance rather than the order of their happening. As you mature, the long, exciting days of your youth pass before your eyes as in a montage; a montage of the events that were important in making the real you—the *now* you.[14]

Such affectionate reminiscence is most easily undertaken from the perspective of a later, comfortable life embraced and internalized. "I think," said Hoagy Bix, "he needed to feel that he was not gonna go back to Indiana, to the cold, to the no money, to the moving around. To the insecurity of life that he felt as a kid there. He'd got security, and plenty of it."[15]

The security allowed him to consolidate his ties to what a later generation would call his roots. That included reaffirming and solidifying his relationship with Indiana University, as both successful old grad and favorite son. In 1937 he'd presented his "Chimes of Indiana" to his alma mater, in dedication to William Lowe Bryan, university president during Hoagy's years at the school. He premiered the song that May 5, during an hour-long, coast-to-coast NBC broadcast in honor of the university's Founder's Day. "I want you to know," university president Herman Wells wrote to him that autumn, "how beautiful and stirring your 'Chimes of Indiana' is. When the band plays it in the stadium, the entire crowd is profoundly impressed."[16]

Contact with the school became more frequent, particularly with one-time campus drummer George F. "Dixie" Heighway, now president of the Alumni Association; August of 1941 found Carmichael home again for personal appearances at three IU scholarship dances. "With him," the alumni magazine reported at the time, he brought a photo of Hoagy Bix, age three, who would "someday be a great trumpet player and star fullback, two of the few ambitions that his illustrious dad never was able to realize."[17]

He brought both boys with him on a June 1942 visit to parents and grandmothers. Their first meeting with "Ma" Robison, their great-grandmother, proved their last. Her death in September, followed by Cyclone Carmichael's passing a year later, seemed if anything to tighten Hoagy's embrace of the region and its people. In November, when sister Georgia married fellow-Hoosier Robert George in San Francisco, Hoagy was there *in loco parentis* to give the bride away, playing his trusty "Wedding Waltz" at the ceremony.

Sisters Georgia and Martha began urging their mother to give up the Indianapolis house and follow the sun west to California. Lida resisted, stubbornly at first, less resolutely as time went by. In one letter she agonizes about uprooting herself, yet confesses that even simple household chores now tire her. Almost casually she reveals her doctor's warning that chronic bronchitis has made her easy prey for tuberculosis, but questions whether living in San Francisco (where Georgia's marriage had taken her) will be any better for her health. Overall, the thought of moving

> makes me nervous and upset, I get sick . . . I am even at the stage now where I can't sleep at night for thinking, and I can't last long at that. I have lost weight worrying about it, and I think the lesser of

two evils is just to let me stay put where I am. I won't be as happy or I won't live as long, but "that doesn't make no never mind..." For example there are 300 records that no one wants to pack.[18]

Mortality, inexorable and unforgiving, is beginning to encroach. All the more important that *The Stardust Road* helps hold the line, keeping at bay a "world of cold realities that was sweeping us into its grip," which no amount of California sunshine could dispel. As *Melody Maker* reviewer Henshaw is quick to note, the phrase "the years have pants," Hoosier variant on *tempus fugit*, occurs at least fifteen times in the text. Here, at least, Hoagy can suspend the formative moments of his life in silence and slow time, and finally do what he's longed to do for a decade and a half: reject the catastrophic news of Bix Beiderbecke's death. The Beiderbecke cornet mouthpiece resting in a glass case on Carmichael's California mantel is more than a keepsake. Talisman and totem, it preserves a link with the living Bix who still inhabits his friend's every day.[19]

Wad Allen, by then vice president and chief of public relations for the Johns-Manville Corporation, provides an epilogue, speaking a few slightly less gauzy truths to and about his pal "Hogwash McCorkle."

You made your greatest success as a composer by *not* writing songs about love. You gained popularity in radio and records by singing: yet you have no voice. How do you do that? It worries us. You got interested in movie acting about a year ago and now you are in that. Every time you put your mind to something you really get on the outside of it before you let go.[20]

The films, and "McCorkle's" contributions to them, bear him out. *Canyon Passage*, in fact, introduces three new Carmichael songs. "Rogue River Valley" and "I'm Gettin' Married in the Morning" are gussied-up cowboy ditties of the "git along, little dogie" variety. The third, however, teams him with British-born lyricist Jack Brooks, just beginning a successful career writing material for Bing Crosby, Bob Hope, Fred Allen, and other stars.[21]

Hoagy called it "Ole Buttermilk Sky." Title and concept came, he said, as "a bolt from the blue," one of those all-at-once revelations so common in Hollywood depictions of the songwriting process but so rare in reality.

"It was the most inspirational thing that's ever happened [in] all the time I've been writing songs, and I just believe somebody up above just handed me that title." He and Brooks "finished that song before the afternoon was over."[22]

But careful listening, he added, yielded doubt. "I said, 'Ooh, it's corny. It's a corny song. I don't like [*sic*] to put it in the picture.'" He put his case to producer Walter Wanger, imploring him to drop the song from *Canyon Passage*. Wanger barely gave the entreaty a thought. "Hoagy, that's going into the picture and you're going to sing it" was his quick and categorical rejoinder. Carmichael moaned, sighed, pouted, and protested—all in vain. Wanger stood firm, and the song stayed in.[23]

To the composer's astonishment, "Ole Buttermilk Sky" took off, vaulting right onto the *Billboard* record charts and staying an impressive five months. Bandleader Kay Kyser's record, with vocal by future TV host Mike Douglas, reached number one; Hoagy's own version occupied the number two slot for four weeks, and records by other artists, including Paul Weston and Connee Boswell, also did well.[24]

And, to complete an improbable saga, "Ole Buttermilk Sky" landed an Academy Award nomination as best movie song of 1946. "Well," Hoagy commented some years later, "every time I see [Wanger] I shake his hand for insisting that it go into the picture . . . I love the man." In the end, "Buttermilk" lost out to "On the Atchison, Topeka, and the Santa Fe," written by Harry Warren and Johnny Mercer for MGM's Judy Garland musical *The Harvey Girls*. Don't worry, Hoag, Mercer reassured his "Skylark" collaborator; we'll get together soon and win one, count on it.

"Ole Buttermilk Sky" is both a Carmichael "character song" and a love song, in the sense that "Skylark" is a love song: both exhort nature to smile on the singer's loved one. The very evocation of a sky whose color and texture evoke buttermilk is of a piece with the imagery of "Memphis in June," "Moon Country," and "Lazybones."

It's also a departure, the first major Carmichael song which, in both its structure and *faux*-western rhythmic underpinning, lends itself only awkwardly to use by jazz players and singers. Subtly but noticeably, the emphasis has begun to shift. Figure shapes are still recognizably jazz-derived, as in the notes he uses to express "can't you see my little donkey and me" in bars 10–11 of "Ole Buttermilk Sky":

"Ole Buttermilk Sky" (2 bars), 1946

But the flavor and sense are different. The change is equally apparent in "Doctor, Lawyer, Indian Chief," written with Webster in 1945 for extrovert singer-actress Betty Hutton to belt out onscreen in *The Stork Club*. Carmichael's worksheet reveals that he conceived the first eight bars as a jazz paraphrase of the melody of "Isle of Capri." But the finished song, fifty bars in length, introduces elements new to Carmichael music: the first eight bars, or "A" section, for example, become nine, with addition of the sort of extra, phrase-separating "breathing" bar more common in folk and country songs and in the blues. Though it has been recorded by jazz artists (singers Bob Dorough and Barbara Lea perform it well on a 1981 record), it is too long for jazz use and belongs to quite another genre. "Doctor, Lawyer, Indian Chief," in fact, reads and plays more like a Broadway show song, something Irving Berlin could have written for *Annie Get Your Gun*, produced around the same time. And like such *faux*-primitive Berlin tunes as "Doin' What Comes Natur'lly," it did well with the public, Hutton's record scoring high on *Your Hit Parade*. For many listeners who came of age in the 1940s, it remains strongly associated with Hoagy Carmichael.

However well it sold, Hoagy's record of "Ole Buttermilk Sky" was not his most successful mid-1940s performance on disc. That honor belongs to a song by another, and a not-unlikely, candidate: Kansas-born Clancy Hayes had grown up singing and playing both piano and banjo in jazz bands around San Francisco, attracting attention toward the end of the 1930s as a founder of the Bay Area's traditional revival. In 1946 he collaborated with New Yorker Kermit Goell on "Huggin' and Chalkin'," an upbeat novelty singing the praises of a sweetheart named Rosabelle McGee "who tips the scales at three-oh-three."

Hoagy Carmichael recorded the song for Decca with backup singers and a band led by Vic Schoen; by the end of November it had begun a fifteen-week stay on the Hit Parade, including some time in the number one spot. So vivid was its impression on the public, and so characteristic Hoagy's performance, that to this day many who remember it mistakenly think it a Carmichael song.

(Johnny Mercer recorded "Huggin' and Chalkin' " at about the same time for Capitol, backed by Paul Weston's orchestra. That record also sold well—prompting more than a few to contend that Mercer had written it, perhaps in collaboration with Carmichael. To this day, there are fans who refuse to believe that neither man had anything to do with creating "Huggin' and Chalkin'.")[25]

      ✳   ✳   ✳

Randy Carmichael preserves a child's clear memory of his father at work. "In Dad's den there was a piano," he recalled recently. "Not a grand—we had one of those in the living room—but an upright. Actually it was the middle size; what do they call them, consoles? To the left of it was this wonderful large writing desk."

"The den was a large room, with telescoping doors that folded back— three panels. When those doors were closed you just didn't go in; that meant strictly 'off limits.' But if one of the doors was open you could knock and enter, but only if invited. I'd sneak in and sit in one of those big wing chairs and listen. Or I could walk up right near the piano and watch him work. But I was very quiet—oh God, you had to be. Not a peep."

"It went on for hours. Just plink plink. Write it down. Plink plink some more. He'd change something. Agonize over it. Pace. Write it down again. He was incessant: when he was writing something it was twenty-four hours a day. He'd work so hard over a two-week period that he'd be a basket case at the end. Unbelievably labor-intensive. I was fascinated, even if I didn't really know what he was doing. Just that this guy, my dad, was sitting there creating something. I didn't know it was something called 'a *song.*' That was beyond me. It was just that he was *there*, all the time, making all these things."

"Then, when he was finished, he'd go play golf, go out and party, and drink and carry on as if nothing had happened. That made the whole thing seem even stranger."[26]

Both sons remembered the parties and celebrity guests, among them actors Clark Gable, John Hodiak, Lee Bowman, Tyrone Power, Robert Montgomery—and such neighbors as Bing Crosby, Roger Converse (of the athletic shoe dynasty), and movie producer Benedict Bogeaus. "Hedy Lamarr lived down the street somewhere," said Randy. "And at the foot of Charing Cross, which is shaped like a horseshoe, was one of the entrances to a huge mansion that also had an entrance on Mapleton Drive. It's now the Playboy mansion, Hugh Hefner's place."

"As children we'd go down there to see if the Charing Cross gate was open, then go up to Mapleton and ride our bikes lickety-split through the property—because the butlers, Germans mostly, that [*sic*] we thought were ogres in those days, would come out and growl at us: 'It iss not allowt zat you komm into ziss property.' Of course we'd go whizzing through as often as we could."[27]

Carmichael the songwriter was branching out, experimenting with phrase lengths, motivic ideas, structural variations. "Ivy," written for a 1947 film of the same name starring Joan Fontaine, anchors its melody to a pair of half notes, a fourth apart, which occur six times in a chorus of forty-one bars (a standard thirty-two with a nine-bar coda).

Conventional song histories regularly identify Hoagy Carmichael as the songwriter who did *not* write often about love. Examination of his output reveals many standard-issue love songs: but with a few exceptions they were not commercially successful, and therefore remain little known. "Things Have Changed," written with Webster, is an ode to love gone wrong. It's heard on the soundtrack of *Ivy*, along with "Put Yourself in My Place, Baby," lyric by singer Frankie Laine; the latter song is preserved on a particularly effective record by Duke Ellington's orchestra.

Such earlier efforts as "There She Was" and "I'm Only Happy, That's All" are well crafted, with appealing melodies and capable lyrics. Though "I Should Have Known You Years Ago" had a featured spot in the 1941 movie *Road Show*, it failed to take off—surely owing in part to the dispute which kept ASCAP-controlled songs from vital radio play during that year. Even "The Three Rivers," a Carmichael-Webster collaboration, which generated a momentary *frisson* of publicity over the lyric's faulty grasp of Pennsylvania geography (the Allegheny, Susquehanna, and Monongahela never meet), didn't quite catch on with the public. Others, even some later efforts with Johnny Mercer, remain obscure.

For better or worse, and excepting "The Nearness of You," the only love songs for which Hoagy Carmichael is known include a song about a song about love ("Star Dust"), about love as symbolized by a bird ("Skylark"), about the memory of love ("I Get Along Without You Very Well"), and about the effects of a wayward eye on an avian love relationship ("Baltimore Oriole").

Perhaps the least heralded, but certainly most distinctive, of Hoagy's love-song collaborators during this time was none other than his departed friend Bix Beiderbecke. Musicians throughout the years had remarked that various of Bix's solos, at the piano as well as on the cornet, lent themselves conveniently to use as songs. The genesis of such Carmichael melodies as "Skylark," "Blue Orchids," and, above all, "Star Dust" surely lies in Beiderbecke.

And, too, the quietly contemplative middle strain of *In a Mist* seemed to invite use in a song. Hoagy has left no indication of when the idea occurred to him, but at some point in the 1940s, he converted the *In a Mist* melody into "Someday Soon," a twenty-four-bar love song with an original verse and a lyric by Webster. Then, unaccountably, he let it lie.[28]

✻   ✻   ✻

With the films doing well and more than a few songs on and off the Hit Parade, Hoagy took time off for a month of performances at British variety theatres, under the aegis of impresario Bernard Delfont. It had been fifteen years since the composer of "Lazybones" had tripped anonymously through London and a half-dozen other European capitals; this time, as in Hollywood, he returned as a star.

Press reaction was mixed. A front-page *Musical Express* review of his opening night at the London Casino took him to task for using prompt cards, for calling to the orchestra to get out parts for "Memphis in June," even for drinking a glass of water onstage. "What he gave us was a recital," the reviewer sniffed. "He should have cut a lot of the cackle and could have played all his beautiful numbers, singing them in his fascinating, irresistible style, one after another, until the cows came home and we would have roared our approval." True, the reviewer added in a direct address to producer Delfont, "there is only ONE Hoagy Carmichael and you are very astute in having booked him. But there's one thing even you can't do—and that is turn a recital into a production."[29]

Backed by a quartet of veteran British musicians including jazz veteran Bill Wiltshire on drums, Carmichael also played weeks at popular cabaret halls in Lewisham and Golders Green, with one-night concerts in Hastings-on-Sea, Liverpool, and Leicester. A *Melody Maker* review, perhaps written by either Laurie Henshaw or Max Jones, praised "the most easy-going and unpretentious act ever presented at a West End variety theatre . . . To call his presentation an 'act' is a misnomer. It might better be called a half-hour casual labour."

As part of the act he introduced "The Monkey Song," alternately titled "King ReBop," a long musical tale about a king "down in the jungle" who dreams about a drummin' monkey, busily engaged in recruiting a jazz band; into this bizarre situation strolls a Bible-toting missionary, who sees commercial possibilities in such an attraction. Carmichael even manages to slip a reference to Bix into the lyric. In all, it's something of a shaggy-monkey story, a piece of character material in the "Hong Kong Blues" tradition, which he ended up singing onscreen some years later in *The Las Vegas Story*.

"Film roles make him out to be a saturnine character of philosophical bent," *Melody Maker*'s Max Jones declared. "When you meet him, though, you realise that he's a reasonably normal American; a good talker and great story-teller, and a quieter dresser than most."

Jones, a jazz saxophonist in his own college days, quickly got his visitor talking about what he knew best: hot music and the craft of songwriting. "None of my songs," Hoagy began, "could have been written without I'd had [*sic*] a jazz background. But that doesn't mean I write jazz. I write *melodies*, and those tunes are conditioned by my musical environment, which means some were directly inspired by jazz." As examples he cited "New Orleans," "Rockin' Chair," "Georgia on My Mind," and "Hong Kong Blues," among others. "I can tell you, it took a jazz education to enable me to write 'em."[30]

In all, the weeks in Britain left a lasting impression. "I guess no artist would be treated so good in the States," he told a Leicester reporter, echoing the pronouncements of countless visiting Americans before and since. "Seems that back home we're all too much bound up in our own affairs. But even in London folks go so nuts about you, you'd think they had never seen a show before."[31]

✳   ✳   ✳

If hit songs are any criterion, the rest of 1948 was a relatively unexceptional time for Carmichael. No films, apart from a cameo appearance in the William Bendix prison drama *Johnny Holiday*, singing his own "My Christmas Song for You," improbably enough, for an audience of inmates. But there was no new Carmichael tune on the Hit Parade, no instant standards in the sense of "Memphis in June" or "Ole Buttermilk Sky."

Yet it was not a fallow period. With "Just a Shade on the Blue Side," he returned to a blues-based sound and flavor he'd first explored in 1932 with "Sing It Way Down Low." The result is a melodically fetching little gem with a hornlike melody, set up in two episodes of sixteen bars each, laced together with a four-bar interlude. Harold Adamson's lyric, if not memorable, nevertheless catches and develops the mood of a song deserving of wider recognition.

Part of a songwriter's craft involves spotting trends and responding to them. So it was with Peggy Lee's satiric, *faux*-Mexican spoof "Mañana," which topped the mid-1948 Hit Parade. Among those who followed up was Hoagy Carmichael: he labeled his "Too Much-a-Mañana," with a lyric by Helen Meinardi, a "jazz samba." And a samba it was, in the sense of Ary Barroso's "Brazil," a major U.S. hit earlier in the decade—fast-moving, rhythmic, catchy. Another effort inspired by a south-of-the-border craze was "Bubble-Loo Bubble-Loo," done in collaboration with Paul Webster. The title was a pun, distant echo of "Babalu," popularized in the early 1940s by Xavier Cugat and other bandleaders. Even a Capitol record by Peggy Lee, whose photo appears on the published song sheet, failed to generate enough interest to lift the song from obscurity.[32]

These months also found Hoagy at work on a project that had absorbed him since his New York days. It had begun as *Echo[es] of the Opera*, a series of free-associative piano improvisations in a late-Romantic style, recorded on three home acetate discs in 1933. Now, in 1949, Carmichael began negotiations with Russian-born Fabien Sevitsky, who since 1937 had been principal conductor of the Indianapolis Symphony Orchestra. Nephew of longtime Boston Symphony Orchestra conductor Serge Koussevitsky, Sevitsky had been salting his programs with works by contemporary American composers, more than a few of which he'd commissioned himself.

His association with Carmichael began with a November 1949 centenary tribute to James Whitcomb Riley. Seven American composers, among them Morton Gould, Paul Creston, and Broadway veteran Robert Russell Bennett, were invited to contribute what the conductor termed "musical sentences"—brief pieces evoking aspects of the great Hoosier poet's life and works. Carmichael's offering, an especially poignant moment for him given his boyhood encounters with Riley, was his setting of "When the Frost Is on the Punkin'." As one rather breathless report put it, "That popular song writer, who might be thought more at home in a jam session than in a symphony concert, stole the show."[33]

A month later, in the same Murat Concert Hall, Sevitsky and his musicians premiered *Brown County in Autumn*, announced as a tone poem inspired by the fall foliage in a particularly beautiful patch of Indiana countryside east of Bloomington. As enthusiastic press reviews made clear, Carmichael's pastoral themes had come a long way from *Echo[es] of the Opera*.

"It opened with a slightly somber daybreak," a *Time* magazine reviewer wrote. "The music went into full action with the purples and reds of the leaves, rose to a peak in the description of the yellows, then slowly died away." Another remarked that "Carmichael has transferred these colors to the varied timbers [*sic*] of orchestral instruments with a nice degree of success . . . His themes are simple and mellifluous. His mood is wistful, perhaps nostalgic."[34]

In the program notes, Hoagy names as his inspiration a Brown County painting by Indiana artist T. C. Steele. It was an appropriate, culturally resonant, choice. Theodore Clement Steele (1847–1926), member of the Hoosier Group of American regional impressionists, held the chair of Honorary Professor of Painting at Indiana University from 1922 until his death in mid-1926—concurrent with Carmichael's time at IU. Steele's Bloomington studio was in the attic of what was then the library building, directly across the street from the Book Nook.

His paintings hang in the IU Student Union and in other buildings throught the campus, many of them landscapes strongly evocative of the Indiana countryside at its most varied and beautiful. There can be no doubting that Hoagy and his Book Nook friends, particularly Bill Moenkhaus, were aware of Steele and his work, and that in later life Carmichael visited the artist's Brown County home, "the House of the Singing Winds."[35]

The *Indianapolis Sunday Star* proclaimed *Brown County in Autumn* unequivocally a "Big Success," predicting that Hoagy's "skill in weaving simple melodic themes into a rich fabric is going to floor the skeptics." The unbylined reviewer praised "sweet, expressive music, with just enough sentiment to make it right. The feeling it leaves is that of peace and contentment . . . not even a suggestion of the austere or acutely modern about it. Its appeal is direct to the ear and the heart and it makes listening a pleasure." The work "will not bring him such handsome royalties as 'Stardust'—maybe he'll never make a penny on it—but it's a work of which he can be justly proud. Let's hope he goes on from there—we need composers who compose for the public's enjoyment."[36]

Henry Butler, in the daily *Star*, struck a more guarded note, pronouncing *Brown County* "a nice composition with pleasing melodies, but no great profundity . . . I'll say that it probably will do better in Indiana than elsewhere, since music critics are notoriously harsh on innovations that don't crash and blast and illustrate some 'chic' musical doctrine."[37]

His words proved prophetic. Introduced by Sevitsky and the Indianapolis orchestra at Carnegie Hall two months later, *Brown County in Autumn* fetched undisguised scorn from New York reviewers. Olin Downes, veteran classical music eminence of the *New York Times*, dismissed Carmichael as having "neither the technique nor the mind of musical thought which makes it possible for him to express himself adequately in this medium." Francis D. Perkins of the *Herald Tribune* decried "the derivative nature of the music . . . [which] found him less at home than in his more familiar spheres of activity." Only popular orchestra leader Andre Kostelanetz spoke out on Carmichael's behalf, declaring that such efforts "must be encouraged. The audience likes it and it was played so beautifully."[38]

Such treatment was nothing unusual in New York, particularly for a first "serious" effort by a composer hitherto best known as a songwriter. It had been the same Olin Downes, after all, who suggested in 1924 that George Gershwin's *Rhapsody in Blue* showed "a young composer with aims that go far beyond those of his ilk, struggling with a form of which he is far from being a master." Lawrence Gilman, in the *Herald Tribune*, had been more harsh: "How trite and feeble and conventional the tunes are, how sentimental and vapid the harmonic treatment . . . so derivative, so static, so inexpressive."[39]

But Gershwin was made of sterner stuff than Hoagy Carmichael, working from a confidence apparently rooted in superficial technical sophistication. To Carmichael the autodidact, such criticism of *Brown County*, rather than a spur to greater effort, constituted a setback comparable to *Walk With Music*. Forget Broadway, the opinion-makers seemed to be saying; forget the concert hall and stick to doing what you do best, writing popular songs. Rather than resist such dismissal, husbanding his energies to try again, he quietly caved in. "I knew my limitation," he confessed later, referring to the entire episode as a musical defeat. "I'm not a student of music."*Brown County in Autumn* disappeared from sight and hearing.[40]

Heard now, Carmichael's nine-minute tone poem stands as a work of no little charm, using homespun themes in shaping a sort of visual imagery consonant with the best of his songs—and evocative of the wistful tone associated with Steele and other Hoosier Group artists. Program is all, subjugating even thematic development and structural progression. The music operates like a motion-picture camera, panning slowly across a richly hued landscape. There is every reason to expect that, had he tried again, made himself more at home with orchestral resources, Carmichael might have explored this unified, programmatic form with ever greater success.

"But you know," said Randy Carmichael, "I think he'd rather have played golf, or tennis, than have to go to school to learn orchestration or anything like that. The guy didn't slough his life off—but I do think he pissed away a good deal of it. Of course he never said anything about this: Dad was very tight-lipped about a lot of things, didn't open up a great deal, especially about feelings."[41]

And, too, the comfort of his life cushioned him from such setbacks as the failure of *Brown County in Autumn*. His songs were earning secure and steady royalties. His two sons were growing up fast, showing incipient musical talent. Ruth kept the Carmichael social calendar full, made certain the invitations to Hollywood parties kept coming in. "I can't tell you the people she drew to that house," said Hoagy Bix. "Full of stuff, and jokes. Quite pretty, in a red-hair-and-freckles, young-cute sort of way. Hazel eyes."

"She wasn't a housekeeper or homemaker in any traditional sense. She liked the parties, the funnin' around, and all that. And remember, we'd had Eva since I was very small, so Mom got off: she wasn't really in charge of running the house. After Eva there were others—people on staff, you know, taking care of all that. Mom was able to socialize, go places, shop for the house. And she had immaculate taste."[42]

The CBS radio series had ended in mid-1948, but Hoagy kept making records, both of his own songs and those of others. Most were overtly commercial affairs, with large studio orchestras and backup singers. But December 9 brought a return to familiar and musically comfortable surroundings: a nine-piece jazz band led by clarinetist Matty Matlock, including tenor saxophonist Eddie Miller, guitarist George Van Eps, Chicagoan Joe Rushton on bass sax, and the pioneer drummer-bandleader Ben Pollack. On trumpet was Indiana-born Dick Cathcart, a clear-toned stylist in the Bix tradition. Both "That's a Plenty" (with a new Ray Gilbert lyric) and "At the Darktown Strutters' Ball" find Hoagy relaxed and obviously happy.

Both performances burst with high spirits, good rhythmic singing, and first-rate instrumental solos.

Still, there can be little doubt that the *Brown County* episode, like *Walk With Music* before it, had stung. But for every setback in one area, Hoagy Carmichael's career seems to have provided an advance in another. In this case the impetus came, if indirectly, from his long-dead friend Bix.

Plans to film *Young Man With a Horn* back in 1938–39 had come to nothing, and the project had been shelved. Now, a decade later, Hollywood was taking renewed interest in Dorothy Baker's best-seller about a jazz trumpet player and his fruitless quest for the perfect chorus, for figures and sounds no one could play on a horn.

In a brief foreword, author Baker declares that "the inspiration for the writing of this book has been the music, not the life," of Beiderbecke. To some degree the statement is disingenuous: while storyline and characterization owe little to the real-life Bix, more than a few career points resemble those of Baker's model.

Now, at last, it was time to think about filming *Young Man With a Horn*. How fitting, inevitable even, that one of the first casting choices should be Hoagy Carmichael. Bix, it seemed, was still taking care of his own.

✳ XVI ✳

Tide: Rise and Ebb

The opening credits to *Young Man With a Horn* have hardly faded from the screen when the camera pans down and catches Hoagy Carmichael, seated at an old upright piano in a deserted ballroom. He glances up, as if acknowledging a visitor, then calmly lights a cigarette.

"My name is Willie Willoughby," he says, "but they call me 'Smoke.'" He takes a drag, blowing it out slowly as if to emphasize the name. "I play piano in a run-of-the-mill dance band. Kind of monotonous, but there were times when I got my kicks, and not so long ago, either.

"Like when I palled around with Rick Martin, the famous trumpet man. What a guy!" These sentences flow naturally, conversationally. The ear abruptly realizes that this exposition, with its fast-moving inner cadence, is not the standard-issue work of a Hollywood scriptwriter.

It's Hoagy Carmichael talking. Even the phrase "What a guy!"—with its ringing echo of "I Get Along Without You Very Well"—strikes the ear the way a passage from *The Stardust Road* might. No accident, too, that "Willie Willoughby" scans exactly the way "Hoagy Carmichael" does, two syllables and three, accent on the first of each name.

Change all "Rick Martin" references to "Bix Beiderbecke," furthermore, and the result is Hoagy, looking back with affection on his own, deeply missed, early jazz years.

"'Course Rick is practically a legend now. People ask me about him and those times. Ordinarily I don't talk much about it. But I think a lot about it. He had a lot of friends. In a way he had no friends at all. He was a lonely kind of guy always, I guess, from the time he was a kid . . . he never did get much out of school, and he made very few friends along the way."

Though one or two of these expository ideas appear in the Dorothy Baker best-seller on which *Young Man With a Horn* is based, the phrasing, tone, and cadence are not hers. If Baker's prose resembles that of anyone at all, it is her close friend and inspiration Otis Ferguson, the short-lived critic and essayist who coined the title to introduce two outstanding magazine pieces on Beiderbecke, the first of their sort published after his death.

The character Smoke had appeared in Baker's novel. But he was a drummer named Jordan, and black. When it came to Carmichael's attention that long-dormant plans to turn the book into a movie were again on the boards, he moved quickly. According to one magazine article, he began lobbying producer Jerry Wald and director Michael Curtiz for the part. "He heard about Miss Baker's description of the character being cast. It read, in part: 'He was a thoughtful boy, inclined to philosophy, and his movements were precise and slow.' Carmichael felt as if someone had described him personally, and declared that all he had to do was to play himself."[1]

Wald, in fact, had cast Hoagy for the film as early as 1946, engaging Stephen Longstreet—later to collaborate with Carmichael on *Sometimes I Wonder*—to write a screenplay. Early plans had called for John Garfield to play the role of Rick Martin, but the latter's departure from Warners sank that idea. Other actors under consideration included James Stewart, Dane Clark, and even Ronald Reagan. Several times the project seemed about to capsize, remaining afloat only through Wald's belief in its ultimate success. Two separate scripts were offered—with even studio head Jack Warner getting into the act, doggedly insisting on a happy ending rather than Miss Baker's, which has the Martin character dying, like Bix, of the effects of alcoholism.[2]

As director of *Casablanca*, Curtiz well understood the dramatic value of the pianist-singer who functions as sounding board and foil for the leading man (Bogart), giver of advice for the heroine (Bacall), and casual outsider commenting on the main action. Carmichael's friend Howard Hawks had been quick to adapt the *Casablanca* idea for *To Have and Have Not*, casting

Hoagy in the role played by Dooley Wilson in the earlier film. Now Curtiz was claiming it back.

But who would play Rick Martin? What actor could marshal sufficient intensity and focus to fit the portrait of single-minded obsession envisioned by Curtiz? An answer came in early 1949, with the extraordinary success of thirty-three-year-old Kirk Douglas in the boxing drama *Champion*. Douglas, clearly emboldened by his box-office popularity, had his own ideas about how certain scenes should play out. Somehow he, Wald, Carl Foreman, and Curtiz reached a compromise, and shooting began in July.[3]

Though cast as a pianist, Hoagy performs none of his own songs in the film and does none of the soundtrack piano work; that credit belongs to ever-faithful Buddy Cole. Carmichael does no singing, save for a moment when he and Douglas, driving along in an open car, deliver a rather bibulous duet on the 1922 Milton Ager–Jack Yellen favorite "Lovin' Sam, the Sheik of Alabam."

Even that scene echoes Hoagy and Bix, toodling along the National Road to Richmond, described so evocatively in *The Stardust Road*. Perhaps Smoke and Rick don't fill the air with the "banners of melody" so lovingly portrayed in Carmichael's book, but the exuberance, a sense of something precious momentarily grasped, is hard to miss.

As released in February of 1950, *Young Man With a Horn* retains relatively little of either the flesh-and-blood Beiderbecke or the tragic hero of Miss Baker's book. As a *Time* magazine reviewer put it, "Enough of the book has stuck to the picture to point up the lost opportunities." There's even a passage—again, Carmichael's guiding hand is apparent behind the words—when Smoke heads off for Christmas at home with his family, leaving his friend Rick in the big city.

"Maybe I'm getting too old for this music racket," he says before boarding the train. "It's not much fun any more, and you can't sell it for a bag of peanuts. Sure you won't come with me? Indiana's awful nice this time of year."

"You mean out to old Aunt Mary," the trumpeter says, in a mock-Hoosier accent.

"Aw, stop kiddin'," his friend replies. "You'd like my folks. We got plenty of room."

"Naw, thanks. I'd only be in the way."

As with Smoke's opening soliloquy, this exchange is an interpolation, occurring nowhere in the Baker novel. Krin Gabbard is squarely on target when, in *Jammin' at the Margins*, he remarks that Carmichael "transforms *Young Man With a Horn* into something entirely different than [sic] it would have been without him. Because he is more outside the film than within it, he can safely and positively signify 'jazz' in a film that has no real use for the music."[4]

The one single factor that might have identified *Young Man With a Horn* as a film seriously concerned with jazz and those who play it was the trumpet player selected to "ghost" soundtrack solos for Rick Martin. According to a perhaps apocryphal, yet persistent, music business story, one of the chief candidates at first was Bobby Hackett, whose lyrical stylings might have embodied the vulnerable lyricism identified with Bix—which Baker surely had in mind in declaring, "The inspiration for the writing of this book has been the music . . . of a great musician, Leon (Bix) Beiderbecke, who died in the year 1931."

By the mid-1940s Hackett had emerged from a struggle with alcoholism into a personal and professional rebirth, his work demonstrating new strength and luster. He was recording widely, and in some cases—as on two titles backing Frank Sinatra—memorably. But he'd been a drinker at the time he ghosted solos for Fred Astaire in Paramount's 1940 *Second Chorus,* and it hardly strains credibility to suggest that Hollywood's memory for such details outstrips its curiosity about anything so arcane as a career renaissance.

The job went instead to Harry James. As early as 1941, word circulated throughout the movie gossip mills that James was being considered for the assignment. He was riding high as a bandleader, thanks to such records as "Ciribiribin," "The Flight of the Bumblebee," and a sugary "You Made Me Love You." Unlike Hackett, whose reputation was largely confined to jazz insiders and fellow musicians, James had the kind of name recognition that registers at the box office.

Douglas took his role seriously, turning to both James and Warner staff trumpeter Larry Sullivan for coaching. "I even learned to play some songs on the trumpet," he reflected in his autobiography. "You can't make a sound out of a trumpet just by blowing in it. You have to develop what they call an embouchure. I've still got it. It's quite a strain on the facial muscles."[5]

According to a February 1950 news feature the actor "got so much into the swing of things that he kept blowing his horn during breaks in the shooting and after hours in his dressing room, much to the distress of the rest of the cast." A fan of hot jazz, Douglas was indeed musically inclined and had even played some banjo in his teenage years. Photographs still exist of him visiting Eddie Condon's New York nightclub, horn in hand, presumably picking up pointers from Pee Wee Russell, Sidney Bechet, and pianist Art Hodes, then "jamming" with trombonist George Brunies, clarinetist Peanuts Hucko, and fellow sitter-in Buddy Rich on drums.[6]

Musically, the choice of James as Rick Martin's "ghost" was regrettable. While he brings a compellingly fevered intensity to an up-tempo jam version of the old favorite "Limehouse Blues," his florid arabesques on other numbers, including a climactic "With a Song in My Heart," backing an equally miscast Doris Day, irreparably compromise any sense of Martin as—in the words of one magazine reviewer—an "artist who abandons the world to worship in the loneliness of his own inner shrine."[7]

Far more effective, for all James's screen billing as "musical adviser," is big band veteran Jimmy Zito, ghosting the solos of black trumpeter Art Hazard. Clearly intended as a kind of Louis Armstrong role model to Martin's Bix, Hazard is the only character besides Smoke who manages, dramatically and musically, to transcend the screenplay. Puerto Rican–born Juano Hernandez, who had brought eloquence to a 1949 film adaptation of William Faulkner's *Intruder in the Dust*, imbues Hazard with quietly understated dignity; Zito, best known for his work on Les Brown's 1946 hit record of "I've Got My Love to Keep Me Warm," solos with Louis-like majesty on "I Gotta Right to Sing the Blues" (reprised later, less effectively, by James), "Moanin' Low," and an unidentified stomp built on the changes to the old favorite "Shine." Bar for bar, he is heard more during the film than is James: even during a nightclub sequence intended to show his decline he gives a thoughtful account of "The Blue Room."

Critical reaction to the film was mixed. But Carmichael, again playing a variant on the character he'd perfected in *To Have and Have Not*, won unanimous praise. While *Time* found his performance "effortless," and *Look* suggested the role was "almost autobiographical," *Variety* averred that the composer of "Star Dust" was "as good an actor as he is [a] tunesmith, and as a piano-pounder who narrates the plot he adds much to the credit side of the picture."[8]

How *Young Man* would end seems to have been unresolved until very late. Wald wanted Rick to die, as he does in the novel. Jack Warner objected, in all probability on the grounds that such a denouement would seem too downbeat. As Carmichael recalled it, "The story conferences became so intense that they even called me in to see if I could think up an ending. Mike Curtiz's idea of just letting Kirk die of alcoholism finally won out."[9]

But it didn't. In the picture as released, Martin—improbably—recovers, wins Doris Day's girl-singer-with-heart-of-gold, and trumpets away into the sunset. But not before one final, obviously Carmichael-generated peroration from Rick's pal Smoke Willoughby:

At the top, 1948. (ATM)

Relaxing with Bogie, Bacall, and Walter Brennan on the set of *To Have and Have Not*, 1944. (ATM)

With Dana Andrews and Merle Oberon in publicity still for *Night Song*, 1947. (ATM)

Publicity still from *Canyon Passage*, 1946. Others include Andy Devine (center) and Ward Bond (right). (ATM)

With cornetist Jimmy
McPartland, who replaced
Bix in the Wolverines, 1945.
(MARIAN MCPARTLAND
COLLECTION)

Giving sons Randy (left)
and Hoagy Bix (right) a
couple of musical point-
ers, c. 1946. (ATM)

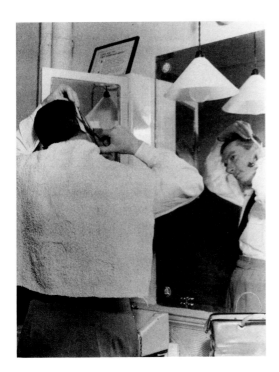

Cutting his own hair, early 1950s. (ATM)

A moment's respite in the sun, late 1940s. (ATM)

A tense scene with Kirk Douglas in *Young Man With a Horn*, 1950. (ATM)

Academy Awards ceremony, 1951. Left to right: Johnny Mercer, Hoagy, Donald O'Connor, Franz Waxman. (RMS)

Serenading a class of schoolchildren, 1950s. (ATM)

At the wheel of one of his beloved Dual Ghias, 1956. (ATM)

At an Indiana University football game, 1950s. (ATM)

At the Bel Air Country Club, c. 1960, with Randy (holding clubs) and Hoagy Bix (at drums). (PHOTO BY STAN LEVEY—ATM)

With John Smith and Robert Crawford, Jr., on *Laramie* set, 1959. (ATM)

After the *Hatari!* setback: with Henry Mancini and Judy McHugh, daughter of song-writer Jimmy McHugh, at a 1961 ASCAP awards ceremony. (ATM)

Rehearsing *Johnny Appleseed Suite* with Charles Bud Dant, 1962. (ATM)

One last hurrah: Louis Armstrong's 70th birthday party, July 3, 1970. (PHOTO BY L. LEVINE, FROM RMS COLLECTION)

Receiving honorary doctorate from Indiana University, 1972. (IUA)

A distinguished late portrait, 1970s. (ATM)

With Hoagy Bix and TV host Fred Rogers (seated at piano), 1978. (ATM)

With Wanda (Dorothy) McKay at Thunderbird Country Club "Western party," mid-1970s. (ATM)

Hoagy receiving New York City Certificate of Appreciation, with the author (center) and Wanda (Dorothy) McKay, June 1979. (PHOTO BY HOLLAND WEMPLE, FROM RMS COLLECTION)

You see, Rick was a pretty hard guy to understand, and for a long time he didn't understand himself. But the desire to live is a great teacher, and I think it taught Rick a lot of things. He learned that you can't say everything through the end of a trumpet, and a man doesn't destroy himself just because he can't hit some high note that he dreamed up. Maybe that's why Rick went on to be a success as a human being first—and an artist second. And what an artist.

As Krin Gabbard points out, the passage echoes a comment about Bix in *The Stardust Road*: "Bix, the incomparable genius, but a human being with it all, subject to the ills of the flesh, the tortures of the spirit. And no way to say it except with the horn and the horn *wouldn't say it all* [emphasis added]."[10]

Shortly after filming began, Wald dropped Carmichael a note thanking him "for the superb job you did up to date on the script. . . ." Curtiz followed six weeks later with thanks for "your help with the story, with the acting, with my work and everybody's work." It takes no cryptographer to read between the lines: Carmichael has indeed "helped" with the script—and, presumably, with other things as well. It's all reminiscent of Howard Hawks telling Hoagy Bix Carmichael, "Your dad kept chasing me around the studio, offering his own ideas about the script, his part, and everything else. His innovation couldn't be contained."[11]

✻   ✻   ✻

The first months of 1951 found Carmichael back in in London, this time for a two-week stand at the famed Palladium, immediately before a much-heralded—and ultimately triumphant—four-week run by Judy Garland. The bill was set up in the manner of a music hall program, with Hoagy the final, culminating act in an evening that also included American vocalist Savannah Churchill, billed for the occasion as "the Sepia Songstress."

As in 1948, the format was simple: just Hoagy, a piano, and an instrumental quartet to back him. "I wore a hat on the back of my head and no tie, with a cigarette drooping from my lips, and lazied through the entire performance." He came onstage, the humor magazine *Punch* reported,

looking like a tired small-town doctor on his way to play golf: short, neat, leathery, confident, and, as I said, tired. The oily egotism which is the burden of so many successful crooners is notably absent. He has an intelligent pair of eyes, and when his lean casual face cracks into a smile you are suddenly friends. His behaviour at the piano is that of an uncle who has been told to play to the children for half an hour but not get them too excited . . . but behind all this calculated informality there is an acute sense of rhythm and timing.[12]

Max Jones, who had interviewed him so effectively in 1948, was on hand for the return engagement as well. "Carmichael hasn't much of a voice," he opined in a *Daily Mirror* feature, "and is the first to admit it. 'I guess it's a kind of foggy baritone,' he told me. 'What I call a shaggy-dog voice.' "[13]

Ruth did not accompany him on this visit to Britain—a decision which was to have far-reaching consequences. Though the particulars are remembered differently by friends and family members, all agree that at some point during the engagement the composer met, and was smitten by, twenty-two-year-old English actress Jean Simmons. Born in 1929, Miss Simmons had been making movies since her teen years, winning critical acclaim for such films as David Lean's 1946 Dickens adaptation *Great Expectations*, in which she played Estella, and as Ophelia in Laurence Olivier's 1948 screen production of *Hamlet*.

As Hoagy Bix Carmichael tells it, Simmons "knocked on Dad's dressing-room door and introduced herself . . . Dad took her to the Savoy [Hotel] and bought her an egg breakfast—she hadn't had an egg since before the war, and—well, they fell in love for three weeks." The recollection is suspect on several counts. The "egg breakfast" story and reference to the actress's age as nineteen place these events in 1948, when Ruth accompanied her husband to Britain and—if contemporary news features are any indication—was present and visible everywhere he went. It is hard to imagine Hoagy having enough time for a three-week fling, even with a glamorous young British movie star.[14]

Rather more plausible is that the affair occurred in 1951, particularly in view of Miss Simmons's career status at the time. After a spectacular beginning, she had appeared in a string of British films, among them the pleasant but forgettable *Adam and Evelyne*, the excellent Somerset Maugham adaptation *Trio*, and the Victorian fantasy *So Long at the Fair*. Her reputation had crossed the Atlantic, and her ambition grown apace. By 1951 it was obvious that the logical next step for a young actress with her Elizabeth Taylor–like beauty was Hollywood.

Eva Ford Chatman, ever the Carmichael family confidante, professed later to have known about the affair almost from the moment Hoagy returned home. In her words, the actress "was a very—well, pressing kind of lady . . . knew what she wanted, [and] was determined to have her way. I think she kind of pushed herself on him." Simmons was "using him as a way to get into American movies. She was very beautiful, and had a way of making people do the things she wanted them to do. I think she just made up her mind she was going to have this man or else, and went about doing just that."[15]

Eva and the Carmichael sons seem unanimous in dating the disintegration of the storybook Carmichael marriage to this time. "They had words about what had happened," said Eva. "But I don't think they made much of it, at least on the surface. In those days you didn't; you just accepted things and went along."

"For a long time I didn't get Dad's side of that story," said Hoagy Bix. By that time he and Randy had been shipped off to the Chadwick Seaside School, a California boarding school catering to Hollywood's rich and famous. Whatever internal upheavals had been set in motion were now being played out between Hoagy and Ruth—with Eva at least some of the time within hearing and confiding distance. But as she later put it, "no one talked about those things." Carmichael's private life remained locked securely away from public view.

Carmichael left a vivid impression on another Briton during the 1951 Palladium visit. When, two years later, Ian Fleming published his first James Bond novel, *Casino Royale*, he had fellow-agent René Mathis describe the suave, amoral Bond as "very good-looking. He reminds me rather of Hoagy Carmichael, but there is something cold and ruthless in his"—at which point an explosion shatters the window of the office in which the conversation is taking place. The description is left unfinished. Later in the novel Bond examines his reflection in a mirror and concludes, "Not much of Hoagy Carmichael there."[16]

❖   ❖   ❖

Among projects coming Hoagy's way at the start of the 1950s was a new collaboration with Johnny Mercer, thanks to Betty Hutton. Hollywood's "blonde bombshell" had been a hot commodity since the early 1940s, starring in a string of box-office successes, among them *The Fleet's In, The Miracle of Morgan's Creek,* and *Incendiary Blonde,* in which she'd played extrovert roaring twenties nightclub hostess "Texas" Guinan. She'd given high-kilowatt treatment to the Carmichael-Webster "Doctor, Lawyer, Indian Chief" in *The*

Stork Club, had triumphed again in *The Perils of Pauline*, based on the career of silent-film heroine Pearl White, and was being considered for the Annie Oakley role in a planned film version of Irving Berlin's *Annie Get Your Gun.*

In 1949, while she was making *Red Hot and Blue* (no relation to the Cole Porter show), Paramount was scrambling to find additional properties for her. One project had her playing Sophie Tucker, another Theda Bara, yet another '20s "It" girl Clara Bow. A more likely subject than any of these was Mabel Normand, a leading comedienne in silent films and a key figure in one of the great Hollywood scandals of the 1920s.

On February 2, 1922, a handyman named Henry Peavey found the body of William Desmond Taylor, chief director of the Famous Players–Lasky studio. He'd been shot, one small-caliber bullet to the heart. Though another actress, Mary Miles Minter, garnered most of the publicity with declarations of grand passion for the deceased, Mabel Normand apparently had been the last person actually to see Taylor alive. For a short while her name turned up everywhere in accounts of the case, and those determined to condemn Hollywood sexual depravity (the third trial of movie comedian Roscoe "Fatty" Arbuckle was making headlines at the same time) attacked Minter and Normand with equal fury. Still, Normand's career continued to thrive. She starred in Mack Sennett comedies, played opposite Charlie Chaplin—and became embroiled in at least two other scandals before her death of tuberculosis, at thirty-three, in 1930.

The result of Paramount's brainstorming was *The Keystone Girl*, ostensibly about Sennett but actually built around Hutton in the Normand role. Carmichael and Mercer were signed to write songs and got right to work. Within a few weeks they'd produced, among others, the rhythmically humorous "Queenie the Quick-Change Artist" and the lighthearted "He's Dead, but He Won't Lie Down." The nostalgic waltz "My Cadill-liddle-ol-Lac" and the *alla breve* "But They Better Not Wait Too Long" vividly reflect the film's silent-era subject matter.

If "I Guess It Was You All the Time" is a charming but unexceptional love ballad, "Any Similarity (Is Just Coincidental)" manages to be better than that. Built on a series of ascending stepwise phrases, it develops its lilting melody over a slow, casual harmonic progression, Mercer's spare lyric enhancing the romantic mood. It's a song of considerable charm, which performers in search of overlooked Carmichael-Mercer gems might do well to explore.

Driving down to Palm Springs for a *Keystone Girl* work session at Mercer's home, Hoagy happened to remember an old story that a friend of mine years before had told me, and it was the story about the jackass. The lion, the king of the jungle, [wanted] everybody to come to his party, and finally everybody showed up except the jackass. The King of the Jungle sent some little fellow to go get the jackass. He went out and said, "The King of the Jungle wants you at his party." The jackass was smoking his pipe and he says, "Tell the King of the Jungle that in the cool, cool, cool of the evening I'll be there." And I told the story to Johnny Mercer and immediately he took it up as a song.[17]

The Sennett-Normand project went unproduced, and the Carmichael-Mercer King-of-the-Jungle song into the trunk, but not for long: director Frank Capra, after working at Paramount for years, was getting restless. He'd just finished *Riding High*, a remake of his own 1934 *Broadway Bill*, this time with Bing Crosby in the lead played originally by Warner Baxter. But the constraints of big-studio filmmaking had taken their toll on the man who had conceived and executed *Mr. Deeds Goes to Town*, *It Happened One Night*, and *It's a Wonderful Life*.

"I knew that filmgoers did not see my films just to enjoy comedy, pace, or other entertainment excellencies," Capra wrote. "They came ahungering for soul food . . . Without that spiritual meat my films were, as stated before, just blue-plate specials." So it was that after *Riding High*, Capra informed Paramount chief executive Y. Frank Freeman that he felt like leaving. Not moving to another studio. Just quitting the business. Out.[18]

Okay, said Freeman, have it your way. But remember, you still owe us two more pictures. Tell you what: do one more for us, it'll count as two, and you can go wherever you want after that. Nobody's fool, Freeman realized Capra would be hooked the moment he read the screenplay for what shortly turned out to be *Here Comes the Groom*.

The story was standard fare, following the fortunes of a reporter, fresh back from World War II with two war orphans in tow, trying to keep his lady love from marrying a stuffy millionaire. Bing Crosby was a natural as the reporter, Franchot Tone as the society guy, fourteen-year-old Anna Maria Alberghetti as one of the kids. And the leading lady? "Much to my delight," said Capra, "I discovered that Jane Wyman—short nose, long legs, big heart, and all talent—had a rarely used flair for singing and dancing . . . I *had* to have a great song for Jane to do with Bing. But you don't just find great songs lying around on shelves."[19]

But they did. Or, at least, Joseph Sistrom, one of Capra's closest friends and most trusted advisers at the studio, did: he remembered the failed Sennett-Normand project, and the "Jackass" tune written for it by Carmichael and Mercer. A bit of digging in Paramount's archives yielded a lead sheet and acetate demo disc, with Johnny singing and Hoagy backing him on the piano. Capra liked it right off. Crosby liked it. Jane Wyman, too. With a few minor adjustments to the lyric, "In the Cool Cool Cool of the Evening" was in.

It won an Oscar for 1951, beating out the Bert Kalmar–Harry Ruby–Oscar Hammerstein "A Kiss to Build a Dream On." Johnny Mercer had delivered at last on the promise he'd made to Hoagy when "Ole Buttermilk Sky" had lost to "On the Atchison, Topeka, and the Santa Fe." "Naturally I was overjoyed at receiving my Oscar," Hoagy remarked, not a little wryly. "I'm not sure that my lyricist, Johnny Mercer, was as overjoyed as I because he already had a vulgar display of three Oscars at his home from former years."[20]

In quite another, less widely publicized, way, "In the Cool Cool Cool of the Evening" made movie history. Crosby and Wyman recorded the song on Capra's shooting set, singing to an accompaniment—piped in via tiny short-wave radio receivers in their ears—provided by an orchestra on a sound stage several blocks away.

Here Comes the Groom scored with both the critics and the public. *Variety* hailed it as "a smash hit . . . a cinch to be one of the studio's biggest grossers . . . Capra at his best . . . a rapturous event for his final production chore at Paramount."[21]

The verse of "In the Cool Cool Cool of the Evening" turns on a device charming in its ability to sound simpler than it is: beginning in D on the published sheet (even so many years later, Carmichael still favored this key), it changes key every four bars, moving to E♭, then to B♭, winding up in C— which in turn becomes the dominant to F, "home" key for the sixteen-bar refrain. Because the progressions are natural the ear accepts them, just as it accepts the movement of the tonal center which makes Jerome Kern's melody to "All the Things You Are" an imperishable miracle.

Less noticed by 1951 American audiences was a more venturesome Carmichael effort, performed by the composer himself in *The Las Vegas Story*. "My Resistance Is Low" is a fast jazz waltz, light on its feet, with a catchy melody. Most of its nine-bar "A" section is built on a tonic pedal note which—rather than impart a static quality—drives the melody forward while the lyric, credited to Harold Adamson, deftly catches and amplifies a giddy, dancing mood. The sixteen-bar bridge dwells appealingly on that unlikeliest of scale tones, the eleventh, before giving way to the kind of repeated three-note phrase that makes such other popular waltzes as Rodgers and Hammerstein's "A Wonderful Guy" so memorable:

"My Resistance Is Low" (bars 37–52), 1951

"My Resistance Is Low" caught the attention of Alec Wilder, who pronounced it (in *American Popular Song*) one of "the high points of Carmichael's writing," expressing particular fondness for the little eighth-note "escape" that binds the bridge to the rest of the song. Perhaps because of the publicity blitz surrounding "Cool Cool Cool" and Carmichael's Oscar, "Resistance" never quite caught on in the United States; but it became a major hit in England, where it remains popular to this day.

✧   ✧   ✧

The early 1950s marked the emergence of television as a mass entertainment medium. From its first experimental stages in the late 1920s, it had developed steadily, with the National Broadcasting Company taking an early lead in both technology and programming. By the outbreak of World War II, both NBC and its close rival, the Columbia Broadcasting System, were presenting an increasing variety of programs for the few thousand New York City–area dwellers who owned TV sets.

Though the war, and the needs of defense industries, put a temporary stop to this growth, both TV broadcasting and research started up again in 1946. Dumont Laboratories, which had been experimenting with television technology for years, emerged as a possible third force alongside NBC and CBS; by the late 1940s, all three concerns were linking East Coast regional stations together into networks and presenting regular programming.

Such early scheduling included variety shows, some drama—and, with the 1947 World Series between the New York Yankees and Brooklyn Dodgers, sporting events. By late 1951 the networks had established West Coast links, and the American Broadcasting Corporation (ABC), formed in the 1940s out of NBC radio's old Blue Network, had joined the other television competitors.

Throughout the first half of the 1950s, NBC remained the clear industry leader, boasting the largest audiences. It had Tuesday evening's *Texaco Star Theatre*, with veteran comedian Milton Berle, Wednesday's *Kraft Television Theatre*—and, in the prime 9:00 P.M. Saturday evening slot, *Your Show of Shows*, starring comedians Sid Caesar and Imogene Coca and including such up-and-coming talents as Carl Reiner, Howard Morris, and Mel Brooks.

By autumn of 1952, with *Your Show of Shows* in its third year as the most popular ninety minutes of the TV viewer's week, NBC executives were thinking about a replacement for the following summer. Vacations and travel might deplete summer viewership, but replacement shows still had to be strong enough to hold audiences for thirteen slowed-down weeks.

And who could be more slowed down, some NBC executive appears to have reasoned, than Hoagy Carmichael? Both *Young Man With a Horn* and the Oscar for "In the Cool Cool Cool of the Evening" had kept his popularity high. He'd done capacity business at Boston's Copley Plaza Hotel, the Nicollet in Minneapolis, and other major venues. Soon after Dwight Eisenhower beat out Adlai Stevenson in the 1952 presidential election the word went out that loyal Republican Carmichael would be among the stars performing at the inaugural, alongside Caesar and Coca, Ethel Merman, Edgar Bergen, the Nicholas Brothers, and others.

In building a summer variety show around him, the network revived *Saturday Night Revue*, the original name for the Caesar-Coca show. The format would be simple, not unlike the *Tonight at Hoagy's* radio series of the previous decade: the camera would find Hoagy welcoming visitors to his home in what was clearly meant to be a penthouse apartment. They'd then adjourn to the "Sky Room," portrayed as a nightclub in the same building, where the guests would perform.

"I'm not geared for a show that requires a master of ceremonies to gladhand all the other performers and guests," he told *Los Angeles Times* interviewer Walter Ames. "I've never operated that way, and it's too late in life for me to make the change now . . . I just want people to relax and enjoy themselves for a few minutes out of the week." Big bands, he added, would be a highlight of the series. Among those signed to appear were Les Brown, Buddy Morrow, and trumpeter Ralph Marterie.[22]

"He looks and sounds like he hasn't a care in the world, but don't let that fool you," *Los Angeles Times* TV reviewer Pauline Swanson wrote while he was doing the show. "He's taut as an E-string and a chronic worrier." Randy Carmichael agreed: "Dad worked hard on that show," he said. "Tuesday through Friday were intense rehearsals . . . because this was ninety minutes *live*. No retakes. You had to know your lines."

Saturday Night Revue went on the air that June 6. Surviving video footage shows Carmichael affably hosting a show of uneven quality. Guest artists include comedians Alan King, George Gobel, and Kaye Ballard; but most of the rest are fledgling performers at varying levels of ability, all clearly hoping for a career break on network television. Sketches purporting to show how Hoagy wrote one or another of his hit songs suffer from labored writing and staging. A little boy named Ricky Vera flits in and out of various episodes, clearly hell-bent on squeezing humor out of an exaggerated Mexican accent. Jerry Fielding's studio band gets a brief spot, the leader going through overcooked "conducting" gyrations for the benefit of the camera.

"The pressure of thirteen weeks of a summer replacement just got to him" was Randy's assessment. "Dad said, 'No, it's too much. I'm outta here.'" And that's what happened. *Saturday Night Revue* returned the following summer, but with veteran character actor Eddie Albert as host, and a stronger guest roster. Carmichael's own post-mortem, though understated, was to the point: "I sadly learned it wasn't really my show. It belonged to mysterious people, to directors, cameramen, and stooges."[23]

Hoagy, meanwhile, had plenty to do. *Belles on Their Toes*, Twentieth Century–Fox's attempt at a follow-up to the box-office success of the family comedy *Cheaper by the Dozen*, cast a non-singing Carmichael as a handyman and homespun philosopher. *Gentlemen Prefer Blondes* featured two Carmichael songs, "Ain't There Anyone Here for Love?" and "When Love Goes Wrong (Nothing Goes Right)," both with Harold Adamson lyrics.

Jane Russell sings the former in good-natured exasperation while a men's track relay team, en route to compete in Europe, does calisthenics and swimming practice around her, ignoring her charms until one of them inadvertently knocks her into the swimming pool. As Hawks biographer Todd McCarthy notes, "The gay aspect of this knockout number is so overwhelming that one can't even properly refer to it as a subtext, which may be the reason it is often cut for television airings."[24] McCarthy goes on to suggest that director Howard Hawks deferred in such matters to choreographer Jack Cole, who was gay—and who injected whatever homoerotic content the scene conveys. Cue sheets for *Gentlemen Prefer Blondes* reveal that, presumably at Hawks's behest, Carmichael and Adamson cranked out at least seven additional tunes for the picture.

Hoagy's favorite among them was "Down, Boy," written expressly for Marilyn Monroe. "We had rehearsed the song together and she loved it," he said. "I felt it was her first chance to become a song stylist and soloist like Mary Martin after her singing of *My Heart Belongs to Daddy*." Built on an even more obvious *double-entendre* than the Porter song, "Down, Boy" was dropped from the release (reportedly at Darryl Zanuck's direct order) along with the other Carmichael material. It found a place the following year in *Three for the Show*, sung as a lavish (and no less suggestive) production number by Betty Grable.[25]

Paramount's *Those Redheads From Seattle* offered Guy Mitchell and Teresa Brewer singing "I Guess It Was You All the Time," salvaged from *The Keystone Girl*. "He's Dead, but He Won't Lie Down," another product of the ill-fated Normand-Sennett film, turned up in *Timber Jack*, made in late 1954, which cast Hoagy as a saloon pianist called "Jingles."

Czech-born ice-skating star Vera Hruba Ralston, wife of Republic Pictures CEO Herbert Yates, plays the female lead. "Vera was a very nice person," Hoagy writes, "and I am pretty sure she knew that the necessary talent was not quite there. But she tried hard." A *Variety* reviewer, identifying *Timber Jack* as "a lusty actioner," remarked that "use of Miss Ralston as a cabaret owner-singer is a convenient means of bringing in Hoagy Carmichael as her pianist-accompanist, along with several songs staged as production numbers."[26]

Carmichael can't have realized it at the time, but his career had just crossed its watershed. There would be no hit songs after "In the Cool Cool Cool of the Evening," no film roles after *Timber Jack*. By the mid-1950s, a major earthquake had struck the popular music world. At first the tremors seemed minor, scattered: Bill Haley bawling the rackety rhythm-and-blues number "Rock Around the Clock" under the credits of *The Blackboard Jungle*, a 1954 movie about urban juvenile delinquency; handsome young James Dean preening and sulking his way through *Rebel Without a Cause* the following year; finally, emphatically, the explosion of Mississippi-born Elvis Presley on the national scene.

Just as Hoagy Carmichael's own post–World War I generation had embraced hot jazz as a banner of independence, in clamorous defiance of their parents' authority and conservatism, so did 1950s youth make rhythm-and-blues, now redubbed "rock-and-roll," the soundtrack for their own rebelliousness. The louder it was, the more infuriating to parents, teachers, clergymen, and other elders, the better.

A combination of forces, some of the music's own making, had driven instrumental jazz from the center of popular culture by the end of World War II. Singers were the focus now. Early 1950s pop music was full of capable vocalists, many of them big band graduates, saddled too often with material ranging from the simply trite to the outright infantile. Still, the early '50s were far from a popular music wasteland. Frank Sinatra enjoyed a major career revitalization with albums recorded for Capitol. Louis Armstrong, Ella Fitzgerald, Bing Crosby, and others continued to record quality performances of good material. Excellent by any measure were "Tenderly," a 1952 hit record for Rosemary Clooney, "You Belong to Me," sung by the prodigiously gifted Jo Stafford, "Teach Me Tonight," as sung by Sarah Vaughan, Les Paul and Mary Ford's jazzy duo treatment of "How High the Moon," and Peggy Lee's deliciously erotic reading of Rodgers and Hart's "Lover."

But in the marketing divisions of the recording and publishing concerns, one overriding realization was being gradually, if at times only reluctantly, acknowledged: the new, postwar American prosperity had created a brand-new, impressionable, economically viable adolescent market. Teenagers—mostly white, middle-class and suburban—were now a separate audience, bent on dissociating themselves from their parents' generation. Armed with enough money of their own to buy "product" expressly tailored to their tastes, and reinforced by a relentless capacity for solipsistic self-indulgence, they were ready for something that would mirror their sense of themselves. Above all, something their parents would loathe.

An intergenerational fault line had opened, with standard songs, and those who sang and played them, on one side of the chasm, youth and its preoccupations on the other. From the late 1950s on, traditional pop performers, songwriters, and lyricists would find it increasingly difficult to reach any but a dwindling, and generationally discrete, target audience. Publishers, filmmakers, and record companies began their shift youthwards.

Hoagy Carmichael felt the ground move. Among his personal papers are songs written between the mid-1950s and early 1970s, some in collaboration with such old associates as Mercer and Webster, attempting to capitalize on emergent trends. A good many are little short of embarrassing.

Amidst all this, the Carmichael marriage finally unraveled. Beyond all else, beyond even the dalliances with Jean Simmons and a mostly still unspecified few others, a host of internal stresses had been growing apace. With both Hoagy Bix and Randy away at boarding school, the only first-hand witnesses to the increasing disharmony between Hoagy and Ruth were the hired help; and, like Eva Chatman, they seemed disinclined to speak of what they heard.

An article in *Screen Stars* magazine, appearing just before Carmichael's fateful second visit to London, had applauded "a wacky and wonderful fifteen years of marriage ... years of laughter, ups and downs, excitement, and never a dull moment." But it wasn't long before a Hollywood gossip columnist sniffed out trouble in Holmby Hills. "Who brushed the *Stardust* off Hoagy Carmichael?" Mitch Anstruthers asked in *Uncensored* magazine. "No one knows the answer, but his best friends wouldn't be surprised if the title of his next tune is something like 'Wild Oats.' Hoagy's 55 but has been sowing them like a colt in his teens for the past year—from the elegant gin mills of Manhattan's East Side to the loud and brassy nighteries along movieland's famed Sunset Strip. And what Hoagland used to get out of a piano, he's been getting from time to time out of a bourbon bottle."

Citing no specific sources, the writer reported that Hoagy's "carrying-on has been enough to make his wife of 18 years a mighty miffed mama. Back in November, 1954, she packed up, leaving the movie colony aghast over what appeared to be the imminent breakup of what had been considered one of its rock-solid marriages." The article went on to describe Carmichael's appearance at a fashionable Manhattan restaurant in company with two glamorous women, neither of them his wife. The evening degenerated into a melee, glassware and epithets flying freely and the police arriving to break up what had become a small-scale brawl.[27]

Ruth filed for divorce in September of 1955, charging mental cruelty. Her husband had been "cold and indifferent and continually complained about family expenses," and was absent for protracted periods without explanation. "It was more or less a culmination of many things," she told California Superior Court judge Edward R. Brand, "and I would give my life if I didn't have to state them specifically."[28]

Odessa Halstead, identified as a nurse at the Carmichael home, was more forthcoming. "They had no family life and no real marriage," she said in a deposition. The composer, she added, had threatened to "knock his wife cold" and to fire the doctors and nurses attending her.

Closer inspection reveals that this situation, in common with most other marriage breakups, was far from simple or one-sided. "My mother had chronic insomnia," said Randy Carmichael. "She'd sometimes go a week, even ten days, without sleeping."

But insomnia, as Hoagy Bix observed, is a symptom, not a cause.

At one point shortly after the Jean Simmons episode, he said, Ruth went to visit her friend Ann Embricos in Barbados. "Annie gave her some sleeping pills, something to calm her down: that was the beginning."

Randy: "Remember, my father was not exactly an openly loving person. It's not that he was openly playing around—but by the time I went off to

Chadwick [boarding school], maybe as early as 1948, I had some sense that this woman was in trouble."

Hoagy Bix: "Sure, Dad philandered, as a man will when nothing is going on at home. In the end they didn't have any life at all together."

Helen Meinardi Stearns: "Things got pretty bad [between them] for a while there . . . he parted with money pretty hard for anyone but himself, so if Ruthie wanted to go to lunch, she had to ask him for it . . . I said, 'You're going to lose Ruthie if you don't do something because you're a pain in the neck about money.' "

Hoagy Bix: "Dad had learned the hard way that money was hard to get ahold of. You used your talent or your hands . . . He could be difficult about that, about money. You'd go to dinner with him, and he'd order small portions for everyone, and half-desserts for people, without consulting them. He imposed his will."

Randy: "My mother was not what you'd call an artistic woman, at least in the sense of music or art. Socializing was her gift. Giving parties. Even shopping—she loved to shop."

Helen Meinardi Stearns: "She knew if she wanted to hurt him, the best thing to do was to go to I. Magnin's [department store] and charge three or four thousand dollars . . . She used it as a weapon and to him it was all-important."

Randy: "Eva got married around that time. She'd come over on day trips, but by that time we had a woman named Ada Dockery. Tall, thin gal who wore her hair in a bun. Little rimless glasses. All very prim and proper. My mother would be up for days . . . [and] Ada would lock her in her suite in the house, where she could bounce around and break everything, instead of in the rest of the house."

Hoagy Bix: "She was great. But Mom fired her. The first eleven or twelve years of their marriage had been great. Everything was fine. Then the balloon, this little fantasy of hers, burst, and she was simply unable to cope with that."

Randy: "There was a doctor in Los Angeles who became our physician for our family. His name was Vern Mason, and he'd been Howard Hughes's doctor."

Hoagy Bix: "He'd been in charge of the Army Medical Corps during the war."

Randy: "All the stars had him. The story was that he was treating Mother for her 'insomnia.' But whether the pills, as my Aunt Helen called them, were all that was available, I don't know. Was it dope? I don't know that either. For all I know they could have been just placebos. I wasn't told."

Hoagy Bix: "She found pretty quickly that she could stay in this little drug-laden cocoon and keep the real world at bay, and that's what she did. There were weekends, lots of them, when she was supposed to come up to Chadwick to see Randy and me, and didn't show, and we only learned later that she'd been in the hospital. Looking back, I just think her sister was right in suggesting she was ill-suited to taking the bumps on the road of life. When things were good she'd ridden the waves, but when the going got heavier—well, she just didn't know how to sort through it."

Randy: "Later on, after the divorce, she married Vern Mason. That's a movie all of its own: young model, beautiful, meets songwriter, hobnobs with Gershwin, becomes social hostess in Hollywood. But she has this thing, this insomnia or whatever it was, and it ruins her social career. Divorces her first husband, meets this doctor, twenty years or so older than she is. He gives her an entire new life, which she hadn't had for God knows how many years."

Hoagy Bix: "She married him, and he made sure she got the pills she wanted. But then he died, leaving her in awful shape. Worse than before. Wandering around the house at night, spending most of her days in bed, avoiding personal contact. At one point she took a freighter to Italy: in those days you could book passage on a freighter. But they had to make a side trip and disembark her in England, I think, because she was so sick. She flew back. It was pathetic."[29]

❖   ❖   ❖

The terms of the divorce awarded Ruth 30 percent of Hoagy's overall income, with a mimimum of $1,250 (about $7,500 in today's money) a month. They maintained joint custody of their sons, both of whom were at Chadwick, best known through Christina Crawford's 1978 best-seller *Mommie Dearest.*

Hoagy moved out of the Holmby Hills house and into a two-bedroom luxury apartment at 9126 Sunset Boulevard, near Doheny. The office of media mogul David Geffen later occupied the space.

Conductor Lyle "Skitch" Henderson, a frequent guest at Carmichael parties during the good years, remembered "Cream" as "the genteel side of Hoagy, always the fixer, a warm, gentle woman. She smoothed all the edges for him, made everything easy and wonderful. Charming woman."[30]

Hoagy Bix concurred. "She really helped Dad immeasurably in his career. She got the very highest marks for social skills—in fact, I don't know what he would have done without her. When things were going well for them, she was fine. But if you placed her on a balance scale and put all life's problems on the other side, it wouldn't have taken more than a feather's worth of weight to throw her off balance."

"In the end that's what went. The balance. After that—well, it was up and down, mostly down. Just sad. What a waste."

✳ *XVII* ✳

Period of Adjustment

The Past is gone, together with its formal arts, its rhetoric, and its institutions,
and in its place there has risen something rootless, abstract, and alien,
I think, to human experience.
—HENRY BESTON, *Northern Farm,* 1948

For a while, at least, Hoagy's life went on more or less as before. He appeared on several dramatic television shows, among them a reprise of *Casablanca* on the *Lux Video Theatre,* with himself in the Dooley Wilson role. He'd filmed "Death in the Snow," a half-hour episode in NBC's *Joseph Cotten Show: On Trial,* and figured in a production on the same network's short-lived *Gulf Playhouse,* an innovative series that cast the camera as a first-person narrative voice. On ABC's *Telephone Time* series he'd played himself in a fictionalized account of the composition of "I Get Along Without You Very Well," with Walter Winchell re-creating his role in the search for "J.B." Asked at show's end how it felt to portray himself, he replied, " 'Hoagy Carmichael' is a character I've specialized in for many years."

With Ruth staying on at Holmby Hills, Hoagy began exploring residential possibilities in Palm Springs, some 140 miles southeast of Los Angeles. A luxury playground for Hollywood people since silent-movie days, it was now a popular, rapidly growing area. Hoagy had spent the 1937 Christmas holidays there and taken to it, even inquiring about buying a house. But Ruth, convinced they should be closer to Hollywood social life, had balked.

In those days, he told a 1965 interviewer, land in the desert outside town was readily and cheaply available. But no one then could have fully imagined the development that would soon transform Palm Springs and its environs into an affluent residential community.

> Riding across the dunes, he'd look out over the sand and mesquite and exclaim, "What a useless waste!" . . . and he'd be looking at land that he could have bought for $10 an acre . . . He did buy it later for $500 an acre and it's worth four times that now. When Tony Burke showed him plans for a golf course where the Thunderbird Dude Ranch stood, he didn't go in as a charter member."[1]

By the mid-1950s "the Springs" was enjoying a full-blown bonanza, with the Thunderbird Country Club established at its heart. By mid-decade Carmichael had bought two homes, one on the eighth fairway, the other not far from the third hole, and by mid-1965 he owned 152 priceless Palm Springs acres and was a golf-addicted Thunderbird regular.

Very often, said Bill Wellman, son of pioneering film director William Wellman, Hoagy would put up in one of his houses, installing his sons at the other. "They were close . . . you could walk across a couple of fairways to them . . . Not like next door or anything, but you know, a hundred yards apart approximately."

Wellman and Hoagy Bix met in the mid-1950s, when they played on opposing prep school baseball teams. "We became lifelong friends, and of course I spent a lot of time with—I called him 'Mr. C.'—a lot of time on the golf course but also at his place in Los Angeles. Many nights I sat there and listened to him playing the piano, tunes that he was still writing," even after any chance of getting them published had passed.[2]

But just as sure as Hoagy's personal life was changing in ways he could never have anticipated, so was his life in music. Toward the end of 1956, his Decca recording contract, in force since 1938, finally expired. A full listing of Decca titles between August 19, 1946, and his final session, October 2, 1956, shows consistent attempts to follow up the success of "Huggin' and Chalkin'." Most of the records are overproduced, with backing bands led by Billy May, Lou Bring, Sonny Burke, and others, often gift-wrapping his vocals within chirping vocal groups.

Still, recording made a steady and reliable outlet. Some Carmichael songs—among them "Hong Kong Blues," "Two Sleepy People," "Doctor, Lawyer, Indian Chief," and "Ole Buttermilk Sky"—had made it to the Hit Parade. Such old-fashioned, non-Carmichael material as "Huggin' and

Chalkin'," "The Coney Island Washboard," "The Old Piano Roll Blues," and "Aba Daba Honeymoon" also scored well with record buyers. To some extent, Decca had also given him latitude to promote his lesser-known catalogue items, including the lightweight but fetching "Casanova Cricket," "The Sad Cowboy," and a surprisingly tender "Rogue River Valley," one of three other *Canyon Passage* numbers lost in the buzz surrounding "Ole Buttermilk Sky" and its Oscar nomination.

Just as often, Carmichael turned his stylized, "flatsy through the nose" delivery to such vehicles as "Ten to One It's Tennessee," by "Huggin' " composer Clancy Hayes; the Harold Arlen–Leo Robin "For Every Man There's a Woman"; and Frank Loesser's lovely but seldom heard "A Tune for Humming," which also gave him ample opportunity to demonstrate his whistling skills.

He'd enjoyed even greater artistic freedom in the mid-1940s with the short-lived, Hollywood-based ARA (for "American Recording Artists") Company and in making wartime "V" Discs, produced expressly for U.S. servicemen at home and abroad. Among Carmichael songs recorded during this period were "A World of No Goodbyes," "Somewhere on the Via Roma" (used in the Italian film *Io T'ho Incontrata a Napoli*—"I Met You in Napoli"), "Ginger and Spice," "Walk It Off," "Yum Yum," and "Billy-a-Dick," which remained unpublished until after the composer's death.

After "In the Cool Cool Cool of the Evening" won its Oscar he recorded a pair of titles with Jane Wyman, attempted to capitalize on the honky-tonk piano craze with the "Crazy Otto Rag," and reprised "Hong Kong Blues" backed by Les Brown's "Band of Renown," all to no special effect. One of his final dates, in autumn 1956, included a "cover" version of a current country hit, Johnny Cash's "I Walk the Line." Another, produced by old Indiana friend—and Decca executive—Bud Dant, revisited 1930's "Barnacle Bill, the Sailor."[3]

However inauspicious a way it might have been to end so long and fruitful an association, it also formed a prelude to one of Hoagy Carmichael's finest moments on record. Richard Bock, owner of World Pacific Records, had been a fan for years; now, with Hoagy free of record-company commitment, nothing prevented him from recording the songwriter in a new and challenging setting.

New Yorker Johnny Mandel had done his band business apprenticeship playing trombone with, and arranging for, Jimmy Dorsey, Boyd Raeburn, Buddy Rich, Woody Herman, Artie Shaw's short-lived 1949 bebop band,

and—perhaps most telling of all—Count Basie. He'd worked as a radio staff arranger in New York, studied at Manhattan School of Music and Juilliard, contributed scores to NBC television's *Your Show of Shows*, arranged an album for singer Dick Haymes.

Bock's idea was simple: feature Carmichael singing his own songs, backed not by slick studio bands, tack-in-hammer pianos, or warbling vocal trios, but by a tightly knit group of ranking modern jazzmen, playing carefully textured and swinging arrangements.

"We went out to visit him," said Mandel. "Forget now whether it was in Hollywood or Palm Springs. Found him there behind the bar, mixing drinks; really hospitable and gracious. We just got right to talking. He had pretty clear ideas of what he wanted to do, and what he *didn't* want to do. He realized he wasn't a straight ballad singer, didn't want to do things like 'One Morning in May,' that had all sorts of sustained notes and big intervals. He didn't try to sing 'I Get Along Without You Very Well,' for instance. But he could always do the character-type ballads, like 'Baltimore Oriole,' 'Georgia,' and the rest."[4]

Mandel, in the process of winning respect as a master songwriter in his own right, chuckled at the memory of those first "brainstorming" sessions. "Hoagy hated bebop . . . I remember he came to hear Woody's band when it was really hot, and said something like, 'Aw, give me an old bass horn any time.' He meant it, too.

"When I was with Basie, around 1953 or so, we came to town and Hoagy was there—he was doing this TV show, *Saturday Night Revue*. He just kinda walked around thinking, with his tongue in his cheek, looking kinda glum, and I took him for just a kind of moody guy. Also, some of the guys on the band had told me he was a real far-right Hoosier-type Republican, kind of an Indiana cracker. Johnny [Mercer] was a bit like that too, I guess—though I never saw it in either of them."

Hoagy Sings Carmichael was recorded at three sessions, September 10, 11, and 13, 1956—with a band full of outstanding jazzmen: trumpeter Don Fagerquist had been in Les Brown's brass section for the 1955 "Hong Kong Blues" date; Harry "Sweets" Edison was an honored Basie veteran, then enjoying a career renaissance through his muted obbligato work on the arrangements Nelson Riddle was using to showcase Frank Sinatra; Jimmy Zito, another Brown alumnus, had ghosted the "Art Hazard" solos for *Young Man With a Horn*.

Alto saxophonist Art Pepper was new to Hoagy, as were pianist Jimmy

Rowles and drummer Irv Cottler. An old Carmichael friend, Nick Fatool, replaced Cottler on drums for the third session. Said Mandel: "I spotted his vocals wherever I thought they'd be most effective, stuck 'em in the middles, usually. Remember, I didn't have a big band there—rather, a small band trying to sound big. So voicings were important.

"As a singer? He was a natural. Knew what to keep and what to throw away. Didn't try to be a capital-S singer: more often he approached the songs conversationally, like an actor, like Walter Huston doing 'September Song.' And you know, those are really the most effective readings for those sorts of things, rather than somebody doing something with a straight baritone. You never knew beforehand how he was gonna sing something: when he was going to talk it, where he was gonna leave spaces."

He not only leaves spaces, but on several songs confines his vocals to a decidedly secondary role, giving the major melody expositions to the band. Again and again, his vocals strike the ear as measured, thoughtful, Carmichael taking his time, never pushing his vocal resources beyond their limits. He opens "Two Sleepy People" with only Al Hendrickson's unamplified guitar; carries "Rockin' Chair" away from its familiar role as a piece of quasi-vaudeville material and returns it to its origins as an end-of-life valedictory, with Rowles, on celeste, underscoring its reflective, pastoral quality.

Art Pepper gets most of the solo space and is particularly distinctive on "Ballad in Blue"—incredibly, the song's first vocal treatment on record since its publication twenty-two years before. "Two Sleepy People" teams him with a cup-muted Fagerquist for a closely intertwined duet, distantly echoing the long-ago "chase" choruses of Bix and Frank Trumbauer.

But the saxophonist's—and perhaps the album's—most stirring moment belongs to "Winter Moon," newly published at the time, with one of Harold Adamson's most affecting lyrics. Pepper establishes the melody, a heartfelt cry in icy emptiness:

> Where is love's magic?
> Where did it go?
> Is it gone like the summertime
> That we used to know?

(The song remained in his mind. Twenty-two years later, his life shattered by heroin addiction and a decade in prison, Pepper recorded it again.

293

Though cushioned by strings and rhythm, it is a performance of almost unbearable intensity, glowing in a clear, glacial light, hypnotic, agonized.)

The line of descent from "Ballad in Blue" to "Winter Moon" is clear. The desolation of love lost shadows both lyrics, casting both melodies in minor-mode darkness. But unlike its predecessor, "Winter Moon" allows no ray of light to penetrate its interior. Melodically and harmonically sophisticated, emotionally complex, it is a work of its composer's maturity, a regretful backward look at a brighter past, "a kind of art song," in singer Barbara Lea's words. "Not at all what you'd think of as 'typical' Hoagy Carmichael except in its air of longing, something once had and now lost."[5]

Mandel concluded *Hoagy Sings Carmichael* with a swinger, a Basie-inflected recasting of "Lazy River" with a sassy, strutting trumpet solo by Sweets Edison. Again, Hoagy rises to the task. "You could tell from that, especially, that he would have been a great jazz musician," the arranger said. "In singing 'Lazy River,' he . . . didn't try to sing the line exactly, [because] he realized what would fit his range and vocal quality, especially at that tempo. He was very smart about that, [and] his approach was very jazzy."

George Frazier's sleeve essay spoke for all concerned in declaring that

> it strikes me as enormously reassuring that an individual who in bygone years made music with men of approximately his own age, background and attitude should be sufficiently uninstitutional to record with a group of musicians (with one exception) so lately undiapered that some of them had not yet been born when *Star Dust* was becoming the theme song of a whole era. To me, the results of this collaboration sound absolutely marvelous.[6]

Hoagy's visits to Indiana became more frequent, as his home state took on a talismanic quality in his imagination; whatever might change in the present, Indiana—his Indiana—would remain inviolate, uncorrupted by time and mortality. Gradually, the harsher aspects of his early Bloomington years had faded from reminiscence, eclipsed by images of the Book Nook, Monk, and—perhaps most of all—the golden yesterdays with Bix. Labor Day weekend 1957, for example, found him in the resort town of French Lick, for a "real old-fashioned Hoosier Hoedown"—built around a tribute to his songs, opening event in the first annual French Lick Music Festival. Bill Wellman found it fascinating that "he continued to write songs [though] he was not happy with the music industry . . . he would write these songs and never try to get them published. You could hear them, he would play them for you. They were wonderful. I always thought that was kind of sad but he never seemed to be [made] sad by it. He always was an optimist."[7]

Surely that optimism prompted his return to a project begun in the mid-1940s. Among twenty-five numbers he'd recorded between 1944 and 1946 for the ARA label was "The Whale," a children's song in 6/8 time with a text by the poet Geoffrey Dearmer. It had proved unexpectedly popular, selling well and reaching a wide radio audience thanks to disc jockeys and to Hoagy's own programs.

By 1946 he'd written melodies for verses by such prominent children's authors as Marchette Chute, Fredrika Shumway Smith, Nancy Byrd Turner, Julia Bingham, and May Morgan. From Isaac T. Headland, best known for juvenile books on China, came the charming "Little Mousey Brown." But once he'd assembled, and copyrighted, this small collection, Hoagy appears to have done little with it until the mid-1950s, when he added melodies to poems by literary figures A. A. Milne ("In the Fashion," from *When We Were Very Young*) and Christina Rossetti and such children's authors as Inez Hogan, Patience Strong, and Agnes Louise Dean.

He wrote words and music to several more, and in 1957 the Golden Press published twenty-three such items as *Hoagy Carmichael's Songs for Children*. With two songs added, and artwork by a different illustrator, the same collection appeared a year later as *Sing and Play With Hoagy Carmichael*, published by the Silver Burdett Company.

Though his collaborators in this venture include some of the most celebrated children's authors of their time, it seems not to have occurred to his publishers to use the names in marketing the collection. An introductory note to *Sing and Play* makes no mention of the texts, telling readers only that the melodies reveal "another facet" of Carmichael's creative talents.

The tunes are fetching and have lost none of their appeal. Surely it would have enhanced sales to announce that the composer of "Star Dust" had written music to poems by so many celebrated young people's authors. With the disappearance of the Golden Press and the 1962 absorption of Silver Burdett by the giant Time-Life Corporation, lines of inquiry have been lost.

"Although he has not had a hit in some time," Richard Lamparski wrote in the third of his five *Whatever Became of . . . ?* books, the tunesmith continues to work at his craft. While his sound is still appreciated by many, Carmichael's songs no longer attract young people ... However, his is still very much in evidence among the big names in the music world on the West Coast even if they don't sing his new songs.[8]

If any one song reveals Hoagy's frame of mind in those days of uncertainty and dwindling expectation, it's the gently nostalgic "Serenade to Gabriel," registered for copyright on New Year's Day 1957. The lyric is credited jointly to Hoagy and Vick Knight, a California advertising agency executive, pop songwriter, and much-decorated World War II veteran who had first attracted entertainment industry attention writing scripts for the War Department's *Command Performance* series. Knight rose fast in postwar radio, scripting such shows as the CBS *Columbia Workship* dramatic series and NBC's *Halls of Ivy*, as well as producing and directing for comedians Eddie Cantor, Fred Allen, and Jack Carson. He apparently entered Hoagy's life through Bud Dant, a frequent radio collaborator.

"Serenade to Gabriel" is a charmer: tender, evocative—and above all melodically typical of Carmichael's best work. Bars 6 and 7, for example, could have been extracted from an instrumental jazz solo.

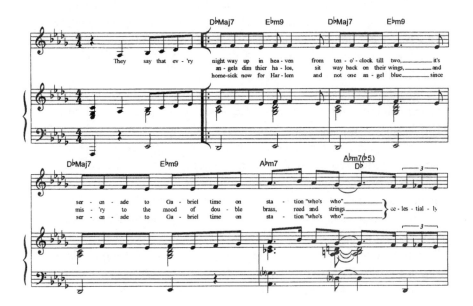

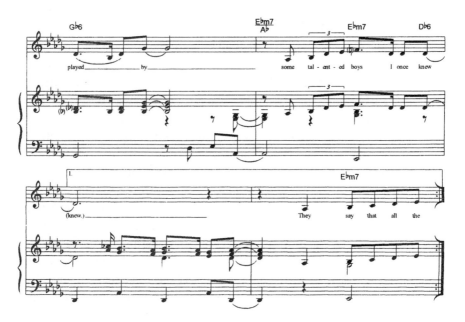

"Serenade to Gabriel" (bars 1–8), 1957

Heard now, the song seems not only an homage to such departed jazz-men as Bix, Bunny Berigan, Eddie Lang, and Fats Waller, but Hoagy's lament for the clarity and simplicity of his own young days. The narrator looks forward to being reunited with his old jazz pals someday soon in heaven.

But not quite yet. On November 10, 1958, he guested on an NBC *Timex Jazz Spectacular*, sharing star billing with old friends Louis Armstrong, Gene Krupa, Lionel Hampton, Woody Herman fronting Les Brown's band, Chico Hamilton's quintet, singers Anita O'Day and Jane Morgan, and—perhaps most welcome of all—an all-star reunion of Bob Crosby's "Bobcats," including Yank Lawson on trumpet, Bud Freeman on tenor sax, and trombonists Lou McGarity and "Cutty" Cutshall.

One sequence finds Hoagy at the piano, jauntily rendering "New Orleans" before exhorting Crosby to "Take it away, Bob" for a rousing "Royal Garden Blues." Watching him, it's impossible to miss his joy in just being with these seasoned and dedicated jazzmen. "Dad had jazz licks in his hands, in his head, that he never, never would have been able to divorce himself from," said Hoagy Bix. "Was he a jazz writer in the forties and fifties? Well, no. Decidedly not. Did he divorce himself from it, throw jazz out with the bathwater? No, not at all: I don't think he could have."[9]

On the strength of *Hoagy Sings Carmichael*, Richard Bock brought him in on an ambitious World Pacific Records project, a jazz-and-poetry LP with a selection of top California-based modern jazzmen providing musical backgrounds for readings of poems by beat-generation poets Lawrence Lipton, Philip Whalen, and Lawrence Ferlinghetti, as well as Walt Whitman, Langston Hughes, and Dylan Thomas. In preparation, Carmichael attended one or two of the jazz-and-poetry sessions run by Lipton at the Ash Grove, a small folk club at the less fashionable end of Melrose Avenue.

Among Grove regulars was a young pianist-singer-songwriter named Bob Dorough: born in Arkansas and raised in Texas, he'd admired Hoagy since boyhood, confessing to amazement at seeing the composer of "Star Dust" and "Georgia on My Mind" at the Grove. "It was such a wild thing for Hoagy to be doing, coming in from left field like that," he said. "I'd always thought of him just as—well, the guy who sat at the piano and wrote songs, you know. This was really something new."[10]

With a quintet led by bassist Ralph Pena (and including Dorough, saxophonist Bob Hardaway, and drummer Larry Bunker) playing original music behind him, Carmichael recorded William Carlos Williams's 1917 *Tract* and the great doctor-poet's brief *Young Sycamore*, written in 1927, the latter in duet with Hardaway's a capella tenor saxophone.

"The beat generation are no strangers to me," Hoagy wrote in *Sometimes I Wonder*. "I was part of a Beat Generation in the twenties that rebelled against being forced to study the classics in ivy-walled colleges, take jobs in old firms, or live in a square world"—which is of course just what he'd wound up doing before committing himself entirely to music.[11]

The jazz-and-poetry session appeared on *Jazz Canto Volume One*, a World Pacific LP also featuring saxophonists Gerry Mulligan and Jack Montrose and the Chico Hamilton Quintet. It is difficult not to be struck by the power in Carmichael's reading, especially of *Tract*; a steeliness in the voice, a deliberateness of pacing, finding reserves of bitterness in Williams's richly ironic verse.

> I will teach you my townspeople
> how to perform a funeral
> for you have it over a troop
> of artists—

unless one should scour the world—
you have the ground sense necessary.[12]

Carmichael's interest in the Hamilton quintet provides a clue to his state of mind at the time. Los Angeles born, the percussionist had attracted critical and audience interest with an instrumentation built around Buddy Collette's woodwind-doubling skills and New Yorker Fred Katz, hitherto known mostly as a pianist and arranger, on cello. Guitarist Jim Hall and bassist Carson Smith rounded out what historian Ted Gioia calls "one of the most stylized groups to emerge on the West Coast scene."

Hamilton and Katz employed their instrumentation in intricate compositions and arrangements full of colorful effects, unusual time signatures and forms. The leader conceived of his drums as "very soft, graceful in motion as well as sound: a sensuous feminine instrument." Katz, who had studied cello with Pablo Casals, contributed originals, the first of which was a brooding, Zen-like specialty he called simply "The Sage."[13]

"That was one of my favorite Hamilton numbers," said Hoagy Bix, who heard the group often at club appearances, bought their records—and had hoped to interest his father in them. When "I played it for Dad," the elder Carmichael indeed seemed more than a little interested.

Answering his phone one day not long afterwards, Fred Katz was astonished to find himself speaking to a caller with an unmistakably familiar voice. "It was Hoagy, calling me—well, out of the blue," he said. "He wanted to meet at his apartment in Hollywood—on Sunset, I think. It was only about a forty-five-minute drive from the Valley, where I lived, so I said okay."

After appropriately deferential small talk, Carmichael got to the point: he'd written a lyric to "The Sage." Even before he heard it, that struck Katz as an odd thing to do. By this time rock-and-roll had narrowed and—to use the phrase of a time yet to come—dumbed down the songwriting field. No one was tackling material as recondite as "The Sage."

"He played and sang it for me," said Katz, "and you know, it was good. I loved it—all while realizing that this was the wrong time to be doing this. And I'm still sorry that I turned out to be right: not even Hoagy Carmichael could get it performed."

His only complaint was with some alterations Carmichael had made in the ending. "I remember telling him I thought it should be this or that, you know, and he seemed—well, let's say a little chagrined. But nothing serious. After about half an hour of talking about the song and various other things we parted company. I never saw him again."

Comparison between the Hamilton Quartet's recording and Carmichael's lead sheet shows that he altered a lot more than just the ending: he seems to have restructured the piece entirely, omitting and reordering melodic elements to fit a more conventional song form. Even at that, his rendering of "The Sage" contains enough irregular phrases and large interval jumps to make it forbidding to the casual singer. Above all, however richly atmospheric of melody and lyric, "The Sage" had no target audience in the popular music world of the late 1950s. It sat undiscovered, unpublished, and unperformed, for decades.[14]

✻   ✻   ✻

In early 1959, clearly shaken by his diminished ability to place his songs, Hoagy engaged an agent. Nacio Herb Brown Jr., himself the son of a celebrated Hollywood songwriter, seemed to be on a first-name basis with everyone of any significance in the music publishing and recording business; Harry Warren, Al Dubin, Harry Ruby, and Sammy Fain were among his clients. Each time he traveled to New York it was with a tape recorder in his briefcase; he'd then make the rounds of record companies, bandleaders, and radio program directors, playing demos of songs he was trying to place.

Two newer Carmichael efforts, "Music, Always Music" and "Mediterranean Love," are in the repertoire for Hoagy's last full LP, issued as *Ole Buttermilk Sky* on the Kapp label. Newly launched by Dave Kapp, brother of Decca pioneer Jack, Kapp Records numbered pianist Roger Williams and society *chanteuse* Jane Morgan among its contract artists. A return to the studio orchestra and vocal-group backings of his Decca years, the album finds Hoagy singing strongly and confidently through a dozen of his own songs, including the seldom-recorded "Rogue River Valley," "When Love Goes Wrong," and "The Monkey Song" and such older favorites as "Moon Country" and "Baltimore Oriole."

"When I'm pinned down to what recording really has the best quality, I am not ashamed of my singing in the Kapp album called *Ole Buttermilk Sky*," he wrote, adding that he thought it "the best vocalizing of my life." On the strength especially of this "Oriole" and a particularly surefooted "My Resistance Is Low," he would seem to have a case. Regrettably, the

Kapp LP achieved relatively limited circulation and has never been reissued. It remains something of a Carmichael rarity.[15]

✲   ✲   ✲

Things began to look up in spring of 1959, with an offer to join the cast of a brand-new television series being launched by NBC. "Big" cowboy dramas seemed a coming TV trend: *Rawhide,* with young Clint Eastwood, had made its debut that January 9, in response to ABC's phenomenally popular *Wagon Train.* Such series as *Gunsmoke, Maverick, The Life and Legend of Wyatt Earp, The Rifleman,* and *Have Gun, Will Travel* had cleared the way, demonstrating that slickly produced westerns, full of vivid characters and sometimes complex human-interest situations, could draw prime-time viewers.

The new NBC series was to be called *Laramie* and set on a Wyoming ranch in post–Civil War days. The projection included a role for a general cook and handyman, apt to wax philosophical and even deliver a song now and then. Hoagy got the nod. His songs might not be selling, but his on-screen presence remained a strong one.

Even here, at so bright a moment, came dark reminders of time and change. Lida Carmichael had been increasingly unwell and showed no sign of getting any better; she'd come west in the mid-1950s, living first near daughters Martha and Georgia outside San Francisco. By mid-1956 all three were in Los Angeles, living in a house Hoagy had bought for them on Doheny Drive, on the perimeter of Beverly Hills within walking distance of his own Sunset Boulevard apartment.

But it was becoming obvious Lida wasn't going to last long. As she began to fail, "she called us to her bedside," her son wrote in *Sometimes I Wonder.* "Although [she was physically] weak, her faculties were crisp and clear." It was time, she seemed to be saying, to be "getting out of our way." On March 17, 1959, the very day Hoagy signed his *Laramie* contract, Lida Carmichael died. "At five came a frantic call and at five-fifteen I was holding Mother in my arms," he wrote. "In two minutes she was gone." She was prepared, he said, and was at peace with the idea: "I know that when I'm put beside Dad, he'll just reach over and put his arm around me," she said shortly before the end.

Ever-faithful Eva came and tied a ribbon under her chin. Randy played *The Lord's Prayer* on the piano, and Hoagy followed with "One Morning in May," his mother's favorite among all his songs. Dressed in a red robe given her by her son, Hoagy Carmichael's beloved "Mommy Doll" was laid to rest at Bloomington's Rose Hill cemetery on Friday, March 20, 1959. Her no-nonsense attitude toward even death, "the will to die, the beauty of it, and the easy manner of its accomplishment was all too much for me," her son added. "I can only say it was another example of ruggedness I may never attain."[16]

Laramie, meanwhile, faced stiff competition when it went on the air for NBC September 15: *Bonanza*, making its debut the same week, was similar in its emphasis on one ranch and a troupe of closely knit characters, in the latter case a family, to carry the action forward. Given the speed with which *Bonanza* established such principals as Lorne Greene and Michael Landon as stars, it's hardly beyond imagining that John Smith and Robert Fuller, *Laramie*'s two young leading men, saw their show as a potential ticket to TV stardom.

Carmichael played Jonesy, ranch hand for the Sherman family, who had helped raise the boys, Slim (Smith) and Andy (Bobby Crawford), after their father's death. Smith, who had begun his career as a messenger boy at MGM, came to the show after a role in 1955's *The High and the Mighty*. Fuller, born in 1933, had begun as a dancer, played a bit part in *Gentlemen Prefer Blondes*, and studied acting with, among others, Richard Boone, who created the role of Paladin in *Have Gun, Will Travel.*

From their perspective, and even from that of young Crawford (whose brother had made a name for himself on *The Rifleman*), having Hoagy in the cast must have been at best a mixed blessing. He was a star, an established show business figure, his presence sure to draw attention and good reviews to the show—and, potentially, away from the young, as-yet unknown lead actors. From the start, too, Carmichael fell into the patterns he'd displayed while filming *To Have and Have Not*, lobbying incessantly for more to do in each episode—more room to introduce and perform his songs, more time on camera. "He was always noodging," said Fuller, "trying to say, 'Well, here's a spot. Why can't we do a song here? Why can't I play here? Why don't you write it in that I do a song?' "[17]

A *Variety* review began by calling *Laramie* "one western that has virtually nothing to recommend it" and, after a few grudgingly complimentary words for Fuller and guest-star badman Dan Duryea, complained that "Carmichael doesn't have much to do and never gets a crack at that relaxed style that's been his trademark over the years."[18]

On the episode aired September 22, Hoagy sings his own "Marry Me in

Laramie," written expressly for the show. Between takes, said Fuller, the composer entertained the cast at a piano on the set. Carmichael worked hard, he added, learning and performing his scenes with polish and professionalism. But behind the actor's outwardly affectionate reminiscences is a shadow-image of Carmichael constantly badgering producer John Champion for more exposure.

"John Champion and I had been friends since third grade," Nacio Herb Brown recalled. "John called me one day and begged me to rein Hoagy in. We all knew he was the only one on the show who had any real presence: a strong personality and a strong actor. But he was pushing too hard, and it was beginning to create problems.

"I told him, 'Just calm down, Hoagy. Just sit there for a year, do what you're assigned to do. Don't start anything. People will realize how good you are and you'll get what you're after. They won't be able to drop you, unless some fluke happens.'

"But he didn't stop. Part of it was also the drinking. Now Hoagy wasn't a drunk, not what you'd call an alcoholic. Far from it. He just liked his little nip, and when he'd had his little drink he'd start up with 'I want to do this song' or 'I want to do this or that' and start pushing people. It didn't take much to get on their nerves."[19]

At a remove of more than four decades, it's impossible to document exactly what forces or individuals prompted NBC's decision not to renew Hoagy's contract at the end of the first *Laramie* season. But it comes as no surprise that by June 1960 he was out. That autumn, when *Laramie* went on the air for its second season, *Variety* quickly took note of "Jonesy's" absence: "The defection of Hoagy Carmichael from the regular cast this season has left *Laramie* bereft of its single offbeat feature, and the series started its second season last week in totally undistinguished fashion." The show lasted three more seasons, with some cast changes and generally abysmal ratings, before NBC pulled the plug; not even the addition of respected veteran actress Spring Byington to the cast arrested the downward spin. *Laramie* without Carmichael remained what *Variety* dismissed as "a flat formula western."[20]

✻   ✻   ✻

If 1960 dealt Hoagy a defeat with *Laramie*, it also brought an unexpected, if brief, resurgence of songwriting attention. Georgia-born singer-pianist

Ray Charles, riding high on a series of rhythm-and-blues hits, was looking hard at the mainstream pop market. In 1959, after many albums and count-less singles for Atlantic, he signed with ABC Paramount, which offered him both a producer's royalty and ownership of his master tapes. Millions knew Charles's throaty voice and rhythmic drive through such hits as "What'd I Say" and "Hallelujah, I Love Her So," but only by recording better-known standards was he going to transcend the R&B niche in which a category-conscious pop music industry had placed him.

His first major project for his new label was a "concept album," to be titled *Genius Hits the Road.* Content and concept were simple: twelve songs with names of states (or major cities, or such landmarks as Basin Street) in their titles. Sessions of March 29 and 30, 1960, included such otherwise unlikely chestnuts as "Alabamy Bound," "California, Here I Come," "Carry Me Back to Old Virginny," and "Moonlight in Vermont"—and, gloriously, as it turned out, "Georgia on My Mind."

Backed by a band including alto saxophonist Hank Crawford and tenor favorite David "Fathead" Newman, playing an arrangment by Al Cohn, Charles delivers Hoagy's 1930 song in an impassioned, gospel-flavored man-ner. Released as a single, "Georgia" soon hit the pop charts and by mid-November had climbed to the number one spot. It won two Grammy Awards, for Best Male Vocal and Best Popular Single of 1960. All at once, it seemed, fans who had no more than a vague idea who Hoagy Carmichael was, who had never heard "Star Dust" (or dismissed it as hopelessly tied to their parents' generation), now embraced this 1930 musical relic as their own. The combination of a song hit with Georgia in its title, sung by a Peach State native son, was too alluring to resist: the wheels of Atlanta bureaucracy creaked into motion, and in 1979 the state of Georgia adopted "Georgia on My Mind" as its official song.[21]

Speaking with jazz critic Leonard Feather, Hoagy confessed to being "quite discouraged" with developments in popular music. Time was, he said, "I could go most any place and say, 'Listen to this new thing of mine,' and they'd listen. But after rock and roll started, I never even got a phone call from an A&R man about anything . . . Nevertheless I still write as well as I ever did."[22]

Carmichael songs of the early 1960s bear him out. If "The Ballad of Sam Older" (1959) is a *faux*-cowboy trifle most at home in a *Laramie* ep-isode (it was copyrighted less than two weeks before the series went on the air), "A Perfect Paris Night," written with Johnny Mercer in 1960 and due for an unexpected role two years hence as "Just for Tonight," is rather more than that. The lead sheet is marked, "Moderato, with a continental lilt," and that's just what the song conveys, in somewhat the charming manner of "Charade," Mercer's 1963 movie collaboration with Henry Mancini.

Where Hoagy's own "Behold, How Beautiful" is a nostalgic, faintly generic waltz, "Big Town Blues" offers a wryly disillusioned lyric:

> I arrived with dreams of a penthouse just made for two,
> High up on the thirty-second floor;
> But where is my penthouse, and where's the view?
> I'm in a bargain basement with a sidewalk skyline . . .

In 1963 Carmichael joined forces with Carolyn Leigh, whose work with pianist Cy Coleman ("Witchcraft," "Young at Heart," "It Amazes Me") had helped make her one of the most talked-about lyricists of the 1950s. Their "Bamboo Curtains," perhaps inspired by the success of *Sayonara* (1957) and other Hollywood films with Far Eastern subjects, is Japanese in attitude and sound, its melody conforming largely (as had that of "Hong Kong Blues" two decades before) to the steps of the pentatonic scale.

"Close Beside You," copyrighted 1963, found Hoagy writing again with Harold Adamson, and once again hitting his stride. It's a thoughtful ballad, with a particularly appealing shift of tonal center in bars 13 to 16:

"Close Beside You" (bars 1–16), 1965

But there is little evidence that any of these songs caught the attention of publishing and record company executives. "I'll betcha I have twenty-five songs lying in my trunk," Carmichael told CBC interviewer Tony Thomas in 1964, "new ones that I've written in the last five or six years . . . It's a strange thing if people don't even call me to ask me if I've got a good song to record . . . I'd think that once in a while they would come to me and say, 'Have you got a real good song for such-and-such an artist?' But they don't."[23]

The early 1960s found Hoagy with more free time than he'd had in years. Accordingly, he turned his attentions to other pastimes. Some, among them golf and coin collecting, may have begun as little more than hobbies, but he tackled them with an energy and concentration typical of his musical pursuits. He won news media attention through his advocacy of the "Clarney," a custom-tailored shirt incorporating ascot neckwear; captured headlines by taking out a patent on what he called "shorties," half-length cigarettes for smokers used to only taking a few puffs at a time. In 1960 Hoagy corresponded with bankers, lawyers, and a circle of potential investors about buying and developing the small Hawaiian island of Kahoolawe, a former U.S. Navy bombing range off the southwest coast of Maui. He even began tentative steps toward buying back the copyrights to his songs.[24]

Inevitably, too, there were women, among them an aspiring actress named Rita Cahill. He'd first become involved with her in the early 1950s, while his marriage was stumbling, and had secured a bit part for her in *Timber Jack*. "She was depicted in the movies as an Indian squaw," Randy Carmichael recalled. "Glorious, striking woman—gorgeous, big-eyed. But she was—well, how shall I put it? A box of rocks? Dumb?" Hoagy nevertheless seemed to find her irresistible. "With Rita he wasn't discreet at all. He was very flagrant, which was at least part of the reason, I think, for the divorce."[25]

But Hoagy Carmichael's chief preoccupation in those early 1960s years lay elsewhere. The 1949 failure of *Brown County in Autumn*, however discouraging, had not quenched his determination to write a "big" musical work, a piece that would expand and transcend the confines of the popular song form. As early as 1949 he'd set his Indianapolis cousin Ruth Grant to work researching the life and deeds of John Chapman (1774–1845), the farmer of post-Revolutionary days known in song and story as "Johnny Appleseed."

Born in western Massachusetts, son of a captain in George Washington's army, young Chapman had settled first in rural Pennsylvania, where he made a practice of dispensing apple saplings and seeds to families moving west. The early years of the nineteenth century found him living in Ohio, traveling regularly through what is now the American Midwest, sowing apple seeds as he went. For four decades he ranged the territory, helping farmers nurture and harvest apple crops of their own, thereby earning himself the "Appleseed" sobriquet.

As one biographical entry has it, "His ragged dress, eccentric ways, and religious turn of mind attracted attention, and he became a familiar figure to settlers." He was a disciple of the Swedish theologian Emanuel Swedenborg (1688–1772), whose teachings fused faith and science, and who still ranks as a pioneer in the modern disciplines of physics, paleontology, and molecular biology.[26]

By most accounts, Chapman sowed the seeds of Swedenborg's teachings about the interrelation of soul and body, spirit and science, as readily as he did apples. One writer compared him to "a Hebrew prophet, tramping from cabin to cabin, spreading the gospel as he went." According to some accounts, he helped American forces during the War of 1812 by traveling great distances as a courier, summoning reinforcements to battles that were going badly.[27]

Part of Johnny Appleseed's "beat," legend has it, was the future state of Indiana. One popular description pictures him as "a small man, with sun-shriveled, weather-beaten face, framed by untrimmed, ragged, graying hair. It was his eyes, of a vivid blue, that best described the man inside, ever-observant, trusting, innocent of evil thought or intent . . . and a metal cooking pot with a handle, was worn as a hat, with the handle in the back!"[28]

The idea of Chapman as a wanderer, spreading fructification of mind and nature as he went, has captivated children and adults for generations, and it enthralled Hoagy Carmichael. Throughout the 1950s, Ruth Grant sent him clippings, photostats, and transcriptions of old newspaper and magazine articles about Johnny Appleseed. "If you have any questions or wish additional material," she wrote, "scream. Twas fun to read and know you can weave his life threads into a suite or who knows—even an 'Ole Settlers' opera."[29]

Shortly after the end of his *Laramie* association, Carmichael got to work on his Appleseed project, expanding and developing the concept in earnest. The result was a twenty-minute orchestral suite, performed in Indianapolis December 8, 1962, by the Indianapolis Symphony. After Hoagy's spoken introduction, Bud Dant conducted orchestrations by Nathan Van Cleave, an established figure in film and radio scoring.

Fortunately, *The Johnny Appleseed Suite* survives in several forms, including a tape recording of the 1962 premiere, a 1964 *Bell Telephone Hour* television broadcast, and a version of October 18, 1984, part of a "Jubilee Concert" of Carmichael music at the Murat Theatre in Indianapolis. Additionally, in 1970, Hoagy Bix Carmichael shot extensive film footage of his father at the piano, playing and discussing the suite's component themes.[30]

Each version shows *Johnny Appleseed* at a different stage of development, with Hoagy endlessly tinkering, adjusting, reordering. He seems fascinated with the idea that seeds sown throughout a long and itinerant life will ultimately flower, in perennial affirmation of the sower's life and work.

Did the onetime Indiana boy have himself in mind in shaping this *chef d'oeuvre*? Hoagy Bix, among others, is convinced of it. "It's Dad's *Porgy and Bess*" is his assessment, "and very roots-driven: young guy grows up in Midwest, goes out, plants his apple trees—that is, plants his music— and comes back later in life to see what he's accomplished. To me that's obvious."[31]

Perhaps the suite's most melodically eloquent moment is its climactic "Serenade" theme, assigned to solo cello in Van Cleave's setting. Other melodies are arresting, if derivative: the elegaic "Prayer" theme recalls Grieg; the overarching "Cathedral" motif owes a certain debt to Rachmaninoff, and through him the neo-Romantic Hollywood scoring of Alfred Newman, Ernest Gold, and Max Steiner. If the sprightly "Appleseed" *Leitmotif* is weightless, a generic cousin to "Yankee Doodle," the climactic "Fulfillment Music" strongly recalls both Aaron Copland (*Appalachian Spring*) and, less directly, Rodgers and Hammerstein ("Climb Ev'ry Mountain," from *The Sound of Music*). From time to time Hoagy's jazz side peeks cautiously through all this underbrush: the "asleep in the woods" sequence, for example, recalls Bix's impressionist probings.[32]

Johnny Appleseed's major problems are with structure and development, a weakness it shares with long works by others whose strengths lie in shorter forms, among them jazz figures James P. Johnson, Tadd Dameron, and the later Duke Ellington. Carmichael seems at a loss to develop complexity and momentum through absorption of individual motives into a larger, more organic structure. *Appleseed* differs in that particular from *Brown County in Autumn*: the earlier tone poem succeeds as a landscape painting succeeds, its single image incorporating its elements. *Appleseed*, by contrast, fails to knit its components into a unified, integrated larger identity. It remains stubbornly episodic.

The *Johnny Appleseed Suite* was far from Hoagy Carmichael's final composition. He would continue writing songs throughout the next two decades, if to little public acknowledgment. But it's clear he envisioned *Appleseed* as a major statement, even a summing-up. Too soon, this wedding of story and melody would begin to sound for all the world like a valedictory address.

* XVIII *

Loss

Even when I try to divest it of the halo which I know always surrounds the past,
I am unable to create any other impression than that it was fresh and clean.
—CALVIN COOLIDGE, 1929

Loss, progressive and pervasive, shadowed Hoagy Carmichael through-out the 1960s. His younger sister Martha, unable to regain her footing since the death of her husband, novelist John Bell Clayton, was the first casualty.

Georgia, with whom she was staying at the Doheny Drive house, found her body on Sunday morning, August 6, 1961. The sisters and Hoagy Bix had dined together the previous evening, and Martha had excused herself early, saying she was tired and wanted to turn in early. She'd drunk a bit during dinner, and before going to bed had apparently taken a sleeping pill, from which she'd never awakened. Though no mention was made at the time, family suspicion lingered that her death had not been accidental.

She and John Bell Clayton had enjoyed "a very secure, strong relation-ship," said Hoagy Bix. "Really loved each other, were real partners. When he died, she was lost—didn't know what to do." She'd come down to Palm Springs and worked alongside Hoagy Bix in Barbara Wells's interior decorat-ing shop. "She was very depressed, very down. Some fluctuations, sure: but in general there was this feeling of 'This was my life and now it's all gone.' "[1]

Martha had been at the bedside in 1959 when Lida died and after that, though only in her forties, seemed to give up, receding gently from view.

For Hoagy himself there seemed no doubt that after Clayton's death Martha "gathered up his papers and manuscript and made another book for him, and then one night while still young and healthy she quietly let go." It cannot have escaped his notice that her death, at forty-six, fell thirty years to the day after that of a figure even more central to his life, his friend Bix Beiderbecke.[2]

✳   ✳   ✳

Stuart Gorrell had been ill for some time, and word of his death at sixty-one on August 9, 1963, if not a shock, nevertheless came as a blow. Living in New Jersey, working in Manhattan as public relations director for the Chase Manhattan Bank, he hadn't been much in contact with Hoagy. But ties between them had remained, particularly with the renewed popularity of "Georgia on My Mind."

Above all, Gorrell had been a vital link to Hoagy's past, the shared memory providing solace as time and change worked their inevitable mischief on the present. In that context, "Serenade to Gabriel" becomes a *cri de coeur*, as much about Hoagy, Stu, and the rest of the youthful Bent Eagles as about the jazzmen they all so admired and missed.

Two other deaths, within days of one another toward the end of 1964, dealt another one-two punch. Buddy Cole had been pianist of choice to countless singers and radio stars, working closely and often with Hoagy. George "Dixie" Heighway, a campus drummer when Carmichael was at IU, had run the university's Alumni Office for years. Now, suddenly, both were gone.

Loss of *Laramie*, too, had been a setback. Had Nacio been right? Could Hoagy have prevailed by just delivering his lines and letting his skill and popularity yield their own rewards? Probably, said Hoagy Bix. "But Dad remained Dad. Nothing was gonna change him just like that."

On its surface, the living remained easy. The songs—above all "Star Dust," "Georgia on My Mind," "Skylark," and "Heart and Soul"—were bringing in a combined annual royalty income somewhere in excess of $300,000, well over a million dollars in today's currency. He also invested heavily, in everything from oil deals to potentially revolutionary new inventions.

"Dad loved a new gimmick," said Hoagy Bix. "He was fascinated by inventions. For example, a guy up around San Francisco developed what he called a 'linear motor,' with only two moving parts. It never went much of anywhere, but Dad was fascinated with it."[3]

His life remained full of sunny socializing, punctuated now and then by television appearances. In "The Hit Songwriters," a particularly charming episode in the animated *Flintstones* series, he introduced his "Yabba Dabba Dabba Dabba Do," composed specially for the occasion; he did two installments of *Burke's Law* and a few original TV dramas, including *The Man Who Bought Paradise* (1965) and *The Farmer's Daughter: Oh Boy, Is the Honeymoon Over!* (1966); he was even in one of the *Name of the Game* adventures (1970).

His golf game had taken on polish, winning him a place in Bing Crosby's Pebble Beach invitational. He was proud of his status as an eight-handicapper—and, in his not-always-understated way, keenly competitive with his golf-playing elder son. At one point he made a few headlines by announcing that his "explosion swing" would add power and distance to anyone's drives. There was an offer from Fred Waring to compete in the Bill Waite Memorial Tournament at Shawnee, Pennsylvania, the bandleader's self-proclaimed "golf capital of the East."

But sometimes the Hoosier in him got to reflecting that none of it seemed quite real. "One wonders sometimes if California is not an ironic trick, something someone is laughing at and not much concerned about," he mused at mid-decade. Subtract the sunshine, subtract the leisure, subtract the diversions and even the glossy TV shows, and how much remained of the life of music and creative effort Hoagy Carmichael had once so easily inhabited?[4]

✻   ✻   ✻

Ruth Carmichael, meanwhile, had married Vern Mason and moved to Miami, where the doctor founded a medical institute for Howard Hughes. In a richly ironic twist, Jean Simmons and her husband, director Richard Brooks, now owned what had been the Carmichaels' Holmby Hills house, with Ruth's bedroom claimed by her erstwhile rival. Simmons and Brooks had met and fallen in love while filming *Elmer Gantry*, on which twenty-one-year-old Hoagy Bix had worked as a "second assistant director"—in practice, a gofer.

The elder son had made up his mind that he would only be able to become his own man far from his father's world, far from Sunset Boulevard and Palm Springs, and a leisured existence he found increasingly stifling. He headed for New York. "I'll never forget the day I left," he said. "We're at the top of the stairs, Dad and me. I've got my bag with me and Dad is standing there, tears just racing down his face. He wasn't real good at talking about how he felt, what he wanted you to do, what you meant to him. Not his strong suit at all."[5]

Hoagy kept writing songs, some of substantial quality. But, to paraphrase one of his own titles, things had changed. By the early 1960s, according to pop historian Donald Clarke, the tastemakers of earlier times—bandleaders, songwriters, publishers—had simply abdicated, supplanted by a teenage generation "encouraged to think that people with talent were kids just like them," and uninterested in anything on the other side of the great divide.[6]

For Hoagy and his fellow-songwriters, the most keenly felt loss was that of ready access to an immediate and accepting movie market. A new wave of young cinema composers, exhaustively skilled, had moved in; their scores, freely incorporating modern jazz and even more exotic elements, often included appealing individual themes easily converted into hit songs—which, in turn, took on lives of their own.

The names of Johnny Mandel, Michel Legrand, Henry Mancini, Oliver Nelson, Lalo Schifrin, and others were appearing on more and more film credits and winning Oscars. They had displaced two discrete groups: such established, largely European-trained composers as Max Steiner, Franz Waxman, Miklos Rosza, and Dmitri Tiomkin, and the songwriters who had supplied individual tunes to complement their quasi-symphonic scores.

Seemingly at a stroke, but actually over a decade, the new film scoring—evolving from such seminally "modern" soundtracks as Elmer Bernstein's music for *The Man With the Golden Arm* (1955) and Mandel's no less powerful writing for the 1958 Susan Hayward melodrama *I Want to Live,* among others—had rendered both the symphonic old guard and Carmichael's breed of songwriters-for-hire obsolete.

One case amply illustrating the point was *Hatari!* It began with a call from Howard Hawks: he was producing and directing an action adventure about big game hunters, to be set and filmed in Africa; would Hoagy be interested in writing the music? Called *Hatari!*, from the Swahili word for "danger," it required a jazz-based score that would be by turns dramatic, exotic, and tuneful.

According to Hawks's biographer Todd McCarthy, *Hatari!* had already gone through months of changes and delays. Early plans, back in 1960, had called for Clark Gable to co-star with John Wayne; but Gable died that November, shortly after finishing *The Misfits,* and the search for a co-star— ultimately fruitless—had consumed months. Hawks's first choice for the music was the veteran Tiomkin, who had scored all his films since *Red River* in 1948. But the director didn't want a "traditional, bombastic, swell- ingly exciting soundtrack for this picture, and he instructed the composer to use native instruments when possible and absolutely avoid strings or woodwinds."

Tiomkin, born in Russia and trained in Europe as a concert pianist, thought Hawks was pulling his leg, told him so—and found himself off the job. The director then tapped his old pal Hoagy. Though Carmichael has left no documentation of what went on between them, his papers include music and manuscript material for *Hatari!,* indicating work on a main theme, a song, and bits of connective tissue.

Randy Carmichael, staying at the Sunset Boulevard penthouse at the time, remembered lying awake nights listening to his father working on *Hatari!* "Three in the morning and he'd belt outta bed, go to the piano and start playing. 'Hey Dad, what's goin' on?' And he'd answer, 'I just came up with this great idea.' And I'd get up and sit with him while he worked on it." In Randy's recollection his father wrote a lot of vivid music ("You'd hear it and you'd *know* you were seeing an elephant, *know* you were in Tanganyika!") and showed the result to Hawks, who decided—inexplicably, says the younger Carmichael—to try his hand at editing some of it, or at least handing it to another composer for remedial work.

McCarthy doesn't describe these events, never mentions Carmichael's name, referring only to "a wrong turn with another composer." But the meaning is obvious. Hawks's ultimate choice was Mancini, whose major *Hatari!* theme, under the title "Baby Elephant Walk," went on to become an instrumental record hit and, later, a popular song.[7]

Randy, eternally and vocally his father's champion, remembered the in- cident with undisguised rancor. "They screwed my dad" was his assessment. "About a week after [Hawks] took Dad's music home he came back with some lyrics, and it was like a seven-year-old coming up with 'See Spot Run.' And Dad said, 'Kiss my ass,' and that was it. Blew him off."[8]

Though major *Hatari!* music credits went to Mancini, Hawks did use some Carmichael music in the picture, chiefly the song "Just for To- night," written the previous year as "A Perfect Paris Night," with a Johnny Mercer lyric.[9]

Hoagy appeared to shrug off the disappointment, turning his attention to other projects. In mid-1963 he wrote to his old friend Paul Summers, at Jim Bingham's Indianapolis law firm, about possibly selling his collection of children's songs to the Indiana public school system. Summers answered encouragingly, suggesting an approach to the system's supervisor of vocal music and mentioning the Boy Scouts, Campfire Girls, and other organizations. There is no indication that Carmichael ever followed through.[10]

He returned to tinkering with *Johnny Appleseed,* changing the order of themes, writing the patriotic text sung by Robert Merrill on the 1964 *Bell Telephone Hour* performance. In autumn 1964, and at the urging of his sons, he took time out to visit the 1964 Tokyo Olympics—greatly enhanced, it appears, by a brief affair with a Japanese woman. "They had a ball," said Hoagy Bix. "He saw Japan with her, had great seats for the events. We have all these photographs of Dad standing next to this little Japanese woman. He was having a helluva time."

A news photo published in the English-language *Japan Times* shows Hoagy signing autographs for female admirers, telling reporters that "his time is fully occupied in the U.S. with television shows (he has played 'Jonesy' in 'Laramie'), movies and both vocal and instrumental recordings." It is at once revealing and sobering to realize that at the time he made this statement he had been off *Laramie* nearly four years, hadn't made a record in five, hadn't done a movie for a decade.[11]

Women wandered in and out of his life. In the mid-1950s, fresh out of his divorce, he'd bankrolled an interior decorating shop set up in Palm Springs by one such inamorata, even pressing sister Martha Claire and teenage Hoagy Bix into service as employees; stationery from this enterprise carries the inscription "Barbara Wells, Inc., Interiors. Hoagy Carmichael, President."

His affair with the eternal ingenue Rita Cahill ended in recrimination and, on her side, alcoholic excess and quarrels over money. There was a woman, one of a set of twins in the San Francisco Bay Area, remembered only as "Tiger." At one point Hoagy Bix introduced one of his own girlfriends, a starlet named Connie Dane, to his father—only to watch in consternation as "Dad" smoothly appropriated her affections. Only later did the son find out that the father and Miss Dane had written a song together, though "From Nikki's Garden" is anything but a highlight of the Carmichael catalogue.

The consort who seemed to last was a minor actress known as Wanda McKay. Born Dorothy Ellen Quackenbush in Portland, Oregon, she'd grown up there and in Missouri and Texas before gravitating to Southern

California in 1940. She'd starred in 'B' movies, beginning with a Hopalong Cassidy western and moving through such titles as *Bowery at Midnight* and *The Black Raven* to *Monster Maker* and *Jungle Goddess*. She'd worked as a model and had parts in episodes of *The Lone Ranger* and *The Cisco Kid* on television. For Hoagy, the woman he dubbed "Quacky" or "Dottie Quack"—he took mischievous pleasure in her obvious annoyance at such nicknames—seemed less a grand passion than a comfortable companion; but she remained for the rest of his life. They were married in 1977.

Hovering about all such Carmichael liaisons is a sense of time—time open and time filled, time expended on diversions. His day-to-day life bore few of the trappings of Hollywood celebrity: his name remained in the Los Angeles phone book, his car parked in a public lot. "I don't think he even owned a pair of sunglasses," his son recalled. His circle of friends was as likely to encompass people outside show business as in. One such, a never-quite-successful businessman named Von Moffatt, was held in much affection by the Carmichael family.

"We loved Von," both brothers agreed. "No-profit Moffatt. Called himself 'short, shiftless, and shabby,' always looking for some new venture, something to do. He was very funny: had terrific energy. Wonderful guy to be around. For a while he had a Chrysler dealership: he was the one who got Dad interested in the Dual Ghia, a new sports car being built in Europe under Chrysler supervision.

"They cost about twelve thousand dollars a pop back then [about $75,000 in today's money]," said Hoagy Bix. "I remember Von and his son, and one other guy, bringing three of 'em down [to Palm Springs] for Dad to see. Gave him his choice. This is long before Sinatra and the Rat Pack bought 'em." At one point Hoagy owned five. "Sure, the indulgence was excessive in a way, but it was fun for him, a bit of a signature. The way I look at it, if he wanted to collect Dual Ghias, or coins, or open a brothel—it was all the same to me. All this talent and energy, and nowhere to go with it—so *do* something, Dad, do *anything*. Just use that energy."[12]

✻   ✻   ✻

Prizes and recognitions were beginning to come Carmichael's way, tokens of appreciation for a lifetime's music-making. There was a "Distinguished Hoosier" award, presented during the 1964 New York World's Fair and eliciting warm thanks from such officials as Indiana's liberal Democratic Senator

Birch Bayh. *Cue* magazine listed Hoagy among the honorees for its scheduled second *Salute to American Composers of Popular Song*, to be held at New York's Philharmonic Hall. When Indiana University began to discuss plans for its upcoming 150th anniversary, Carmichael—who had endowed the school regularly and richly—was one of the first invited to participate.

And, all agreed, it was high time the composer of "Stardust" told his story between the covers of a book. Not another *Star Dust Road*—that small memoir had been little more than a roseate portrait of its author's early life, ending abruptly in 1931 with the deaths of Bix and Moenkhaus. Hoagy's subsequent rise from piano-playing jazz insider to world-famous song-writer, performer, actor, and public personality awaited chronicling.

During the 1950s he'd conferred with Indiana-born Ralph Hancock, a former *New York Times* foreign correspondent who had written popular books on subjects as diverse as actor Douglas Fairbanks Sr., Hollywood's Forest Lawn Cemetery, and the emergent states of Central America. Memos and letters suggest that for a while, at least, Hancock planned a biography; but there is no evidence that he ever converted his notes and interview transcripts into a manuscript.

As contracted with its publisher, the new book came with a built-in collaborator. Stephen Longstreet had distinguished himself as a novelist and Hollywood scriptwriter, on such films as *The Jolson Story, The Greatest Show on Earth*, and *The Helen Morgan Story*. They got started, and as the manuscript developed, the subject made it clear he was not going to just sit back and let someone else, even so skilled a craftsman as Longstreet, tell his story. Editorial changes, revisions, and even complete rewrites, all in his distinctive hand, festoon the typescript which became *Sometimes I Wonder* (Farrar, Straus & Giroux)—its title reportedly suggested by singer Peggy Lee during an airplane trip.

Any expectation of an orderly, chronologically based biography recounting the facts of Hoagy Carmichael's life and career was doomed to disappointment. Appearing in 1965, *Sometimes I Wonder* was in great measure a successor to *The Stardust Road*: written in the first person, it free-associates and leapfrogs across decades, leaving few signposts to orient the reader.

The Stardust Road's lyric cadences give way here to an Indiana monologue, equal parts reminiscence and philosophizing, Abe Martin chewing on a toothpick while moving from crackerbarrel to piano keyboard. Carmichael as narrator is older now, more worldly-wise: rueful, contemplative, he reflects on jazz, on Hollywood and his life there, even on the beat-generation writers of the 1950s—though, curiously, never mentioning his *Jazz Canto Volume One* adventure.

Most of the oft-told tales remain in place: the garden-wall genesis of "Star Dust," the inspired lunacy of the Book Nook, Bix, Monk. But the Bloomington town pals and other ancillary characters glimpsed in *Jazzbanders* remain absent and unaccounted for. A review in the *Bloomington Herald-Times* remarked that Hoagy "just talks the story . . . Be prepared for nostalgia when reading 'Sometimes I Wonder'—there's plenty of it."[13]

Republican Senator Barry Goldwater, a Carmichael friend, hailed the new book as "a precious thing . . . Reading over the things he has often talked with us about is just as if he were sitting in the room again picking at the piano and talking about the great days of music he has lived through." A brief note from Ralph Hancock, implying the demise of the earlier project, congratulates Longstreet on "a masterful job . . . Here's hoping it sells a million."[14]

But awards and books, even books that sold respectably, proved no surrogate for a musically active life. "Music was what turned Dad's crank" is Hoagy Bix's verdict. "And he was denied music. Opportunities to get out in front of the public, as part of the entertainment business, just weren't coming along."

Barely into his sixties, physically trim and healthy, his faculties unimpaired, the composer of "Star Dust" seemed increasingly a racer with no race to run. On more than a few occasions, his son said, they'd be together at a restaurant or lounge that had a piano, and "he'd be at it within ten minutes. Camp out at it. Hold court. To tell the truth it used to embarrass me; not because he wasn't wonderful at what he did. He was. But it was so blatant, so obvious that he needed the attention."[15]

        ❊   ❊   ❊

For Ruth Carmichael, "beautiful Cream," as Skitch Henderson and so many others had affectionately called her, life had tumbled steadily downhill. Vern Mason died suddenly in late 1965, leaving her bereft of course or compass. "He'd given her an entire new life," said Randy. "A twenty-four-hour-a-day life, which she hadn't had for God knows how many years. A first-class life, the kind she was used to having, and now, with him, she could enjoy it. Then he died—and she went straight down the drain."[16]

In Hoagy Bix's view, Mason had been what a slightly later generation would call "an enabler. He made it possible for her to get the drugs—the uppers and downers and the rest—on which she'd been dependent. Without him, she just slid back into that dependency." Repeatedly and firmly, the elder Carmichael son rejected any idea of sleeplessness as an identifiable condition in his mother's case; for him, Ruth's drug addiction had begun in the early 1950s, been nurtured by Mason, then spun out of control after his death. "She didn't know how to handle that," he said. Helen Meinardi had been right in fearing that her sister lacked the resilience to weather the storms of her marriage, or of life in general.[17]

Ruth wandered back to California, putting up at the home of a dentist friend near Los Angeles International Airport while having work done on her teeth. She spent nights walking, wraith-like, throughout the house, often sleeping through the days. Her attempt to sail away as a passenger on a freighter had ended disastrously, and she'd come home in worse shape than when she left. She looked bad—wan, haggard, her once beautiful features lined with strain. There were often tears, days at a time when she would be by turns volatile and remote, hostile and inconsolable. Even close friends seemed at a loss to say or do anything.

Her final escape came with an overdose of sleeping pills. "They found her in a second-floor bedroom, fully dressed, with Vern's picture propped against the headboard," said Randy. No one was in any doubt that she had simply had enough: enough living, enough demons. Enough struggle.

Hoagy's reaction was muted, whatever feelings he may have had internalized, under tight control. "I'm sure he felt bad about and for Ruthie, as he always called her," said Hoagy Bix. "But he didn't show much, and anyway—by then I think there'd been too much history between them . . . he'd pretty much given up on the possibility of doing much for her."

❊ ❊ ❊

However sporadically, Hoagy Carmichael was still occasionally "finding" and writing out songs. When Indiana University's football team won a place in the vaunted 1968 Rose Bowl game, he responded with "To the Team," a musical tribute to the gridiron heroes and their school. Robert E. Stoll's sixty-six-voice choir, the Singing Hoosiers, performed it at various runup events to the big game; with Hoagy and the team as guests of honor they sang it at a December 29 Hollywod Big Ten Club commemorative dinner. Carmichael's lyric is richly affectionate:

> The big, tall maples on the Campus
> Lift their branches proudly to the sky,
> And while they're swayin' they keep sayin'
> We'll be even taller bye 'n bye . . .

More than a few other 1960s Carmichael titles and lyrics, heard now, hint at a darker view. In 1962 it was "I'm Gonna Try It One More Time," Carmichael music and lyric, including the lines:

> Love's unkind, Love's uncouth,
> Highly overrated dream of youth.
> It doesn't make sense in reason or rhyme,
> But I've gotta try it one more time.

His lyric to Randy's melody on "How Sweet It Was" (1965) reads, in part:

> All along a distant shore the marks of time are gone completely,
> But mem'ries seem to linger on
> And though your love is gone,
> Dear thoughts of you remain to warm a winter's rain
> Like kissing does . . .

A collaboration with trombonist Reg DuValle Jr., son of Hoagy's piano-playing early mentor, produced "Where Are You Now?"

> Where shall I go? What can I do?
> Should I pretend that I will spend the rest of my life with you?
> Maybe the memories will see me through somehow . . .

Johnny Mercer's lyric to their 1968 "Song of Long Ago" refers specifically and unmistakably to Carmichael's starlit youth:

> I should forget
> But I will let
> Little mem'ries overflow.
> Then through the tears,
> And misty years,
> Back to Stardust days I go . . .

Song publisher Howie Richmond, long a Carmichael admirer, reunited Hoagy briefly with Mitchell Parish for an ode to Christmases past, published as "The White World of Winter."

> I can't wait till we skate on Lake Happy
> And sup a hot buttered cup in the afterglow . . .

Perhaps most telling of all was an anecdote Hoagy related to jazz critic Leonard Feather. "Many years ago," he said, "I played tennis with George Gershwin and after the game we got to talking about songs. We shook hands and solemnly agreed we'd never write a Hawaiian song." This, he added, was in 1937, when Harry Owens's cloying "Sweet Leilani" beat out Gershwin's own, far superior "They Can't Take That Away from Me" for an Academy Award.

"Well," Hoagy concluded with a shrug, "two of my recent tunes are 'Hawaii, Pearl[s] of the Sea,' recorded by [pianist] Roger Williams, and 'Hawaiian Evening Song'." It had come, at last, to that. Unsurprisingly, neither song got very far, and neither even begins to approach Carmichael in peak form. Better, though no more successful commercially, is "Close Beside You," written (in Hoagy's beloved key of D-major) with Harold Adamson.[18]

Richmond brought him another interesting opportunity. Traveling in Italy, the publisher had heard a movie theme, a fetching little waltz called "Senza Fine," which translates as "without end." Bringing it home, he first showed it to composer Alec Wilder, who crafted an English-language lyric based on Gino Paoli's Italian text. At that point, for reasons he no longer remembered after thirty-five years, Richmond sent the original and Wilder's revision to Hoagy Carmichael.

Hoagy wrote back on January 27, 1962, explaining his intention to "improve the lyric in one way or another and possibly make some musical changes." He lists reasons for thinking the Italian text untranslatable, then gets down to the real point of his letter. Wilder's lyric, he says, is

> a very good thing from a conventional point of view. I might have made a few minor suggestions for it, but who am I to criticize someone else's work, especially Alec's . . . [but] after seeing the English interpretation I got to thinking the other night and determined that perhaps a more heroic (??) approach, lyric-wise, should be attempted

at least, and I went to work. It was not my thought to impose my small talents upon you, especially since I have not had Alec's consent or yours—but sometimes things strike me in a way that give [*sic*] me cause to do something I might like whether it is ever used or not."[19]

Hoagy's "heroic" approach involved not only a new text but the sorts of changes in notation and phrase order he'd imposed on Fred Katz's "The Sage." Explaining them to Richmond in detail, he ends with a somewhat disingenuous assurance that "it's Alec's baby, and if he feels that my efforts are complicating matters, or if he feels that he'd prefer having his own lyric rather than working as a threesome . . . then I shall have to forget it."[20]

Republished in 1964, "Senza Fine" wound up on the soundtrack of the adventure film *Flight of the Phoenix*—and, when it started to capture public attention (mostly thanks to a record by Peggy Lee), was republished a second time in 1966 as "The Phoenix Love Theme," music and Italian text credited to Paoli and English lyric by Wilder.

✻   ✻   ✻

In 1967, with his career seemingly at a standstill and the emotions stirred by Ruth's passing still fresh, Hoagy decided on a change of scene. Texas businessman Bill Ford and his wife, actress Arlene Dahl, had offered their Park Avenue apartment to him whenever they weren't using it. He "had the run of the place," said Hoagy Bix.

He was in New York a lot around this time, and on more than a few occasions, especially with a few scotches under his belt, his professional frustration bobbed unbidden to the surface. At Carnegie Hall for a Rudolf Serkin all-Beethoven piano recital, "Dad started saying, audibly, things like 'I can write better stuff than that!' You could hear him two or three rows behind. It was pretty embarrassing, and we got him outta there by the coattails at intermission."

Afternoons he'd wander over to the old Manhattan Savings Bank building, at Madison Avenue and East 47th Street. "The bank—it's gone now—had a very unusual and enlightened management," said Hoagy Bix. "They had ice-skating, a woman ice-skating *inside* the lobby. And there was a piano in there." Fortified with a nip or two, the elder Carmichael would stroll into the bank, make himself comfortable at the keyboard, and start playing. "Customers would come in, and he'd just nod and say, 'Hi!' Wouldn't stand up and say, 'Hey, I'm Hoagy Carmichael, and I'm playing my famous songs, why don't you come adore me.' Nothing like that. He'd just go in there and play.

"Thinking of it now, I realize that even *he* didn't know any more who he was—and he *needed* that outlet . . . He didn't deal with things, with rejection, the way other people might. Didn't know how. Mind you, he never reached any kind of meltdown—no throwing rocks at studio executives' windows, or anything like that. He wasn't like that. But he felt— well, abandoned."[21]

In 1968 Hoagy Bix landed a job at Boston public television station WGBH, pacesetter in the educational TV field. Like his move to the East Coast, it was a courageous shot: he'd been working at the Park Avenue brokerage house of McDonnell and Company, decided it was a dead end, and one day just cold-called the Boston station. "I asked them, 'If I come up at my own expense will you take me on as a volunteer? If I don't prove myself in six months I'll leave.' "

Miraculously, they agreed. Pouring his belongings into a U-Haul, the younger Carmichael headed up Interstate 95 to Boston. Less than halfway into his six-month trial period his new employers realized they'd gained a hard and resourceful worker and took him on full-time. Soon—as was to be the pattern throughout his adult life—he was immersed in a project aimed at featuring and promoting his father.

The children's songs had languished since their composer's unsuccessful bid to place them in the Indiana public schools. "I'd always loved them," said Hoagy Bix, "and was determined to get them out there in any way I could." Much planning and brainstorming yielded *Hoagy Carmichael's Music Shop*, an educational series showcasing the songs in new, fashionably rock-flavored settings devised by vibraphonist-arranger Monty Stark and played by a small group including guitarist John Abercrombie.

Each fifteen-minute program took the form of a musical lesson, reinforced with one of the songs. "Here's this guy—Dad—who owns a music shop, and three kids who hang around . . . The idea was to take the tunes, play and sing them—and explain something about time signatures, quarter notes, or whatever."

They recorded far more of the music than they needed for the show, but enough to fill a possible LP for the nascent jazz-rock market. The son's hopes for parental approval are obvious when he writes to his father, "Your music has turned a lot of people on here, including some school children to date . . . Have a listen and tell me what you think."[22]

Hoagy tackled his part conscientiously, though not without a certain amount of father-son friction. "Let's just say he wasn't as collaborative as you might have wanted" was Hoagy Bix's summation. "There were times when he'd let things go, and others when he dug in his heels and just wasn't gonna budge. Prickly, you know. That made it a little difficult sometimes for me."

In the midst of shooting, the elder Carmichael decamped abruptly for some vacation time on Spain's Costa del Sol, leaving Hoagy Bix, Monty Stark, and the rest of their crew with no choice but to await his return. At the end, said his son, "It wasn't quite the kind of experience for him that I'd hoped it would be. I'd have liked him to dig in more."

The *Music Shop* ran on PBS stations throughout New England during the 1970–71 season and in reruns for several seasons thereafter. Twenty-four of the songs came out again as a *Hoagy Carmichael's Music Shop* book, arranged for voices and piano, with a companion study guide. But any hopes for wider distribution ran aground in late 1970, thanks to a decision from the office of Educational TV executive Robert Fox. "This action was a shocker to me," Hoagy wrote to a friend in a rare display of bewildered anger.[23]

Bill Wheatley, a colleague at WGBH, became a Hoagy Bix friend and confidant around that time. Listening to him talk, said Wheatley, "I often felt that he was the father, the older guy. Not that their roles were reversed: it wasn't quite that clear-cut. I guess you could best say that Hoagy Bix felt he had to take responsibility for his father. I remember him talking about his dad doing a commercial, for instance, and saying, 'What the hell is he doing *that* for? He doesn't need the money.' He thought it was demeaning."[24]

Often, he said, the son gave the impression of feeling the situation more keenly than did his father. Though active in a number of fields—among other things, he was building a specialist reputation as a designer of fly-fishing equipment—Hoagy Bix appeared to regard his father's welfare as his personal mission. In addition to creating and producing *Hoagy Carmichael's Music Shop*, he set out to raise funding to develop *Johnny Appleseed* into a fully realized dramatic work.

In this connection the two friends flew to Los Angeles, where Wheatley met the composer about whom he'd heard so much and began to see the complexity and emotional layering of Carmichael's relations with his sons. "I'd been prepared to meet a fairly pathetic man," he said. "To tell the truth, I have to say I don't think he seemed as pathetic as his son had described him." Disenchanted, perhaps, more than a little wry in regarding the turns and twists of outrageous fortune. But "I was surprised that he wasn't more vocally bitter about it." On the surface, Wheatley said, there was charm, even humor—and above all a winning gentleness.

As a teenager, Hoagy Bix had showed enough promise as a drummer to take lessons with jazz great Stan Levey. "He got to the point where he was so good he'd scare you to death," said brother Randy. "Maybe he wasn't as good as, say, Shelly Manne or Max Roach, but then, who was? He was damn good."

"Well, I played a lot" was Hoagy Bix's mildly self-effacing reply. "And I got to the point where I was pretty proficient, but somehow I think it always sounded better to Randy and Dad than it really was. I knew what my limitations were, had to admit to myself that in the end I didn't have what it takes." Rather than risk falling short of some unattainable standard, he walked away from it, never to return.

Levey remembered young Hoagy Bix showing up often at the Lighthouse, the club in Hermosa Beach where he and other California modern jazz figures worked in the 1950s. "Real nice kid. Came to the house all the time, too: we were like a second family to him, kinda took care of him, like one of our own kids. I guess I showed him some stuff, too, but I can't remember him ever playing with a band." At one point, Levey said, he had the Ludwig Company ship a set of drums to the youngster, and "I photographed him with them at—I think it was the Bel Air golf course, him and his father."[25]

Randy, by contrast, shaped himself into a pianist and singer specializing in his father's songs. But his brother "would never play with me, because I was just a bullshit piano player—couldn't play jazz, couldn't keep time. Still have a problem with it to this day."

Above all, in embracing music Randy risked coming off second-best in his father's regard, perpetuating a lifelong pattern. On the very night of his birth, June 27, 1940, Indiana businessman Wendell Willkie had astonished the nation by winning the Republican presidential nomination. "So there's Dad in the hospital waiting room, his ear glued to the radio, listening to the results. The nurse comes in and says, 'Mister Carmichael, I want to tell you that you're the father of—' and he says, 'Shhhh! Be quiet! I'm listening!' So even right at the start I'm second banana. They even took their time finding me a name. A couple of weeks went by before they got around to naming me."

At his mother's urging he began piano lessons early; but what notice his father took was hard to measure. "You'd say you were gonna do something and he'd just stand back and watch, see how you did it; wouldn't comment whether it was good or bad. Let you fall on your face, if that was what you were gonna do. Like playing poker, he never gave anything away. He used to come to some of my piano recitals. I was generally very good, so he was generally proud. He'd express that by taking me around to other people's homes like Exhibit A, to play the piano. My mother, of course, thought I walked on water, because I was this classical pianist, and she respected that." But when, as a teenager, the prodigy discovered girls and other adolescent diversions and began to move away, "Well, it just blew her bubble."

To Bill Wheatley, the boys' relations with their father incorporated a strong need for approval, a fine edge of never-quite-explicit competitiveness, and a no less obvious warmth. "When all three of them were together I felt real affection. They communicated in this special kind of language they shared." Both sons acknowledged and understood their father's self-centered inability to see them and their lives through any prism but his own; his innate, too often ill-concealed, sense of competitiveness. Each found his way of dealing with it.

"Because Hoagy senior was quiet, with that laid-back Indiana quality, people could misread him, fail to see the steel in him, the persistence and perfectionism," said Wheatley. That extended to most other areas of his life: to dress and grooming, for example. He cut his own hair, and for a long time that of his two sons. He was careful in selecting his wardrobe, even to wearing only hand-sewn trousers and designing his own variations on the ascot-and-shirt "Clarney." Inviting family, friends, and colleagues to a restaurant, however exclusive, he often insisted on advising his guests what to eat and in what quantity, even going so far as to arrogate all ordering to himself.

"At one point," said Wheatley, "we went out to shoot some film footage of him on the Thunderbird golf course, there at Palm Springs. His house was right on the edge of the course, and it was all very scenic, with the mountains in the background. 'C'mon, Dad, let's find a spot,' Hoagy Bix keeps saying. But of course right away his father's the director, shaking his head. 'No, no, no. We don't wanna do it there. Come on over here and I'll show you where we'll do it.' So they walk around awhile until his father finds the right spot. And you know—this is the important part, I think—the spot he found was in fact the right one.

"That's just it: he had this way of being *right* about things. Maybe that's what got people's backs up. Lots of people, most people maybe, just don't take to the idea of some guy, some busybody outsider, telling them what they should and shouldn't do, and then having the nerve to be right about it."[26]

✢   ✢   ✢

As the 1970s got under way, Carmichael seemed to have ever less to do. Sportscaster Chris Schenkel, a fellow-Hoosier and lifelong fan, got him a shot on ABC's *American Sportsmen* series, being filmed cane-pole fishing in an Indiana river. But the small burst of publicity it generated subsided quickly.

Hoagy returned to painting, which he'd first taken up in the early 1940s. His 1941 *Miami Skyline With Thunderheads* established him as a talented craftsman, particularly remarkable for having been self-taught. The cover of a later edition of the Carmichael children's songs, published after his death as *Raffles and Other Singing Stories*, features a vividly stylized still-life, a San Francisco rooftop scene painted in 1952 as *Crusaders: Richard the Lion-Hearted*. According to the caption, Hoagy

> did not see the air conditioning and other pipes as such. Instead his imagination transformed them into a group of medieval knights in armor conferring beside a turreted wall with a watchful sentry on guard . . . Although Hoagy never studied art he often captured things he saw, real or fancied, on canvass [*sic*].[27]

If his 1950s *For Sunlovers* and *Sunlight on Brick: The Charing Cross House* seem somewhat pedestrian in their rendering of various aspects of his Holmby Hills life, *Serenade to a Blue Nose*, depicting a guitar-playing ceramic figure, a scotch bottle, and a bottle opener, displays a healthy feeling for abstraction. A study of the young Hoagy Bix treats the boy in a plain, even stark manner reminiscent of the midwestern archetypes of Grant Wood. *Out of This World* portrays a "Persian Garden scene."

From 1969 to 1972 Carmichael corresponded with Miss Clara Hangary, a lifelong resident of New Albany, at Indiana's southeast corner near Louisville. His aim: to assemble a body of information and photographs about the venerable "Constitution Elm" at nearby Corydon, the original state capital. The framers of the state constitution did their work in the tree's capacious shade.

He visited New Albany, spent time with Miss Hangary and other townsfolk, examining photos and inspecting the site. "All that remained," he wrote in a brochure accompanying his painting of the elm, "was most of the trunk and a couple of feet of the huge branches, all of which had the bark removed and creosoted to prevent decay."

As conceived and executed by Carmichael over three years, the Constitution Elm is a stark presence; though represented in high summer, it is without leaves. "Leaves come and go," he wrote, "and in this case would have been so abundant that they would have dominated the entire scene." The trunk and naked branches "should be seen to give the viewer a more striking display of greatness and a knowledge of what age has done." Still an imposing image at five feet by seven, *Constitution Elm* hangs today in Indiana University's Memorial Union building.[28]

On the evidence of these oil paintings, Hoagy Carmichael seems a natural peer to such musician-artists as jazz clarinetist Charles "Pee Wee" Russell, similarly self-taught, and even the drummer George Wettling, an accomplished student and disciple of the jazz-influenced abstractionist Stuart Davis.

❊   ❊   ❊

An emphatic reminder of time passing, and loss adumbrated, came in mid-1970 in the form of what seemed, on its face, a signal honor. Louis Armstrong was due to turn seventy—at least according to his "official" birth date of July 4, 1900—and a nationwide series of celebrations was scheduled. Festivities began in earnest the hot, humid evening of July 3, with a mass, all-star tribute concert staged at the Los Angeles Shrine Auditorium, an event which, in the mind of at least one reporter, "stole the thunder from the larger affair."[29]

Despite a noticeable lack of air-conditioning in the cavernous hall, a capacity crowd of 6,700 fans turned out to listen and cheer as trumpeters spanning several generations—from West Coast pioneer George Orendorff to Teddy Buckner to Clark Terry—joined Benny Carter, Matty Matlock, Barney Bigard, Nappy Lamare, Louis Bellson, Tyree Glenn, Sarah Vaughan, Ray Brown, Red Callender, and Joe Marsala, among dozens of others, including visiting Frenchmen Maxim Saury and Claude Luter, all paying musical tribute to the one and only Louis Armstrong.

Days earlier, as the Association of Southern California Jazz Clubs and producer-coordinator Floyd Levin made their preparations, word had gone out: as host Louis especially wanted his old friend and colleague of years past, Hoagy Carmichael. Not surprisingly, the request met with something less than universal enthusiasm in some quarters.

"That was the time of the Black Panthers," said Hoagy Bix. "Black Power, and all that. There was a lot of pressure on Louis to get a black guy in there instead, you know, but Louis stood his ground: said this wasn't about race, it was about music. He wanted Hoagy, and if it wasn't Hoagy he wasn't gonna do this thing. And that was all there was to it."

In the end, though officially sharing hosting honors with California disc jockey Benson Curtis, Carmichael had the best moments. When a delegation of admirers brought out a white wicker rocking chair, Armstrong did a broad double take. "I ain't got to that stage yet," he quipped.

"Try it for size," Hoagy suggested. "You know, Pops, you've slimmed down. Lost some weight or something?"

"Naw," Armstrong shot back. "I just take Swiss Kriss every night. My slogan is 'Leave it all behind me.'"

When Hoagy remarked that he was some months older than Louis, and "perhaps I should be sittin' in the rockin' chair," Armstrong parried with "No, no—you got too much money for that."

At which point Hoagy launched into his part of an a capella vocal duet with Louis on "Rockin' Chair," pretty much as they'd done it in the OKeh studios one December day back in 1929.

Louis rose handsomely to the occasion, clearly enjoying himself, betraying no hint of the heart and kidney troubles that had already undermined the iron Armstrong constitution. Came the midnight hour, and at Hoagy's signal a giant birthday cake—eleven feet high, six tiers, weighing some eight hundred pounds, capped with a statuette of a trumpeter—was wheeled onstage. With Hoagy steadying the stepladder, Louis clambered halfway up to cut a slice, confiding to the audience that it was for trombonist Tyree Glenn: "You always want the first piece." Finally, capping it all, he delivered

"When It's Sleepy Time Down South," "Blueberry Hill," and "Hello, Dolly" with the verve of a man half his age, decisive rejection of time and change, laughter in the face of his own mortality.

Photos taken of Louis and Hoagy that night show two old comrades, in the true sense of that hoariest of expressions, having a high-spirited, all-stops-out good time, exulting in one another's company. As journalist Harvey Siders put it, "The two masters of wise-cracking asides just stood there, playing ad libsmanship, and the crowd ate it up."[30]

Little more than a year later, with the cheering still resounding in memory, Louis Armstrong was gone, and a discouraged Hoagy Carmichael had begun his lonely walk through the final, twilight decade of his own passage.

✳ *XIX* ✳

Ev'ntide

It may be that I'm a dreamer,
But I can't help feeling that some day
We'll find a world, just you wait and see,
A world of no goodbyes...
—HOAGY CARMICHAEL AND RAY GILBERT,
"A World of No Goodbyes," 1944

Slowly, reluctantly, like a piece of precision machinery turning over despite an encrustation of rust, Hoagy Carmichael's songwriting mind kept working; the melodies might be harder to find now, fewer and farther between. But he was still reaching.

Whatever they had or hadn't been, the glory days were long gone. No effort by Hoagy Bix, Nacio Herb Brown, Howie Richmond, or anyone else who still believed in Hoagy Carmichael would change that, or revive a market where none now existed.

Older Carmichael songs were still being played and recorded by artists rooted in pre-rock times. Among the best LP collections was *The Music of Hoagy Carmichael*, organized and led by Bob Wilber, a standout among the young postwar jazz traditionalists. A clarinetist, onetime protégé of New Orleans grand master Sidney Bechet, Wilber had developed the rare curved soprano saxophone into a lyrically potent second solo voice.

Bill Borden, founder-owner of the energetic little Monmouth-Evergreen label, and widely respected since his arranging days with the Claude Thornhill Orchestra, gave Wilber all the creative latitude he needed. The band was chosen with care: Bud Freeman, on tenor sax, had known Hoagy since the 1920s and recorded with him on Bix Beiderbecke's last session. Yank

Lawson, Bernie Privin, Buddy Morrow, and Lou McGarity were big band veterans whose paths had crossed Carmichael's many times. As vocalist, Wilber's and Borden's unanimous choice was Maxine Sullivan, her cool, understated style much admired among musicians since the 1930s. Musically excellent, *The Music of Hoagy Carmichael* found more favor with the critics than with the public. Though nominated for a Grammy, it lost out to a more fashionable album by Quincy Jones.

Too many of Carmichael's newer efforts, meanwhile, came out sounding as tired as their titles indicated. Anyone listening to "Chirp, Chirp, the Baby Burped" and other trivia could be forgiven for assuming the creative fires had been banked, but every now and then, just when it seemed he had nothing further to offer, the Old Music Master came up with something fresh and good.

A 1971 social afternoon with Johnny Mercer, who for all his versatility seemed to be faring little better in the marketplace himself, yielded the remarkable "Fleur de Lys." Hoagy's melody reaches for upper chordal voices in the manner of "Ballad in Blue" and "Winter Moon," as Mercer introduces some particularly imaginative bird imagery. It is by any standard a quality song, poignant and just a bit exotic—and with no discernible commercial market. To paraphrase Fred Katz's remark on hearing Carmichael's reworking of "The Sage," the time seemed strange to be writing such a song.

It was 1971, after all. Among the year's major record hits were two rock performances, "Joy to the World," performed by the rock group Three Dog Night and not to be confused with the similiarly titled Christmas carol, and "Maggie May," bawled by Rod Stewart—and Carole King's *faux*-folk "It's Too Late." There seemed little or no place for exotica such as "Fleur de Lys."

The same year saw Hoagy inducted into the newly formed Songwriters' Hall of Fame in New York, along with Duke Ellington and eight other major figures, and a letter from John W. Ryan, president of Indiana University, brought news of a singular honor: after years of Carmichael visits, financial donations, commemorative songs, and other acts of loyalty, his alma mater had decided to award him an honorary doctorate in music. The ceremony, scheduled for April 16, 1972, would coincide with dedication of the university's long-awaited new Musical Arts Center, which his largesse had helped build.[1]

He took some weeks to reply, and when he did, on January 12, his tone was at best equivocal. He'd read Ryan's letter, he said, "congratulated myself and rather roughly placed your letter under a pile of other things more urgent to attend to (by hand) during the holiday season, such as Xmas cards, etc. Which reminds me that I had you on my list but when I got to the R's I had used up all my cards."[2]

A curious and cavalier statement for a letter to the president of Indiana University. Yet perhaps it is only too comprehensible, given the honoree's state of mind at the time. Hoagy Bix, especially, knew the frustration of trying to offset his father's ennui. He'd never let up trying to kick-start things, get "Dad" interested in anything to break the inertia; but "sometimes it seemed there was nothing at all you could say to him to move him four feet—even one foot—in any other direction." In his January 12 letter, Carmichael does admit to being "deeply honored" and promises to "certainly be there, God willing, and please express my thanks to the committee of initiation."

Come April, he was in Bloomington, accepting his doctorate alongside German-born musicologist Willi Apel, opera tenor James McCracken, and conductors Izler Solomon, Margaret Hillis, and Mark Hindsley. The citation hailed "the force of his creative urge, combined with the versatility of his talents," singling out fourteen songs, among them "Star Dust," "Georgia on My Mind," and even "Chimes of Indiana," several of the movies, his two books, and the *Johnny Appleseed Suite*, identified as "a salute to Indiana's folk history."

Then it was back to California, the days of sun-washed indolence passing ever more slowly. "He didn't know how to get off his butt," said Hoagy Bix, still exasperated at the thought. "Take some of that energy, Dad, and *do* something with it. Not all day and all night long: you don't have to cut your ear off for it just to prove your dedication. But don't go around saying, or believing, your life's not worth living. Go out and institute something, anything."

Why not resume correspondence with fellow–Bent Eagle Wad Allen, whose most recent letters had gone unanswered? "Aw, Wad's living in the past," came the dismissive retort. But he, too, dwelt in the past, doted on it, reminisced constantly about his lost early years.

More than once, the son suggested endowing a chair in his father's name at UCLA. Or getting him to teach a course, conduct a master class in songwriting. "It would have been such a natural. Right down Sunset Boulevard, nine miles from his place, no freeway driving. Home for lunch. They would have given him what he needed: a room, a piano, two or three students. Or have him come in once a month and lecture, explain how he found all those weird chords; answer questions. 'How do you do this?' 'Why did you do that?' Easy. He wouldn't have had to lift a finger.

"But no: he just passed it off, pissed it away. 'Nah, I don't want to do that.' Never gave it a thought. Used to absolutely frost my ass."

Things reached critical mass one early 1970s evening in New York, when he met Hoagy Bix and some mutual friends for dinner at Jimmy Weston's popular East 52nd Street restaurant. A piano, guitar, and bass trio was playing standards in a corner, and "as usual, Dad got up from dinner and walked over. They recognized him right off, and the piano player got the idea: 'Time for me to get up and let Carmichael sit down.'"

"Dad went right into his stuff—instead of 'Blue Moon' and the rest it was now gonna be 'Ole Buttermilk Sky.' He got through that song and maybe one more before realizing to his dismay that the room wasn't quieting down the way rooms usually did when he performed. Nobody knew he was there. Nobody noticed or gave a damn. And right there—you could see it on his face—he decided, 'Well, to hell with this.' Got up, mid-tune, and you could hear him audibly say, 'Well, if they don't care, I'll be damned if I'm gonna play for 'em.' And he came back to his table."[3]

Back in California there were lunches and dinners at Chasen's or Scandia, golfing days at Thunderbird, bibulous high jinks with such old pals as fellow-Hoosier Phil Harris. And much too much scotch. Bob Wilber recalled playing a Thunderbird date with Lawson, Bob Haggart, and the rest of what was by then attracting attention as the "World's Greatest Jazz Band," and being alerted that two club members were "born troublemakers." At a private party some weeks before, his hosts warned, "these two drunken guys gate-crashed and upset everybody. I hope nothing like that happens tonight."

Wilber promptly forgot the admonition. Dinner over, they were setting up the bandstand when the saxophonist noticed pianist Ralph Sutton "in an unusually convivial mood." He'd encountered Harris in the bar: Martinis, wine, and extrovert bonhomie had worked their mischief, and Sutton, it seemed, would be pretty much *hors de combat* for the evening. They kicked things off anyway, Haggart's bass and Gus Johnson's drums laying out the time.

"I was doing my solo on Hoagy's *One Morning in May*," Wilber recalled later. "It sounded a little empty without Ralph's usual brilliant accompaniment, but suddenly I heard some very strange chords behind me. [They] were right, but they didn't sound like Sutton at all. I looked around, and there was Hoagy Carmichael sitting at the piano, his head weaving from side to side, obviously four sheets to the wind. He looked up sheepishly and said, 'Ish shat okay, man? I wash jush tryin' to help.' "[4]

Carmichael's need to control every situation, and his reported tightness with a buck, made for more than a few stories making the rounds of Palm Springs and Las Vegas in those days. "We'd go out to dinner," said Nacio Herb Brown Jr., "and the waiter would bring ice water. Now I liked ice water, liked it with my meal. But he'd call the waiter over and say, 'Get all the ice water off the table.' Or he'd say, 'Sam, I'm gonna order a steak. Let's split it: I'll take half and you take half.' And we'd even each have half a salad."[5]

Vignettes, the small observations of others, form a telling composite portrait.

NACIO HERB BROWN JR.: "Sometimes we'd be out somewhere, and he'd introduce us to people. You could tell he hated to say, 'This is Nacio Herb Brown Jr.' Instead it was just, 'I want you to meet the Browns.' Didn't want to say the name, or acknowledge that my father had been a songwriter too, a really famous one. He couldn't deal with that."

RANDY: "There were still some good times. Like one Christmas Day, when Johnny and Ginger Mercer came over. Dad's sitting on the piano bench, with Johnny right next to him facing out. And they do *two hours*, nonstop, every song they ever wrote and everybody else ever wrote. Right off the tops of their heads, ad lib. Nobody misses a lyric, nobody misses a note. Everything's perfect, and they're laughing and carryin' on, having the best time."

BILL WELLMAN: "It seemed like he always had some cause he was try-ing to further . . . One time it was telephone poles. He was trying to outlaw telephone poles. He said, 'They're ugly, they're a blight on this beautiful country.' He had a petition, and he had lots of names and every-thing."

HOAGY BIX: "Weeks would go by and I wouldn't hear from him. I'd call him, and we'd have a conversation, and I'd be trying to boost him up, telling him, 'C'mon, Dad; do this, or do that. This sounds like a lot of fun. Why don't you give it a try?' "

BILL WHEATLEY: "There was a point, during the seventies, when Hoagy Bix worked for a while out in Pittsburgh, on the *Mister Rogers' Neighborhood*

TV show. I got the impression that his father just vaguely knew where he was . . . That disappointed him, because he was really proud of working on the show. The son knew everything about his father's accomplishments, while the old man seemed oblivous to his."

And, too, the passing of time was bringing its own inevitable necrology, a growing roll call of those who had inspired Hoagy and his generation: Louis Armstrong in 1971; Clancy Hayes, composer of "The Witch Watch Song" and "Huggin' and Chalkin'," the following year; Gene Krupa and Eddie Condon in 1973. On May 24, 1974, the seemingly indestructible Duke Ellington succumbed to lung cancer; the next years claimed, seemingly in rapid succession, singers Lee Wiley and Connee Boswell, cornetist Bobby Hackett, and, least believable of all, Johnny Mercer.

Alec Wilder's monumental *American Popular Song*, published in 1972 and quickly hailed as definitive on its subject, declared Carmichael "the most talented, inventive, sophisticated, and jazz oriented of all the great craftsmen." Wilder, himself a composer of distinction, expressed surprise that after *Walk With Music* Hoagy never again tried to write for the Broadway stage. "I have a hunch that he simply wasn't interested in anything less than writing unattached, isolated, independent great songs," he wrote, concluding that "pop music is the richer for his decision to stay out of the theater."[6]

New generations of musicians kept discovering—or rediscovering—the joys of Carmichael songs. On November 17, 1976, New York jazz presenter Jack Kleinsinger staged *A Jazz Portrait of Hoagy Carmichael*, featuring vocalist Helen Merrill, pianist Jimmy Rowles, and other notable figures. The following May 22 brought *One Morning in May*, a Carmichael evening in Washington as part of the Smithsonian Institution's Popular Song Series, with ex–Ellington singer Joya Sherrill, pianist-vocalist Max Morath, and guitarist-entertainer Marty Grosz, all backed by an all-star band including pianist Dick Hyman.

A 1978 appearance, in tandem with Hoagy Bix, on Fred Rogers's *Old Friends, New Friends* public television show afforded a look at the often tense relationship between Carmichael *père et fils*. "His life is like a corridor," Hoagy Bix said of his father, "a long corridor, with doors in it. And you are behind one of those doors, and other people are behind one of those doors," each representing another part of his life.

"And always at the end of that corridor is his music. Every once in a while that person, my father, comes and opens up my door and does something with me, or opens up another door and does something with [one of the] other people. But you know, you always know, the main event, the big thing in his life, is whatever is at the end of that corridor—and that is a truth that doesn't always feel good."

What of the son's accomplishments as a widely admired designer and manufacturer of handcrafted fishing rods? *A Master's Guide to Building a Bamboo Fly Rod*, his book on the craft, had become standard reading; he had produced a widely praised documentary film honoring his mentor, Everett Garrison. Within this specialized, arcane but quality-driven field he was a celebrity, a figure honored in his own right. Time and hard work had shown him that he, too, could "create something from nothing," as his father did with music. Couldn't the elder Carmichael take pride in that?

The answer, apparently, was no. "He hasn't seen [any of] that. I can't get him to come east and spend a weekend with me in Vermont or anything, because—well, he's settled in what he does. Doesn't want to travel. But he *will* travel to go to the Olympics."

In a particularly revealing sequence filmed in a Palm Springs cocktail lounge, Carmichael senior sits at an out-of-tune spinet piano, chording through "Small Fry," while exhorting Hoagy Bix to sing the lyrics. When the son falters—as anyone not immediately conversant with the lyric might—the father's expression, manner, even body language, fairly shout at him, "You incompetent ninny!"

✻   ✻   ✻

Little by little, Carmichael's health began to deteriorate. Cataract surgery diminished his eyesight, curtailing his ability to play golf. Traveling, even to his beloved Bloomington, had become a chore. "Thank you so much for your personal invitation to attend the coming festivities in honor of Hoagy's 75th birthday," sister Georgia wrote to the university president in October of 1974. "However, neither Hoagy nor myself can attend, sorry to say. He is still having quite bothersome eye problems—hence my having to answer all correspondence."[7]

In early 1979 came what seemed a heaven-sent reprieve. Impresario George Wein's Newport Jazz Festival was planning a star-studded Carnegie

Hall concert for June 27, honoring Hoagy in his eightieth year. National Public Radio would record the event for a two-hour eightieth-birthday special, to be aired that November 22. The office of Mayor Ed Koch declared June 27 "Hoagy Carmichael Day" in New York, with presentation of a plaque at City Hall. ASCAP announced a lifetime achievement award, to be presented onstage by the organization's president, erstwhile Carmichael lyricist Stanley Adams. Several record companies, including RCA Victor, planned commemorative LP releases.

"I'm a bit disappointed in myself," he confessed to *Washington Post* writer Hollie West before the concert. "I know that I could've accomplished a hell of a lot more . . . I could write anything, any time I wanted to. But I let other things get in the way." For a long time, he said, his songs had allowed him to live the good life, but the rock revolution had "just knocked me out. I just quit almost on account of rock 'n roll . . . I haven't had a hit since 'In the Cool, Cool, Cool of the Evening' . . . I've just been floating around in the breeze, I guess."[8]

The Stardust Road—A Hoagy Carmichael Jubilee was a triumph, a signal moment in the composer's latter career. Headliners included singers Kay Starr and Jackie Cain (the latter appeared solo, without husband and partner Roy Kral) and pianist-singers Dave Frishberg and Max Morath. Bob Crosby made a genial, if occasionally bumbling, host, fronting an edition of his Bobcats co-led by trumpeter Yank Lawson and bassist Bob Haggart, and featuring fellow-brassman Billy Butterfield, saxophonists Wilber and Eddie Miller, guitarist-singer Marty Grosz, pianist Dave McKenna, trombonists Vic Dickenson and George Masso, and drummer Bob Rosengarden.

They swung happily through several Carmichael instrumentals, including "Riverboat Shuffle" and "March of the Hoodlums." At one point during the latter number, Hoagy leaned over to Joe Lang, a young jazz fan seated farther over in the second row. "Did I write that?" he asked. Assured by Lang that he had indeed written "Hoodlums," he laughed out loud. "Y'know, I don't remember a note of the damn thing." But in Lang's recollection, "he seemed to be enjoying himself thoroughly."[9]

Trumpeter Jimmy Maxwell brought Armstrong-inspired majesty to "Ev'ntide." Dave Frishberg revived "Lyin' to Myself," with a silver-toned assist from Billy Butterfield. Max Morath's reading of "Moon Country" struck an appealing balance between sentiment and stoicism, and Kay Starr brought an appropriate sense of drama to "Washboard Blues." At the end, after all the singers and instrumentalists had joined trumpeter Maxwell for a rousing, Louis-inspired "Jubilee," Crosby motioned the guest of honor to join him onstage. Hoagy needed no coaxing. Sitting down beside Mike Renzi at the piano, he went through an impromptu performance of his Bix-flavored confection "Piano Pedal Rag." Then, all but overcome with emotion, he walked from musician to musician, stumbling over words of thanks for each one, finally giving up and blurting out a rapturous "Yeah! Here we are! We had a chance to do it!"

Pointing first to old friend Eddie Miller, then the rest of the band, he looked out over the audience and announced: "Y'know, that's a great orchestra. Everybody's great—" then a quick chuckle and, almost sotto voce: "I'm great, too."

As one, 2,800 souls in the packed house rose to their feet in cheering, roaring, seemingly endless agreement.

Even as this memorable night was unfolding, more honors were on the way. British poet-playwright Adrian Mitchell had read and admired *The Stardust Road* during his undergraduate days at Oxford. After attracting attention with a body of outstanding and unconventional work, including an English-language adaptation of the Peter Weiss *Marat/Sade*, he returned to Carmichael's book. Working with a small British theatre company, the Wakefield Tricycle, he opened out *The Stardust Road* into what he called a "drama with music."

Under the rather cumbersome title *Hoagy, Bix and Wolfgang Beethoven Bunkhaus*, it opened on October 18, 1980, at the newly remodeled Indiana Theatre, the very building in which Bix Beiderbecke and Frank Trumbauer had joined Paul Whiteman's orchestra, with Hoagy Carmichael in attendance, thirty-three years before.[10]

Not surprisingly, Mitchell found the Book Nook crowd and their Dadaist high jinks particularly appealing, linked in his mind to the lineage of British humor typified by Edward Lear, the Goon Shows, and even the zanier side of the Beatles. It runs through *Bunkhaus*, focusing on the three-way friendship of Bix, Monk, and the young, as-yet-unformed Carmichael. Lengthy chunks of Moenkhaus verse and playlets, lifted from *The Vagabond*, jostle and bump in the script alongside delicately purple *Stardust Road* passages— all to the dismay of most critics. In one reviewer's words, "What sounds good in the mind coming off the pages . . . seems occasionally stilted and self-consciously 'poetic' coming out of the mouths of actors."[11]

Bunkhaus moved on to Los Angeles, where it opened January 15, 1981, in a far more lavish production at the Mark Taper Forum. Hoagy, visibly diminished by illness and encroaching blindness, attended opening night, sitting onstage as the cast—including cabaret singers Amanda McBroom and Neva Small, Broadway star-in-the-making Harry Groener, Frishberg, and guitarist Howard Alden—played and sang his songs.

To Frishberg, widely respected as a songwriter-performer greatly inspired by Carmichael, play and music emphasized

> the same kind of thing that I dwell on all the time: the days of lost camaraderie and lost moments, and how everything was different back then . . . I don't even know how much of that is real, and how much is imagined in my own head, but I feel pretty driven by those sentiments myself. When I start to write a song I immediately slip into that mode. I tried to write a song about the future once, and it turned out to be nothing but people in the future reminiscing about the past."[12]

Hoagy, Bix and Wolfgang Beethoven Bunkhaus played at the Taper for two months. Critics praised the music (nineteen Carmichael songs, plus "Singin' the Blues" and other numbers associated with Bix) more than Mitchell's play. It struck Duane Byrge, writing for the *Hollywood Reporter*, as "one protracted *Happy Days*. Like a note held too long that spills into measures and disrupts other chords, so too does the constant prolonged emphasis on this period of Carmichael's life disrupt and distort our grasp of Carmichael's artistic progression."[13]

In England, where *Bunkhaus* had begun, yet another project was waiting in the wings. Singer Georgie Fame, a Carmichael fan since boyhood, teamed with Annie Ross, still riding high on her Lambert, Hendricks, and Ross popularity, for *In Hoagland, 1981*, an album of Carmichael songs done with a fresh, contemporary approach. Backed by a tightly arranged small big band, they reconceived "The Old Music Master" as a rhythm-and-blues feature in the Fats Domino manner, complete with muscular tenor sax solo. If "Georgia on My Mind" echoed Ray Charles, and "Lazy River" the Las Vegas shuffle of Louis Prima, "Two Sleepy People" came off memorably, an affectionate vocal duet over light-footed bossa nova rhythm.

A Carmichael rarity, the 1943 "Drip Drop," gets a lusty R&B workout in the album, and Annie Ross combines intelligence and bittersweet longing on "I Get Along Without You Very Well," backed only by Martin Kershaw's guitar. Synthesizer and electronic keyboards are used to sometimes telling effect—especially on an effective "Star Dust," also featuring Peter King's boppy alto sax.

Hoagy himself appears briefly, singing "Rockin' Chair" to his own piano accompaniment, while explaining how a couple of characteristic figures found their way into his recorded performances of the song.

In Hoagland ends with its title song, Georgie Fame's contemplative, heartfelt valentine to the composer:

> Play a little song for me
> Take me to where I should be
> No one seems to care for me
> Except you, Daddy . . .
>
> Won't somebody change the key?
> Turn me loose and set me free,
> Hoagland's where I ought to be
> I hear you, Daddy . . .

Though it received nothing like the critical or popular reception it deserved, *In Hoagland* stands up well today as a particularly successful attempt to recast Carmichael's songs in a manner familiar and appealing to latter-day, rock-oriented audiences.

❖   ❖   ❖

In early 1981, amid a burst of new music business attention, came an offer that Hoagy, delicate health or no, was not about to refuse. CBS was offering to send a camera crew to Palm Springs and film him in a local theatre for an hour-long prime-time special, singing and talking about his songs with country diva Crystal Gayle. The pair would then introduce Ray Charles, reprising his hit record of "Georgia on My Mind."

"Hoagy had been sick awhile and we knew it," Crystal Gayle recalled. "I could tell when I first saw him that he wasn't feeling good. Sometimes he seemed to be in real pain. But when that camera came on, there was absolutely no way of telling that. He was a real pro, a born entertainer. You could watch him for just a few seconds and you'd think, 'Here's a man who loves what he does, loves life.' You could tell it through his music."[14]

Born in Kentucky but raised in southern Indiana, the country singer—younger sister of "Coal Miner's Daughter" Loretta Lynn—"was very nervous at first, really in awe of Hoagy. I kept screwing things up, then apologizing to him, but it never once bothered him; he'd just kinda laugh and shrug it off, while all the while making sure I was comfortable and at ease. It didn't matter if I blew a line, or dropped a lyric: nothing was going to go really wrong. And of course it didn't."

For their moment together on *Country Comes Home,* the two performers sat on stools, chatting easily and performing a running medley including "Lazybones," "Ole Buttermilk Sky," and "Lazy River." They took frequent breaks, she said, allowing Carmichael to rest and conserve his energies.

"Miz Gayle," as Hoagy addressed her, was entranced with her partner's singing. "He didn't think he had much of a voice, but there was such character there, I thought. He knew how he wrote those songs, and how they should feel and sound. For me it was a special, unforgettable moment, a wonderful experience."

It led, eighteen years later, to *Crystal Gayle Sings the Heart and Soul of Hoagy Carmichael,* a lovingly wrought CD featuring the singer on fifteen Carmichael favorites backed by full orchestra. Fellow–country star Willie Nelson, whose own records of "Star Dust" and "Georgia on My Mind" had made the charts in 1978, joins her in an affectionate duet on "Two Sleepy People."

Country Comes Home turned out to be Hoagy's last public appearance. He weakened noticeably over the summer and autumn, and by the time Hoagy Bix and Randy arrived to spend the Christmas holidays, "it was clear to everyone that he was going downhill." There were urinary tract problems, said Hoagy Bix; prostate cancer had been diagnosed. "He was just getting weaker, and moving along those lines pretty quickly. By Christmas he was—well, an old man."

He seldom wanted for attention. "Dottie Quack," now his wife, hovered nearby, constantly ministering to his needs. Hoagy Bix and Randy kept him talking, engaged. If a friend or two dropped by he'd always rise to the conversation. "He enjoyed us being there," his elder son recalled. "Took everything in. Was part of the gang, as long as it was in front of his chair. Didn't move around much; just sat there, sometimes reading, sometimes talking, but mostly just looking out at people."

Something, some vital spark, had quietly winked out. At one point during the holiday weekend he started talking about Eva Ford. Had to see her, he said. Repeated it twice, three times. But Dad, don't you know that Eva's got a family of her own now, hasn't been part of your household for years? No matter: he wanted Eva, and only Eva would do.

Hoagy Bix: "It wasn't any kind of casual thing. It wasn't 'Wouldn't it be fun to see Eva.' Anything like that. Not at all, not a bit. He wanted, really needed, her there, categorically. So we called for a car service, and she came. It may have been Christmas Day itself."

Next day, December 26, they ate dinner together as a family: Hoagy, Dottie, the two sons, Hoagy Bix's fiancée, perhaps an additional friend or two—and, deeply welcome, Eva Ford Chatman. After dinner the two of them, Hoagy and Eva, sat and talked. In later years, memory dimmed by time and illness, Eva seemed unable to dredge up specifics of that exquisitely private moment. "But I know they got into some depth" was Hoagy Bix's recollection.

Leaving for the night, the son's last image was of his father, motionless in a living room chair, nodding his head as he listened again and again to George Shearing's new record of "Lazy River," played in a style deliberately evocative of 1930s keyboard master Bob Zurke.

✳   ✳   ✳

Shortly after nine the following morning, Hoagy Bix and Randy returned to find their father, seemingly renewed, up and about, rustling around the bathroom in his robe and looking forward to watching a New York Jets football game that afternoon. After greeting his sons, he turned and shuffled back into his bedroom to get dressed.

"We had a nurse there for him during the days," said Hoagy Bix. "She went right into the room after him—but after a minute or so came running back into the living room, really upset, saying something like, 'There's something wrong with Mister C! You better come quick.' Dottie went in with her, and in a second she came out and said—or somebody said— 'Call emergency! Call Eisenhower [Medical Center]!'

"Within seven minutes they were there: ran in and started jumping on his chest, putting tubes in, all that kind of horrible stuff. They put him in the van—I mean the ambulance—and I remember one of the guys saying, 'It doesn't look good,' before they drove off. In that moment I think I knew, just *knew*, I'd never see him again. I remember going out on the lawn and just *screaming*, 'Don't, don't, don't bring him back!' "

On Sunday morning, December 27, 1981, at exactly 10:22 A.M., Hoagland Howard Carmichael, composer of "Star Dust" and myriad other beloved songs, actor, and embodiment of a once-upon-a-time American dream, was pronounced dead of "cardiac problems" in the emergency room at Eisenhower Medical Center.

✳   ✳   ✳

Now, at last, he would come home to Bloomington to stay. Indiana would welcome him, honor him as it had in life—and, when all the words had been spoken and the songs played, it would be Indiana that laid him to rest.

He'd last been there in 1972, to receive his honorary doctorate and dedicate the new Musical Arts Center. It seemed only fitting that his memorial should be in the building's grand foyer, built with his donations.

Monday, January 4, 1982, dawned bitter cold in Bloomington, but couldn't keep away throngs of family members, friends, and admirers crowding the grand foyer to say farewell. The three hundred folding chairs filled rapidly; an additional two hundred onlookers lined the rear and sides. The radio and TV networks were there, alongside A-team representatives from newspapers and magazines. Even on this wintry day, giant sprays of flowers sent by President Ronald Reagan, Senator Barry Goldwater, and members of the Kappa Sigma fraternity limned the coffin in brilliant summer color.

Voice barely audible at times, Wad Allen wiped away a tear as he remembered the long-ago hot jazz days and giddy evenings at the Book Nook. "Hoag," he said softly, "you said so long, and it won't be long until I'll be seeing you." Chancellor Herman Wells, a classmate, told of

> sitting by a swimming pool in hot and steaming Lagos, Nigeria, at the end of the day, talking with the young pool attendant, a handsome Nigerian. I looked up at the sky filled with fleecy white clouds just as the sun was coming down behind the dark tropical foliage, and I said to this lad, "That is a buttermilk sky, the kind that a friend of mine in college wrote a song about. You probably don't know about buttermilk skies." Then, smiling with smug delight, he broke into a full rendition of "Ole Buttermilk Sky."

A faculty band, including tuba virtuoso Harvey Phillips, trumpeter Dominic Spera, and music department head David Baker, played a medley of Carmichael songs. Hoagy himself had asked that "Serenade to Gabriel" be sung at his memorial, and voice professor Roger Havranek obliged. The emotional climax, inevitably, came with soprano Sylvia McNair's single chorus of "Star Dust," with Charles H. Webb, dean of the School of Music, at the piano. Her voice soared and drifted out, up, suffusing the moment in the richly nostalgic glow of melody and memory.

Hoagland Howard Carmichael was laid to rest in Bloomington's Rose Hill Cemetery alongside his father and mother, and near the grave of little Joanne, whose loss so many long years before had marked him for life.

Among the many tributes in newspapers and magazines, on radio and television, a few stood out. Hoagy, said the Bloomington *Herald-Telephone*,

> was inducted into the Monroe County Hall of Fame last summer. But where is Hoagy Carmichael Lane in Bloomington? Where is Stardust Square? Where are the reminders to Bloomington and Indiana University that something that originated here sprinkled stardust on the lives of millions of Americans in a dreary time: the depression of the '30s, the horror of worldwide warfare in the '40s?"

In one emotionally charged eulogy, second cousin George Wade Carmichael noted that tears at the service "came slowly and quietly. These were tears not known since Vietnam. They were not the tears of one who has lost so much as they were the tears of one who understands and can do nothing. Move on. I hear you, Hoagy."

Perhaps the most affecting words of all, and the most revealing, came from a carefully restrained Hoagy Bix. "Our family," he wrote to Herman Wells later that week, "is one that has, for the most part, centered around one man, my father, and now that he is gone there is a feeling of leaderlessness and a belief that somehow, by some form of everlasting magic, he will come back. It is not true, we know that, but I can tell you that I find it almost unbelievable that I cannot pick up the phone and call my own Dad."[15]

Hoagy didn't die, the memoirist of *The Stardust Road* might have written. I can hear him from here, hear him in the songs and their images, idealized echoes of an American past forever longed for, remembered even if never personally experienced; the sights and fragrances they evoke; even the character, so deceptively simple, he came to portray so effectively in public life.

How fitting that it should have been Duncan Schiedt, a Hoosier poet living comfortably in the austere vestments of a historian, who found the words everyone longed to utter. "As this is being written," he reflected, "snow and ice grip his beloved Indiana and much of the nation. For a moment, at his passing . . . cold fingers must have touched the heart of music lovers everywhere, as 'our' Hoagy, a supremely mortal American figure, joined the pantheon of his departed colleagues in immortality."

"But surely, as it always must, the sense of grief gives way to a warming of the spirit, as we look back on a long life of creativity, and a legacy of musical production that transcends the sorrow of the moment. We are, in the end, happy to have lived in his time."[16]

And through his music, it need only be added, his time has been granted the benison of eternal life.

NOTES

Abbreviations Used in the Notes

ATM Archives of Traditional Music, Indiana University, Bloomington

IU Indiana University, Bloomington

JB Hoagy Carmichael, *Jazzbanders: A Rhapsody in Mud*. Unpublished manuscript on file at ATM. Chapters individually paginated. References are given as chapter/page: e.g., I/3.

SIW Hoagy Carmichael with Stephen Longstreet, *Sometimes I Wonder* (New York: Farrar, Straus & Giroux, 1965)

SR Hoagy Carmichael, *The Stardust Road* (New York: Rinehart, 1946)

Chapter I

1. *Indianapolis News*, December 16, 1902, quoted in Sylvia C. Hendricks, "Indiana: 60 Years on Center," *Indianapolis Star Magazine*, March 7, 1982.
2. Duncan Schiedt, *The Jazz State of Indiana* (Pittsboro, Ind.: Self-published, 1977), p. vi.
3. Some information from Jim Walsh, "It's Always Moonlight on the Wabash," *Indianapolis Star Magazine,* December 9, 1951.
4. *SR*, pp. 93–94.
5. Harry Orchard, letter to Robert D. Hamontre, dated May 3, 1983, ATM. Carmichael himself says (in *SIW*, p. 6) he was named after Harry Hoagland, a railroad surveyor, who was boarding at the home of some Carmichael relatives.
6. *SIW*, p. 4.
7. Florence Carmichael quote from Kathleen Van Nuys, "Hoagy Has Warm Spot in Heart for Indiana," *Indianapolis Times*, November 18, 1962. Hoagy Carmichael quote from *SIW*, p. 7.
8. *SIW*, p. 5.
9. Harry Orchard, letter to Robert D. Hamontre, dated May 3, 1983, ATM.
10. *JB*, I/3.
11. The exact address has been open to some dispute. In a letter to James T. Maher dated June 7, 1960, administrative assistant F. L. Templeton of the Bloomington

Metropolitan Schools cites it as 214 North Dunn Street. But Bradley D. Cook, IU reference specialist and photograph curator, notes emphatically that the Carmichael home was at 214 *South* Dunn Street.

12. *JB*, I/3.

13. Bradley D. Cook, IU reference specialist and photograph curator, offers the following: "The Jordan River was [indeed] named after ex-President David Starr Jordan; [it] was known by that name during Hoagy's days, and had been since 1891. The previous name was 'Spanker's Branch' (unknown who Spanker was) [but] very few people knew it by that name. It was not officially named the Jordan River until the Board of Trustees did so on Aug. 6, 1994. Most of the time you can get across the Jordan without getting your knees wet. And in some places without getting your ankles wet."

14. *JB*, I/7.

15. *SIW*, p. 8.

16. *JB*, I/12.

17. Harry Owens, *Sweet Leilani: The Story Behind the Song* (Pacific Palisades, Calif.: Hula House, 1970), p. 7.

18. Hoagy Bix Carmichael, conversation with the author, January 27, 1999.

19. *JB*, I/12.

20. *JB*, I/9.

21. *JB*, I/9.

22. *JB*, I/13.

Chapter II

1. In 1893, student Joseph T. Giles, pressed to come up with something for the first IU Glee Club to sing at an Indiana State Oratorical Contest, had borrowed the melody of "Annie Lisle," a sentimental Scottish ballad already used by Cornell for its alma mater, and added his own text. Its highlight—or weakness, some complained—was the phrase "Gloriana, Frangipana," the "Gloriana" from a football yell, "Frangipana" from the name of a perfume then in vogue, made from a variety of jasmine. Both words were there for one reason only: they were among the few that rhymed with "Indiana." No surprise that students soon took to identifying "Hail to Old I.U." informally—and not without a certain wry affection—as "Indiana Frangiapana."

2. Correspondence between the university and the McShane foundry, dated June 15, 1905, refers to the set of eleven bells being in the key of E-major. Theoretically this is true, in that the bells describe an E-major scale, with A♮ and D added. But the range of notes, from E to F# a ninth above, would have made it impossible to play "Hail to Old I.U." in E-major (too low) or B-major (too high). The melody lies comfortably in A-major, however, with all the necessary accidentals in place.

3. *SIW*, p. 7.

4. Information from Indiana University reference specialist and photograph curator Bradley D. Cook, 1999.

5. *JB*, II/1.

6. *SIW*, p. 9.

7. Harry Orchard, letter to Robert D. Hamontre, dated May 3, 1983, ATM.

8. *JB*, I/10.

9. *JB*, II/1.

10. *JB*, II/2. The original Beta Theta Pi house no longer stands. Today two buildings, the Acacia and Alpha Tau Omega houses, straddle the same property, at the corner of South Fess and Third Street, just west of the main campus. The Acacia House parking lot now occupies the former location of the 300 block of South Fess Avenue.

11. *JB*, II/3. Though he graduated in 1914, Hanna remained in Bloomington, married in 1917, and made his home at 828 Atwater Street, directly around the corner from the Carmichaels' South Fess Street home. According to IU alumni files, he died in Akron, Ohio, August 12, 1934.

12. Pete Martin, "Star-Dust Troubadour," *Saturday Evening Post*, November 8, 1947. *SIW*, pp. 76–77.

13. *SIW*, p. 29.

14. Neil Leonard, *Jazz and the White Americans*. (Chicago: University of Chicago Press, 1962), pp. 21, 21–22 (Damrosch), 22 (statistics).

15. Predictably, among America's growing black bourgeoisie, children of physicians, academics, attorneys, and other professionals, then as now, were encouraged to attend college and direct their lives to more "respectable" callings than that of the entertainer. Invariably, religion played a major role in the lives of such families and also actively discouraged talented youngsters from pursuing a life that would find them among prostitutes, gangsters, and other *demimonde* types.

16. Booth Tarkington, *The Magnificent Ambersons* (1918; Bloomington: Indiana University Press, Library of Indiana Classics, 1989), chapter 1.

17. Kenneth Cline, "Star Dust Memories," *Indianapolis Star Magazine*, November 28, 1982.

18. It is not clear at what point "Hoagland" evolved into "Hogie" (or "Hoagie") and then into "Hoagy." Carmichael told it differently on different occasions, usually assigning baptismal responsibility to some early girlfriend. But in most reminiscences by family members and friends, the nickname simply evolves over time. Only his mother held out for "Hoagland"—though in letters to him later in life even she shortens this to "Hoag."

19. "Hoagy Carmichael's Music Played Throughout the World," *Indianapolis Sunday Star*, December 10, 1933.

20. Charlie Davis, *That Band From Indiana* (Oswego, N.Y.: Mathom Publishing, 1982), p. 54. *JB*, III/10. Wells, a Bloomington native, studied at Indiana University for three years but did not graduate. IU *Arbutus* yearbooks for 1915, '16, and '17 show him playing violin in the University Orchestra. By the end of the 1917 school year, President Woodrow Wilson had brought the United States into the "Great War." Wells joined up and shipped out, serving with a field artillery unit. He came home in 1919 with Indiana's 42nd "Rainbow" Division but apparently never returned to school (IU Archives).

21. Duncan Schiedt, *The Jazz State of Indiana* (Pittsboro, Ind.: Self-published, 1977), p. 50. Charlie Davis reprints what he suggests is Wells's own manuscript for "Falling Star," with lyrics, but that attribution is open to question. The notation is crude, and the key signature incorrect, indicating the key of C when the melody is clearly in F. Wells, as a trained musician, would not have written so inaccurately. Davis, *That Band From Indiana*, pp. 154–55.

22. During the late 1920s, East teamed up with banjoist-singer Ralph Dumke, who also had worked for Davis (who credits "Big Ed" with naming the jazz standard "Copenhagen"). Their duo act formed the basis for the radio show *The Quality Twins*, known more familiarly as *Sisters of the Skillet*, broadcast over Chicago station WGN. Basically a nonsense show, it offered parodies of the sort of "advice to the housewife" programs common on early radio. Their regular characters included "Pat Plenty, love expert extraordinaire," who offered ways to handle unruly children or keep husbands from snoring. During World War II, East and his wife recycled the idea in a show called *Ladies Be Seated*, broadcast on NBC's Blue network. John Dunning, *On the Air: The Encyclopedia of Old-Time Radio* (New York: Oxford University Press, 1998).

23. Bill Kenney, undated letter to Carmichael, ATM. The song referred to is surely "The Little House Upon the Hill," written in 1915 by Ballard MacDonald, composer of "Indiana" and "On the Banks of the Wabash," in collaboration with Joe Goodwin, best known as the lyricist for "When You're Smiling," but whose mid-1920s efforts also include the aforementioned "Hoosier Sweetheart."

24. *SIW*, p. 34.

25. *SIW*, pp. 35–37.

26. *SIW*, p. 36.

27. *SIW*, p. 35, and *JB*, II/10.

28. Reg DuValle Jr. disputes descriptions of his father playing the banjo. "I don't know where they got that from," he told the author. "He played piano, of course, and accordion. But never the banjo." Asked what instrument his father would have played with Smith, the younger DuValle confessed to being mystified. "Perhaps accordion, or second piano," he said. The personnel given for the Smith band by Indiana historian Duncan Schiedt (in *The Jazz State of Indiana*) includes banjoist Elmer "Babe" Herron. Confusing matters even fur-

ther is the fact that the Texas-born banjoist and saxophone doubler Ben Holliman, a lifelong friend of the elder DuValle, may also have worked with Smith.

29. According to one account, white singer-entertainer Tess Gardella, who billed herself as "Aunt Jemima," heard DuValle play and offered him a job as her accompanist. He turned her down, preferring to remain with home and family.

30. *SIW*, p. 31.

31. *SIW*, pp. 31, 33. A similar account in *SR* has DuValle saying ". . . you'll never get hostile with yourself"—the version usually quoted by DuValle Jr. in discussing his father. Carmichael's *Jazzbanders* manuscript, written in the early 1930s, deals with DuValle less lengthily and contains no version of the conversation reproduced here.

32. *JB*, II/10. DeMarcus quote from long autobiographical letter to George W. Kay, undated, in the possession of Indiana historian Duncan Schiedt. Used with permission. Carmichael's reference to DuValle's thumb hitting the seventh as both a harmonic and, presumably, rhythmic device resembles a similar trick as demonstrated by Hank Wells, which the latter uses several times on the home recording cited earlier in this chapter. Both pianists appear to be thinking in terms of a pivot, striking the chord on the strong beat (or downbeat), the extra note as a counterbalancing eighth on the "and" beat, producing the exaggerated four-to-the-bar effect shortly to be identified as "sock-time."

33. Reginald DuValle Jr., telephone conversation with the author, February 9, 1999, tape in author's possession. DuValle's claim that his father composed at least part of the jazz band standard "Copenhagen," though unsubstantiated, is at least plausible. It is one of the facts of 1920s life that songwriters of both races often sold ideas to colleagues, especially those who might be better connected with music publishers, for fees that were nominal at best. Rumors persist that such Jimmy McHugh hits as "On the Sunny Side of the Street" and "I Can't Give You Anything but Love" were actually Fats Waller melodies—and even that the verse to Carmichael's crowning "Star Dust" was the work of his friend bandleader-arranger Don Redman. Such reports are notable both for the stubbornness with which they persist and the failure of generations of researchers to turn up corroborative evidence.

34. In later years, the elder DuValle worked days for the Linco Gas Company and nights as a pianist, sometimes in duo with his old friend banjoist Ben Holliman. He never recorded commercially, though a hotel location recording, on an acetate disc, is rumored to exist.

35. As a matter of interest, the same program offered poet Countee Cullen reading a selection of his own verse and baritone Walter Price singing spirituals, as well as "Trees" and other popular favorites. The location was Caleb Mills Hall, in Indianapolis.

36. Bill Kenney, undated letter to Carmichael, ATM. Kenney also remarks somewhat mysteriously, "His folks would not let him play the stuff he wanted to play," prompting visits to the Kenney parlor piano. Possibly his maternal grandmother, Mary C. "Ma" Robison, had less patience with the boy's keyboard "pounding" than did his mother.

37. *JB*, I/2.

38. Photograph on file at ATM. Joanne Carmichael is buried, beside her parents and brother, at Bloomington's Rose Hill Cemetery. The simple stone marker bears no date of death save the year, 1918.

39. Handwritten note to Ralph Hancock, c. 1957, ATM.

40. For further particulars, see Alfred W. Crosby, *America's Forgotten Pandemic: The Influenza of 1918* (New York: Cambridge University Press, 1989), and Lynette Iezzoni, *Influenza 1918: The Worst Epidemic in American History* (New York: TV Books, 1999).

41. *SIW*, pp. 34, 45. In an exquisite irony, the flood of American fighting men also carried the new and mysterious plague to the European front. Unknown to young Carmichael and thousands like him, and understandably not reported by the Army in those war-hungry days, it struck with particular virulence at U.S. military training camps.

42. War information from Fred S. Cavinder, *The Indiana Book of Records, Firsts, and Fascinating Facts* (Bloomington: Indiana University Press, 1985), pp. 311–12, and Moshe Y. Sachs, ed., *The Worldmark Encyclopedia of the States* (New York: Worldmark Press, Harper & Row, 1981), pp. 169–84. Hanna information from *Daily Telephone*, July 8, 1918.

43. *SIW*, pp. 41, 42. Radio newscaster H. V. Kaltenborn, in his autobiography *Fifty Fabulous Years* (New York: G. P. Putnam's Sons, 1950), describes using much the same method in an (ultimately unsuccessful) 1899 attempt to join up for service in the Spanish-American War.

44. *SIW*, pp. 41–42.

45. U.S. National Archives and Records Administration, citing "Report of the Adjutant General of the Army," *War Department Annual Reports, 1919*, vol. 1, part 1. Source for Sunday closing: Ray Cunningham, University of Illinois. Further source for enlistment policy: Doran Cart, Liberty Memorial Museum of World War I, Kansas City, Mo., citing Marvin Kreidberg and Merton G. Henry, *A History of Military Mobilization in the U.S. Army* (Washington: U.S. Dept. of the Army, 1955). All in correspondence with Indiana University reference specialist and photograph curator Bradley D. Cook, spring-summer 1999. Draft cessation: Iezzoni, *Influenza 1918*, p. 103.

46. Harry Orchard, letter to Robert D. Hamontre, dated May 3, 1983, ATM.

47. All Carmichael quotes from *JB*, III/4–7.

Chapter III

1. Robert Leffler, "Old Nooks, New Nooks." *Indiana Alumni Magazine,* January-February 1982. The Candy Kitchen, officially named the Greek Candy Company, was located at 112 North Walnut Street, on the east side of the square, some five blocks west of Indiana Avenue, location of the Book Nook.

2. *JB,* II/5–6.

3. *SIW,* p. 55.

4. Biographical material on DeMarcus from Duncan Schiedt, *The Jazz State of Indiana* (Pittsboro, Ind.: Self-published, 1977), pp. 24–25.

5. *JB,* III/9–10.

6. Correspondence, all undated, between Bradford "Batty" DeMarcus and George W. Kay, and letters to Duncan Schiedt from DeMarcus and Johnny Johnson, c. 1960s. All in the possession of Duncan Schiedt and cited with permission.

7. DeMarcus's career on records, both at home and abroad, has remained curiously underdocumented. His correspondence with both Kay and Schiedt names dozens of specific records he made as a member of Yerkes's Novelty Five, Bailey's Lucky Seven, Gene Fosdick's Hoosiers, the All-Star trio, and various other units under the directorship of Sam Lanin, Gus Henschen, Harry Reser, Ross Gorman, Eddie Elkins, and others, as well as accompaniments to such singers as Cliff "Ukulele Ike" Edwards and vaudeville star Marion Harris. At various times he substituted for such well-known saxophonists as Bennie Krueger and Don Parker on records issued under their names. But without exception, such leading discographers as Brian Rust have missed Batty DeMarcus entirely: the personnels of the records he names are sometimes listed as being the work of others, most often simply as "unknown." The same fate has befallen his work with the Savoy Orpheans and other leading British groups. Yet the exactitude of DeMarcus's information, often corroborated by fellow-musicians, leaves no doubt as to his achievements. His rich, varied career is ripe for investigation.

8. Schiedt, *Jazz State of Indiana,* p. 26. One of the best of the 1920s college units was Princeton's Triangle band, organized to play for shows sponsored by a student dramatic organization—the Triangle Club—founded by none other than Indiana writer Booth Tarkington.

9. *SIW,* p. 57.

10. *JB,* III/11. Carmichael surely misremembers "Fate" as the pianist's warmup number. "Fate" was composed in 1923, long after the events recounted here, by Byron Gay (1886–1945), best known for such hits as "Oh!" (1920), "Horses" (1926), and "Four or Five Times" (1927), particularly favored by jazzmen of the era. Several earlier songs also bore the title "Fate," including one by Victor Herbert and another by British composer Horatio Nicholls; but it seems unlikely that a dance

band out of Louisville would have been playing these. Jordan has been variously, and erroneously, identified as "Louis" or "Joe," but Pen Bogert, reference specialist of the Filson Club Historical Society of Louisville, wrote on March 29, 1999, "I have done extensive research on early Louisville jazz musicians, and the name Louis Jordan has never come up. [But] there was an African-American saxophone player and bandleader named Howard Jordan, who was active here beginning around 1914. During the 1920s and 1930s he led the Howard Jordan Orchestra, which was the most popular band in the area."

11. *JB*, III/11–12. It is useful, at this early stage, to note that the present text makes no concession to what has become known as "political correctness." Beyond dispute, such terms as "dinge" used to describe blacks are now considered demeaning and no longer used in civil discourse. But things were different in the America of 1919, and for many years thereafter; in the author's view, any attempt to alter or eviscerate the speech conventions of the era amounts to tampering with the historical record. Nor should such usages, and the assumptions about race which, in bygone years, often underpinned them, be cited deliberately to reflect ill on those who used them. They were men and women of their times and cannot be expected to have anticipated changes in linguistic or sociological fashion. Carmichael's descriptions, and the language in which they are couched, belong to their time; as will be seen again and again, his enthusiasm for black music and musicians is genuine, untainted by any note of condescension.

The "Russian Rag" referred to in this connection was a widely popular 1918 adaptation of the opening theme of Sergei Rachmaninoff's *Prelude in C-Sharp Minor* by George L. Cobb (1886–1942). Born in upstate New York, Cobb was equally known for technically demanding piano rags and for such popular songs as "Alabama Jubilee" and "Are You From Dixie?" Cobb did so well with the "Russian Rag," writes ragtime historian David A. Jasen, that he followed it up with a "New Russian Rag," using more thematic material from the same *Prelude*.

12. *JB*, III/12–13.

13. Even as late as December 13, 1924, the *Indiana Daily Student* was advertising a Christmas dance at Phi Omega Pi fraternity house with music by "Jordan's Harmony Kings." Carmichael's Collegians played a double-header the same Saturday, working a tea dance from 5:30 to 8:30 and a Christmas party at a residence hall immediately thereafter.

14. *JB*, III/13–14.

15. Kenneth Cline, "Hoagy: Bloomington Remembers," *Bloomington Herald-Times*, January 3, 1982.

16. His financial situation was indeed perilous. In a letter to classmate Harry Carlton, dated August 15, 1921, Carmichael remarks, "I hope you are making the dough. I'm sure not. Haven't made but $45 all summer. I'm going to have a

lot of trouble even getting to enter [school]. I owe lots. If you could possibly lone [*sic*] me $50 by the time school starts or if you think you can now, let me know. Mother even advised that I not go to school until Xmas." Letter on file at Lilly Library, IU.

17. Kenneth Cline, "Hoagy: Bloomington Remembers," *Bloomington Herald-Times*, January 3, 1982. Kenneth Cline, "Star Dust Memories," *Indianapolis Star Magazine*, November 28, 1982. As will shortly be seen, Kathryn Moore appears regularly throughout Carmichael's Indiana story, as recounted in his various memoirs. She is first seen as "Kate Cameron," one of his early crushes, and later as "Dorothy Kelly," credited as his "inspiration" in writing "Star Dust."

18. M. William Lutholtz, *Grand Dragon: D. C. Stephenson and the Ku Klux Klan in Indiana* (West Lafayette: Purdue University Press, 1991), pp. 22–27. Moshe Y. Sachs, ed., *The Worldmark Encyclopedia of the States* (New York: Worldmark Press, Harper & Row, 1981), pp. 169–84.

19. Eagleston information from Fred S. Cavinder, *The Indiana Book of Records, Firsts, and Fascinating Facts* (Bloomington: Indiana University Press, 1985), p. 226.

20. *SIW*, p. 69.

21. *JB*, IV/7.

22. Urged on by a Republican Party push for temperance, Indiana entered the ranks of "dry" states relatively early. By January 16, 1919, thirty-six of the forty-eight states had ratified the new Eighteenth Amendment to the Constitution, making Prohibition the law. "The great social experiment" was adopted nationally, over President Wilson's veto, January 16, 1920.

23. Carmichael never makes clear whether the drummer and booker Glen Woodward mentioned here is in any way connected with the "Mr. Woodward" who had played drums with Lida Carmichael on various of her college dance engagements. Band personnel information from Carmichael letter to Wad Allen, dated November 18, 1944, ATM.

24. *JB*, IV/10. As Carmichael's narrative here suggests, many officially "dry" states, Indiana among them, tended to be lax about enforcement. Even after national ratification, loopholes in Prohibition laws were plentiful, wide, and sometimes impossible to plug. Rural communities, particularly, seemed well endowed with local sources, and officials frequently discovered it was in their best interests to let them get on with activities.

25. *JB*, IV/11. As Geoffrey Perrett notes in his *America in the Twenties* (New York: Simon & Schuster, 1982), "The people who resented Prohibition most were probably the working class, considering it class legislation, which to a large degree it was. The upper classes had supported Prohibition in order to save the workers by denying them drink. They never intended it to apply to themselves" (p. 177).

26. *JB*, IV/13.

27. *SIW*, p. 60.

28. Letters from Ed Whetsell to John Cravens, dated September 12, 1920, and September 23, 1920, IU Archives.

29. *JB*, IV/13. Again, a point of chronological detail: though both "Margie" and "Wang Wang Blues" were recorded in 1920, the best-selling records (by the Original Dixieland Jazz Band and Paul Whiteman's orchestra, respectively) were made toward year's end. Here, as elsewhere, Carmichael elides matters of time: beyond during the spring and summer, as he asserts.

30. Hoagy Carmichael, address to IU alumni, undated, IU Archives.

Chapter IV

1. Some accounts suggest that Miss Palmer actually secured the booking, bringing in musicians who had accompanied her on her 1921 Midwest tour, canceled after the risqué side of her act incensed guardians of local morality. This band included clarinetist Leon Roppolo and trombonist George Brunies, both from New Orleans, and Iowa banjoist Lou (or Lew) Black. According to this version, Mares joined them when the Friars' Inn engagement began. Some published reports add that Miss Palmer and her husband *pro tem*, pianist Al Siegel, decamped after a few weeks at the Chicago cabaret, leaving the job to the band. At this remove it's difficult to establish which account hews closer to the facts.

2. George Beall, "The New Orleans Rhythm Kings," *Swing Music*, March 1936.

3. *JB*, V/7.

4. Carmichael has described these events in his three memoirs, with varying degrees of embellishment. His accounts are seldom rigorous about establishing times. Philip R. Evans, in researching the life of Bix Beiderbecke, has come as close as anyone to a plausible chronology. Those in search of further detail are invited to consult his *Bix: The Leon Bix Beiderbecke Story* (Bakersfield, Calif.: Prelike Press, 1998).

5. *JB*, V/14.

6. *JB*, V/15.

7. Hoagy Carmichael, letter to Stanley Slome, dated January 26, 1980. Until recently few seem to have questioned the glaring illogic of the Beiderbecke family decision to send young Leon to a school just outside Chicago. Widely famed as the "dancin'est city" in America, and an incubator for the very music which had reportedly caused the trouble at home, Chicago was the last place they would have chosen for him—unless their reasons had nothing to do with music. Evidence in the Davenport, Iowa, city records indicates that young Beiderbecke had encountered difficulty of quite another nature, a complaint alleging improper sexual conduct with a female minor, which necessitated his removal from Davenport with all dispatch. For reasons not difficult to infer (given his

close association with the Beiderbecke heirs), the late Philip R. Evans chose not to publish this information in his 1998 Beiderbecke book, though it had been in his possession for some time.

8. Evans indicates this was a Sigma Nu fraternity dance at Northwestern University, held Saturday, May 20th, 1922 (information from *Bix: The Leon Bix Beiderbecke Story*, as above, p. 109). This event Carmichael identifies (in *JB*, IX/14, and *SIW*, p. 102) as a Sigma Alpha Epsilon dance: he and saxophonist Gene Fosdick crashed, he says, just for the purpose of hearing Beiderbecke play the cornet. His description in *Sometimes I Wonder* asserts that "Bix dumbfounded me and the band was more than I could believe," and speaks of the band as if it were the Wolverines—which came into existence more than a year later. He has clearly elided this evening with a much later epiphany.

9. Richard M. Sudhalter and Philip R. Evans, *Bix: Man and Legend* (New Rochelle, N.Y.: Arlington House, 1974), p. 71.

10. Bradley D. Cook, IU reference specialist and photograph curator, conversation with the author, March 8, 1999.

11. *JB*, V/16.

12. *JB*, V/13. It is not without relevance here that following George Johnson's death his widow quickly consigned all his memorabilia—scrapbooks, correspondence, photographs, records, newspaper clippings—to the trash. Jazz researchers approaching her with questions about the early years, and especially his association with Bix Beiderbecke in the band known to posterity as the Wolverines, were summarily turned away.

13. Correspondence between Hoagland Carmichael and U. C. Smith, dated August 30, 1921, and June 28 and 30, 1922, IU Archives.

14. Orchard diary entry in letter to Robert D. Hamontre, dated May 3, 1983, ATM.

15. *JB*, VI/2. In a 1973 interview with Philip R. Evans, Carmichael suggested that Beiderbecke was to have been part of the Palm Beach band. As related to Evans, he left Bloomington in early January and stopped off first at the Friars' Inn, where he, Johnson, Moore, and Beiderbecke hatched plans for the trip. Then, he said, they continued on to the South Side, spending the rest of the evening at the Lincoln Gardens listening to King Oliver's Creole Jazz Band. There is no mention of this episode, or of Bix's inclusion in plans for the Florida adventure, in *Jazzbanders*, written in the early 1930s, soon after Bix's death. Was Carmichael conflating several evenings, yarn-spinning as he went, because he knew that was what his interlocutors had come to hear?

16. *SIW*, p. 95.

17. *JB*, VI/4.

18. Newspaper clippings, undated and unidentified, ATM.

19. *JB*, VI/4. At one point Carmichael mentions that "Lucky" had worked in a band led by Ed East. In a November 18, 1944, letter to Wad Allen, Carmichael recalls

the band with which he played campus dances while still at Bloomington High School. At one point he refers to one "Leonard Luck," who "pranced up and down the Student Bldg. stage warbeling [*sic*] 'Won't You Be My Baby' and brandishing his violin and bow in the air." Can this be the hapless "Lucky" referred to in *Jazzbanders?*

20. *JB*, V/5.

Chapter V

1. Material derived from assorted clippings and obituaries, ATM. These include articles in the *Indiana Daily Student* (August 4, 1928; September 2, 1929; January 20, 1931) and various issues of the *Indiana Alumni Quarterly*.

2. It is useful to remember that the years 1921 through 1924 saw the most dramatic and ultimately romantic phase of the assault on Mount Everest. The exploits of George Leigh Mallory, particularly, seemed to capture public imagination: his participation in the 1921 and '22 Everest expeditions and his disappearance, with Andrew Irvine, on the high slopes in 1924, made headlines and have fascinated readers ever since. The thought of associating any inexplicable aspects of Moenkhaus with so romantic and mysterious a calling must have come naturally.

3. *JB*, VIII/3.

4. Phillip Rice, "The Miraculous Deeds of Bunkhaus," *Vagabond,* March 1931, p. 13.

5. Dean B. Winfred Merrill, "William Moenkhaus," *Vagabond,* March 1931, p. 12.

6. "Dadaland," in *Arp on Arp: Poems, Essays, Memories* (New York: Viking, 1972), p. 234. These ideas soon found expression in print, in an anthology titled, appropriately, *Cabaret Voltaire*. By the time, a year later, the periodical *Dada* first appeared, Ball had moved on to new pursuits.

7. Tristan Tzara, "Lecture on Dada" (1922), translated from the French by Robert Motherwell and published in Motherwell, ed., *Dada Painters and Poets*, 2d ed. (Cambridge: Belknap Press of Harvard University, 1989), pp. 73–98.

8. Some art historians will argue that Dadaism as a freestanding "anti-art" movement was passé by 1922, absorbed into the greater tide of emergent surrealism. But Tzara's famed "Lecture on Dada" dates from that very year; safe to say, moreover, that in the early 1920s, any corpus of new ideas spread slowly, especially over great expanses of geography and culture. The pioneering work of Ball and others found its legatees in such later figures as Kurt Schwitters, in whose hands it was metamorphosed into constructivism, reduction of language to its elementary parts without the demolition which lay at the heart of the Dada movement.

9. The title, if not the content, is an obvious—if irreverent—gesture toward George Gershwin, whose *Rhapsody in Blue*, premiered at New York's Aeolian Hall that February, had been the talk of the music world.

10. "Gedunkhaus" springs from the German *Gedanken,* meaning "thoughts" or "ideas." Hence, "a house of ideas."

11. *SIW,* p. 65.

12. Kathy Walsh, "The Nook: Biography of a Campus Hangout," *Indiana Alumni Magazine,* November–December 1985, pp. 8–11.

13. Ibid., pp. 8–9. *SIW,* p. 54.

14. "Book Nook Demolished," *Scandal Sheet,* dated "Prom Day, 1928," IU Archives.

15. Duncan Schiedt, *The Jazz State of Indiana* (Pittsboro, Ind.: Self-published, 1977).

16. According to an article ("The Era of Sock, Part II") in *The Vagabond* for May–June 1924, Stiner's group, including Allen and Harry Williams, a campus drummer and xylophone player, played a Pacific cruise around this time, with stops in Hong Kong and Shanghai. Carmichael makes no mention of this in his memoirs and refers to competitor Stiner (sometimes Steiner) only in passing.

17. *JB,* VIII/4–5.

18. *SR,* p. 40.

19. *JB,* VIII/11.

20. Tod Owlin (Wad Allen), "The Life and Death of Bunkhaus," *Vagabond,* May–June 1926, pp. 54–59.

21. "Campus Idols Return: William 'Bill' Moenkhaus," *Indiana Daily Student,* August 4, 1928.

22. "Ike" Bercovitz, letter to Duncan Schiedt, dated May 20, 1977.

23. Headlined "Down College Avenue," this article (or column) seems to have appeared in either the *Indiana Daily Student* or *Bloomington Record* shortly after Moenkhaus's death in 1931. It is signed only with the initials "K.W.F." and an Indianapolis dateline. The item is on file at the IU Archives.

24. *JB,* VIII/8.

25. Booth Tarkington, *The Conquest of Canaan* (rpt. Upper Saddle River, N.J.: Gregg Press, 1970), p. 185.

26. It is useful in this connection to recall that Switzerland offered a haven for countless artists and intellectuals during World War I. Among them was V. I. Lenin, who inveighed regularly and publicly against the war—whose ultimate beneficiaries, he charged, would be the hated bourgeoisie. His insistence that Socialists "transform the imperialist war into a civil war" found expression in his landmark 1916 tract, *Imperialism, the Highest Stage of Capitalism.*

27. "Campus Idols Return," *Indiana Daily Student,* August 4, 1928.

28. Kathy Walsh, "The Nook: Biography of a Campus Hangout," *Indiana Alumni Magazine,* November–December 1985, pp. 8–11.

29. Ibid. "Book Nook Commencements," *Bloomington Daily Herald Stonebelt Magazine,* June 1, 1948.

30. As such events will, the Book Nook "commencements" made a quick transition from rebellion to respectability. By contrast with 1927, the 1928 event was well

organized, even choreographed and a little predictable. The size and calculated absurdity grew self-conscious as the Nook celebrations became a standard feature of IU life. For all practical purposes, the idea of the Bent Eagles as an intimate, even gnostic, circle had been overtaken by events—and by the characteristic American urge to market a saleable idea. In 1929 the Bloomington police obligingly roped off the parade area. The fourth, last—and most lavish—"commencement," with faculty, students, and almost everyone else in sight getting into the act, was held in 1931; but by this time the Poolitsan family had raised the rent, and the Costas brothers were looking for a new location.

31. Moenkhaus obituary (unsigned, but unmistakably by Allen), published in IU *Alumni Quarterly*, April 1931. "Best friend" quote from Allen letter dated February 7, 1969.

32. Dean B. Winfred Merrill, "William Moenkhaus," and Phil Rice, "The Miraculous Deeds of Bunkhaus," both in *Vagabond*, March 1931.

33. *SR*, p. 143.

34. As late as 1979, the character and writings of "Bunkhaus" captivated English poet Adrian Mitchell, who found in their flights of surrealistic fancy an affinity with the writings of Edward Lear and even—a stretch, this—some of the more imaginative efforts of the Beatles. Mitchell's "play with music," *Hoagy, Bix and Wolfgang Beethoven Bunkhaus*, was staged in London, in Indianapolis, and at the Mark Taper Forum in Los Angeles; it took "Bunkhaus" off the pages of *The Vagabond*, putting his verses and aphorisms in the mouths of various Book Nook–related characters, staging some of the plays, and turning others into miniaturized marionette shows. The musical side of the play consisted entirely of small-band arrangements of Carmichael songs, plus such 1920s jazz band staples as "The Jazz Me Blues." Reviewers praised the music and singled out various performers—but missed, overall, the tragicomic side of the "Bunkhaus" character and writings.

35. According to Bloomington researcher William Weaver, someone—no one seems to know who—still puts flowers from time to time on William Moenkhaus's grave.

36. "In Memoriam," *Vagabond*, March 1930, p. 43.

Chapter VI

1. *JB*, IX/15.

2. *SIW*, p. 116.

3. *JB*, IX/14.

4. In *Jazzbanders*, Carmichael remembers them arriving on a Saturday and playing the Kappa Sig formal that night. As usual, he appears to have elided the dates. The Kappa Sig dance was a week later, on May 3, and was their fourth Bloomington date. Additionally, "Dippermouth" is a standard twelve-bar blues and

has no break "in the middle of the chorus." Even at this early date, Oliver's three-chorus (thirty-six-bar) solo on the number has become part of the standard way of playing the tune, and it is likely that Beiderbecke would have rendered some adaptation of it. As customarily played by cornetists, the first *four* bars of Oliver's second, or middle, blues chorus are rendered as three short breaks. Perhaps this is what Carmichael remembers.

5. *JB*, IX/16.

6. Carmichael statement to Brigitte Berman in *Bix: Ain't Nobody Played Like Him Yet*, documentary film, released commercially 1994.

7. Letters to John Cravens from Lida Carmichael, dated April 25, 1924, and from Georgia E. Carmichael, dated September 8, 1924, IU Archives. According to IU records, Georgia Carmichael did not enter at midterm in the 1924–25 academic year but matriculated in September of 1925. She withdrew that December, never to return.

8. Letter from U. C. Smith to Hoagland Carmichael, dated April 30, 1924, IU Archives.

9. Fiddler "Ike" Bercovitz recalled at least once when Bix and Hoagy "parked themselves on the balcony at the Book Nook and listened for hours" to a recording of *The Firebird*. Letter to Duncan Schiedt, dated May 20, 1977.

10. *JB*, X/1–2.

11. *JB*, X/3.

12. *JB*, X̌/3. A rather more embellished account in *SIW* (p. 133) has him beginning it at the Nook, finishing at the Kappa Sig piano. The use of the word "blues" in the context of the 1920s has little to do with the blues as a discrete, identifiable form. Like "jazz" and even "dixieland," it was a form of shorthand, telling the lay public that a given piece of music was in the "hot" idiom and could be danced to in the agitated manner of the day. Such nicknames as the "High-hatted Tragedian of the Blues" (Ted Lewis) and the "Rajah of Jazz" (Paul Ash) had less to do with musical content than with marketing placement. By contrast, those in the know understood that the title "Empress of the Blues," bestowed on Bessie Smith, or "Father of the Blues" (W. C. Handy) represented a musical reality.

13. The handicap of his inability to read or write music would follow him throughout the decade, as his relationship with the musically trained cornetist Charles "Bud" Dant and the latter's account of the genesis of "Star Dust" clearly indicate. Not until Carmichael arrived in New York and signed with Mills Music did the situation change. As a Mills employee he had constant access to trained arrangers and copyists, able to work with him in correctly notating his melodies. That was equally true of his tenure with Ralph Peer's Southern Music Co., as will be seen. Manuscript worksheets to his later songs, on file at Indiana University, suggest that he never completely mastered the skills of exact notation—

a factor that surely hampered his later attempts to compose more ambitious music. Even after Carmichael's death, in 1981, Bud Dant returned to Indiana to organize and orchestrate (with Nathan Van Cleave) the fragments of his friend's long-planned *Johnny Appleseed Suite*.

14. *JB*, X/4.

15. *JB*, VIII/12.

16. Information from Bradley D. Cook, reference specialist and photograph curator, IU Archives, based on advertisements in the *Indiana Daily Student* and other publications and documents.

17. *JB*, X/4–5.

18. *SIW*, p. 127.

19. *JB*, X/9.

20. Duncan Schiedt, *The Jazz State of Indiana* (Pittsboro, Ind.: Self-published, 1977). pp. 128–30. Charlie Davis, *That Band From Indiana* (Oswego, N.Y.: Mathom Publishing, 1982), p. 35.

21. The Wolverines returned to Bloomington for one weekend, April 24–25, 1925, with Jimmy McPartland on cornet in place of Bix.

22. *JB*, X/5.

23. Affidavit supplied by, and on file at, IU Archives.

24. *Indiana Daily Student*, undated clipping on file at IU Archives and quoted entire in *JB* (X/6), *SIW* (pp. 130–31), and *SR* (pp. 73–74).

25. *JB*, X/7. Similar accounts in *SIW* (p. 131) and *SR* (p. 74).

26. Hoagy Carmichael, handwritten memo prepared c. 1957 for Ralph Hancock, who had spoken extensively with the composer about writing a biography, ATM. Hoagy's passion for the cornet may have abated somewhat over the years, but his fascination with it never died out. Harry Evans's "Hollywood Diary" column in the July 12, 1940, *Family Circle* magazine describes one of Bing Crosby's "Westwood Marching and Chowder Club" parties, with music by "the Come-and-Bring-Your-Horn Boys," an *ad hoc* ensemble including songwriter Johnny Burke at the piano, Benny Goodman on clarinet, and—standing alongside studio trumpet virtuoso Mannie Klein—Hoagy Carmichael with his battered old horn.

27. *SR*, p. 77.

28. *SIW*, p. 132. *SR*, p. 77. Carmichael's various accounts of this incident are a typical, semi-fictionalized mess. *SIW* has Wad Allen telling Hoagy, "Monk just did this pretty little play for *The Vagabond*," and reading *Culp's Down Feltment* (which did not appear in that journal until October 1929); Carmichael then repeats it to Bix, who utters, "I am not a swan." In *The Stardust Road*, the reader is Hoagy himself, the occasion an informal gathering at the Book Nook with Bix present, and the text is Monk's *Wheatena Test*. But the "test," unpublished in *The Vagabond*, also appears in *Jazzbanders*, in an earlier conversation between only Carmichael and Moenkhaus; Bix is neither present nor referred to.

29. *SIW*, p. 115.
30. *JB*, IX/16.
31. *JB*, XI/1.
32. *JB*, XI/8.
33. *JB*, XI/9. Last Bix quote from Evans, *Bix: The Leon Bix Beiderbecke Story*, p. 179.
34. *SIW*, p. 151.
35. Hoagy Carmichael and Frank Loesser, "Small Fry." Copyright 1938, Famous Music, Inc. Renewed 1965.
36. *SIW*, p. 139.

Chapter VII

1. *JB*, XI/4–5.
2. *SR*, p. 86.
3. Duncan Schiedt, *The Jazz State of Indiana* (Pittsboro, Ind.: Self-published, 1977), p. 75. The Happy Harmonists played three dates in Bloomington in early 1925: Friday, February 27; Saturday, May 9; and Friday, May 15, four days before the Gennett date. At a guess, it seems plausible that Hoagy "demonstrated" his new piece for Hitch on May 9, giving the band ample time to learn it.
4. *JB*, XI/5. Curt Hitch told interviewer Bob Harrington in 1982 that "Hoagy did not have a name for his first number. We were trying to come up with something when [banjoist] Arnold Habbe picked up a piece of newspaper. On it were the words about an automobile boneyard, and he said, 'Why not call it "Boneyard Shuffle"?' And that's the true story behind the song title." *Mississippi Rag*, February 1982, p. 5.
5. *SR*, p. 87.
6. *JB*, XI/7.
7. The three-against-four pattern, moreover, occurs frequently in *The Firebird*. It is easy to imagine Hoagy, thinking about composing while listening to the Stravinsky ballet music with Bix at his side, absorbing the concept. Given his inability to read and write music, he probably perceived it intuitively as a sound, a "feel." More "schooled" songwriters, George Gershwin paramount among them, were using such juxtapositions freely; his 1924 "Fascinating Rhythm," for example, builds on a pair of eight-bar three-against-four sequences. But it uses mostly eighth notes, and in its obviousness strikes the ear as a piece of clever artifice. Several early ragtime pieces, among them Euday L. Bowman's 1914 "Twelfth Street Rag," use three-note eighth-note clusters against a 4/4 rhythm, a practice known as "secondary rag." But the idea of using such a device in unaccented quarter notes, as part of the melody of a popular song, and incorporating a change of tonal center, is an innovation belonging to "Washboard Blues" alone. Remarkably, a listener follows the melodic line without difficulty, unaware that the composer has just made use of an unusual and sophisticated *trompe l'oreille*.

8. The original text, in common with those from such stage works as *Show Boat* and *Porgy and Bess*, appears in black dialect. For the purposes of clarity in discussion, and with no political or other extramusical intent, it is reproduced here with some of the spellings adjusted to "conventional" usage.

9. "Washboard Blues" got off to a curious start. The first sheet music edition, published in 1926 by Mills Music, contains a different notation and harmonization of the "rubbin', scrubbin' tubbin' " section from that played on the Hitch record. Instead of following the notation of the original manuscript (signed by Moenkhaus and dated May 18, 1925), this version substitutes a passage less venturesome melodically and harmonically. A republished version, copyrighted 1928, returns to the original form. What might otherwise be an inexplicable mystery becomes somewhat clearer with Carmichael's own first vocal record of November 18, 1927, accompanied by Paul Whiteman's orchestra. In both issued takes of this performance he sings and plays the "simplified" version—reinforcing his own recollection that he was nervous at the session, and leading to the conclusion that, at this early stage of his development as a performer, he may have had trouble "hearing" and singing the passage the way he wrote it. Batty DeMarcus's description of Carmichael's visit to the Mills Music offices, described later in this chapter, makes sense if the song is indeed not "Rockin' Chair" but "Washboard Blues."

10. "Nobody," words by Alex Rogers, music by Bert Williams, published 1905, quoted by Ann Charters in *Nobody: The Story of Bert Williams* (New York: Macmillan, 1970), p. 9.

11. Carmichael himself sometimes gave in to his fancy in tracing the origins of his songs. Talking with a newspaper reporter in 1927, he identified "Washboard Blues" as "a colored spiritual, adapted to modern jazz." As he told it, the inspiration was "a colored cook and laundress at the Kappa Sigma house . . . her singing in time to work on the washboard brought the selection, the time of which is the same." "Popular Hoosier Composer Is Learning to Read Music," *Indianapolis Star*, April 13, 1928.

12. Historians Marshall and Jean Stearns, in their groundbreaking *Jazz Dance* (1968), trace the Charleston's origins back to at least the turn of the century. They quote numerous witnesses, including James P. Johnson and bandleader-entertainer Noble Sissle, who remembered seeing it performed by black dancers as early as 1903. According to Johnson, it was a "regular cotillion step [with] many variations—all danced to the rhythm everybody knows now." It turned up in several black musicals before attracting national attention in *Runnin' Wild*. And, as *Variety* writers Abel Green and Joe Laurie Jr. noted, it wiped out the distinction "between popular dances to watch, and popular dances to dance."

13. "Young Peoples' Dancing Is Natural: Moenkhaus," *Indiana Daily Student*, February 10, 1926.

14. *SR*, p. 103.

15. Charles "Bud" Dant, shortly to play a substantial role in Carmichael's life, later remembered "Watch Your Hornin' " as "a medium fast rhythm tune" which his band at Indiana University would use "if we got a little tired and wanted to end [a] dance early." The dancers, he said, "would all do 'The Indiana Hop' in which they would all go up and down in unison. The supports of the floor [in the girls' gym of the Student Building] were weak and we could watch the floor go up and down with the dancers! The chaperones would immediately stop the music and the dance—everybody would make a hundred yard dash for the Book Nook. I don't think any other band besides Hoag's and mine ever played 'Hornin'.' " Conversations with the author, October 19–20, 1998.

16. *SIW*, p. 158.

17. Ibid. and *JB*, XI/16. For many years, and despite all accounts, test pressings of these two selections have been rumored still to exist. As of this writing, neither has turned up. But discovery of other "lost" tests, from two later Carmichael Gennett dates, has helped sustain a belief among record collectors that "Watch Your Hornin' " and its companion will someday reappear.

18. Even at this relatively late time, the spelling of Carmichael's nickname still fluctuates, and will continue to do so for a while. Only when it begins appearing regularly on records and sheet music as "Hoagy" will the spelling be standardized.

19. Trumbauer diary quoted in Philip R. Evans and Larry F. Kiner, *Tram: The Frank Trumbauer Story* (Metuchen, N.J.: Scarecrow Press, 1994), p. 56.

20. Harry Orchard, diary excerpts as contained in letter to Robert D. Hamontre, dated May 3, 1983, ATM. Contents of Beiderbecke letter courtesy of Lilly Library, IU. Used by permission.

21. This and other 1925–26 information in this section from IU Archives, courtesy of reference specialist and photograph curator Bradley D. Cook.

22. Mark Sullivan, *Our Times: The United States, 1920–1925*, vol. 6, *The Twenties* (New York: Scribner's, 1935), p. 647.

23. Ibid.

24. *SIW*, p. 157.

25. Ibid.

26. *JB*, XII/2.

27. Batty De Marcus, who in many letters showed himself to be an accurate, often shrewd, observer, adds the following: "Hoag had the lyrics to 'Rockin' Chair' on a piece of yellow scratch paper and the tune in his head, so I took him to see Irving Mills, and Hoag got right in the middle of the thing and decided he would work over a couple of bars for awhile to make a few chord changes. Irving Mills had never run into anything of this nature and said so. Then he told me to bring this guy back when he knew his own tune." The story makes

no sense applied to "Rockin' Chair," first recorded a year later as an instrumental, under the title "When Baby Sleeps." Evidence here points to "Washboard Blues," especially considering Carmichael's difficulties in singing his own melody on his 1927 record with Paul Whiteman's orchestra. DeMarcus to George W. Kay, undated letter in the possession of Indiana historian Duncan Schiedt. Used with permission.

28. *SIW*, p. 166. Assuming Hoagy left Bloomington by Sunday, April 18, and if his accounts of getting stuck in snowdrifts and being waylaid by West Virginia police are true, he can't have arrived in Washington before the 20th. Two more days of seeing old friends bring him to the 22nd. Perhaps he's in New York by the 24th and sets out for Florida two days later, on the 26th. Given the state of American roads in 1926, the thousand-mile trip from New York to Palm Beach will have consumed several days. Yet the Florida Bar Association is categorical in saying it received Carmichael's application in April. Had he sent it by mail from Bloomington? Regrettably, no further documentation has come to light.

29. *SIW*, p. 168.

30. *JB*, XII/3.

31. *JB*, XII/5.

32. *JB*, XII/5–6.

33. *JB*, XII/6, and *SIW*, pp. 171–72. Nichols plays a substantial role in the "Washboard" story. One day, during Hoagy's last year at IU, "I returned from an equity class [and] found Red Nichols sitting on the davenport in the Kappa Sigma house. We jumped all over each other and spent the afternoon exchanging licks, so to speak. First he'd give the eastern interpretation of 'Dinah,' then I'd give mine. Red had heard Bix play in New York, and he was more excited over jazz than ever" (*JB*, XI/12). Nichols's two records of "Washboard," whle bringing the song to a wide audience, are a mixed blessing. They rachet up the tempo, rearrange the structure, excise the three-against-two, drop the extra bar, and substitute "hot" solo breaks for the arpeggiated "my man's sleepin' " section. Of the majesty and depth so strongly suggested by the Hitch record, little trace remains.

34. Letter from Florida Board of Bar Examiners to James T. Maher, dated June 10, 1960, and signed "James B. Tippin, Jr., Executive Director."

35. *JB*, XII/6.

36. Letter quoted in *SIW*, pp. 172–73.

37. Dant material from conversations with the author, recorded in Hawaii October 19–20, 1998. Also see Mike Pearson, "The Genius of Hoagy: Dant Believes Carmichael Merits Distinctive Place in Musical History," *Bloomington Sunday Herald-Times*, October 6 or 13, 1984.

38. This song became Carmichael's "One Night in Havana," which he recorded several times (the last in 1930), without notable success, then recycled in 1934

as "In the Churchyard," again to minimal public response. Only as "Chimes of Indiana," its main melody slowed down and extended to hymn-like character, did it find a permanent home. Carmichael presented it to the university in 1937; in 1978 it took its place as an IU alma mater beside "Hail to Old I.U.," the melody that had started young Hoagland Carmichael along his path to music so many years before.

Chapter VIII

1. Charles "Bud" Dant died shortly before work on this book was completed and after favoring the author with a long and detailed interview, not to mention a file folder bulging with informative follow-up letters, most of them typed impeccably despite rapidly failing eyesight. He remained a bright presence, clear-minded and vibrant, right to the end.

2. Dant recalled it as a job for a relief band playing opposite Duke Ellington's orchestra at Roseland Ballroom. Most chroniclers place Ellington on tour in New England throughout most of early 1927, and there is no account of a booking at Roseland. Still, Fletcher Henderson, the resident bandleader, was also on tour during those weeks, and the Roseland management was filling in with other bands. The possibility of a job that fell through cannot be ruled out, and the Duke's men had not yet landed the opportunity at the Cotton Club that would establish their fortunes forever. Dant's recollection may be accurate.

3. Bar information from letter to James T. Maher from Harriette Bailey Conn, deputy attorney general, State of Indiana, dated June 2, 1960. Carmichael letter to Nikki Schofield, librarian, Bingham, Summers, Welsh & Spilman, received October 12, 1979. In a 1979 letter, founder-partner Jim Bingham disputed Hoagy's "auto damage claims" story, adding, "We did some of that sort of work for some insurance companies on their claims in damage cases and in cases where the companies had claims against their assureds." But that, he said, was all. Letters in possession of Bingham, Summers, Welsh & Spilman.

4. Charles "Bud" Dant, conversation with the author, October 20, 1998. In later years, Carmichael credited his IU roommate Stu Gorrell with thinking of the title. The published sheet music of "Georgia on My Mind" (1930) credits him as lyricist.

5. SIW, p. 183.

6. SR, pp. 123–24.

7. Hoagy Carmichael, memo to Ralph Hancock, c. 1957, ATM. Many of these memos, cited throughout the text, are fragmentary, handwritten in note form. Words in brackets have been inserted to render his thoughts more comprehensible.

8. Linda Williams, "Pyle: 'Stardust' Wasn't Written Here," *Indianapolis Daily Star*, February 17, 1982. Ernie Pyle, "Insomnia and Stock Market Plague Composer

of Song Hits," *Washington Daily News*, July 7, 1936, syndicated column. Hoagy statement from Gene Handsaker syndicated "Hollywood" column, April 6, 1946. All material on file at IU Archives.

9. Mary Ann Sebrey, "Memories in Music: Hoagy's Friends Recall His 'Star Dust' Years," *Indianapolis Sunday Herald-Times*, December 26, 1982.

10. Duncan Schiedt, *The Jazz State of Indiana* (Pittsboro, Ind.: Self-published, 1977), p. 69.

11. Letter and telegram in ATM.

12. *JB*, XII/9. Perhaps it happened this way, perhaps not. Bloomington pianist Amos Ostot, as quoted by Duncan Schiedt, recalled watching Carmichael play the Gennett record to Whiteman long-distance over a telephone at a fraternity house, presumably Kappa Sig (*Jazz State of Indiana*, p. 84). Herb Sanford, writing in the early '70s, told of Whiteman and Jimmy Dorsey, with Carmichael in tow, invading his Indianapolis hotel room to use a small portable organ he'd brought along for arranging. Sitting down at it, Carmichael plays and sings "Washboard Blues." "Get this down," Sanford has Whiteman telling Challis. "We'll do it in Chicago." Sanford, *Tommy and Jimmy: The Dorsey Years* (New Rochelle, N.Y.: Arlington House, 1972), p. 33. In an interview with Crosby biographer Gary Giddins, Challis told essentially the same story as Sanford, but remembered the hotel room as his own.

13. As noted in Philip R. Evans and Linda Evans, *Bix: The Leon Bix Beiderbecke Story* (Bakersfield, Calif.: Prelike Press, 1998), p. 300. The waltz seems to have been a personal favorite of its composer. He recorded it again the following May 2, this time with Bud Dant on cornet; files identify it variously as "One Last Kiss" and "Wedding Waltz." It was finally published in 1935, under the title "Wedding Song."

14. Maurice "Maury" Bennett, taped interview, undated, supplied by Indiana collector Robert L. Floyd.

15. Byron Smart quoted in Orin Blackstone, "The Emil Seidel Band of 1928," *Jazzfinder* (New Orleans), December 1948. A rejected alternate take of "Friday Night," in the hands of Carmichael collector Michael Kieffer, has Hoagy playing in an even more uninhibited manner, "blowing up to" Smart in volume level and, at least once, in range.

16. Maurice "Maury" Bennett, taped interview, undated, supplied by Indiana collector Robert L. Floyd. The song, not yet published, is listed as "Stardust" (one word) on the Gennett label.

17. The spelling of this song's title has been, and in some cases remains, a matter of some confusion. At the time of first copyright registration, January 5, 1928, it was identified as "Stardust" (one word), and Gennett's "Permit to Record" sheet for the Seidel date, consigned by Carmichael and an S. R. Jackson, uses the single word. It became "Star Dust" on January 29, 1929, when reregistered by

Mills Music for its first publication. In the interests of consistency this text will use the published "Star Dust" throughout except in quoted references and the title of Carmichael's 1946 memoir, *The Stardust Road.*

18. The piano solo, as issued, actually runs thirty-three bars, extending the song's first eight bars to nine. An unissued alternate take, and a 1933 Victor recording, show this elongation to be no fluke but an extra "breathing" bar to complete Carmichael's phrase, part of what is obviously a carefully prepared set piece.

19. As will be seen, several Carmichael songs written in later life, as well as the longer "concert" works *Brown County in Autumn* and the *Johnny Appleseed Suite,* may be heard as explorations of this territory.

20. It is tantalizing to note, in this connection, that Lida Carmichael's family name was Robison. Given the obvious affinities between many of Hoagy's songs and those of Willard Robison, establishment of some blood tie between them would be only fitting. The author's inquiries along these lines have yielded no result.

21. J. Walter Wilson, M.D., letter to Duncan Schiedt, dated July 12, 1977. Used by permission. Wilson errs about the published key, though it is easy to see why. The published sheet music appeared in C and remains in that key to this day. But the publisher's "stock" orchestration, on which several notable "Star Dust" records are based, is in five flats. Accordingly, this has long been musicians' "standard key" for the song. Nor does the matter end there. Hoagy's own manuscript and the first records are in D, but Georgia Maxwell later maintained that her brother worked the chorus out in B♭, then transposed it to D when adding the verse. A lead sheet written out in later years by Bud Dant to show both the original melody and Hoagy's own lyric was indeed in B♭. Such evidence, however circumstantial, gains weight with the supposition that a technically limited campus jazz band in the 1920s, jamming on the changes of Hoagy's melody, might have gravitated more naturally to a flat key (concert B♭ is C for cornet and G for alto saxophone), with its easier fingerings, than to a sharp one. Concert D would have put the cornet into the technically trickier key of E (signature four sharps), and the alto sax into B (five sharps). Dant lead sheet courtesy of Duncan Schiedt.

22. Robert D. Robinson, letter to Duncan Schiedt dated January 25, 1975. Used by permission.

23. These include even what appears to have been a *pro tem* adjustment in the melodic line. The orchestra plays the central section of the "Up to de washin' soap" theme, beginning with bar 9, as originally written, the three-against-four melody moving up a major third. But Hoagy, singing it to his own piano accompaniment, goes up a fourth, and even at that sings the melody only approximately. On the originally issued take −1, he gets by with it—but on take −4 (which first appeared on a 1960s LP), he loses his way the last time through,

veering off pitch. By December 22, 1933, when he next records a vocal-and-piano version of "Washboard" for Victor, he's far more secure, comfortably using the "correct" melody and harmonic sequence. (For further discussion of this anomaly, see note 9 to chapter 7).

24. *SIW*, p. 189.

25. Ross Russell, *Jazz Style in Kansas City and the Southwest* (Berkeley: University of California Press, 1971), p. 8.

26. In a related note, it was to the Pla-Mor that Jack Kapp came looking for a hot black band to help Brunswick compete with the success of Bennie Moten's great Kansas City outfit on Victor. Other bands active around "Kaycee" at the time included those of Walter Page and George E. Lee, elder brother of singer-pianist Julia Lee.

27. *JB*, XII/13.

28. Carmichael's remarks to Schiedt were handwritten responses to an interview conducted by the historian with members of Hoagy's 1928–29 Columbia Club band. Schiedt then inserted them into the finished conversation, as published in *The Jazz State of Indiana*, pp. 89–91. The original and the Hancock document are on file at ATM.

29. Carmichael letter quoted in article on Gene Fosdick, printed in unidentified article published March 20, 1952, clipping on file at IU Archives. The phrase "double on elephant" was a musicians' joke, poking fun at the fact that musicians' union regulations allowed extra pay for those who "doubled" on other instruments in the course of a broadcast, recording, or concert. "Sock cymbal" was an early name for the combination of two cymbals on a post, which soon became known by its more familiar name, the hi-hat.

30. *Indianapolis News*, April 13, 1928.

31. See note 28 above.

32. Hoagy Carmichael, memos to Ralph Hancock, c. 1957, ATM.

33. *JB*, XII/15.

34. Charles "Bud" Dant, conversation with the author, October 19, 1998.

35. Mike Pearson, "The Genius of Hoagy: Dant Believes Carmichael Merits Distinctive Place in Musical History," *Bloomington Sunday Herald-Times*, October 6 or 13, 1984.

36. Redman letter on file at Lilly Library, IU. Used by permission.

37. Arnold Habbe, letter to Duncan Schiedt, dated March 28, 1969. Used by permission.

38. Schiedt, *Jazz State of Indiana*, p. 85.

39. *SIW*, p. 189.

40. In early 1999, Dant listened to his solo on "One Last Kiss" for the first time in seventy-one years. His response: "Not bad." His years as a recording executive told him at once why "Shimme-Sha-Wabble" and the rest had been withheld

from issue: "The balance was just awful. I was undermiked, and 'Yah' [Murray] was so close to the microphone he almost blew it apart with his solo." Dant letters and conversations, 1998–99.

41. Quoted in Schiedt, *Jazz State of Indiana*, p. 153, and in person by Dant himself during conversation with the author, October 19, 1998.

42. J. Walter Wilson, M.D., letter to Duncan Schiedt, dated July 12, 1977. Used by permission.

Chapter IX

1. *JB*, XII/16–17.

2. From the *Indianapolis Star* of July 26, 1925, quoted by Marjie Gates Giffin in *If Tables Could Talk*, official history of the Columbia Club (Indianapolis: Columbia Club, 1988), pp. 81–82. "Austere marble floors" passage also from *If Tables Could Talk*.

3. Letters from Ed Beauchamp to Duncan Schiedt, undated, late 1960s.

4. Ray Conolly, "Now, as I Recall It . . . ," *Columbian*, January 1965, pp. 8–9.

5. Many early cornets came with a series of removable crooks, tubes of various lengths that connected the mouthpiece to the rest of the instrument. The standard crook pitched the instrument in its standard key of B♭, but of hers permitted instant transposition to A, B♮, and C.

6. Columbia Club band alumni conversation, 1960, moderated, recorded, and transcribed by Duncan Schiedt and published in *The Jazz State of Indiana* (Pittsboro, Ind.: Self-published, 1977). Mr. Schiedt allowed the author to work from the original transcript. Lindbergh Indianapolis visit of January 16–17, 1929, documented by *Indianapolis Star*.

7. Herein lies a small mystery. In a 1974 reminiscence, Betty Harper, wife of saxophonist George Harper, spoke of a scheduled Gennett recording session at Richmond. En route, she said, the car Hoagy was driving was in a major crash. "We've had an accident," a dazed Carmichael told her on the telephone, "and I can't find George." The saxophonist turned up shortly afterward at a nearby farmhouse. The session, if scheduled at all, never took place. This was apparently Carmichael's second auto mishap: Ruth Carmichael Grant (letter dated September 6, 1957, ATM) mentions a "Ford wreck" nearly a decade earlier, involving herself, Ruth Orchard, Hoagy, and Trevor "Buck" Geddes, another Bloomington friend unmentioned in any Carmichael memoirs.

8. Carmichael letter to Duncan Schiedt, quoted in Schiedt, *Jazz State of Indiana*, p. 88.

9. Ibid., p. 91. For the information of collectors, several of the titles done that day have turned up in multiple takes throughout the years. When Bob Vollmer says, "I don't know how many tests we made, but there sure were a hell of a lot of them, I'll tell you," he is not exaggerating. Vollmer also raises a small mystery:

in the group conversation he is insistent that the band recorded *nine* titles that day, rather than the seven listed in standard discographies, and that "Star Dust" was among them. According to archivist and record producer Michael Brooks, no indication of such additional titles exists in Victor's files.

10. Hoagy Carmichael, handwritten note to Ralph Hancock, c. 1957, ATM.

11. Hoagy Carmichael, "Wanted—A New Theme," *Rhythm*, September 1932, p. 33. Several versions of the "Rockin' Chair" story will be found in assorted clippings and interview transcripts on file at ATM.

12. Barbara Lea, conversation with the author, March 30, 1999.

13. "Hoagy Carmichael, the Lawyer," *Indiana University Law Update* 4, no. 1 (Spring 1994), pp. 10–11.

14. Hoagy Carmichael, typewritten reminiscence, c. 1955, apparently an addendum to a letter, IU Archives.

15. *JB*, XII/18, and *SIW*, p. 190.

16. *JB*, XIII/1.

17. Contrary to some assertions, *King of Jazz* was not Hollywood's first all-color musical; that honor belongs to Warner Brothers' *On with the Show*, produced in 1929. Among its attractions: a young Ethel Waters, singing "Am I Blue?"

18. *JB*, XIII/3.

19. "Beverly Hills" quote from handwritten note to Ralph Hancock, c. 1957, ATM.

20. Lyric worksheets on file with Carmichael holdings at ATM. Used with permission.

21. In a personal journal of those years, Al Rinker suggests that Carmichael asked Whiteman for a job. He may well have done so, given the success of "Washboard Blues"; but it must have seemed, even to Hoagy, a long shot, given Carmichael's inability to read music—not to mention the fact that the orchestra already included two pianists and, with Mildred Bailey added, a total of seven vocalists. Gary Giddins, conversation with the author, June 7, 2000.

22. *SIW*, pp. 166–67.

23. *JB*, XIII/5–6.

24. *JB*, XIII/6–7.

25. Letter from Hoagy Carmichael to Hugh Niven, undated, ATM.

26. Harry Orchard, letter to Robert D. Hamontre, dated May 3, 1983, and Carmichael, handwritten note to Ralph Hancock, c. 1957, both ATM.

27. Letter from Hoagy Carmichael to Hugh Niven, undated, ATM.

28. *JB*, XIII/8.

29. *SIW*, pp. 213–14. Handwritten note to Ralph Hancock, c. 1957, ATM.

30. Harry Orchard, letter to Robert D. Hamontre, dated May 3, 1983, ATM.

31. *SIW*, p. 221.

32. Dow Richardson, "New York Neighbors Stop and Listen While Hoagie Carmichael Is at Work," *Indianapolis Star*, n.d. 1930, ATM.

33. Another Carmichael anomaly. As originally published by Peer, the verse of "Georgia on My Mind" is sixteen bars long, its text as given here. Later editions, including the version newly edited and corrected in the 1999 *Centennial Collection* of Carmichael songs, have shortened the verse to eight bars and altered its text. It is the author's view, and that of several performers of Carmichael songs, that the later version sacrifices much of the passage's evocative power.

34. This example uses the melody as published by Peer in 1930, rather than the later Carmichael revision, in a different key, that appears in the 1983 *Stardust Melodies* collection published by Belwin-Mills. The reason for this surprisingly altered later version appears to lie in a copyright dispute between the two companies.

35. "Hoagy," Bud Freeman, in conversation with Irving Kolodin, *Saturday Review*, June 28, 1969, pp. 44–45. Also excerpts from Freeman's notes to *The Music of Hoagy Carmichael*, Monmouth-Evergreen LP MES/6917, 1969.

36. In *Sometimes I Wonder* (p. 216), Carmichael speaks of thinking up both melody and lyrics for "Georgia on My Mind," adding that "Stu Gorrell, one of my roommates, pitched in and gave me some help. As a result I gave Stu an interest in the song." Gorrell, it will be remembered, was the Kappa Sig fraternity brother and longtime Carmichael friend who had first suggested the name for "Star Dust."

37. Mitchell Parish, conversation with Brian Priestley, June 28, 1985.

38. Close study of these three late-1920s records is useful in tracing the conceptual evolution of "Star Dust." Redman's version, recorded for OKeh October 13, 1928, retains the written key of D-major, but fills out sectional voicings considerably for the larger McKinney's Cotton Pickers personnel. Clearly with dancers in mind, it also interjects rhythmic brass figures borrowed from the newly popular tango and reinforced in the rhythm. A quite rare version recorded about a month later (November 8) in New York by an Irving Mills group moves the key up half a step to E♭ and slows the tempo to a ballad-like ♩ = 120, as compared to the ♩ = 136 of the Carmichael Gennett and the even brisker ♩ = 156 of the Redman. Another Mills version, recorded more than a year later with the composer at the piano, predictably returns the tempo to Hoagy's original. But Mills's arranger, identity unknown, rescores the Carmichael piano chorus as a three-saxophone passage under Jimmy Dorsey's alto lead, leaving Hoagy to play as a piano solo what had been a clarinet paraphrase on the Gennett.

39. Breyley material from James T. Maher, in a note to the author dated March 11, 2001.

40. Handwritten note to Ralph Hancock, c. 1957, ATM.

41. The name "Harvey" seems to have had a humorous significance for Carmichael. A pet canary became "Harvey II," a later pet monkey (!) "Harvey III."

42. "My Sweet" was recorded again in 1938, by Django Reinhardt and the Quintette of the Hot Club of France. But there is no vocal, and the melody statement by violinist Stephane Grappelly is obviously derived from the Armstrong record.

43. Several earlier records, by Ben Selvin's Columbia studio orchestra (April 22, 1931), the Mills Blue Rhythm Band (May 1, 1931), and a "Ted Wallace" date contracted by California Ramblers founder-manager W. (for Wallace) T. "Ed" Kirkeby (May 29, 1931), draw on the same Mills "stock." All are slower than the Armstrong version, necessitating extensive cutting and pasting. Significantly, all performances allocate generous solo space to trumpet, muted and open. In contrast to the Armstrong, the Selvin and Kirkeby records present the verse, entire or in part, but only instrumentally, with vocals on the chorus. The Blue Rhythm Band attempts a fusion, incorporating a few bars of the stock in a performance closer in spirit to the Isham Jones record.

44. Mills staff arranger Jimmy Dale, whose name is on the published "stock" of "Star Dust," is generally credited as the first to suggest playing the piece at a slower tempo. Indeed, the original printed parts are marked "slowly, with expression."

45. Watson was in charge of New York releases for Victor's "race" catalogue. It was his invitation that brought young Henry "Red" Allen north from New Orleans in mid-1929 to record for Victor, after which the trumpeter joined Luis Russell's orchestra at the Saratoga Club. Watson also arranged Victor dates for Russell's musicians in 1930 (under Higginbotham's name) and again in 1931, after OKeh failed to renew the pianist-leader's contract. Watson deeply admired Miley's plunger work with Ellington and helped bring the Ellington orchestra to Victor in 1927. After leaving Ellington, Miley picked up work with Noble Sissle and others, but spent much of his time out of work. Watson continued to offer help, recording "Bubber" as unbilled soloist with Leo Reisman's society orchestra on the debut recording of "What Is This Thing Called Love?" and booking him for a date under his own name five days before the Carmichael session. The titles done at both the Miley and Carmichael dates were released as "race" items. By this time Miley was seriously ill with tuberculosis and all but destitute. He died, age twenty-nine, in early 1932.

46. Hoagy Carmichael, remarks to the author, September–October 1979.

47. *JB*, XIII/16.

48. *SR*, p. 3.

Chapter X

1. *SIW*, p. 213.

2. See Drew Page, *Drew's Blues* (Baton Rouge: LSU Press, 1980). Informally, Arodin and fellow-musicians in New Orleans had taken to calling the number "Lazy Nigger." Many of today's readers will wince at his casual use of what is now a proscribed epithet, but this, again, must be understood in its historical, demographic, and geographical context. Born and raised in New Orleans, perhaps of part Creole or Cajun extraction, the clarinetist played regularly with both white musicians

and black, friendly with, and respected by, both. As Miller and others attested, his employment of the term is closer to that long used by blacks among themselves with a wide and flexible range of meaning, even to include obvious endearment.

3. William Zinsser, "From Natchez to Mobile, From Memphis to St. Joe," *American Scholar*, Spring 1994, p. 259.

4. Some, inevitably, have heard this as evidence of anti-Semitism in Carmichael, a contention hard to support; though the original lead sheet, dated 1925 and on file at IU Archives, is clearly titled "Jew-Boy Blues," and Carmichael in later years occasionally inveighed against the practices of such Jewish businessmen as Irving Mills and various Hollywood executives, there is no evidence of any more generalized bias. Certainly his relations with (and admiration for) such Jewish fellow-musicians as Benny Goodman, Artie Shaw, and Mannie Klein, not to mention fellow-songwriters Berlin, Harold Arlen, and above all George Gershwin, appear to dispel such notions. It seems safe to assume that Hoagy, in common with most gentile Americans of those years, indulged in a certain amount of stereotyping of allegedly "Jewish" mannerisms and business practices. But there is little sign of anything beyond that.

5. Hoagy Carmichael, letter c. 1946, addressed to Mark Saxton, editor at Rinehart and Co. Publishers, ATM. Saxton appears to be the editor who helped Carmichael assemble the manuscript of what was published as *The Stardust Road*. If Carmichael's judgment of Peer seems harsh, it is useful to remember that his only prior experience with New York publishing had been with Irving Mills, a relationship that had ended in acrimony.

6. Born in Battle Creek, Michigan, in 1899, Charles "Sunny" Clapp first played saxophone, appearing with the Six Brown Brothers saxophone sextet, among other groups. After switching to trombone, he played with Arthur Pryor and John Philip Sousa; worked extensively throughout the Southwest with white "territory" bands; wrote such songs as the popular waltz "Girl of My Dreams"; contracted and played on New York record dates for both Irving Mills and Ralph Peer. He died in 1962. John Randolph, "Sunny's Sunshine Jazz," *Jazz Journal*, December 1954, pp. 14–15.

7. *JB*, XIII/12–14. Portions of this text also appeared in *Metronome* magazine in July and August of 1933.

8. *SIW*, p. 223.

9. *SIW*, p. 215.

10. Harry Orchard, letter to Robert D. Hamontre, dated May 3, 1983, ATM.

11. "Gin Agin," handwritten worksheet, ATM.

12. Newspaper clippings, n.d. 1930–33, preserved in scrapbooks assembled by Georgia Carmichael Maxwell and on file at ATM. Paul D. Miller, "Song Hits and Royalties Cause Hoosier to Devote Full Time to Piano Keyboard," *Indianapolis Sunday Star*, December 10, 1933.

13. Part of the opening phrase occurs at the start of "The Shadow of Your Smile," written in 1965 by Johnny Mandel for the film *The Sandpiper*. According to a widely circulated account, Johnny Mercer was to have written the lyric to Mandel's tune, but balked because he thought the melody a "steal." While Mercer may have cited this as his reason for backing out, turning it over to Paul Francis Webster, strong inferential evidence suggests only that he failed to come up with a lyric satisfying the needs of the movie. Long after "The Shadow of Your Smile" had become a hit, he showed Mandel the lyric he'd tried to write: "It was the saddest, most terrible lyric he'd ever done," the composer said (conversation with the author, August 24, 2000). "Something about a bird with a broken wing . . . just terrible. He used to sing it at parties in a medley of 'things I screwed up.' "

While the first six notes of Mandel's tune are indeed those of "New Orleans," their uses could not be more different: in "Shadow," five of the six are a long pickup to a downbeat; "New Orleans" uses only a one-note pickup, the other five inside the double bar as the song's first phrase. Lying easily under the hand, the figure traces a chordal movement common in popular song. Even the suggestion that Mandel "stole" so fragmentary a phrase is as groundless as the canard that Don Redman wrote the verse of "Star Dust."

"One day, years later," said Mandel, "Hoagy said to [Mercer], 'How come you never wrote "The Shadow of Your Smile?" ' And Johnny told him about that whole thing, saying 'It's like "New Orleans." ' And Hoagy said, 'I never noticed.' " Also relevant in this connection is the fact that Mandel arranged and conducted Hoagy's 1956 Pacific Jazz LP *Hoagy Sings Carmichael*, on which the composer turned out poignant vocal performances on ten of his own songs, including "New Orleans."

14. Johnny Mercer, unpublished autobiography, Mercer (Popular Music) Collection, Pullen Library, Georgia State University. Chapter V, pp. 11–12; Chapter XIII, pp. 3–4. Used by permission.

15. *SIW*, p. 239. Hoagy Carmichael, letter to Mark Saxton, c. 1946, ATM.

16. The role of the Casa Loma Orchestra in the popular music world of the early 1930s was great and pervasive. Formed out of a Jean Goldkette unit, it was crisp, well rehearsed, impressive even in appearance and demeanor. Arranger Gene Gifford seemed equally adept at richly scored ballads and up-tempo jazz instrumentals. Perhaps more than any other single writer, he set the stage for the mid-1930s swing band eruption, with arrangements that played brass and reeds off against one another in question-and-answer fashion, using repeated motivic figures, or riffs. The orchestra's immense popularity between 1931 and 1934 virtually guaranteed attention and major exposure for a new song of any promise. That included such Carmichael efforts as "Lazybones," "New Orleans," "Moon Country," and "Judy."

17. Thomas A. DeLong, *Pops: Paul Whiteman, King of Jazz* (New York: New Century Publishers, 1983), p. 170. Ella Logan was another Youth of America winner, her prize a six-month token movie contract with MGM.

18. A silent movie titled *Lazybones*, featuring cowboy star Charles "Buck" Jones in the title role, played Bloomington's Princess Theatre December 18–19, 1925. Described by film critic Leonard Maltin as a "poignant evocation of small-town life from the turn of the century into the 1920s," it follows the fortunes of an amiable ne'er-do-well. Carmichael was in Bloomington at the time, must have been at least aware of the film, and may even have seen it; perhaps the hometown concept embodied in the very word "Lazybones" appealed as much to him as to Mercer.

19. Carmichael account from biographical letter, n.d. 1933, to "Tom," probably Cincinnati-based fan Tom Adler, ATM. Mercer, see note 14 above. Excerpt used by permission of Gene Lees.

20. Roger Hewitt, "Black Through White: Hoagy Carmichael and the Cultural Reproduction of Racism," *Popular Music 3: Producers and Markets* (Cambridge: Cambridge University Press, 1983).

21. Barbara Tuchman, lecture to National Archives conference on research in the Second World War, June 1971; first published in *Maryland Historian*, Fall 1971, anthologized in *Practicing History* (New York: Ballantine, 1982).

22. Krin Gabbard, *Jammin' at the Margins: Jazz and American Cinema* (Chicago: University of Chicago Press, 1996). Authorship of the "Old Man Harlem" lyric remains open to question: Rudy Vallee introduced the song on the radio, presumably in return for co-composer credit à la Irving Mills. Carmichael himself, in his 1933 letter to "Tom" (see note 19 above), containing material obviously intended for publication, credits Vallee. But in a 1946 letter to *Stardust Road* editor Mark Saxton he identifies Mercer, not yet the commanding presence he soon became, as the real lyricist. Both letters, ATM. The only lyric sheet on file at IU is in Carmichael's unmistakable hand.

23. Hoagy Bix Carmichael, conversation with the author, September 27, 1999.

24. Carl T. Rowan, address at Johnny Mercer memorial tribute, Music Box Theatre, New York City, July 22, 1976.

25. Hoagy Carmichael, letter to Mark Saxton, c. 1946, ATM.

26. Ibid.

27. Memo to Ralph Hancock, c. 1957, ATM. Mercer quoted by John Edward Hasse in notes to *The Classic Hoagy Carmichael*, boxed CD set compiled and issued by the Indiana Historical Society, 1988, p. 58.

28. Memo to Ralph Hancock, c. 1957, ATM. *SIW*, p. 240.

29. Alec Wilder, *American Popular Song* (New York: Oxford University Press, 1972), p. 377.

30. Hoagy Carmichael interview by "Sherry" on *CBC Showcase: There's More to Hoagy Carmichael Than Stardust*, CBC (Canadian Broadcasting Corporation) Radio, Toronto, c. 1965, tape on file at ATM. Several singers, accompanied by a large studio orchestra, perform Carmichael hits.

31. For an altogether more satisfying representation of the song it is best to turn to an April 5, 1934, record by the British orchestra of Ray Noble, with a vocal by crooner Al Bowlly. They make no attempt to "swing" the song, instead presenting the melody over a smooth *alla breve* rhythm. An invigorating performance.

32. Paul R. Summers, letter to Georgia Carmichael Maxwell, dated December 11, 1962, ATM.

33. Carmichael's use of the term "bolero" in this context is puzzling and perhaps inaccurate. In its original form, and as adapted by Maurice Ravel in his famed 1928 orchestral piece, the Spanish dance is in 3/4 time. A 2/4 variant, with African elements added, achieved great popularity in 1920s Cuba, where Carmichael may have heard it; but it is most often played more slowly than *Phrases* would indicate. The letter is on file at ATM.

34. Score and parts on file in the Whiteman Collection, Williams College. Copies in the possession of the author.

35. Paul R. Summers, letter to Georgia Carmichael Maxwell, dated December 11, 1962, ATM.

36. In their unpublished Whiteman biography, *The Whiteman Years*, historians Warren W. Scholl and Lee Chadwick note that the Sunday evening Cascade Room dinner concerts began in December 1933, only days after repeal of Prohibition.

37. The themes, and overall elegaic shape, of *Echo[es] of the Opera* reemerged fifteen years later as Carmichael's orchestral tone poem *Brown County in Autumn*, premiered at Carnegie Hall. Critical reaction to the work, indicative of unfathomed depths in this composer's musical consciousness, was harsh, apparently discouraging him from further such efforts. Fortunately, Carmichael had the New York performance recorded: heard now, *Brown County* seems a highly promising work, more ambitious by far than the piecemeal *Johnny Appleseed Suite* that occupied his thoughts in later years. Both works are discussed at greater length later in the text.

38. Howard Phillips Lovecraft, letter to E. Hoffmann Price, 1934, quoted by Jim Turner in introduction to *Eternal Lovecraft: The Persistence of HPL in Popular Culture* (Collinsville, Ill.: Golden Gryphon Press, 1998), p. xiv.

39. Richard G. Hubler, "Hoagy Carmichael: Melancholy Minstrel," *Coronet*, November 1954, p. 116. Willson quote from unindentified 1935 news item in Carmichael scrapbook, ATM.

40. Duncan P. Schiedt, "Hoagy Carmichael: Some Afterthoughts...," *Mississippi Rag*, February 1982, p. 1.
41. Manuscript, undated, ATM.

Chapter XI

1. Eva Ford Chatman, conversations with Patricia Kellar, March 3 and 4, 1996, and the author, October 23, 1998.
2. *SIW*, pp. 248–49. Here and elsewhere, Hoagy also mentions having a roommate at the time, Richard "Dick" Huber, and that the two of them found Eva by advertising for a maid. Huber was indeed one of several friends who roomed at the 52nd Street apartment from time to time; if he was a full-time resident at all it was only briefly, and there is scant independent substantiation for the "maid" story.
3. Draft of *SIW*, p. 283, ATM.
4. Eva Ford Chatman, conversations with Patricia Kellar, March 3 and 4, 1996, and the author, October 23, 1998.
5. Charles Schwartz, *Gershwin: His Life and Music* (New York: Bobbs-Merrill, 1973), p. 47. Edward Jablonski, *Gershwin* (Boston: Northeastern University Press, 1987), p. 48.
6. Harry Evans, "Odds and Ends," *Family Circle*, September 1934.
7. The irony in this comparison is too profound to be ignored. Gershwin's various biographers are unanimous in acknowledging his technical and theoretical shortcomings. Isaac Goldberg, the earliest (1931), states categorically that Gershwin knew "as much harmony as could be found in a ten-cent manual." From all accounts his early studies with Artur Bodanzky, Edward Kilenyi, and Rubin Goldmark, and later with Joseph Schillinger, Wallingford Riegger, and Henry Cowell, left little imprint. "Notwithstanding Gershwin's enormous facility at improvising," biographer Charles Schwartz (1973) writes, "there were many gaps in his musicianship besides his limited knowledge of harmony." Schwartz cites the composer's haphazard sight-reading and limited grasp of counterpoint and orchestration, branding him "an indifferent music student—self-indulgent, dilettantish, often casual and uncertain in his musical approach, and at times inept" (pp. 53–56). Carmichael, of course, knew none of this: he saw only the face that Gershwin, with his all-consuming energy and bravado, turned to the public—and which so thoroughly intimidated him. And, too, there was another dimension: Carmichael's Indiana youth had left him with an ill-defined ambivalence toward Jews. Small bits of testimony—from friends, colleagues, even his sons—make clear the degree to which admiration and envy, respect and outright mistrust, coexisted in his relations with Jewish colleagues and business associates. While he could admire the prodigious gifts of a Benny Goodman or Richard Rodgers, he

regarded such businessmen as Irving Mills and Jake Shubert with suspicion. It is not hard to imagine the conflicting emotions triggered in Carmichael by Gershwin's flashiness and flair for apparently limitless self-promotion.

8. Richard M. Sudhalter and Philip R. Evans, *Bix: Man and Legend* (New Rochelle, N.Y.: Arlington House, 1974), p. 211.

9. Hoagy Carmichael, conversation with the author, spring 1979, combined with *SIW*, p. 248.

10. *SIW*, p. 248.

11. Eva Ford Chatman, conversation with the author, October 23, 1998.

12. No such date is listed in the Wolverines itinerary compiled by Beiderbecke scholar Philip R. Evans. The Wolverines did play a brief noon dance at the Starr Piano Company's downtown Indianapolis showroom on Saturday, May 31, 1924. Perhaps it is this date that she remembered.

13. Neal Gabler, *An Empire of Their Own: How the Jews Invented Hollywood* (New York: Crown, 1988), p. 223.

14. Helen Meinardi Stearns, conversation with Patricia Kellar and Peter Davies, February 26, 1996. Used with permission.

15. Ibid. A slightly different version of these events will be found in Alice Craig Greene, "Happy Anniversary to Hoagy Carmichael," *Screen Stars*, February 1951, pp. 70–88.

16. Hoagy Bix Carmichael, conversation with the author, April 20, 2000.

17. Helen Meinardi Stearns, conversation with Patricia Kellar and Peter Davies, February 26, 1996. Used with permission. Additional matter from *Screen Stars* article and from author's telephone conversations with Stearns.

18. *SIW*, p. 249.

19. Helen Meinardi Stearns, conversation with Patricia Kellar and Peter Davies, February 26, 1996. Used with permission.

20. Hoagy Bix Carmichael, conversations with the author, September 27 and December 16, 1998, and March–April 1999.

21. Helen Meinardi Stearns, conversation with Patricia Kellar and Peter Davies, February 26, 1996. Used with permission.

22. Helbock had approached Carmichael back in the early 1930s as a possible investor in the new club, to open after repeal. "Turned it down: otherwise would have made young fortune" was Hoagy's wry account of it (Hoagy Carmichael, letter to Mark Saxton, c. 1946, ATM).

23. All citations from Pete Martin, "Star Dust Troubadour," *Saturday Evening Post*, November 8, 1947.

24. Quote from letter saved by Carmichael, ATM.

25. Article, title unknown, in *Melody Maker*, October 11, 1934, on file at Institute of Jazz Studies, Rutgers University, Newark, New Jersey.

26. With the exception of the composer's own performance on the 1956 *Hoagy Sings Carmichael* LP, "Ballad in Blue" went all but unperformed until 1981, when singer Barbara Lea unearthed and recorded it as part of a Carmichael tribute LP. Her darkly brooding interpretation can easily be regarded as definitive. When, in 1998, representatives of Peermusic, latter-day descendant of Peer's Southern Music Corp., prepared a CD and CD-ROM Carmichael sampler, Barbara Lea was the only artist besides the composer represented on three of the twenty-five tracks— with "Ballad in Blue," "Sing It Way Down Low," and "Winter Moon."

27. *SIW*, p. 247. In the weeks between leaving Peer and signing with Warners, Hoagy apparently dashed off "Song of Spring," its sustained notes, Kern-like intervals, and nostalgic lyric ("Love is perfume we'll always wear, dear . . .") an obvious follow-up to "One Morning in May." He quickly sold it to the Brill Building firm of Santly Brothers.

28. Lyric sheet on file at IU Archives. Given the context and the nature of Carmichael's emendations, Heyman may well have meant "rhyme scheme."

29. Hoagy Bix Carmichael, conversations with the author, September 27 and December 16, 1998, and various dates during 1999.

30. "In My Wildest Dreams," copyrighted at the same time (and not to be confused with the 1937 Johnny Mercer–Arthur Schwartz collaboration), appears not to have been published at all. A lyric sheet on file at IU indicates that Carmichael wrote both music and words.

31. Thomas A. DeLong, *The Mighty Music Box: The Golden Age of Network Radio* (Los Angeles: Amber Crest Books, 1980), p. 229.

32. Ernie Pyle, "Insomnia and Stock Market Plague Composer of Song Hits," *Washington Daily News*, July 7, 1936.

33. Wilfrid Mellers, *Angels of the Night: Popular Female Singers of Our Time* (New York: Basil Blackwell, 1986), p. 44. "Bread and Gravy" was finally published in 1999, as part of the Hal Leonard Corporation's *Hoagy Carmichael Centennial Collection*.

34. Helen Meinardi Stearns, conversation with Patricia Kellar and Peter Davies, February 26, 1996. Used with permission.

35. Description excerpted from contemporary newspaper and wire service news items, from *SIW* (p. 253), and from various Bud Freeman accounts including *You Don't Look Like a Musician* (Detroit: Balamp, 1974).

36. Joe Bushkin, conversation with Peter Davies, December 1996. Used by permission.

37. *SIW*, p. 254.

38. Like "Bread and Gravy," "Lyin' to Myself" first saw publication in 1999, in the *Hoagy Carmichael Centennial Collection*. "Ev'ntide," copyrighted but still unpublished at this writing, contains a musically interesting *trompe l'oreille*, an

auditory illusion rare in popular song and found nowhere else in Carmichael's music. In the written key of E♭, the melody at first suggests a resolution in F, then pivots on a single chord to resolve in E♭.

"Ev'ntide" (bars 1–8), 1933

The device occurs only once in the song, resulting in what might be identified as an ABCB[1] structure.

Chapter XII

1. Edward G. Robinson with Leonard Spiegelgass, *All My Yesterdays* (New York: Hawthorn, 1973), p. 109.
2. Niccolò Machiavelli, *The Prince* (New York: Modern Library, 1940), pp. 60–61.
3. Neal Gabler, *An Empire of Their Own: How the Jews Invented Hollywood* (New York: Crown, 1988), p. 322.
4. Jerome Chodorov, William Wiener Oral History Library, American Jewish Committee, quoted ibid., p. 323.
5. Patricia Dubin McGuire, *Lullaby of Broadway: The Life and Times of Al Dubin* (Secaucus, N.J.: Citadel, 1983), pp. 111–12.
6. Richard Rodgers, *Musical Stages: An Autobiography* (New York: Random House, 1975), p. 165.
7. *SIW*, pp. 192, 254.
8. Hoagy Bix Carmichael, conversation with the author, September 27, 1998. *SIW*, p. 254.
9. Helen Meinardi Stearns, conversation with Patricia Kellar and Peter Davies, February 26, 1996. Used with permission.
10. Otto Friedrich, *City of Nets: A Portrait of Hollywood in the 1940s* (New York: Harper & Row, 1986), p. 14.
11. Donald Bogle, "Louis Armstrong: The Films," in Marc H. Miller, ed., *Louis Armstrong: A Cultural Legacy* (Seattle: University of Washington Press and New York: Queens Museum of Art, 1994), p. 161.
12. Armstrong's performance is all the more admirable for the ease with which it surmounts the song's inherent weaknesses. Several passages in Carmichael's thirty-six-bar melody, played at the faster tempos prescribed by the content and

thrust of the lyric, lie awkwardly on the trumpet. Played or sung, the figure spanning bars 5–8, for example, is hard to negotiate cleanly without a loss of rhythmic flow. Vocally, Armstrong glosses it by flattening its contours; on trumpet he plays it, but subordinates it—and then, in his final chorus, discards it altogether; drawing on his unerring instincts he fashions a counterline that actually *enhances* Carmichael's ungainly figure. Another 1937 record, by the popular band of Larry Clinton, solves the same problem with a more prosaic—if nonetheless effective—expedient: pulling the tempo back to a perky $\downarrow$ = 174, thereby allowing vocalist Bea Wain ample room to reshape Adams's somewhat clumsy lyric into a coherent thought. For all its unevenness (the bridge, by contrast, is well suited to Armstrong's aria-like conception), "Jubilee" has long appealed to jazzmen in a manner not unlike Jerome Kern's earlier "Pick Yourself Up." The tonal center shifts every eight bars, the second eight pitched a major third higher than the first, and the final "A" section combines four bars of the original with an eight-bar "tag," or coda.

13. Elliot Norton, "Laugh Hit of the Year at Shubert," *Boston Sunday Post*, November 8, 1936.

14. James T. Maher, conversation with the author, April 24, 2000.

15. Søren Kierkegaard, *Either/Or*, vol. 1 (New York: Doubleday, 1959). Lillian Smith, *The Journey* (New York and Cleveland: World Publishing, 1954), p. 20.

16. Alec Wilder, *American Popular Song* (New York: Oxford University Press, 1972), p. 378.

17. Helen Meinardi Stearns, conversation with Patricia Kellar and Peter Davies, February 26, 1996. Used with permission.

18. Hoagy's infatuation with tennis led him, during a mid-1941 Bloomington visit, to suggest an innovative idea to alumni director George "Dixie" Heighway. Why not develop tennis into a major sport, both at IU and throughout the Big Ten? As he envisioned it, each school could employ a top tennis pro for three or four months a year at a fee of about $2,500 (the equivalent of nearly $30,000 in today's money). He'd discussed the idea, he said, with some ranking pros, including his frequent Westwood Tennis Club partner Don Budge, and enlisted their interest. Heighway, it turned out, was listening. In early 1942, with the country now at war and the government expanding physical education programs at major colleges and universities, he decided tennis might well be worth considering. "If all students are to participate in some form of competitive sport," Heighway wrote to IU director of athletics Zora Clevenger, "it seems to me that some thought might be given to the stimulation of tennis as part of this plan." Letter dated January 20, 1942, IU Archives.

19. *SIW*, p. 256.

20. Helen Meinardi Stearns, composite from conversations with the author and with Patricia Kellar, 1996.

21. Ibid.

22. As usual, the true division of labor on the text is hard to determine. A penciled lyric sheet in Carmichael's hand, on file at IU, contains crossed-out lines, alternative couplets, numerous rhyme schemes. It all suggests that, though Helen Meinardi surely supplied the title and much of the imagery, the actual lyric-writing may well have been by Carmichael.

23. Nor is this a difficulty unique to Hoagy Carmichael. More than a few finely wrought songs by instrumentalists or arrangers have failed to capture public fancy for no reason other than that they are too hard to hum or sing. For example, "Restless," a 1935 melody by pianist-arranger Tom Satterfield, has long enjoyed popularity among jazz musicians, but remains all but unknown to the public. Johnny Mercer, aware of such problems, sharply attenuated the intervals of Eddie Miller's 1938 tenor sax feature "Slow Mood" when converting it into a popular song. As "(Love's Got Me in a) Lazy Mood," it achieved great popularity in 1947.

24. Recording in 1987, singer Marlene VerPlanck found a wistful appeal at the core of "Old Man Moon" by slowing it down to ballad tempo and restructuring it slightly. Regrettably, her performance—issued only on the Indiana Historical Society's 1988 boxed set *The Classic Hoagy Carmichael*—has not yet inspired other singers to "discover" the song.

25. Some accounts have suggested that "The Nearness of You" was scheduled for, then dropped from, a 1938 Paramount feature, *Romance in the Dark*, starring singers John Boles and Gladys Swarthout and a tottering John Barrymore. But studio cue sheets, consulted by Ken Bloom in the preparation of his massive *Hollywood Song*, make clear that this was not so.

26. Max Wilk, *They're Playing Our Song* (New York: Zoetrope, 1986), p. 251. Susan Loesser quotes a similar account in *A Most Remarkable Fella: Frank Loesser and the Guys and Dolls in His Life* (New York: Donald Fine, 1993), pp. 26–27.

27. *SIW*, p. 260.

28. Wilk, *They're Playing Our Song*, pp. 252–54. *SIW*, p. 260. Perhaps with Irving Berlin's example in mind, the Carmichael-Loesser partnership also founded a joint publishing venture, Frank Music. Carmichael eventually pulled out, under circumstances now lost to memory. But to this day, Frank Music controls a number of major Carmichael songs, among them "Hong Kong Blues," "Doctor, Lawyer, Indian Chief," "My Resistance Is Low," "Ole Buttermilk Sky," and "The Lamplighter's Serenade."

29. Benny Green, *Let's Face the Music* (London: Pavilion, 1989), pp. 143–44.

30. In the sheet music they are rendered not specifically as quarters but as, in order, a brace of eighths ("old"), a quarter ("Hong"), and a phrase-ending half-note ("Kong"). However the effect is achieved, the placement of these notes lends them the emphasis and functional value of quarters.

31 John McDonough, conversation with the author, September 25, 1999. Used by permission of National Public Radio.

Chapter XIII

1. Robert Kee, *The World We Left Behind: A Chronicle of the Year 1939* (London: Weidenfeld, 1984), p. 10. Charles Schwartz, *Gershwin: His Life and Music* (New York: Bobbs-Merrill, 1973), p. 287.
2. Identity of "Stephen Powys" from items in *New York Times*, September 24 and October 26, 1939. Loretta Young information from *New York Herald Tribune*, November 19, 1937, and Fox press release of March 12, 1938. Later movie adaptations of *Three Blind Mice* include *Moon Over Miami* (1941), with Betty Grable, and *Three Little Girls in Blue* (1946), with June Haver, Celeste Holm, Vivian Blaine, and Vera-Ellen.
3. Different versions of this incident mention Carmichael pals Stu Gorrell, Harry Hostetter, and Wad Allen among other candidates. The friend, whoever he is, clips the poem out of the magazine—or, according to another version, scrawls it on the back of a manila envelope—and hands it to the composer. Another, perhaps less likely, retelling has the poet herself sending it to him. All accounts agree that Carmichael read it and liked it enough to save among his papers.
4. "Except Sometimes," published in *Life*, May 18, 1922, p. 5.
5. Clearly the use of "like" in this context disturbed Carmichael. In various personal appearances, and in a television re-creation of the circumstances of the song's birth, he pointedly substituted the more grammatically appropriate "as": "I've forgotten you just as I should..."
6. Alec Wilder, *American Popular Song* (New York: Oxford University Press, 1972), pp. 381–82. Lees from conversation with the author, June 30, 2000.
7. Neal Gabler, *Walter Winchell: Gossip, Power, and the Culture of Celebrity* (New York: Knopf, 1994), p. xi.
8. Walter Winchell, program of November 27, 1938, pp. 3–4, script on file at Library of the Performing Arts, New York Public Library. Here, as in his other broadcast material, Winchell has punctuated his script as it will be read, with little reference to either grammar or syntax. The passages quoted here have been repunctuated in the interests of clarity and the demands of the printed page.
9. Ibid., December 4, 1938. In biographer Gabler's words, the "Oddities" section of each Winchell broadcast included "offbeat stories that would have been regarded as filler in a newspaper or magazine."
10. Walter Winchell, "On Broadway," *New York Daily Mirror*, Tuesday, December 27, 1938.
11. Ibid., January 3, 1939.

12. Roger S. B. Hinsley, "Except Sometimes: A Research Foray Into the Affairs of Jane Brown Thompson and Hoagland Carmichael." Typescript, unpublished, ATM.

13. *SIW*, p. 261.

14. "Hoagy's Mother 'Swings That Bass' in Radio Debut," *Indianapolis Star*, March 2, 1939. Herb Sanford, *Tommy and Jimmy: The Dorsey Years* (New Rochelle, N.Y.: Arlington House, 1972), p. 149.

15. Sanford, *Tommy and Jimmy*, pp. 155–56.

16. Julia McCarthy. "World of Swing O.K. to Burgess Meredith," *New York Sunday News*, November 19, 1939, p. 54.

17. Information based on file correspondence in the archives of the Shubert Organization, New York City.

18. Letter from Shubert attorney Adolph Kaufman to Walter Greaza, Actors' Equity Association, dated February 26, 1940, on file in Shubert Organization archives.

19. "Inner circle" quote from Robert Pollack, unidentified, undated clipping on file at Rodgers and Hammerstein Collection, New York Public Library.

20. Jerry Stagg, *The Brothers Shubert* (New York: Random House, 1968), pp. 337–38.

21. Review by Brooks Atkinson, *New York Times*, June 5, 1940.

22. Reviews by Richard Watts Jr. (*New York Herald-Tribune*), John Anderson (*New York Journal-American*), Burns Mantle (*New York Daily News*), and John Mason Brown (*New York Post*), all dated June 5, 1940, and on file at New York Public Library, Performing Arts Collection.

23. Kitty Carlisle Hart, conversation with the author, May 18, 2000. Betty Lawford, referred to here, was a replacement for Mary Brian.

24. Brooks McNamara, *The Shuberts of Broadway* (New York: Oxford University Press, 1990), p. 194.

25. Johnny Mercer, unpublished autobiography, Mercer (Popular Music) Collection, Pullen Library, Georgia State University. Chapter X, pp. 3–4. Used by permission.

26. *SIW*, p. 265.

27. "All in Fun" reemerged after 1944, when George Murphy sang it in the Hollywood musical *Broadway Rhythm*. It is now performed occasionally as a valued but minor standard.

28. Kern's song performs similar harmonic sorcery. At one point, emerging from the release in E-major, it converts a G sharp, third step of the E-major chord, to an A♭, third of an F-minor seventh, returning the melody easily to its home key of A♭. Both songs move forward on consciously "poetic" texts.

29. *SIW*, p. 256.

30. Kitty Carlisle Hart, conversation with the author, May 18, 2000.

31. Quoted in David Ewen, *George Gershwin: His Journey to Greatness*, 2d ed. (New York: Ungar, 1986), p. 275.

32. Carmichael gave Broadway one more try, if a small one. He and lyricist Paul Francis Webster collaborated on "If You Don't Love Me," scheduled for use in the 1950 revue *Alive and Kicking*. By the show's January 17 opening night the song had been dropped, and *Alive and Kicking* folded after only forty-seven performances. It's now best remembered for its cast of talented youngsters, among them dancer Gwen Verdon and comedians Carl Reiner and Jack Gilford.

Chapter XIV

1. Editorial, *Time*, December 15, 1941.
2. Geoffrey Perrett, *Days of Sadness, Years of Triumph: The American People, 1939–1945* (Madison: University of Wisconsin Press, 1985), pp. 205–6, 237.
3. *This Fabulous Century*, vol. 5 (Alexandria, Va.: Time-Life Books, 1969), pp. 201–3. Also Perrett, *Days of Sadness*, pp. 219–20.
4. Purchase price information quoted by Pete Martin in "Star-Dust Troubadour," *Saturday Evening Post*, November 8, 1947. The recollections of Hoagy Bix Carmichael, based on family conversation, place the figure considerably lower, at about $55,000—approximately $625,000 in today's currency.
5. A. M. Sperber and Eric Lax, *Bogart* (New York: William Morrow, 1997), p. 464.
6. Hoagy Bix Carmichael, conversation with the author, September 27, 1998. Randy Bob Carmichael, conversation with the author, November 24, 1998.
7. Hoagy Bix Carmichael, conversation with the author, September 27, 1999.
8. Randy Bob Carmichael, conversation with the author, November 24, 1998.
9. Memo to Ralph Hancock, c. 1957, ATM.
10. Amanda Mercer Neder, conversation with the author, October 24, 1998.
11. Johnny Mercer, unpublished autobiography, Mercer (Popular Music) Collection, Pullen Library, Georgia State University. Chapter XIII, p. 4. Used by permission.
12. Gene Lees and Alan Bergman, conversations with the author, both July 13, 2000.
13. In a curious article published in spring of 2000, the august *American Heritage* magazine adjudged "Skylark" the twentieth century's "most underrated song." Author Max Rudin, publisher of the Library of America book series, goes on at great and flowery length about the song, comparing Mercer's ornithological evocation to those of Shelley and Keats, bearing "a message from a faraway world of evanescent beauty . . . Mercer's American songbird sings of the vanishing American rural life itself, and its beautiful song, like the ravishing, heartbreaking tune Carmichael gives it, carries the impossible sweet ache of intense nostalgia . . . In 1941, on the eve of Pearl Harbor and the enormous transformations to come, the song is like a farewell not only to a lost love but to a vanishing country and a vanishing time."

Rudin's judgment is curious, in that "Skylark" has never been either overlooked or underrated—except, perhaps, by those listeners and performers for whom any consciousness of popular music begins with the coming of rock in the late 1950s. Not surprisingly considering its origins, jazz and cabaret performers have long since made it their own, and it remains a favorite of non-rock instrumentalists and singers, also ranking high in the affections of partisans of what has come to be called the "Great American Song Book."

14. Todd McCarthy, *Howard Hawks: The Grey Fox of Hollywood* (New York: Grove Press, 1997), an informative and estimable biography.

15. Robert Wilson, ed., *The Film Criticism of Otis Ferguson* (Philadelphia: Temple University Press, 1971), pp. 216, 256.

16. McCarthy, *Howard Hawks*, p. 290.

17. Hawks-Hemingway exchange from *Hawks on Hawks*, quoted in Otto Friedrich, *City of Nets: A Portrait of Hollywood in the 1940s* (New York: Harper & Row, 1986), p. 240.

18. McCarthy, *Howard Hawks*, p. 368.

19. Pete Martin, "Star-Dust Troubadour," *Saturday Evening Post*, November 8, 1947.

20. Randy Bob Carmichael, conversation with the author, November 24, 1998.

21. *SIW*, p. 268.

22. Sperber and Lax, *Bogart*, pp. 260–61.

23. *SIW*, pp. 267–68.

24. Quoted in Marjie Gates Giffen, *If Tables Could Talk* (Indianapolis: Columbia Club, 1988), p. 70.

25. James D. Hart, *The Oxford Companion to American Literature*, 5th ed. (New York: Oxford University Press, 1983).

26. Other entertainers who have worked within this Hoosier tradition include radio and television humorist Herb Shriner (1918–1970), born in Ohio but brought up in Indiana, and radio raconteur and storyteller Jean Shepherd (1921–1999). Both drew heavily on Indiana people and events in spinning their folksy yarns, usually in making some basic point about human nature. It is surely no accident that Shriner, who was killed in an auto crash in 1970, named one of his two sons "Kin."

27. Hoagy Bix Carmichael, conversation with the author, September 27, 1999. Hoagy Carmichael interview with Tony Thomas, CBC (Canadian Broadcasting Corporation) Radio, n.d. 1964, tape on file at ATM. "Perfectionist" quote from Richard G. Hubler, "Melancholy Minstrel," *Coronet*, November 1954, p. 116.

28. Bogart quoted in Sperber and Lax, *Bogart*, from interview with Gladys Hall, May 9–10, 1946, Gladys Hall Collection, Margaret Herrick Library, Academy of Motion Picture Arts and Sciences.

29. Lauren Bacall, *By Myself* (New York: Knopf, 1979), p. 95.

30. McCarthy, *Howard Hawks*, p. 377.

31. Hoagy Bix Carmichael, interview with Mark Rowles for BBC Radio documentary *Hoagy on My Mind*, broadcast November 1999.

32. Hoagy Bix Carmichael, conversations with the author, September 27, 1998, and September 27, 1999.

33. Guy Webster, conversations with the author, November 3 and 11, 1998.

34. Hasse from booklet to *The Classic Hoagy Carmichael*, boxed LP/CD set issued by the Indiana Historial Society and the Smithsonian Collection of records, 1988, p. 36. The twenty-four-bar ABA structure also occurs in Carmichael's "Can't Get Indiana off My Mind," but in slightly more complex form.

35. Sheila Jordan, conversation with the author, July 22, 2000.

36. *Indianapolis Sunday Star*, June 14, 1942, p. 34, ATM.

37. Hoagy Bix Carmichael, conversation with the author, September 27, 1998.

38. *Sometimes I Wonder,* first typescript version, p. 311-D, on file at IU.

39. " 'War Song Must Go Deep,' Says 'Stardust' Author," *Los Angeles Times*, undated clipping in possession of Hoagy Bix Carmichael. Used by permission.

40. Like the earlier "I Get Along Without You Very Well," the lyric to "My Christmas Song for You" was based partly on an outside submission. In this case the original was by Furniss T. Peterson, described in a 1944 AP news feature as "an invalid in Tucson," and submitted in letters dated December 1943 and May 20, 1944, sent from a rest home in the Arizona city. Paul Webster, sharing lyricist credit, uses a generous amount of Mrs. Peterson's text, sharpening and focusing it through addition of several lines in the body of the lyric.

41. Among Carmichael's rejected lyrics for this uncompleted tribute are the lines:

> They're the smokin', jokin'
> People who're outspoken
> When you mention Roosevelt's name.
> They're the soda-drinkin'
> Relatives of Lincoln,
> Solid as a hickory frame.

42. Quoted by Pete Martin in "Star-Dust Troubadour," *Saturday Evening Post*, November 8, 1947.

43. Among the more entertaining wartime items heard on the shows is "There's Nobody Home on the Range," dealing with the specifics of the war effort and even managing a cleverly inserted plug for the sponsor, Safeway's Nu Made mayonnaise. Among sample lyrics:

> There's nobody home on the range,
> No, there's nobody left on the range.
> All the pistol-packin' Mamas
> Are at Douglas, buildin' bombers . . .

An archival search at the Library of Congress turned up no trace of the song. In all likelihood Carmichael never submitted it for copyright, judging that its topical content (and relentlessly generic cowboy-style melody) would not outlive the war.

44. Letters and postcards on file at ATM. Webb letter dated July 24, 1945. "Voice-less" reference from *New York Times* news feature dated August 18, 1946.

45. Carmichael quotes from *SIW*, p. 287. Radio information from John Dunning, *On the Air: The Encyclopedia of Old-Time Radio* (New York: Oxford University Press, 1998), p. 321. Buddy Cole's extraordinary career as pianist, arranger, and conductor came to an abrupt and tragic end with his death, of the effects of a heart attack, at age forty-nine on November 5, 1964. Much loved among col-leagues, next to unknown by the general public, he was widely mourned.

46. A handy index of the song's popularity is its use in one of the most celebrated radio broadcasts of the era. At 8:00 P.M. on Sunday, October 30, 1938, Orson Welles and the Mercury Theatre aired a dramatization of H. G. Wells's *The War of the Worlds*. The drama's early moments depict a live remote broadcast in progress, from the imaginary "Meridian Room of the Park Plaza Hotel," where the equally fictitious "Ramon Raquello and his orchestra" are playing popular favorites. Their opening selection, the tango "La Cumparsita," soon segues into a saccharine arrangement of "Star Dust."

Chapter XV

1. *SIW*, p. 269.

2. Krin Gabbard, *Jammin' at the Margins: Jazz and the American Cinema* (Chicago: University of Chicago Press, 1996), p. 263.

3. Harold Russell, conversation with the author, August 29, 2000.

4. *SIW*, p. 272. Hoagy Bix Carmichael, conversations with the author, September 27, 1999, and July 17, 2000.

5. William Wheatley, conversation with the author, December 12, 2000.

6. Intriguingly, Carmichael's original "Memphis" manuscript doesn't contain ei-ther this melody turn or the augmented chord that underpins it. Both were interpolated later, probably to conform with the demands of the lyric.

7. Randy Bob Carmichael, conversation with the author, November 24, 1998.

8. William Zinsser, "From Natchez to Mobile, From Memphis to St. Joe," *Amer-ican Scholar*, Spring 1994, p. 259. Barbara Lea, conversation with the author, July 20, 2000.

9. Sheilah Graham: "Composer Carmichael Becomes Movie Star; May Rival Sinatra in Bobbysoxers' Hearts," *Indianapolis Star*, August 12, 1945. "Acting Is Big Joke to Everyone but Hoagy Carmichael," *Indiana Alumni Magazine*, undated clip on file at ATM.

10. Hoagy Carmichael as told to Ted Toll, "Songwriting Is Luck, Talent, Luck, Hard Work, and Luck: Hoagy," *Down Beat*, May 1939, p. 18. "Star-Spangled Banner"

comment from *Indianapolis Times*, March 22, 1946. In 1957, Carmichael followed through on the idea, publishing his own revised version of the national anthem, its range reduced and large intervals eliminated. The Carmichael "Star-Spangled Banner" is part of the *Hoagy Carmichael Centennial Collection* published in 1999 by the Hal Leonard Corporation.

11. Lida Carmichael, letter to Hoagy Carmichael, undated but presumably c. 1946, IU Archives.

12. *SR*, p. 71.

13. Laurie Henshaw, "Hoagy Carmichael and the Bixian Legend," *Melody Maker*, August 7, 1948, p. 3.

14. *SR*, p. 25.

15. Hoagy Bix Carmichael, conversation with the author, September 27, 1999.

16. Herman Wells, letter to Hoagy Carmichael, dated October 14, 1941; correspondence between Hoagy Carmichael and George Heighway; all on file at IU Archives. Letters in this collection also allude to a November 19 broadcast, in which Carmichael did not participate, but which featured, among other selections, "Chimes of Indiana" and "Star Dust." "Chimes" was in fact not a new melody but the third version of the failed "One Night in Havana," stripped of its syncopation and slowed down to hymn-like tempo.

17. *Indiana Alumni Magazine*, October 1941, p. 13. The article also mentions that Carmichael "brought with him the two newest songs he has written, and gave them their world premiere at the dances sponsored by the alumni clubs of Fort Wayne, Terre Haute, and Evansville." The article does not identify the songs.

18. Parts of two letters from Lida Carmichael to Hoagy Carmichael, undated, but whose content places them in May and June 1945, ATM.

19. Correspondence on file at IU indicates that in late 1947 Carmichael and actor-producer Charles "Buddy" Rogers discussed a possible movie version of *The Stardust Road*, set in Bloomington, with the author playing himself. University officials welcomed the idea and in February 1948 informed Rogers by telegram and letter that the school "extends to you its fullest facilities to make this campus the locale for the movie you are planning on the life of Hoagy Carmichael." For reasons not explained, the film was never produced.

20. Howard "Wad" Allen, epilogue to *SR*, p. 151.

21. Brooks later collaborated with Harry Warren, on "You Wonderful You" (1950), "That's Amore," (1953), "Innamorata" (1955), "The Rose Tattoo" (1955), and "Somebody" (1960).

22. Hoagy Carmichael interview by "Sherry" on *CBC Showcase: "There's More to Hoagy Carmichael Than Stardust,* CBC (Canadian Broadcasting Corporation) Radio, Toronto, c. 1965, tape on file at ATM. Several singers, accompanied by a large studio orchestra, perform Carmichael hits.

23. Ibid.

24. *Joel Whitburn's Pop Memories* (Menomonee Falls, Wisc.: Record Research, 1986), pp. 76 (Carmichael), 264 (Kyser), and 562 (general ranking).

25. During the 1950s, as a member of a popular band led by trumpeter Bob Scobey, Hayes heard from Carmichael again. For some time he'd been singing his own amusing "Witch Watch Song," based on punning uses of the title words, at parties. But according to a friend, Chicago trombonist Jim Beebe, he considered it incomplete, not much more than an amusing fragment, and did little to shape it into a conventional song. Lyric sheets among Carmichael's papers suggest that Hoagy tried to finish Hayes's work and turn "Witch Watch" into a marketable song, perhaps for use in the children's collection published in the late 1950s. Hoagy Bix, in later life, remembered his father's revised version of the lyric word for word—indicating that, for a while at least, "Dad" put in some real work on it.

26. Randy Bob Carmichael, conversation with the author, November 24, 1998.

27. Ibid.

28. "Someday Soon" went unpublished, recorded commercially for the first time (by Carmichael interpreter Barbara Lea) in 1998.

29. "Hoagy Carmichael at London Casino," *Musical Express,* Friday, August 13, 1948, p. 1.

30. Max Jones, "The Old Music Master Says, 'I've No Patience With the Narrow Jazz Boys,'" *Melody Maker,* August 14, 1948, p. 4.

31. "Hoagy Carmichael Comes to Town," *Leicester Evening Mail,* September 6, 1948.

32. According to show business columnist Earl Wilson, the idea for "Bubble-Loo" sprang from a lyric submitted to Carmichael by a fan, a woman whose name the composer couldn't recall. Part of the submission wound up included in Paul Webster's lyric. "Then I couldn't locate the letter or remember the woman's name," Carmichael told Wilson. "I think she was from the Northwest, and was middle-aged." Through Wilson, he promised one-third of royalties to the writer if she would come forward. Despite this publicity ploy, used so successfully with "I Get Along Without You Very Well," the new song created little stir. "Bubble-Loo" was soon forgotten.

33. Corbin Patrick, "Symphony Orchestra Opens Concert Season," *Indianapolis Star,* November 13, 1949.

34. "Indiana Melody," *Time,* December 26, 1949. Walter Whitworth, "Hoagy's 'Brown County' Has All the Color," unidentified clipping on file at ATM.

35. In 1907, Steele and his second wife, the former Selma Neubacher, bought property in a particularly beautiful part of Brown County, where they built their "House of the Singing Winds." According to a biographical sketch provided by the Indiana State Museum, they "landscaped the surrounding hillsides to enhance the beauty of their property. Selma created several acres of gardens around the home. From 1907–21, the Steeles wintered in Indianapolis," estab-

lishing their Bloomington home after the artist's appointment to the university faculty. The Brown County house is now a museum, housing a great number of their works.

36. "Hoagy Concert Debut at Murat Big Success," *Indianapolis Sunday Star*, December 18, 1949.

37. Walter Whitworth, "Hoagy's 'Brown County' Has All the Color," unidentified clipping on file at ATM. Henry Butler, "Concert Marks Triple Triumph," *Indianapolis Sunday Star*, December 18, 1949.

38. "Stick to Jazz, N.Y.C. Critics Advise Hoagy," *Indianapolis Herald*, January 17, 1950. Kostelanetz quoted in *SIW*, p. 286.

39. Downes and Gilman quoted in David Ewen, *George Gershwin: His Journey to Greatness*, rev. ed. (New York: Ungar, 1986), p. 81.

40. "Indiana Melody," *Time*, December 26, 1949, on file at IU Archives.

41. Randy Bob Carmichael, conversation with the author, November 24, 1998.

42. Hoagy Bix Carmichael, conversation with the author, September 27, 1998.

Chapter XVI

1. *New York Sunday Herald-Tribune*, February 5, 1950.

2. James C. Robertson, *The Casablanca Man: The Cinema of Michael Curtiz* (New York: Routledge, 1993) pp. 102–5.

3. Ibid.

4. Krin Gabbard, *Jammin' at the Margins: Jazz and the American Cinema* (Chicago: University of Chicago Press, 1996), p. 75.

5. Kirk Douglas, *The Ragman's Son: An Autobiography* (New York: Simon & Schuster, 1994), p. 168.

6. Around the same time, *Variety* announced that actor Burgess Meredith, who had been closely involved with early plans for bringing *Young Man With a Horn* to screen or stage, had teamed with producer Benedict Bogeaus—Hoagy Carmichael's next-door neighbor in Holmby Hills—planning a film of Eddie Condon's jazz life, with another mutual friend, James Stewart, playing the guitarist and John O'Hara doing the screenplay. According to the item, "Meredith met Condon a few years back when former was due to play Bix Biederbecke [*sic*] in Vinton Freedley's projected legit production of 'Young Man With a Horn.' Play never was put on because of script trouble, but may yet be filmed." Clipping undated, but reproduced—with the two Douglas photographs—in Eddie Condon and Hank O'Neal, *Eddie Condon's Scrapbook of Jazz* (New York: St. Martin's Press, 1973), pp. unnumbered. In later years, Douglas appeared as a banjo player on Jack Benny's radio and TV shows, at least once in an impromptu jam band made up entirely of actors—among them Dick Powell (cornet), Fred MacMurray (tenor sax), and Tony Martin (clarinet).

7. Unbylined review in *Cue*, February 11, 1950.

8. Reviews: *Time,* February 27, 1950; *Look,* March 28, 1950; *Variety,* February 8, 1950.

9. *SIW,* p. 273. Various sources have suggested that Warner also demanded that the film devote less attention to black city life and black musicians. Curtiz and Wald reportedly held their ground, and the "negro" sequences were not cut.

10. *SR,* p. 135.

11. Letter, Jerry Wald to Hoagy Carmichael, dated July 13, 1949. Letter, Michael Curtiz to Hoagy Carmichael, dated August 30, 1949. Both used by permission of the Lilly Library, IU. Hawks quote from Jed Graham, "Songwriter Hoagy Carmichael: His Total Focus Boosted Him to the Top of Popular Music," *Investors' Business Daily,* November 22, 1999.

12. *SIW,* p. 294. *Punch,* April 11, 1951, item unsigned.

13. Max Jones, "Hoagy Is the Man With the Shaggy-Dog Voice," London *Daily Mirror,* March 28, 1951.

14. Hoagy Bix Carmichael, conversation with the author, September 27, 1998.

15. Eva Ford Chatman, conversation with the author, September 11, 2000.

16. Ian Fleming, *Casino Royale* (New York: Macmillan, 1953), pp. 42 et seq.

17. Hoagy Carmichael interview with Tony Thomas, CBC (Canadian Broadcasting Corporation) Radio, n.d. 1964, tape on file at ATM.

18. Frank Capra, *The Name Above the Title* (New York: Macmillan, 1971), p. 418.

19. Ibid., p. 420.

20. Quoted widely: by Susan Sackett, in *Hollywood Sings!* (New York: Billboard Books, 1995), and by Robert Osborne, in *Sixty Years of The Oscar* (New York: Abbeville, 1989), among others.

21. Capra, *Name Above the Title,* p. 420, quoting a report in *Film Daily* and an undated *Variety* review.

22. Walter Ames, "Hoagy Takes Tough Job-Braking Video," *Los Angeles Times,* June 28, 1953.

23. Randy Bob Carmichael, conversation with the author, November 24, 1998. *SIW,* p. 289.

24. Todd McCarthy, *Howard Hawks: The Grey Fox of Hollywood* (New York: Grove Press, 1997), p. 508.

25. *SIW,* p. 271. Other Carmichael-Adamson efforts intended for *Gentlemen Prefer Blondes* included the upbeat, *alla breve* "Love Will Soon Be Here," "My Conversation," "Make Me Make You Mine," "When the Wild, Wild Women Go Swimmin' Down in Bimini Bay," "That's Where I'm So Different," and "April Springs."

26. *SIW,* p. 274. *Variety,* February 9, 1955.

27. Mitch Anstruthers, "Why Stardust Hoagy Carmichael Was Dusted Off," *Uncensored,* March 1955. Alice Craig Greene, "Happy Anniversary to the Hoagy Carmichaels," *Screen Stars,* February 1951, p. 70.

28. "Hoagy Carmichael's Wife Wins Divorce," *Los Angeles Examiner*, November 9, 1955.

29. All Hoagy Bix Carmichael and Randy Bob Carmichael statements quoted here are from conversations with the author, September 27, November 24, and December 16, 1998, and September 29, 2000. Helen Meinardi Stearns statement from conversation with Patricia Kellar and Peter Davies, February 26, 1996.

30. Lyle "Skitch" Henderson, conversation with the author, September 29, 2000.

Chapter XVII

1. *Palm Springs Life*, April 1965, pp. 31–34.

2. William Wellman Jr., conversation with Patricia Kellar, March 4, 1996. Used with permission.

3. Several solo recordings made in 1951 at the Long Island home of Sherman Fairchild also found their way to issue during the 1980s. Among the songs featured are the little-known "Ginger and Spice," written in 1946 but never popularized, and the still-unpublished "Ev'ntide," recorded so effectively by Louis Armstrong in 1936. Another song in this collection bears the title "Gone With the Wind"—not to be confused with the 1937 Herb Magidson–Allie Wrubel standard of the same name. Perhaps predictably, this "Wind" is a plaintive lament for times past:

> Where's that old-time glory road,
> What's become of black-strap and maple gin?
> Where's the South that I once knowed?
> Man, I guess they all done gone with the wind.

Regrettably, the lyric also contains references to "Old Black Joe" and "folks what sing an' grin"—all but guaranteeing that, however heartfelt its sentiments may be, this "Gone With the Wind" will not see publication, at least in the foreseeable future.

4. Johnny Mandel, conversation with the author, August 24, 2000.

5. Barbara Lea, conversation with the author, September 25, 1999.

6. George Frazier, notes to *Hoagy Sings Carmichael*, copyright 1957 by Pacific Jazz Records.

7. William Wellman Jr., conversation with Patricia Kellar, March 4, 1996. Used with permission.

8. Richard Lamparski, *Whatever Became of . . .* , 3d ser. (New York: Crown, 1970), p. 61.

9. Hoagy Bix Carmichael, conversation with the author, September 27, 1999.

10. Bob Dorough, conversation with the author, November 7, 2000.

11. *SIW*, p. 299.

12. A. Walton Litz and Christopher MacGowan, eds., *The Collected Poems of William Carlos Williams*, vol. 1 (New York: New Directions, 1986), pp. 72–73.

13. Ted Gioia, *West Coast Jazz* (New York: Oxford University Press, 1992), pp. 189–90.

14. Fred Katz, conversation with the author, October 25, 2000. In keeping with its subject, the instrumental version of "The Sage" had two lives apart from the circumstances of its creation. Elmer Bernstein used the theme in his soundtrack music for the 1957 Burt Lancaster film *The Sweet Smell of Success*. The Hamilton record also turned up, improbably, on the soundtrack to *Boogie Nights*, an award-winning 1997 film about the porn film industry. "Sickening" was Katz's response. "If it had been within my power, I'd never have allowed that piece to be used in that picture."

15. *SIW*, p. 292. *Ole Buttermilk Sky* appeared as Kapp KL-1086. Produced by Michael "Mickey" Kapp, son of the label's owner, it featured ever-present Buddy Cole at the piano and organ. Arranger and musical director was Philadelphia-based Frank Hunter.

16. Lida Carmichael quotes from obituary notice, *Indianapolis News*, March 19, 1959. Carmichael quotes from *SIW*, p. 297.

17. Robert Fuller, conversation with the author, October 4, 2000.

18. *Variety* review, September 23, 1959.

19. Nacio Herb Brown Jr., conversations with the author, October 23, 1998, and October 15, 2000.

20. *Variety* review, September 28, 1960. Robert Fuller went on to roles in *Wagon Train* and the medical drama series *Emergency*, playing opposite a pair of music stars, pianist-songwriter Bobby Troup and his wife, the late singer Julie London (formerly married to producer Jack "Dragnet" Webb). But he never achieved the prominence, or the bankability, of Greene, Landon, and the rest of the competing *Bonanza* cast.

21. Charles's "Georgia" record also found its way onto the soundtracks of two Hollywood movies: Norman Jewison's *In the Heat of the Night* (1969) and Arthur Penn's *Four Friends* (1981). Hit records by singer Bobby Darin and trombonist Sy Zentner helped bring another Carmichael standard, "Lazy River," to a brand-new audience.

22. Leonard Feather, *The Pleasures of Jazz* (New York: Horizon, 1976), p. 79.

23. Hoagy Carmichael interview with Tony Thomas, CBC (Canadian Broadcasting Corporation) Radio, n.d. 1964, tape on file at ATM.

24. First devised by financier and sometime actor Richard Ney in collaboration with a Turnbull and Asser representative named Clark (hence the name), the "Clarney" was marketed in the 1960s by Brooks Brothers.

25. Randy Bob Carmichael, conversation with the author, November 24, 1998.

26. *Columbia Encyclopedia*, 3d ed., p. 505.

27. Myrtle Barker, "Hoagy Adds Chapter to Appleseed Legend," *Indianapolis News*, December 7, 1962.

28. "Music by Hoagy," *Indianapolis Star*, December 2, 1962.

29. Ruth Carmichael Grant, letter to Hoagy Carmichael, January 11, 1950, ATM.

30. The television broadcast is noteworthy, too, for two added elements: Hoagy's own patriotic text ("Now it is ours, and this is our America"), added to the "Fulfillment" theme and sung by Metropolitan Opera tenor Robert Merrill, and some interpretative dancing by ballet star Edward Villella.

31. Hoagy Bix Carmichael, conversation with the author, September 27, 1998.

32. Curiously, the "Appleseed" theme had a brief life outside the suite, as the marching song "Li'l Pro," adopted by the National Football League. Among Carmichael's trophies was a miniature football helmet, cast in bronze, inscribed with the NFL's thanks for donating the song.

Chapter XVIII

1. Hoagy Bix Carmichael, conversation with the author, January 17, 2001.

2. *SIW*, p. 296. Hoagy Bix Carmichael, conversation with the author, December 16, 1998. John Bell Clayton's last years had brought him a small measure of national popularity, through such novels as *Wait, Son, October Is Near* (1953), chronicling a young boy's adjustment to his parents' divorce. Clayton's fortunes, never good, worsened in the last two years of his life. As Hoagy Bix and Randy remembered it, he finally stopped eating and after that "just wasted away," with Martha unable to arrest the downward spiral.

3. Hoagy Bix Carmichael, conversation with the author, March 7, 2001.

4. *SIW*, p. 279.

5. Hoagy Bix Carmichael, conversation with the author, October 13, 2000.

6. Donald Clarke, *The Rise and Fall of Popular Music* (New York: St. Martin's Press, 1995), p. 427.

7. Todd McCarthy, *Howard Hawks: The Grey Fox of Hollywood* (New York: Grove Press, 1997), pp. 570–90.

8. Randy Bob Carmichael, conversation with the author, November 24, 1998.

9. At some time during the movie's preparation, Carmichael appears to have rewritten the lyric as "All of Your Love," but it was neither used nor published. Ken Bloom, *Hollywood Song*, vol. 1 (New York: Facts on File, 1995), p. 377.

10. Correspondence between Hoagy Carmichael and Paul R. Summers, dated July 3 and 8, 1963, supplied by Bingham, Summers, Welsh & Spilman, Indianapolis.

11. Photo and caption from *Japan Times*, Wednesday, October 21, 1964.

12. Hoagy Bix Carmichael, conversation with the author, October 13, 2000.

13. Unsigned review in *Bloomington Herald-Times*, March 4, 1965.

14. Letter from Barry Goldwater to Dolly Guinther at Farrar, Straus & Giroux, dated February 9, 1965. Letter from Ralph Hancock to Hoagy Carmichael, dated May 9, 1965. Both, ATM.
15. Hoagy Bix Carmichael, conversation with the author, October 13, 2000.
16. Randy Bob Carmichael, conversation with the author, November 24, 1998.
17. Hoagy Bix Carmichael, conversation with the author, January 9, 2001.
18. Hawaii anecdote from Leonard Feather, *The Pleasures of Jazz* (New York: Horizon Press, 1976), p. 80.
19. Hoagy Carmichael, letter to Howie Richmond, dated January 27, 1962, ATM. Used by permission.
20. A letter from Richmond to Carmichael, dated February 12, 1962 (ATM), congratulates him on "quite a beautiful job" but makes clear the publisher's decision to move ahead with the Wilder version. Among the reasons: Wilder's membership in Broadcast Music, Inc., major rival to ASCAP, and Frank Sinatra's interest in and intention to record Wilder's version of "Senza Fine." "Am truly sorry we couldn't find a sound way to wed the song," Richmond concludes.
21. Hoagy Bix Carmichael, conversation with the author, October 13, 2000.
22. Hoagy Bix Carmichael, letter to Hoagy Carmichael, dated May 11, 1970, ATM.
23. Hoagy Carmichael, letter to Wilfred Bain, dean of Indiana University School of Music, dated December 29, 1970, IU Archives.
24. William Wheatley, conversation with the author, December 12, 2000.
25. Stan Levey, conversation with the author, January 5, 2001.
26. Hoagy Bix Carmichael, conversation with the author, December 16, 1998. Randy Bob Carmichael, conversation with the author, November 24, 1998. William Wheatley, conversation with the author, December 12, 2000.
27. From *Raffles and Other Singing Stories by Hoagy Carmichael,* compiled and edited by Helen Meinardi Stearns and illustrated by Clara Urbahn (Camden, Me.: Cricketfield Press, n.d.)
28. Hoagy Carmichael, explanatory brochure for *Constitution Elm,* published by the Indiana State Museum, Division of Historic Preservation, Indiana Department of Natural Resources, Corydon.
29. Harvey Siders, "Los Angeles Love-In for Louis," *Down Beat,* August 20, 1970, pp. 21, 33.
30. Ibid. James Lincoln Collier, *Louis Armstrong, an American Genius* (New York: Oxford University Press, 1983), p. 331. Recording of entire event issued by GHB Records as three-CD set BCD 421–3.

Chapter XIX

1. According to 1970 correspondence between Hoagy and Wilfred Bain, dean of the School of Music, there had been talk of using parts of *Johnny Appleseed* at the opening of the Musical Arts Center, originally scheduled for May 1971, then

postponed first until October, then till spring of 1972. These plans appear to have come to nothing. Correspondence at IU Archives.

2. Hoagy Carmichael, letter to John W. Ryan, dated January 12, 1972. This copy of the letter appears to have been a draft, with alternative word choices notated in the margins. The copy actually sent to President Ryan has been lost. Letter at IU Archives.

3. Hoagy Bix Carmichael, conversation with the author, October 13, 2000.

4. Bob Wilber, *Music Was Not Enough* (New York: Oxford University Press, 1988), p. 114.

5. Nacio Herb Brown Jr., conversation with the author, October 23, 1998.

6. Alec Wilder, *American Popular Song* (New York: Oxford University Press, 1972), pp. 371–72.

7. Georgia Maxwell, letter to John W. Ryan, dated October 26, 1974, IU Archives.

8. Hollie I. West, "Newport Honors Hoagy," *Washington Post*, July 2, 1979.

9. Joe Lang, conversation with the author, January 7, 2001.

10. Mitchell appears to have had a taste for plays with tongue-twisting titles. What became known as the *Marat/Sade* was originally titled *The Persecution and Assassination of Jean Paul Marat as Performed by the Inmates of the Asylum at Charenton Under the Direction of the Marquis de Sade.*

11. Charles Staff, " 'Hoagy' Perfect for New Indiana Home," *Indianapolis News*, October 25, 1980.

12. Dave Frishberg, conversation with the author, September 28, 1999.

13. Duane Byrge, "Hoagy, Bix, and Bunkhaus," *Hollywood Reporter,* January 20, 1981, p. 38.

14. Crystal Gayle, conversation with the author, January 17, 2001.

15. "A Few Reminders of Hoagy," *Herald-Telephone* (Bloomington), December 28, 1981. George Wade Carmichael, "Farewell Hoagy: A Personal View," *Arts Insight,* February 1982, p. 17. Letter from Hoagy Bix Carmichael to Chancellor Herman B. Wells, dated January 9, 1982.

16. Duncan Schiedt, "Hoagy Carmichael: Some Afterthoughts," *Mississippi Rag,* February 1982, p. 1.

ACKNOWLEDGMENTS

Though focused on a single life, a biography is ultimately a piece of history; and writing history successfully depends on the assistance of many people, in ways great and small. All those to whom I've turned have given generously and unquestioningly of time and knowledge.

Archivists are a singularly dedicated breed. They thrive on detail, hunting exuberantly for the one key fact that will close a circle, bring unity and coherence to what was otherwise a congeries of disjunct facts. I'm singularly blessed to have worked with two of these invaluable, yet all too often unrecognized, heroes, both at Indiana University. Suzanne Mudge, at the Archives of Traditional Music, and Bradley D. Cook, at the University Archives, uncovered endless fascinating and revealing—and indispensible—aspects of Hoagy Carmichael's life and career. I called on both of them often and insistently; there was never a time when either failed to deliver. Justin Abene worked with great accuracy in preparing the musical examples for printing.

Thanks, too, to the Indiana Historical Society, to the Lilly Library at Indiana University, to the Lynde and Harry Bradley Foundation, and to the Carmichael and McKay families, whose generosity allowed this project to move ahead. To John R. T. Davies and Michael Brooks, Jeff Healey, and Mike Kieffer, for rare and indispensable recordings. To Dan Morgenstern and his indefatigable staff at the Rutgers Institute of Jazz Studies, responding promptly and with unfailing good nature to many a request, usually panicked and last-minute, for information. To Duncan Schiedt, James T. Maher, and Brian Priestley, who made their own careful research available to me. To Terry Teachout and Bill Kirchner, for patience, encouragement, and good turns on countless occasions.

Perhaps above all, my unbounded gratitude goes to Hoagy Bix Carmichael, elder son of the composer; over nearly four years he shared his time, his memories, his insights with me, and with neither stint nor censure. I know only too well that dredging up certain events can't have been pleasant for him: yet no subject was off limits, no question inappropriate. However often the statement is made, this book would not have been possible without him.

Maribeth Payne and Sheldon Meyer of Oxford University Press believed in this undertaking from the start, and never once wavered. India Cooper, flawless of ear and eye, dealt magnificently and ever-indulgently with what could have been an ordeal of copy-editing. Joellyn Ausanka coordinated with her usual deftness and insight, and Barbara Lea proved yet again that she is as skilled and exacting in the precise discipline of indexing as in her distinguished musical endeavors.

Dorothy Kellogg drew my attention recently to the fact that, in all the years of our shared life, I have always been working on some form of book. That her patience and Scots humor have survived intact is a source of perpetual astonishment and gratitude.

One point demands clarification: my depiction of certain events toward the close of Hoagy Carmichael's life is neither totally objective nor emotionally disinterested. As a featured participant in Jack Kleinsinger's 1976 *Highlights in Jazz* Carmichael evening; producer-director of the Smithsonian and Carnegie Hall events and of the Barbara Lea–Bob Dorough cabaret shows; and musical director for both American productions of *Hoagy, Bix and Wolfgang Beethoven Bunkhaus,* I had an opportunity to work personally with Hoagy Carmichael. All these experiences affected my perception of my subject, yielding many insights which helped shape this book.

Historically minded readers will note that the singer identified here as Connee Boswell was known during the 1930s as Connie and changed the spelling of her name in the early 1940s. The later spelling is used throughout in the interests of clarity.

Finally, my thanks to the following, without whose expertise and generosity the task would have been immeasurably more difficult:

Ella Abney (Medical Society, State of New York)
Steve Allen†
Jim Beebe
Alan J. Bergman
Pen Bogert (The Filson Club)
Nacio Herb Brown Jr.
George H. Buck
Mary Russell Bucknum (Library of Congress)

Randy Bob Carmichael
Eleanor Fell Caulfield
Maryann Chach (The Shubert Organization)
Eva Ford Chatman
Sally Carr Childs
John Chilton
Charles Bud Dant†
Chris Dant
Arlene H. Danville (Williams College)
Nick DeCarlis
Bob Dorough
Reginald DuValle Jr.
Rose Fell
Robert L. Floyd
Dave Frishberg
Robert Fuller
Neal Gabler
Crystal Gayle
Gloria Gibson (Indiana University)
Marilyn Graf (Indiana University)
Thornton Hagert
Chico Hamilton
Kitty Carlisle Hart
Hugh Hefner
Lyle "Skitch" Henderson
Richard Hessney (Reader's Digest Music)
Jane Jarvis
Sivert "Sy" Johnson
Sheila Jordan
Michael "Mickey" Kapp
Fred Katz
Patricia Kellar
Robert Kimball
Joe Lang
Barbara Lea
Gene Lees
Stan Levey
Dan Levinson

Myra Kapp Levitt
David Lewis (Indiana State Library)
Lilly Library Staff
Elaine Lynch (Family Communications, Inc.)
John McDonough
Gillian McManus
Brooks McNamara
Johnny Mandel
Virginia Mayo
Max Morath
Suzanne Mudge (Indiana University)
Amanda Mercer Neder
Chris Paton (Georgia State University)
Vincent Pelote (Institute of Jazz Studies)
Franklin S. Powers
Brian Priestley
Walter Ralphs
Howard Richmond
Richard Rosenzweig
Harold Russell
David Sager
Duncan Schiedt
Nikki Schofield (Bingham, Summers, Welsh & Spilman)
Artie Shaw
Raymond L. Shoemaker (Indiana Historical Society)
Joe Showler (Canada)
Susan Stamberg (NPR)
Helen Meinardi Stearns†
Adrian Sudhalter
Andy Van Sickle
Terry Waldo
Guy Webster
William Wheatley

Thanks to those—Sy Johnson, Hans Eekhoff, Terry Fallon, and Ray March among them—whose sharp eyes detected errors great and small.

Oxford University Press wishes to thank the Indiana Historical Society for their generous support toward the publication of this book.

CREDITS

April in My Heart
from the Paramount Motion Picture
Every Day Is a Holiday
Words by Helen Meinardi
Music by Hoagy Carmichael and Helen
Meinardi
Copyright © 1937, 1938 (Renewed 1964,
1965) by Famous Music Corporation
International Copyright Secured All
Rights Reserved

Ballad in Blue
Words and Music by Hoagy
Carmichael and Irving Kahal
Copyright © 1935 by PSO Limited
Copyright Renewed
International Copyright Secured All
Rights Reserved

Baltimore Oriole
Words and Music by Hoagy
Carmichael and Paul Francis Webster
Copyright © 1942, 1944 by Songs of
Peer, Ltd., and Warner Bros., Inc.
Copyright Renewed
International Copyright Secured All
Rights Reserved

The Big Town Blues
Words and Music by Hoagy
Carmichael
Copyright © 1962 by Songs of Peer, Ltd.
Copyright Renewed
International Copyright Secured All
Rights Reserved

Billy-A-Dick
Words and Music by Hoagy
Carmichael and Paul Francis Webster
Copyright © 1990, 1992 by Songs Of
Peer, Ltd,. and Webster Music Co.
International Copyright Secured All
Rights Reserved

Blue Orchids
Words and Music by Hoagy
Carmichael
Copyright © 1939 (Renewed 1966) by
Famous Music Corporation
International Copyright Secured All
Rights Reserved

Bread and Gravy
Words and Music by Hoagy
Carmichael
Copyright © 1935 by PSO Limited
Copyright Renewed
International Copyright Secured All
Rights Reserved

Close Beside You
Words and Music by Hoagy
Carmichael and Harold Adamson
Copyright © 1965 by Songs of Peer,
Ltd.
Copyright Renewed
International Copyright Secured All
Rights Reserved

Cranky Old Yank (In a Clanky Old Tank)
Words and Music by Hoagy
Carmichael
Copyright © 1942 by Songs of Peer,
Ltd.
Copyright Renewed
International Copyright Secured All
Rights Reserved

Daybreak
Words and Music by Hoagy
Carmichael
Copyright © 1932 by PSO Limited
Copyright Renewed
International Copyright Secured All
Rights Reserved

One Night in Havana
Words and Music by Hoagy
Carmichael
Copyright © 1928, 1929 by PSO Limited
Copyright Renewed
International Copyright Secured All
Rights Reserved

Riverboat Shuffle
Words and Music by Hoagy
Carmichael, Mitchell Parish, Irving
Mills, and Dick Voynow
Copyright © 1939, 1947 by Songs of
Peer, Ltd., and EMI Mills Music, Inc.
Copyright Renewed
All Rights Outside the USA Controlled
by EMI Mills Music, Inc. (Publishing)
and Warner Bros. Publications U.S.,
Inc. (Print)
International Copyright Secured All
Rights Reserved

Rockin' Chair
Words and Music by Hoagy
Carmichael
Copyright © 1929, 1930 by Songs of
Peer, Ltd.
Copyrights Renewed
International Copyright Secured All
Rights Reserved

Serenade to Gabriel
Words and Music by Hoagy
Carmichael and Vick Knight
© 1957 (Renewed) by Frank Music
Corp.
All Rights Reserved

Skylark
Words by Johnny Mercer
Music by Hoagy Carmichael
Copyright © 1941, 1942 by Songs of
Peer, Ltd., and WB Music Corp.
Copyright Renewed
International Copyright Secured All
Rights Reserved

Small Fry
from the Paramount Motion Picture
Sing, You Sinners
Words by Frank Loesser
Music by Hoagy Carmichael
Copyright © 1938 (Renewed 1965) by
Famous Music Corporation
International Copyright Secured All
Rights Reserved

Snowball
Words and Music by Hoagy
Carmichael
Copyright © 1933 by PSO Limited
Copyright Renewed
International Copyright Secured All
Rights Reserved

Song of Long Ago
Lyric by Johnny Mercer
Music by Hoagy Carmichael
© 1969 (Renewed) by Frank Music
Corp., Commander Publications, Inc.,
and Songs of Peer, Ltd.
All Rights Reserved

Star Dust
Words by Mitchell Parish
Music by Hoagy Carmichael
Copyright © 1928, 1929 by Songs of
Peer, Ltd., and EMI Mills Music, Inc.
Copyrights Renewed
All Rights Outside the USA Controlled
by EMI Mills Music, Inc. (Publishing)
and Warner Bros. Publications U.S.,
Inc. (Print)
International Copyright Secured All
Rights Reserved

Two Sleepy People
from the Paramount Motion Picture
Thanks for the Memory
Words by Frank Loesser
Music by Hoagy Carmichael
Copyright © 1938 (Renewed 1965) by
Famous Music Corporation
International Copyright Secured All
Rights Reserved

Washboard Blues
Words and Music by Hoagy
Carmichael, Fred B. Callahan, and
Irving Mills
Copyright © 19254 by Songs of Peer,
Ltd., and EMI Mills Music, Inc.
Copyright Renewed
All Rights Outside the USA Controlled
by EMI Mills Music, Inc. (Publishing)
and Warner Bros. Publications U.S.,
Inc. (Print)
International Copyright Secured All
Rights Reserved

INDEXES

GENERAL

SONGS AND COMPOSITIONS BY HOAGY CARMICHAEL

Note: Page numbers in bold italics refer to musical examples

SONGS AND COMPOSITIONS BY OTHER WRITERS

Note: page numbers in bold italics refer to musical examples